Culture in Policy Making: The Symbolic Universes of Social Action

The book series develops and consolidates the innovative approach to policy-making and politics based on the recognition of the central role played by cultural dynamics, intended as on-going processes of sense making channelled by symbolic resources the cultural environment makes available and through which people make sense to the experience, therefore feel, think, act.

It pursues both a theoretical and practical purpose: the development of the conceptual approach to policy and politics based on the view of human being as *homo semioticus,* as a subject engaged constantly with the need to make meaningful ordinary daily experiences, as well as participation in society.

Maria Beatrice Ligorio
Editor

Technology as Cultural Mediator

Theories and Experiences from Different Contexts

Springer

Editor
Maria Beatrice Ligorio
Dept. of Educational Sciences, Psychology, Communication
University of Bari "Aldo Moro"
Bari, Italy

ISSN 2523-7306 ISSN 2523-7314 (electronic)
Culture in Policy Making: The Symbolic Universes of Social Action
ISBN 978-3-031-97672-8 ISBN 978-3-031-97673-5 (eBook)
https://doi.org/10.1007/978-3-031-97673-5

This Springer imprint is published by the registered company Springer Nature Switzerland AG
The registered company address is: Gewerbestrasse 11, 6330 Cham, Switzerland

The original version of the book has been revised. The author names have been included along with the title “Afterword” in the backmatter to provide credit for their work. The respective title now read as “Afterword by Michael Cole and Maria Falikman”.

Presentation

The text presented in this volume offers many points of interest, and I am pleased to see it published in the *Culture in Policy Making: The Symbolic Universes of Social Action* series. First, this book makes a valuable contribution to the development of a holistic and processual understanding of culture. *Holistic*, in the sense that culture is not just one segment of the social world; rather, it is the fundamental way in which human beings shape their lives. Culture does not exist as a separate dimension that interacts with other dimensions—such as political, social, or economic spheres. Instead, social life is a unified whole, and culture is the form through which this whole evolves while maintaining its continuity over time. *Processual*, in the sense that culture is not an entity but an ongoing activity of sense-making—the continuous process through which the social world comes into existence and takes shape moment by moment, becoming a taken-for-granted reality in the eyes of those who inhabit it.

Through the various perspectives found in its nine chapters, this volume conceptualizes technology as dynamics of sense-making, whose socio-technical properties, functions, and impacts are inherently embedded in and shaped by the social negotiation of its use. Drawing on the concepts of *artifact* and *mediation*, technology is presented as a hermeneutical circle: as a sign that shapes the very process of its interpretation. In doing so, technology channels and constrains the interpretative practices that define its use and impact. At the same time, the social worlds shaped by these uses and impacts feed the semiotic power of technology, that is, its capacity to guide how individuals and groups make sense of it—in an ongoing, endless recursive process.

The holistic and processual perspective on culture is central to the theoretical project of the *Culture in Policy Making: The Symbolic Universes of Social Action* series, and this volume makes an important contribution to its development. By examining the interplay between the socio-technical and socio-semiotic aspects of technology, it underscores the inherent materiality of sense-making, countering the risk of an implicit Platonism that might reduce semiosis to a mere matter of ideas and symbols.

Just as with gravity, sense-making must be studied through abstract models—for example, by mapping sign transitions in a phase space. However, abstract does not mean immaterial. Sense-making is a process that unfolds through changes in organisms and objects—to make sense is to leave footprints in the world. This volume makes it clear that such footprints take on concrete, experiential forms: spaces and times, objects and their resistances, bodies and emotions, economic resources and their distribution, power relations and their weight.

Second, this volume provides valuable insights into the role of technology in our daily lives. Digital devices, communication and transportation systems, the Internet of Things, as well as AI chatbots, robots, universal translators, synthetic organs, and speech neuroprosthetics are just a few examples of the artifacts that people are already experiencing or will soon encounter. These tools do not merely make a shift in the scale of human engagement with the world; more fundamentally, they have the power to reshape the very structure of reality and, with it, our self-perception. Contemporary technology does not just enhance human presence in the world—it constitutes new worlds.

Consider, for instance, AI systems that produce human language and thought. As they develop the ability to govern their own learning processes, reflect on themselves, and even exhibit emotions and values, they blur the boundary between life and non-life, raising fundamental questions about what defines our humanity. At the edge of these emerging realities—sometimes already embedded within them—the analyses presented in this volume demonstrate the value of sociocultural psychology in understanding technology. By focusing on the performative capacity of sense-making of constituting the reality, the theoretical and methodological framework outlined here helps us recognize the role individuals play in constructing the world as it is—rather than seeing its trajectory as an inevitable fate. In doing so, it invites both individuals and society to embrace the opportunity and responsibility of making choices.

This leads to the third point. The rapid development of technology in modernity has fueled eschatological visions, imagining a radically new, post-human world. *2001: A Space Odyssey*, *The Matrix* trilogy, and countless other films and novels reflect a deep-seated anxiety about the reversal of power between humans and machines, with the latter taking control. However, even those who remain optimistic about technological progress cannot ignore the accelerating advancement of AI. The increasing likelihood of AI reaching the stage of super-intelligence—i.e., systems capable of self-directed learning and cross-domain problem-solving—raises serious concerns and, more importantly, calls for urgent attention to the governance of human-machine systems.

This volume does not aim to provide direct answers or policy recommendations on this issue. However, it offers a theoretical framework for thinking about it. The central idea is that technology is not a natural phenomenon but a socio-semiotic construction—both its uses and its development result from the ways people make sense of their interactions with it. This book helps us understand that the scope and the function of technology—the *what, how,* and *why*—are shaped by the cultural forms of the social fabric: technology embodies the crystallized form of the social landscape. In this light, we might ask whether concerns about the unlimited expansion of super-intelligent machines, as vividly illustrated by Bostrom's *paperclip maximizer* argument, can truly be addressed without considering that the very notion of limitless, asymptotic progress is embedded in the fundamental platform of meaning at the grounds of the neoliberal, hyper-globalized organization of society—an institutionalized worldview that, because it is taken for granted, remains largely invisible to those who live within it: its structures—modes of production, power relations, and ways of life—are naturalized as if they were objective facts rather than social constructs.

Against this tendency to naturalize the contemporary forms of life, this volume provides insights for reflective, critical thinking. Technology is both a means by which we make sense of the world and the product of that sense-making. As such, it is not a given fact, but a historical product of societies—ultimately, a political act. Echoing the words of the volume's Editor: If we want to govern what technology does to us, we must first be concerned with what we do to and with it.

Finally, this volume deserves particular attention for the exploration of the use of technology in education. Readers will find theoretical discussions, case studies, and concrete examples illustrating the interplay between two key dynamics: on one hand, the active and constructive role that learners (and teachers) play in shaping the actual form of technological devices through their use and interpretation; on the other, technology's ability to create innovative educational environments that serve as meeting spaces between generations. The culturally guided subjectivization of technology and the technological mediation of intergenerational communication reinforce one another—like the two hands in Escher's famous drawing.

This function of technology is particularly significant in an era marked by an increasing gap between generations. Today's youth are experiencing an anthropological rupture: they do not merely hold a different or even conflicting position within the same world as adults; rather, their subjectivities—expressed in their languages, ways of life, emotional frameworks, and metrics of time and space—appear increasingly alien to those of older generations. One interpretation of this phenomenon highlights the lack of semiotic affordances available to young people in contemporary society. The radical opacity of the modern world prevents them not only from understanding it but, more profoundly, from representing it. As a result, youth subjectivity becomes anchored in the present and in concrete, relational micro-contexts, as these are the only available spheres of experience that can be meaningfully represented. It would be inaccurate to describe this phenomenon as a *crisis of meaning*, since no pre-existing system of meanings has collapsed. Rather, there is a narrowing of the sphere of meaning to what is immediate and concrete. This restriction has severe consequences, leading to a dramatic decline in agency—the perception of oneself as capable of regulating one's relationship with the world in order to establish a position within it. The widespread distress among young people, the prevalence of risky and dysregulated behaviors, emotional illiteracy, cultural impoverishment, the loss of temporal perspective and long-term planning, and the tendency toward concrete thinking and performative communication (where meaning is exhausted in the act itself and in the related emotional gratification) are all signs of this decline.

The outcome of this process is the emergence of younger generations as a form of radical alterity in relation to the languages, values, and ways of life that shape adult subjectivity. This, in turn, significantly weakens the ability of adults to recognize and engage with the worlds of meaning inhabited by young people, as well as their capacity to mediate the process of secondary socialization. This generational divide represents one of the greatest challenges for educational institutions. Educators must design and explore new communicative practices and learning environments capable of bridging the currently incommensurable subjectivities of youth and adults.

What this volume demonstrates is that a culturally informed approach to technology—one that sees it as a context, object, and vector of sense-making—while not a universal solution, can open promising perspectives.

In sum, I thoroughly enjoyed reading this volume, and I believe that many different audiences—scholars of cultural processes, researchers and professionals engaged in the design and implementation of technology, educators, and policymakers—will find it equally valuable. Good reading.

University of Salento (IT) Sergio Salvatore
Lecce, Italy

Contents

Introduction

As this book was being written, two wars (Russia vs. Ukraine and Israel vs. Gaza) were upsetting the world order, and many other conflicts, some that have been raging for a long time, provided further disruptions. Ecological stresses from climate increased the risk of survival for many species, including humans. As one consequence of these intersecting phenomena there is a massive increase in international migration that is upsetting national policies with some countries proposing solutions that put democracies in crisis. These directions are accompanied by a general increase in intolerance (racial, religious, and gender based), interpersonal aggression, psychological instability, depression, and self-injuries. What has technology got to do with all this? In this book, the idea of a tight interconnection between technology and human beings is pursued; therefore, it is natural to wonder what roles and responsibilities technologies may have in these negative scenarios and what possibilities they might offer for positive changes. The debate remains open but the simplest answer is: yes, technologies do contribute to these problems and they have a great responsibility for some of these trends, but technologies are not solely responsible.

Waelbers (2011) suggested that society must take responsibility for the changes technologies cause and find ways to make those changes productive. Waelber discussed responsibility from a sociological and philosophical point of view, posing the foundation of mediation in connection with the idea of freedom of choice. Individuals can be held morally responsible for their choices if they are free, if they are not forced. In this sense, technology itself cannot be called responsible since options are usually restricted to a narrow range of alternatives, as happens with algorithms. Should the responsibility for the choices, then, be attributed to its developers—engineers, computer scientists, programmers—or to the individual or collective end users? Alternatively, ought accountability for technologies lie with those who commission and finance them? This dilemma is somewhat reminiscent of Bateson's dilemma of the blind person with his cane (Bateson, 1972). When a blind person is walking using a cane to navigate, the cane effectively becomes an extension of their body—altering their sense of where the person ends and where the environment begins. This raises a question: should we regard the cane as part of the blind person's "self" or merely as a tool? We can also use this reasoning to wonder, for example, if the cane accidentally breaks something or does something wrong, who is responsible? It is difficult to say, it could be the fault of the person holding the cane because they may have used it badly or the cane might have a manufacturing defect. But it could also be the fault of the context in which the blind person and the stick move that somehow hinders or prevents them from moving well. Bateson uses this paradox to illustrate that our perceptions and cognitive boundaries are not fixed but emerge from the interplay between our biological systems and the external tools we employ. Similarly, we can think that since humans and technology are directly interconnected, the responsibility is also similarly shared by all the participants. It is thus appropriate that Chaps. 1 and 5 of this volume focus on concerns about the mediating roles covered by technology.

This book is mainly dedicated to technology users and scholars. The authors challenge readers to reflect on their own points of view about responsibility for technology. When we use or study technology we make some choices that go beyond the range of possibilities pre-defined by those who design and create the technology. In this way, an intricate scenario of interconnections between humanity and machines is emerging, in line with the thinking of philosophers like Latour and MacIntyre. Latour (1996) analyzed the ways human and non-human actors interact and construct social realities. His ideas, organized within a theory called Actor-Network Theory (ANT), are based on a few key points. First, "actors" involved in the flow of communication can be either humans or non-human entities as objects, technologies and institutions. Technologies do influence social relations since they can "act" and modify human behavior. It follows that society is not a fixed entity but a network of relationships that is constantly changing according to the connections among the various actors—and those actors are also constantly changing. Actors modify and reinterpret information as they transmit it, creating new social configurations and new networks that are constantly being rebuilt. Latour rejects the separation between nature and society as well as the distinction between "social facts" and "natural facts," arguing that science, technology and society are inseparable. ANT is very useful to study how scientific and technological innovations emerge through networks of actors, rather than from individuals or single institution. In short, ANT sees social reality as a dynamic network of human and non-human actors, in which no entity has absolute control, but everything is constructed through relationships and interactions. In this perspective, we can only talk of collective responsibility.

The notion of "actor" in ANT is a bit like the network "node" or "entity" in connectivist learning theory, "a learning theory for the digital age" (Siemens, 2004). In this theory, a node or entity is an information source—it might be a person, or a book or a film or a text message—anything that might store information. Learning occurs when two entities form a connection causing one or both to change: a connection exists between two entities when "a change of state in one entity can cause or result in a change of state in the second entity" (Downes, 2022, p. 60). The similarity between ANT and connectivism is clear—both describe the rapidly changing networked environment that the chapters in this book are responding to.

MacIntyre is a moral philosopher best known for his work "After Virtue" (2013), where he develops an interesting virtue-based theory rooted in Aristotelian and communitarian traditions. He starts from a critique of modern ethics, fragmented and incoherent because it has lost the sense of virtues and moral traditions. Modern moral theories (utilitarianism, deontology) do not provide a solid foundation for morality. According to MacIntyre, humans are narrative beings: our identity is formed through stories and the continuity of our life and morality can only be understood within the context of a life story and a cultural tradition. Therefore, for a "responsible" use of technologies it is necessary to practice positive virtues. These are qualities developed within practices (e.g., art, science, politics), which have their own rules and objectives. A good example is that of a good doctor who is not only technically skilled but who also possesses virtues such as justice and care for the patient. To summarise, MacIntyre views society through the lens of ethics and the historical continuity of virtues whilst Latour sees society as a fluid network of interacting actors, without predefined moral structures.

The works in this volume take a position that in some way reconciles these two visions. In the various chapters comprising this volume, the readers will easily find how responsibility for technology consequences are shared between contexts and actors who engage in morally positive activities. For instance, the concept of shared responsibility clearly emerges in Chap. 4 (Kumpulainen et al.), which explores how digital engagement allows children to investigate and connect with their surroundings in ways that foster a relational orientation towards the world. In this case, technology is used to immerse children in a "more-than-human world," defined by the interconnectedness of humans and nonhumans. Kumpulainen et al. relate how children use an augmented story-crafting app to explore their urban forest, creating and sharing stories. This experience can be considered also as an act of taking responsibility not only for the ways the children use technology but also for their relationship to the natural environment and how technology might be used to protect it. In this way, students' learning about sustainable environmental development is fostered not in a conceptual or abstract way but in terms of becoming active and, indeed, responsible citizens.

The book explores the relationship between culture and technology, highlighting how technological innovations influence social structures, thought and cultural practices. All the authors adopt an interdisciplinary approach, integrating perspectives of philosophy, sociology, education and media studies. This is because the experiences they report are complex, captured by considering the ecological dimension of the use of technology. For example, Chap. 5 (Erstad) problematizes the use of everyday technology, in particular by looking at the tension between experiences of intrusiveness versus affordances in using available technological resources. Despite growing research interest in the fundamental social, institutional and individual consequences of what Erstad calls "platformisation," we know less about how families are transforming with the everyday use of heavily commercialized and globally networked platforms and their algorithms. Erstad synthesizes various researches, some focused on young people's trajectories, others on families living in different European countries, and elaborates two interesting concepts: "learning lives" which describes the spaces learners actively create by blending online and offline activities; and "Platforming," which is the "digital tracing of everyday events across generations" (PlatFAMs). The PlatFAMs project focuses distinctively on intergenerational experiences in relation to the platformisation of family life (teenagers, their parents and their grandparents). The core of the project is the study three-generation families in five European countries (Norway, Estonia, UK, Romania, and Spain) over a 2-year period, across different online and offline spaces. The ambition of the project is to unpack the relational and temporal aspects of digital platforms' wide-ranging social transformation of everyday family practices and inter-generational relations in contemporary societies.

All the chapters share a vision of technology fully embedded into the cultural context as they reciprocally shape each other. All throughout the book it is clear that technology is not only made up of tools and machines, but also includes systems of thought, cultural practices and ways of organizing society. In fact, the book starts with a chapter (Ligorio) in which the nature of technology is extensively explained. The chapter analyses the concept of mediation as able to justify the reference to technologies not as simple functional tools for carrying out some activity but as part of the human process of understanding and modifying the world we live in. This aspect is also addressed in Chap. 5 (Erstad) and analyzed together with the concept of mediatization, more focused on how media become part of societies and cultural developments. In these chapters the term "Artifact" is proposed instead of simply technology. Artifact is used with a broader meaning that embodies any kind of technology, not just digital ones. Furthermore, the label "Artifact" also nicely captures the cultural nature of technology since it underlines the idea that it is made "with-art," conceiving art as a typical human cultural product. As Murphie and Potts (2017) underline, technology is part of our culture and shapes the way we think and act. This is particularly apparent in Chap. 3 (Ritella) that shows how the concepts of space and time change with the use of technology. New spaces combining online and offline are made available, and time seems to go at a different speed when online. Technology allows users to experience being "anywhere" and "at any time," transcending the constraints imposed by the physical environment. By now, we are already used to fast communication and to live the experience of being simultaneously "here" and "there." Simultaneous communications are now the norm: we answer messages on the phone while watching TV and listening to the daily report of our loved ones. Ritella, in his chapter, shows the impact of removing the "traditional" time-space (chronotopes) constraints in education, describing a learning activity based on Minecraft Education, a game based on digital block construction. The case presented in this chapter effectively explains how chronotopes are perceived and navigated; not only based on the users' perceptions but also on several socio-cultural processes that might extend beyond educational settings impacting the learning processes.

The inseparability of culture and technology is recognized in several theoretical frameworks; some very wide such as the socio-constructivism and constructionist theories (for instance, Chap. 1), others more specific such as the post-human theory (Chap. 4), Theory of Mind (Chap. 9), or the Intergroup Contact Theory, invoked in

Chap. 7 (Austin & Hunter). This latter theory is used to address communities in conflict—for example in Northern Ireland and Israel—and, in this chapter, to describe how technology can promote peacebuilding in schools by structuring positive educational contacts between young people who would otherwise lead separate and parallel lives. When educational programs are well managed, unregulated use of the Internet could be contained and significant benefits for all can be achieved. Being in contact could be a great resource, as long as users take their own responsibility and the intentions are clear and positive for anyone involved.

The growth in use of social networks (SN) over the past decade[1] from 970 million in 2010 to 5.24 billion users in January, 2025, has lead to increase attention to the benefits and challenges of online education (Akpen et al., 2024). Together with the portability of the devices, the diffusion of SN certainly determined new dynamics and new issues to be studied. For example, consider the role (perhaps not yet fully understood) that technologies have played in Brexit as an indication of how decisive they can be. The same role has probably been played in elections in various countries by forming opinions and positioning. At an international scale and in our personal lives we have come to depend heavily on technology, sometimes in ways that we are not particularly aware of. For example, for many people, scrolling their mobile phone is the last thing they do when they go to bed and the first one when they wake up in the morning. This widespread diffusion makes it clear that we need to carefully examine the technology-culture relationship. In fact, for almost any action we perform we now need technological support. All these options could be used to improve personal and social lives, as both Chap. 5 (Erstad) and Chap. 7 (Austin & Hunter) demonstrate.

However, our focus in this volume is *not* what we can do with technology—the list would be too long—but rather on the implications of using it in specific contexts. Further, individual chapters here do not concentrate on the design of technologies but rather on the dimensions determining the effects of technology use, with a critical and reflective perspective, so as to be able to offer to the readers both practical and theoretical development ideas. The authors call attention to conditions needed for technology to play a positive role. When these conditions are absent or poorly met, technology may have a negative or null role. A clear case in this sense is reported in Chap. 2 (Whitworth) that explores the fascinating history of the South Atlantic island of St Helena, linked to navigation, colonialism and Napoleon's exile. This case is interesting since it shows how, despite the significant investments in informational connectivity, little impact was felt by the island's community and culture. In fact, the beneficiaries of all these investments still are the colonizers, continuing to relegate the island to the status of a colony.

Chapter 6 (Marti and Recupeo) provides an example of the changing effects of technology by describing a technology that illustrates how older adults with age-related impairments, in nursing homes and day-care centers, can benefit from cultural experiences through sensory museology. Chapter 8 (Lund) explores changing

[1] https://backlinko.com/social-media-users

effects arising from the use of an artificial intelligence technology—Playware—designed to create playful experiences using a combination of robotic and AI-driven systems that create engaging challenges in real-world situations. Users living in disadvantaged national contexts—mainly Africans—and those with severe socio-cognitive limitations can play with innovative technology in ways that enhance cognitive, physical, and social abilities. Here technology is providing a clear added value to people living in situations of limitation because of age or because or health conditions. In both chapters, technology opens up new horizons for people who might otherwise never have those experiences. The ethical value is clear and the activities unfold through a system of activities that includes human agents—from designers to those who assist in the implementation of the activities—and non-human agents.

In Chap. 9, Cangelosi et al. explore the potential of robotics and AI models in several fields, from social assistive robots for health and social care to manufacturing scenarios with human-robot collaboration. This chapter also points out the need to have a trustful relationship with robots, not only because we trust they will never hurt us (see the "first law of robotics" posited by Asimov, 1950) but because, in order to have a fruitful interaction, one must take into consideration not only people's perceptions and beliefs about robots' capabilities, goals, and intentions but also the robots' representation of the human's needs and goals. These are ethical issues that should be taken into consideration when technological applications are designed for successful interactions between humans and technological applications.

The starting point for the order of the various chapters reflects a dynamic focus, initially more on the cultural dimension, discussing the changes (or lack of changes) both in people and in their contexts. In the later chapters, the focus is more directly on innovative technologies. We believe this order will guide a reading free from a priori enthusiasm or skepticism but rooted in the stories documented by the various authors, where the pros and cons are accompanied by critical reflections and proposals for future directions of development. Regardless the degree of technology recognizable in the various chapters, they all have in common the implicit belief that the advancement of technologies cannot be stopped. Therefore, we must equip ourselves as best as possible to bend this advancement to our needs and not to our fears, to the values shared by most (solidarity, inclusion, dialogue) and not to those of a few.

For these reasons, many of the chapters included in this volume stress the importance of education. It is precisely by starting from school that we can influence the processes of technological development. We need to invest much more in schools to pass on to our young people positive and constructive models of use of technologies. This commitment cannot be left to peers (who easily risk negative or counter-productive uses) nor to parents who have no way of developing such models since technologies are new to them too. The only possibility we have, therefore, is in the hands of the school that, with a clear focus on evidence-based research and practice, will be able to develop, model, and transfer positive and productive examples of use, simultaneously taking care of individual and social development. While we are aware that many issues have not been included in this volume—e.g., the digital divide, gender differences, not all types of technologies are considered—we hope this book will serve as an incentive to look at technology as a way to promote those uniquely human skills that machines cannot replicate and which have allowed us to build increasingly sophisticated artifacts.

Finally, our hope is that this volume will help readers to overcome fears and worries about possible abuses of technology, in both in a qualitative and a quantitative sense. Of course, there are some risks, but we need to remember that it is possible to face those risks in positive ways. The stories told in our chapters are great examples in this sense, because they also describe the conditions that determine certain consequences.

The future vision could still worry us but we also know that it is not the first time that we face challenges as important as those that the current society poses to us. All the changes mentioned at the outset of this Introduction may lead to think we are now living an unprecedented revolution. But this feeling is not original at all, we humans have experienced this feeling many other times. Mokyr et al. (2015) examined the history of fears regarding technological change since the Industrial Revolution and concluded that we tend to overestimate the impact of short term harm and underestimate the long term benefits. Resistance to that revolution was so strong that we carry it with us today in the term "Luddite." However, it is clear to us that the history goes back much further. For example, at the turn of the sixteenth century, Copernicus argued that the position of the sun is fixed and earth revolves around it, changing the sense of humans' place in the universe; at the same time Gutenberg's printing press massively changed the way information spreads and Luther defied papal authority putting the church of Rome into crisis. This was a big revolution made possible by technologies we do not fear any more. Berbekar (1988) saw a very early case of technophobia in ancient Greece when she described Hephaestus as "The God We Love to Hate." And yet, we are still here; survivors of all the epochal revolutions that have shaken our foundations. Each time we have found a way to recombine and re-mediate the available technology to create new cultural paths through which to overcome the sense of confusion and fear in the face of the technological revolutions that we ourselves create.

University of Bari (IT)
Bari, Italy

Maria Beatrice Ligorio

References

Akpen, C. N., Asaolu, S., Atobatele, S., Okagbue, H., & Sampson, S. (2024). Impact of online learning on student's performance and engagement: A systematic rebiew. *Discover Education*. https://doi.org/10.1007/s44217-024-00253-0

Asimov, I. (1950). *I, robot* (Vol. 1). Gnome Press.

Bateson, G. (1972). *Steps to an ecology of mind: Collected essays in anthropology, psychiatry, and epistemology*. Ballantine Books.

Berbekar, R. (1988). Hephaestus—The god we love to hate: The lingering pro- and anti-technology debate. *Bulletin of Science, Technology & Society, 8*, 172–182.
Downes, S. (2022). Connectivism. *Asian Journal of Distance Education, 17*(1).
Latour, B. (1996). On actor-network theory: A few clarifications. *Soziale Welt*, 369–381.
MacIntyre, A. (2013). *After virtue*. A&C Black.
Mokyr, J., Vickers, C., & Ziebarth, N. (2015). The history of technological anxiety and the future of economic growth: Is this time different? *Journal of Economic Perspectives, 29*(3), 31–50. https://pubs.aeaweb.org/doi/pdfplus/10.1257/jep.29.3.31. https://doi.org/10.1257/jep.29.3.31
Murphie, A., & Potts, J. (2017). *Culture and technology*.
Siemens, G. (2004). Elearnspace. Connectivism: A learning theory for the digital age. *Elearnspace.org*, 14–16.
Waelbers, K. (2011). *Doing good with technologies: Taking responsibility for the social role of emerging technologies* (Vol. 4). Springer.

Chapter 1
The Human Dimension of Technology

Maria Beatrice Ligorio

1.1 Introduction

The relationships between humans and technology have a long and complex history. To fully grasp the sense of this relationship it is essential to have a clear definition of what we mean by technology. It would not make much sense to use the label "technology" only in reference to what the modern common sense would include into it, that is to say digital devices (computers, smartphones, tablets, etc.), robots, Internet or Artificial Intelligence (AI). To better understand how humans interrelate to technology we need to assign a larger meaning to what we refer to as technology. Of course, all the elements mentioned above can be fully conceived as technology but, at the same time, it is quite obvious that what we include under the umbrella of technology is strongly influenced by a contemporary vision of technology. When assigning a larger meaning to technology, it becomes soon clear that it always existed in the history of humans. From the first stone shaped by primitive people to the complex machines we have today, we can say that humans and technology co-evolved: human intelligence created tools/instruments/technology[1]and the actions we could perform with them sustained human development.

This is confirmed by many perspectives. Historians and anthropologists (Hård & Jamison, 2013), linguists (Stout, 2010), economists (Freeman, 1995), philosophers

[1] Throughout the chapter, for the sake of convenience, I will some time use these terms, along with that of artifact which will be introduced shortly, as interchangeable even though I am aware of their differences.

M. B. Ligorio (✉)
Dept. of Educational Sciences, Psychology,
Communication University of Bari "Aldo Moro", Bari, Italy
e-mail: Mariabeatrice.ligorio@uniba.it

M. B. Ligorio (ed.), *Technology as Cultural Mediator*, Culture in Policy
Making: The Symbolic Universes of Social Action,
https://doi.org/10.1007/978-3-031-97673-5_1

(Jablonka et al., 2012), till the modern cyber-anthropology (Libin & Libin, 2005) they all confirm—from different angles—the inextricable duality of humans-technology. The boundaries between humans and machines are progressively blurred and this is visible both in our 'flesh' and 'spirit'. Think of the advances of prostheses and technological supports that help maintain or enhancing various human functions and, similarly, living style is for many highly influenced by technology (LeMoyne, 2016). A recent Italian survey[2] shows that some people consult their smartphones up to 1200 times a day to make even trivial decisions. In practice, we are no longer able to draw a distinctive line between online and offline so that the philosopher Floridi (2015) proposes the concept of "onlife" to describe "the new experience of a hyperconnected reality within which it is no longer sensible to ask whether one may be online or offline" (p. 1).

It follows that it is impossible to understand humans without looking at how and where we use technology, meant in a larger sense. This instance is at the basis of the contextualist strand of psychology which has its roots in constructivism (Cobern, 1993; Kanselaar, 2002; Fosnot, 2013). According to this approach, the world we live in is never exclusively the faithful reproduction of reality. As already underlined by Plato's myth of the cave, the nature of the world we populate is subjective and constructive and what we see is not the description, reproduction or mirroring of a world that exists in itself but it is rather our personal way of seeing, feeling and organizing our experience in the world. We are metaphorically chained to our own perceptions and we have no access to reality. This allows us to overcome the distinction between humans and context, since the latter one is built by our continuous interpretation of signs or, how Bruner (Bruner and Haste 2010) would say, our sense-making processes. One of the most convincing proof comes from Kirsh (1995) studies that highlight how practice sharpens the perceptive system, so that an expert sees the context in which he works differently from other participants. The expert focuses his attention on some salient properties and, at the same time, uses the context as a resource for action while the less experienced makes less effective and more dispersive selections. This means that the context is not separated from the person but it is actually built by the encounter between what the person has in mind and what is in the environment. This belief underlies the concept of "space for thought", proposed by Perret-Clermont (2004), which refers to a symbolic space into the mind, built and shaped considering expertise, previous experiences, values, interiorized norms, and many other personal and social dimensions. These aspects are interiorized and they work as "frames" guiding what to "see" into the context and to what pay attention to. It is impossible to consider everything composing a certain context; therefore, we own to make a selection that is strongly conditioned by what we have in mind. The metaphor of a frame is not intended in a geometric sense but rather in an artistic, aesthetic sense: the frame limits the painting and, at the same time, it contributes to give it a sense. Assuming a cultural perspective in

[2] https://www.iss.it/-/rapporto-istisan-22/5-dipendenze-da-internet-a-cura-di-adele-minutillo-paolo-berretta-pietro-canuzzi-liliana-la-sala-roberta-pacifici?utm_source=chatgpt.com

analyzing technologies means understanding how they interact with the context within which they are used. So, after accepting that technology has entered human life long before computers and AI existed, we will now exploit the relationship entertained by technology and its cultural-historical frame. To unpack the different meaning technology may assume depending on the cultural-historical point of view, two concepts need to be exploited: the concept of mediation and that of artifact. They will be discussed in the next paragraph.

1.2 Mediation and Artefact

The concept of mediation is preliminary to fully understand what it is meant by artefacts and why this term could be preferred to that of technologies. Also the concept of mediation was made popular by socio-constructivism. As already mentioned in the previous paragraph, this assumption is based on Plato's myth of the cave. Not being able to access an objective reality humans are inevitably led to interpret what they see, going beyond the information given (Bruner, 1973). In other words, humans have a mediated understanding of the world (Bruner, 1997). Mediated by what? Hard to imagine what humans used at the outset of this mediational process but, whatever it was, surely it covered a crucial role. By using mediation tools—either conceptual and material—our spices learnt not only to give sense to the world and also to modify it. We can figure out that a significant step forward was made when humans start to develop their own mediation tools. To mark this evolutionary leap, it was proposed using the term artefact (Miller, 2002)—that is, "made with art" instead of a simple tool given in nature. First introduced in archeology to define any item made or given shape by humans, it acquired a broader meaning when philosophers and human scientists started to reckon upon it. For instance, Luria (1928) considers that it is precisely when we began to create artifacts that the psychological processes that distinguish the modern man emerged. In fact, creating and using artifacts impacts the psychological structure of those who build and use them. In this sense, the artefact par excellence is language which, by becoming an integral part of the actions we carry out, alters the flow and structure of mental functions, just as professional tools alter the production process. Artifacts are the 'externalized' form of mental processes and the manifestation of mental activity that unfolds on two levels:

(a) A concrete level that concerns artefacts actually used to carry out a certain activity. At this level we could just concentrate on the activities performed with the artifact.
(b) A psychological, internalized level, when the mediation action becomes symbolic. The action made possible with an artifact determines cognitive and thought structures which then allow it to think according to the affordance of that tool.

Many authors had developed the idea that using mediational artifacts we may improve our physical and intellectual capacity. Starting from Vygotsky (2012) and his sociocultural approach, it is now commonly accepted that thinking and learning develop through external tools that mediate interactions with the world. Over this point it can be recognized as an agreement between Vygotsky and Piaget's work. According to Piaget (2003), children develop intelligence through processes of assimilation and accommodation, and artefacts can act as stimuli for these cognitive processes. More precisely, Jonassen (1992) claims that artifacts can act as 'cognitive tools' that help people think and solve problems in new ways; whilst for Bruner (Bruner & Haste, 2010) artifacts can function as 'scaffolds' to represent and understand the world. McLuhan (2017), famous for his statement 'the medium is the message', believed that media are not simply neutral tools, but that they expand human capacities; for example, writing enhances memory and the processing of ideas, while digital media transform the way we access and share information, fostering new forms of collective and individual intelligence. In this sense, their use can help develop the cognitive and intellectual skills of humanity in its globality. In addition, the French philosopher Pierre Lévy (1997) believes that the capability of digital networks to create connections between people makes them powerful tools to advance collective intelligences, considered as more than the sum of individual intelligences. From digital networks emerges, therefore, an intellectual capacity generated by the multiplying force of social interaction.

Norman (Zhang & Norman, 1994), a leading theorist of distributed cognition, discussed how technology and media extend human cognitive capacities, making us more 'intelligent' through external support. Jenkins (Jenkins & Ito, 2015) fine-tunes the concept of 'participatory culture' to sustain that digital media, in particular, can develop collaborative and creative intelligences. Along this line, Clark and Chalmers (1998) propose the concept of extended mind to argue that external artifacts extend human mind, increasing its computational, memory and problem-solving capabilities.

Another author who has definitely reflected upon the concept of artefact is Wartofsky (2012) who describes three evolutionary levels to outline the relationship between man and artefacts:

(a) Primary level: concerns material and immaterial objects created to extend man's physical and intellectual potential; for example, plough and hammer strengthen our arms, glasses extend vision. In essence, they can be considered as human prostheses, tools to better and more effectively carry out activities that we are able to carry out even without but with inferior results and with greater effort.
(b) Secondary level: it is made up of artefacts that assemble the primary ones into new artefacts and allow new actions. This is the case of artefacts such as, for example, a recipe, which assembles ingredients and tools and, through specific procedures, this assembly leads to a very different result—a dish—not obtainable by simply putting together primary artefacts.

(c) Tertiary level: they convey representations of abstract worlds, governed by complex cultural and symbolic concepts and rules. Examples include works of art, television formats but also virtual worlds that convey meanings and ways of seeing the world beyond the elements of which they are made of.

If carefully considering this classification, we can understand how it is determined by the specific historical-cultural perspective within which it is carried out. Let me give an example. In our current society it seems obvious to consider the plow as a primary artefact, but let's try to project ourselves back in the historical time in which it was introduced. When we do that, we realize that the plow could have all the characteristics of a tertiary artefact. The plough, by facilitating work in fields, brought better living conditions, relieved fatigue and improved health; therefore, it increased life expectancy and allowed free time to be dedicated to family, leisure or other activities. In short, the plow, by changing the way of working, induced a different vision of life. Aware of this historicization process, Engeström (2001) postulates the cycle of artefacts, that means the same artefact can arise as primary (for example the pen as an extension of the hand to leave signs), become a secondary level artifact (the pen as one of the elements, together with the alphabet and the paper, to write a text) and then become tertiary (the pen as a tool for expressing one's vision of the world in writing).

In summary, artefacts modulate our actions in the world and, at the same time, they change the way we think and reason. In the next paragraph we will look more analytically at how digital technology and human thinking intertwine.

1.3 Specularity Between Technologies and Human Thought

We have so far discussed how terms such as mediation and artefacts can help us to better understand the relationship between technologies and human beings. Going into the specifics of contemporary artefacts—computerized technologies—it is interesting to note the mirroring between how humans' cognitive structures are described by psychologists and technologies features.

For example, behaviorism, which was fundamentally based on the stimulus-response-reinforcement (S-R-R) paradigm, elaborates the idea of teaching machines (Skinner, 1968) (see Fig. 1.1) which presented one concepts at a time (stimulus) and the user, after having read and learnt it, had to answer to a test by selecting one of the answers proposed by the machine (response). Immediately afterwards, feedback is obtained regarding the correctness of the response (reinforcement).

This machine, therefore, translates in a concrete way how behaviorists believe thinking is generated: by external stimulus which conveys a consequent action that makes thinking visible. Soon the accusations of excessive mechanism overwhelmed behaviorism and the cognitive approach became increasingly popular.

According to cognitivists, people do not think following a precise sequence—stimulus-response-reinforcement; rather, thinking is reticular, based on unexpected

Fig. 1.1 Skinner's teaching machine

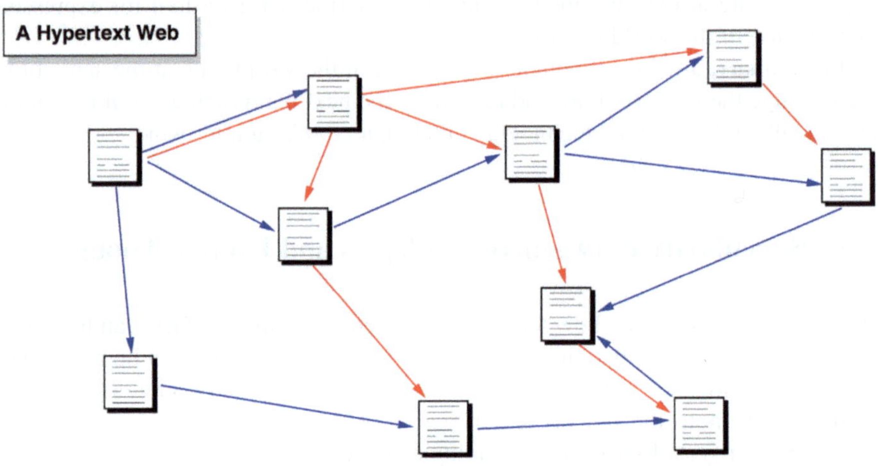

Fig. 1.2. Bush's hypertext structure

and personal connections between information and ideas, determined by motivation, previous knowledge and metacognitive reflection. Therefore, cognitivist technology is characterized by a not-linear structure; it is rather reticular, traversable through freely explorable nodes and connections: this is the concept of 'hypertext'. The first to imagine an hypertextual structure was Bush (1945) which did it prior to the introduction of any digital technology but with just paper cards linked each other by words or ideas in common (see Fig. 1.2). Bush considered the nature of human thinking well represented by such structure.

The attempt to build intelligent machines, increasingly capable of emulating human thought, characterizes a specific line of technological development within the cognitivist stream. From hypertext and hypermedia (which add different formats—images, sounds, animations—to the concept of hypertextuality) up to the most recent developments in technology, it is possible to trace a common thread. Artificial Intelligence, robotics, the so-called machine learning up to the recent Chat-GPT, they all have in common the replication in machines of what psychology, cognitive science and neuroscience are gradually understanding about human reasoning.

At the same time, however, there is also a somewhat contrasting trend that wants a technology that does not limit itself to replicating—even if in a faster and more effective way—what human beings already know how to do. This is a vision of technology at the service and support of human abilities; this is a type of technology meant to make us think better, to enhance our reasoning, our ability to solve problems, supporting interaction and creative processes. The progenitor of this way of seeing technologies can be considered Papert (1980) with its LOGO, an open and unstructured computerized environment where, by giving directions to a 'turtle' that replaces the cursor arrow, users can animate an initially empty digital space. When accessing LOGO, no information to learn or links to click appear, but a sort of white board with a series of tools that allow the users to create objects into the white board (see Fig. 1.3).

LOGO represents a forerunner of those educational environments that could be defined 'empty' because characterized by the idea of having a digital environment initially empty that users themselves have to fill in. This implies a shift of the focus from the content to having tools that allow users to populate the digital space by creating something. A development of this type of technology can be traced into the

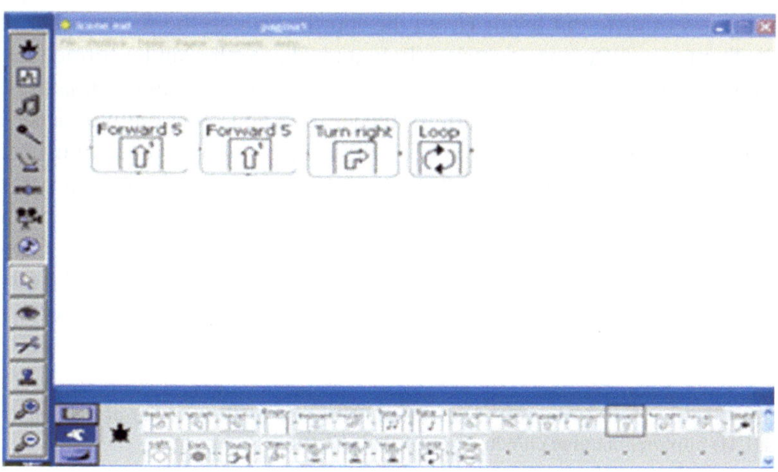

Fig. 1.3 A LOGO screenshot

so called *Multi Users Dungeon* (MUD[3]), text-based multi-user environments very popular between the 1990s and early 2000s, inspired by the famous role-playing game called 'Dungeon and Dragons'. When logged in a MUD, users type a text to describe oneself and, at the same time, to build a digital text-based scenario within which users can play. This results in a sort of digital novel written by several hands in which each user takes up a character and performs actions according to the general metaphor introduced by the creator of the MUD. For instance, it could be a hotel where a murder has been committed and the culprit must be found (Ligorio, 1997), a museum with animated paintings (Usaka et al., 1998), or various educational settings (Slator et al., 2007). In any case, research on MUD can be considered as the first attempt to understand how people interact online, what dynamics are activated when there is no physical co-presence but only remote online presence. These environments were considered innovative for interactions and actions and promised to increase creativity and human interaction at a distance (Ito, 2013).

With the progress in programming, these digital environments quickly moved from text-based to two or three-dimensional virtual worlds where users are represented by Avatars. One of the most used three-dimensional desk-top environments is Second Life[4] (Rymaszewski, 2007) a "3-D social networks, where people can collaboratively create and edit objects in the virtual world (like a collaborative 3-D wiki space), besides meeting each other and interacting with existing objects" (Boulos et al., 2007, p. 233).

While Second Life is a multi-purpose virtual environment, the most decidedly educational one is Active Worlds[5] (AW). Here the metaphor supporting the creative strategies is that of a universe composed of different worlds, built and populated by the users all involved in educational projects. New digital worlds can be created and, from the cultural point of view, it is interesting to observe how communities interact and get organized to have a virtual world actually functioning. Euroland is an interesting case dedicated to the construction of the land of Europe and to support the sense of European citizenship (Ligorio, 2001; Ligorio & Van der Meijden, 2008). Seven schools of different levels (from the fourth grade to the second year of high school), from two different countries (Italy and The Netherlands) formed a virtual community that populated the AW online space, building and animating three-dimensional houses dedicated to art, to music, food and other cultural aspects representative of the two countries involved. To activate collaborative learning processes between remote partners we wanted to avoid each school carved out a part of the task and used the virtual world as a sort of showcase, a window where they would just display their own products. We, therefore, resorted to the principle of 'positive interdependence' (Johnson, 1992), defining the task in such a way that the contribution of others was necessary to complete it. It was envisaged that the cultural houses

[3]A fairly exhaustive list of educational MUDs can be found on the website of the University of Geneva (CH) http://tecfa.unige.ch/edu-comp/WWW-VL/eduVR-page.html

[4]https://secondlife.com/

[5]https://www.activeworlds.com/

of one country should be built by students from the other country; specifically, the Italians had to build the Dutch cultural houses and vice versa (Ligorio et al., 2008). In this way, students were forced to turn to foreign partners to ask for confirmation, to integrate missing knowledge and to complete the construction of the virtual world, initially totally empty, under the guidance of teachers and tutors. Having a common general task—build Euroland—allowed them to decline it in different ways in each class, since each of them had to take the lead of one or more virtual houses composing Euroland. This allowed users to try out on-line dynamics that inevitably impacted also the classroom; indeed, classmates at a distance become an active part of the class in presence, as they are always mentioned and taken into consideration even during offline work (Ligorio & Van Veen, 2006).

The idea of empty spaces to be filled by the users is also at the basis of the most recent Social Networks (SN). At their outset, they were empty spaces provided by tools for the users to gradually and constantly feed them. The difference between authors and users is no longer crucial, so to generate a new label—Users Generated Content (Krumm et al., 2008; Van Dijck, 2009)—to stress out that the contents are generated by the users themselves and no longer by experts that organize the information in advance. Entering digital environments no longer means just searching and finding information or communicating with others remotely; navigating through SN now means to share your own material in different formats: texts, photos and videos. From a psycho-pedagogical point of view, it means allowing everyone enormous visibility of their own work and their personal lives so as to generate groups of sharing and interest. Now the validity of what we think or create is measured in terms of contacts, downloads, and 'likes' received.

But SN differs from environments such as Logo or Active Words for another relevant point. In the case of Logo and Active Words, a coordinated and collaborative work is needed to actually fill in the environment. The users need to coordinate themselves, to define a common project and to implement it. By using SN, the content to share is decided individually and no coordination is needed. Still, the sense of community is there, since users are always fully aware that there is an audience reading, watching, and commenting on their products.

Looking at how technology can be used to support increasingly effective collaboration strategies is the main topic addressed by the study line called Computer Supported Collaborative Learning (CSCL) (Stahl et al., 2006). This research stream has been very active for decades and one of the most interesting outcomes is the recognition that computers (technology in general) would unfold their positive effects only under the condition of using also strong educational models (Jeong et al., 2019). In other words, what is really shaping human-computer interaction is human intention and capability to exploit computers' potentiality to help us in doing better and more. Therefore, teaching a computer what to do has become one of the newest trends. For instance, computers can be trained—under the right conditions—to reliably classify new data, such as patient data. In other words, we moved from the Skinner's teaching machine to machine learning; from machines which contain predefined information to machines that collect information online, systematize it and present it to us when needed. This type of technology (Siri, Alexa, GoogleMaps,

ChatGPT just to quote a few among the most popular) is already very commonly used by a large part of the population; they are already considered as normally part of our daily life. This means that we increasingly think 'with' technologies and that we make decisions about what and how to do it by consulting them. And all this will expand more and more, especially if we consider the perspective of the Internet of Things (IoT) where everyday objects (from means of transport to household appliances) will increasingly be connected online and they will communicate with each other, based on our needs and habits (Mukhopadhyay & Suryadevara, 2014).

The great technological change we are witnessing in recent decades cannot be considered just a product of cultural changes but rather a reason for cultural change; the new technology is producing new culture. The next paragraph is an attempt to better describe the intertwining of culture and technology.

1.4 Historical-Cultural Dimension and Intergenerational Transmission

In modern psychology, the historical-cultural dimension is increasingly taken into account, considered as the cultural "residues" traceable in the various transformation processes of which humans are, at the same time, the product and the creator. To underline the importance of being rooted in the historical-cultural dimension, psychologists propose to call their approach Cultural Historical Activity Theory (CHAT) (Chaiklin, 2001, 2011; Cole & Engeström, 1993). This approach greatly values the role played by mediation objects, considered as artefacts. The reason for this attention is to be found in the capacity, typical and exclusive of humans, to create tools capable of strengthening their own action, to evolve them, and to transmit them from generation to generation. The foundation of the importance of this capacity is to be found in Marx (Friedman, 1974) and in particular in two of his assumptions: the first one considers materialism not in reference exclusively to the object as such, but to the object as capable of subjectively shaping human practices; the second one sustains the need to overcome the opposition between materialism and activity, since in this opposition activity is erroneously defined as abstract, detached from concrete objects. Vygotsky and his collaborators use these concepts to understand human action but also to offer indications on how to improve the human condition. In open opposition to the two psychological currents that were dominant at his time (behaviorism and psychoanalysis), Vygotsky (1978) proposes a psychology based on conscious action mediated by objects and aimed at productive aims. Vygotsky elaborates the idea of mediation in a symbolic and cultural key, considering language as the mediator par excellence and framing the whole thing within the Marxist concept of production. Leont'ev (1981) clarifies the parallelism with Marx specifying that activities are mediated by artifacts and—exactly how it happens with human work—the way these artifacts are used impacts the work flow and allows the creation of many forms of collaboration. In this way, humans enter into a relationship with each other to accomplish complex tasks that allow our development. This became a strong principle for the historical-cultural perspective: the collaborative work carried out to achieve a common and productive objective turned out to be the spark from which the psychological structure of the modern man, aware and conscious, germinated.

Starting from this assumption, Vygotsky (1978) announces his general law of cultural development: the development process starts from the use of artifacts already used by others and the starting point of the development of a new generation may overlap with the arrival point of the previous generation. Therefore, to understand how the development processes of a child start, it is necessary to know the historical-cultural context in which that child is born and grows up. Cole and Engeström (1993) state that such analysis should start from the possible actions in a given context, reaffirming once again the indissolubility between humans and their contexts, and the fundamental role covered by artifacts—without them our set of activities will be very limited and we would not be able to push forward our development (Kaptelinin & Nardi, 1997). This lays the foundation for the general law that regulates development according to which every psychological function always appears twice: first at the social level and only later at the individual level; first between individuals (inter-psychological), then as an internalized form (intra-psychological) (Wertsch & Sohmer, 1995).

The social dimension corresponds to a concrete level, as activities are concretely put into action by cooperating in different ways with others. The internalized form, on the other hand, corresponds to the symbolization of the activity that has now become part of the psychological structure with which we think. Normally, the concrete level is expected to precede the symbolic one. When a technology/artifact appears for the first time in our living scenarios, we first have to learn to use it. This may cost some struggles, not only at an individual level but as a social concern. Later, when the artifact is internalized together with its function, we use it almost without thinking of it, it becomes nearly 'transparent' (Pinch, 2010; Ritella et al., 2015). For example, when we start learning how to use a computer we are initially focused on how it works, how to turn it on and off, how to save our work; later, once we master the use of the computer, we focus on the activities we want to carry out, with a limited preoccupation about the computer functioning. This is true not only at the individual level—when each of us learns how to use a computer—but also at a social level, when a new artifact is first introduced into a certain culture. Whether it is a pen, the press, the television, the cinema, computers or the internet, the appearance for the first time of a new technology worries everyone—so much so that it generates debates and even ideological oppositions (see Eco, 1964).

But what happens when that technology is already consolidated within the culture? Is the sequence first social level then internalized still valid also for those born with that technology already spread in their culture? To answer these questions, we have to look at the intergenerational transmission and, according to Vygotsky, the two levels are reversed: children learn to use that technology first symbolically, through play, for example by pretending to use a computer, and only later they will have access to the concrete use of that artifact. This not only explains the different relationship that younger generations have with modern technologies, but demonstrates the historical-cultural transmission character of artefacts that become progressively more complex because they inherit, capitalize and re-mediate the characteristics of the tools used by previous generations. In this sense, the label "cultural technology" is preferable, so to underline the cultural mediation technology is capable of. This mediation is not based on the objective value technology may have but, rather, on its capability to create culture by re-mediating previous technology upon which the current one is built; for instance, the computer re-mediates the writing capacity acquired with the pen, which in turn re-mediates the culture created previously with the goose feather pen. Furthermore, the label cultural technology better exploits the capability of anticipating and constituting the antecedents of future technology. Following this reasoning, it is evident once more that the impact artifacts/technology may have changed over the course of human history, with a level of complexity gradually increasing. New questions emerge and they are particularly pressing in educational contexts: How to support a cultural vision of technologies? That is, how to escape the polarization that always accompanies the entry of a new technology into society? What does it mean to recognize the cultural value that each new artifact brings along? I will try to answer these questions in the next paragraph.

1.5 Supporting the Cultural Value of Technologies in Educational Contexts

While technology permeates many aspects of our lives, in school there still seems to be a debate about whether to introduce it or not. In Italy, for example, we went from the approach called "Bring your own device" (BYOD)—introduced in 2015 to the 2024 guidelines drawn up by the Ministry of Education that imposes an absolute ban of the use of cell phones in the first cycle (infant, primary, lower secondary), even for educational purposes. This prohibition is justified by the aim to protect the cognitive and social development of younger students, especially in relation to phenomena such as internet addiction and cyberbullying.

What seems difficult for the Italian legislator to understand is that the point is neither to define the quantity of technology allowed nor the right time when to start using it but rather the way it is used. Aside from the fact that bans have never solved any problem, schools *must* address the issue of the use of technology. If school does not do it, there is a risk that models of how to use technology are left to peers. In fact, it is hard to rely on families since they are often unable to offer models of modern technology use because they are new to them too. Again, parents are often pre-occupied by the quantity of exposure to technology of their child, neglecting the idea that there are many ways of using it and that the most relevant issue is that adults should take over the mediational function, whose relevance has been already underlined. Parents often place digital devices (tables; smartphones) into their child's hands already in the first months of their life (Kılıç et al., 2019), delegating to these artifacts a baby-sitter-like function (Pires & Martinho, 2021) without any real mediation. Therefore, first adults should learn how to use technology—not just under a technical point of view (how to turn off or on; where to click, etc.) but rather under a cultural perspective. Only on the basis of a cultural vision of technology (what to do with it) would it be possible to overcome the risks of incorrect uses. What is really needed is a cultural vision of technology, where its functions are exploited at the service of a positive development. To achieve this goal, the adults' mediation is fundamental (Klein et al., 2000) and the elective place where this can be activated is school.

During the emergency period caused by the spread of COVID, educational institutions across the world have resorted to the use of technologies to be able carry out their educational role. Research is still trying to draw up a balance of that experience but it is quite clear that distance learning is no longer a taboo and the positive effects produced are such to believe that it is worth trying to improve it instead of returning to exclusively in-person teaching (Boerchi et al., 2024; Cacciamani et al., 2025; Hebebci et al., 2020; Tarc, 2020). About this, there is a lot of attention on blended teaching (Amenduni & Ligorio, 2022; Graham, 2006) where online and in-presence formats are mixed. Again, it is not the quantity of technology that matters but how the various elements are combined. One of the educational models most suitable to this purpose is the so-called Trialogical Learning Approach (TLA) (Paavola et al., 2012). This approach proposes to take into account three dimensions: (a) the "monological" dimension concerning the individual learning not only in terms of increase of the knowledge a student may have at the end of his/her learning journey but also as appreciation of personal inclinations, talents and attitudes; (b) the "dialogic" dimension, which is realized in social interaction, considering knowledge as emerging from collaborative work and distributed among the participants; (c) the "trialogical" dimension; this is actually the most original part of the TLA because it emphasizes that learning should be channeled towards the construction of concrete objects, which embody concepts and skills learned, and which can be actually used by communities other than those that built them. The application of TLA is guided and supported by six design principles that do not provide rigid prescriptions but suggest indications for teachers and educators to be personalized, depending on their own context (Paavola et al., 2011; Sansone et al., 2016). In synthesis, principle #1 considers as fundamental placing at the center of the activities the construction of shared objects, which have a real utility; the objects should be built by combining individual and group work, so to guarantee the real participation of each member of the group (principle #2); furthermore, it is essential that knowledge creation processes are supported over time, promoting the advancement of knowledge through the continuous review of the objects under construction (principle #3); creativity is encouraged by including moments of collective reflection about what is under construction and why, and the promotion of different forms of knowledge, both practical and theoretical (principle #4); it is also essential to create connections with the communities to whom the object is addressed by investigate their needs, expectations, ways of conceiving the object in question; to this aim also experts can be consulted (principle #5); to implement the previous principles, any technology can be used, preferably those already in the hands of the students so as to capitalize on their knowledge of those tools and show them an educational use of tools that they probably use only for recreational or relational purposes (principle #6). This later principle makes it clear that technologies are fully considered as cultural artifacts since they can cover different roles: they can be mediational tools to build a 'trialogical' objects; they could mediate the connections with the recipients of the objects and all those who may be involved in various capacities in the construction process; and, finally, they can be the end product, the object built.

This approach has been already introduced in many educational situations; for instance, in higher education (Lakkala et al., 2012; Ligorio et al., 2020; Sansone & Grion, 2022), for professionalization and work competences (Karlgren et al., 2020; Stefanova & Vasileva, 2014) as at the compulsory level of school (Van der Veen et al., 2016). A case where the cultural dimension is particularly evident is that of a project where students had the opportunity to redesign a public space, a square nearby their school (Barzanò et al., 2020; Ligorio et al., 2024). Around 200 students (age 7–16) from two schools—a primary school and a lower secondary school—together with 20 teachers have been engaged in tackling the degradation of an important square in Rome (IT). The project needed several stakeholders that contributed to the understanding of critical issues influencing the maintenance of the square; for instance, shopkeepers whose stores overlook the square; babysitters and elderly people who use the benches set up in the area of the square; workers who use the metro stop located there; the faithful who frequent the basilica that stands nearby. A plethora of perspectives that, thanks to the interviews elaborated and administered by the students to all these different users of the square, provides a broader vision than the students' perspective alone. Furthermore, thanks to the collaboration of the various teachers, the square was investigated in different curricula: Italian, to create the interviews; history, going back to the concept of 'agora'; geography, comparing the different squares of the world; science, studying the plants that spontaneously grow there and those that would be useful to plant; math, to analyze the data collected; geometry, to understand the organization of spaces; and even art, given the presence of walls often defaced by urban paintings made by graffiti artists that have definitely attracted the attention of the students.

To realize the final redevelopment of the square, three different generations of students were needed, thus creating an interesting intergenerational interaction that implied not only a continuous re-definition of the project but also a cultural vision of artifacts, used in different ways but always functional to the various aims of all the participants. Smartphones and tablets were not banned but rather their use was encouraged under the supervision of adults experienced, for example in video production or in the management of databases filled by all the documents collected during the three years of the project.

In projects like this one, technology is really an artifact. Re-considering Wartofsky's (2012) classification, we may wonder: on what level a technology with these characteristics would be classified? An answer will be outlined in the next paragraph.

1.6 Towards Fourth-Level Artefacts?

The evolution of the technologies in less than a century—shortly described in this chapter—is remarkable: from teaching machines to learning machines; from individual and occasional use, given the initially poor technical conditions, to collective and capillary tools available almost anywhere at any time. Returning to the three-level proposed by Wartofsky (2012), we may consider that the current technological setting outlines a new, further development of artefacts: a fourth level featured by technology able to create mixed spaces where the distinction between analogue and digital is increasingly difficult to trace. In this space, users not only can find information but they can produce their own information, collective and common projects can be pursued, and anyone can express personal opinions on anything. But the most distinctive feature of the fourth level is the possibility for everyone to define and renew an individuality within a community. This fourth level, therefore, concerns the construction and reconstruction of one's personal world within a specific cultural context. In synthesis, cultural artefacts of a fourth level are those capable of sustaining the construction of one's own 'profile' and 'world' within a blended community.

To better grasp how fourth-level artifacts work the concept of 'positionings' (Harré & Van Langenhove, 1991) could be very useful. This term is proposed as an alternative to that of 'role', socially connoted. A position refers to the personal interpretation of the role, how it is internally represented considering the contexts and interpersonal relationships played around it.

After all, expanding the set of possible positions is one of the objectives of modern psychology as, for instance, suggested by the dialogic approach proposed by Hermans (2003). This approach conceives the self as composed by many different type of positions, always changing depending on the experiences and the situations lived, and in a constant dialogue to each other. The nature of the relationship between the various positions composing the identity scenario is polyphonic (Bakhtin, 2013) and, based on it, configurations of power and/or coordination are established.

This is particularly true in educational contexts; the expansion of the repertoire of positionings and the strengthening of a positive dialogue between them is closely connected to the learning processes (Ligorio, 2010). In fact, learning and identity are closely interconnected: not only do we learn better what impacts our way of being but learning means becoming someone else thanks to the participation in shared practices (Wenger, 1999). What is learned becomes, therefore, a symbolic resource useful for pursuing a global and general change that goes beyond the local and specific learning context and allows one to think of oneself in new and original ways (Zittoun, 2006).

This conception of identity development goes beyond the purpose of learning to 'discover who you are,' as if the lack of knowledge impeded access to the real self. Rather, it aims to build visions of who one can become completely new, not achievable without participation in educational contexts. This is possible because during the process of learning not only the knowledge increases but also the learner changes along. The focus on becoming, typical of educational contexts, allows us to overcome the etymological meaning of the term 'identity' where the etymological root 'id' stands for identical. This moves the attention from the 'center' of the identity, constituted by a sense of unshakable unitary, towards the 'periphery' populated by hypothetical and desired selves; from the deep and intimate towards the surface of the self in contact with the outside, influenced by the social and cultural dimension (Gergen, 1991). This idea is particularly useful in education where a clinical approach to identity development is not suitable and the concept of 'identity positions' can better help sustain an educational self-development.

Many authors (Hermans, 2004; Hevern, 2004; Ligorio, 2010; McCarthy & Wright, 2005; Wegerif, 2013) believe that technology has resources that can offer everyone the possibility of exploring new parts of themselves and, consequently, adding new positions to their repertoire. Online, these positions could be incarnate, for example, by the Avatars and can be easily tracked down since online interactions are often automatically recorded. Users can create 'profiles' that do not totally adhere to reality, for instance, by editing photos or artfully enhancing the description of certain aspects of one's personality (Ramalingam & Chinnaiah, 2018). It does not necessarily mean that users are lying or mystifying about themselves, it could be a sort of experimenting with new ways of being and testing themselves in dialogue with others. For instance, pretending to be of a different gender than that assigned at birth or of a different age could just be a way to see how that feels (Talamo & Ligorio, 2001).

When technology is used in an educational setting, fake profiles and anonymity are not allowed since students need to be recognizable and changes in terms of positions could be also used to assess their performance. In a research I conducted some time ago (Ligorio & Sansone, 2009; Ligorio et al., 2013), university students attended a blended course about e-learning, based on TLA (see previous paragraph). To put in practice this approach, students were required to carry out different activities including, for example, role-taking (Sarbin, 1943), Jigsaw (Aronson, 1978) and the construction and maintenance of personal e-portfolio (Impedovo et al., 2013). During the course, students, in addition to attending the lessons in the classroom, used an online platform to discuss the topics of the course and create and modify documents. The notes posted in the various forums and the content of the e-portfolio became data for the analysis of their positioning. The course was structured in five modules and each of them could be considered as a milestone to detect the state of the art of students' positions. We concentrated our analysis on two aspects:

(a) The transition from individual I-positions versus We-position to test the effect of the collaborative work (Loperfido et al., 2014).

(b) The transition from student-positions versus professional-positions triggered by the trialogical objects built during the course meant for a professional market that forced students to be in close contact with e-learning entrepreneurs (Impedovo et al., 2018; Ligorio et al., 2013).

The results were encouraging, We-positions increased dramatically after participating in group work and, toward the end of the course, professional positions appeared whilst they were totally absent at the outset. Furthermore, the modular structure of the courses allows students to identify critical moments as well as the most profitable ones, thus offering useful feedback for the teacher to reorganize the various activities and pay attention to students in difficulty.

Fourth-level artifacts may also have negative consequences, especially when the educational dimension and the presence of an expert/teacher are missing. For instance, users may find themselves living in a bubble (Fechter, 2007), of being victims of algorithms that let them see only what they like, thus creating self-referential and sometimes toxic communities. Just think of the ability of new technologies to influence (often negatively) political events (Ward, 2008) and various beliefs (often false) (Lazer et al., 2018). The way to escape these dangers is to leverage a conscious human mediation, characterized by a deep understanding of the potentialities of the tools we have in our hands so as to exploit the positive aspects and avoid the negatives ones; furthermore, an educational and cultural model is needed to guide their use. When these aspects are taken into account, the use of technology may result not only as an advantage for learning but as a trigger for self-development.

1.7 Conclusions

The point I wanted to make in this chapter is that technology is part of our being. As such, we should be concerned about what we do with them and not what they do to us. To exploit this point, the term artifact seems to better convey the human nature of technology by putting in the foreground the awareness that they are made by us, that they reflect our abilities and that they are there to realize our desires and our purposes.

I also suggested conceiving a fourth-level artifact to underline how culture changes the perception we have of technologies but still much needs to be understood about our relationship with technologies. For instance, we are moving from a paper-based culture toward a screen-mediated culture where new communication channels are used; written short texts, images and videos instead of books, visual contacts, oral, and nonverbal-communication. This leads to the creation of a new world that needs to be understood critically, highlighting the re-mediation from previous artifacts and from which to extrapolate positive models to pass on to the new generations. Technologies are now widely present in every context of life and scholars should take charge of providing models of positive use, transforming practices and discourses around technologies into opportunities to bring out interests, to adopt new communication methods so that, for example, find the right interlocutors, decide when and how to intervene, accept to challenge beliefs and to confront in a public debate. Instead, technologies are often perceived as a risk factor that generates fears of various kinds. Of course there are risks, but it is the task of research to offer an analysis free from a priori morality as well as unfounded fears or excessive enthusiasm. Technology increasingly thinks and acts like us but is totally devoid of opinions, intentions, motivations and, of course, emotions. Those are ours, the human ones that come into play and, therefore, we are the ones who must influence their trajectory so that from simple tools they become cultural artefacts at our service. If technology increasingly resembles us, it is up to the human sciences—more than computer science—to analyze the psychological and sociocultural consequences of the development of increasingly complex artifacts.

While not denying a certain aprioristic enthusiasm of research, which has not always allowed to take into due account the real difficulties of using technologies and the conditions necessary for their effective use, it has been demonstrated that the introduction of technologies under the conditions of a cultural mediation from adults/experts and an efficient psycho-pedagogical model allows interesting results in terms of improvement of skills, knowledge and behavior not only related to digital but in a more general way, connected to personal and social growth (Costley, 2014; Buntin et al., 2011; Riva et al., 2012). It remains that implementing such use of technology requires big effort, a lot of preparation, flexibility and no prejudice towards technologies, which is often found in educators.

References

Amenduni, F., & Ligorio, M. B. (2022). Blended learning and teaching in higher education: An international perspective. *Education Sciences, 12*(2), 129.

Aronson, E. (1978). *The jigsaw classroom*. Sage.

Bakhtin, M. (2013). *Problems of Dostoevsky's poetics* (Vol. 8). University of Minnesota Press.

Barzanò, G., Amenduni, F., Cutello, G., Lissoni, M., Pecorelli, C., Quarta, R., et al. (2020). When the place matters: Moving the classroom into a museum to re-design a public space. *Frontiers in Psychology, 11*, 943.

Boerchi, D., Cacciamani, S., & Ligorio, M. B. (2024). The role of college study competencies and motivations in determining the acceptance of distance education. *Technology, Knowledge and Learning, 29*(1), 397–411.

Boulos, M. N. K., Hetherington, L., & Wheeler, S. (2007). Second life: An overview of the potential of 3-D virtual worlds in medical and health education. *Health Information & Libraries Journal, 24*(4), 233–245.

Bruner, J. S. (1973). *Beyond the information given: Studies in the psychology of knowing*. W. W. Norton.

Bruner, J. (1997). *The culture of education*. Harvard University Press.

Bruner, J. S., & Haste, H. (2010). *Making sense (Routledge Revivals): The child's construction of the world*. Routledge.

Buntin, M. B., Burke, M. F., Hoaglin, M. C., & Blumenthal, D. (2011). The benefits of health information technology: A review of the recent literature shows predominantly positive results. *Health Affairs, 30*(3), 464–471.
Bush, V. (1945). As we may think. *The Atlantic Monthly, 176*(1), 101–108.
Cacciamani, S., Ligorio, M. B., & Buglass, S. (2025). University students' acceptance of distance education at the second wave of Covid-19: Insights and future perspectives. *QWERTY-Interdisciplinary Journal of Technology, Culture and Education*, 122–145.
Chaiklin, S. (2001). *The theory and practice of cultural-historical psychology*. Aarhus University Press.
Chaiklin, H. (2011). Attitudes, behavior, and social practice. *Journal of Sociology & Social Welfare, 38*, 31.
Clark, A., & Chalmers, D. J. (1998). The extended mind. *Analysis, 58*(1), 7–19.
Cobern, W. W. (1993). Constructivism. *Journal of Educational and Psychological Consultation, 4*(1), 105–112.
Cole, M., & Engeström, Y. (1993). A cultural-historical approach to distributed cognition. In *Distributed cognitions: Psychological and educational considerations* (pp. 1–46).
Costley, K. C. (2014). The positive effects of technology on teaching and student learning. *Online submission.*
Eco, U. (1964). Apocalittici e integrati: comunicazioni di massa e teorie della cultura di massa (Vol. 46). Bompiani. [Apocalyptic and Integrated: Mass Communications and Theories of Mass Culture].
Engeström, Y. (2001). Expansive learning at work: Toward an activity theoretical reconceptualization. *Journal of Education and Work, 14*(1), 133–156.
Fechter, A. M. (2007). *Living in a bubble. Going first class*, pp. 33–52.
Floridi, L. (2015). *The onlife manifesto: Being human in a hyperconnected era* (p. 264). Springer.
Fosnot, C. T. (2013). *Constructivism: Theory, perspectives, and practice*. Teachers College Press.
Freeman, C. (1995). Innovation and growth. Chapters.
Friedman, J. (1974). Marxism, structuralism and vulgar materialism. *Man, 9*(3), 444–469.
Graham, C. R. (2006). Blended learning systems. In *The handbook of blended learning: Global perspectives, local designs* (Vol. 1, pp. 3–21).
Gergen, K. J. (1991). Emerging challenges for theory and psychology. *Theory & Psychology, 1*(1), 13–35.
Hård, M., & Jamison, A. (2013). *Hubris and hybrids: A cultural history of technology and science*. Routledge.
Harré, R., & Van Langenhove, L. (1991). Varieties of positioning. *Journal for the Theory of Social Behaviour*.
Hebebci, M. T., Bertiz, Y., & Alan, S. (2020). Investigation of views of students and teachers on distance education practices during the Coronavirus (COVID-19) pandemic. *International Journal of Technology in Education and Science, 4*(4), 267–282.
Hermans, H. J. (2003). The construction and reconstruction of a dialogical self. *Journal of Constructivist Psychology, 16*(2), 89–130.
Hermans, H. J. (2004). Introduction: The dialogical self in a global and digital age. *Identity, 4*(4), 297–320.
Hevern, V. W. (2004). Threaded identity in cyberspace: Weblogs & positioning in the dialogical self. *Identity, 4*(4), 321–335.
Impedovo, M. A., Ligorio, M. B., & McLay, K. F. (2018). The "friend of zone of proximal development" role: ePortfolios as boundary objects. *Journal of Computer Assisted Learning, 34*(6), 753–761.
Impedovo, M. A., Ritella, G., & Ligorio, M. B. (2013). Developing codebooks as a new tool to analyze students' ePortfolios. *International Journal of ePortfolio, 3*(2), 161–176.
Ito, M. (2013). Virtually embodied: The reality of fantasy in a multi-user dungeon. In *Internet culture* (pp. 87–109). Routledge.

Jablonka, E., Ginsburg, S., & Dor, D. (2012). The co-evolution of language and emotions. *Philosophical Transactions of the Royal Society B: Biological Sciences, 367*(1599), 2152–2159.

Jenkins, H., & Ito, M. (2015). *Participatory culture in a networked era: A conversation on youth, learning, commerce, and politics*. Wiley.

Jeong, H., Hmelo-Silver, C. E., & Jo, K. (2019). Ten years of computer-supported collaborative learning: A meta-analysis of CSCL in STEM education during 2005–2014. *Educational Research Review, 28*, 100284.

Johnson, D. W. (1992). Positive interdependence: Key to effective cooperation. In *Interaction in cooperative groups: The theoretical anatomy group learning*. Cambridge University Press.

Jonassen, D. H. (1992). What are cognitive tools? In *Cognitive tools for learning* (pp. 1–6). Springer.

Kanselaar, G. (2002). *Constructivism and socio-constructivism. Constructivism and socio-constructivism.*, 1–7.

Kaptelinin, V., & Nardi, B. A. (1997). Activity theory: Basic concepts and applications. In *CHI'97 extended abstracts on human factors in computing systems* (pp. 158–159).

Karlgren, K., Paavola, S., & Ligorio, M. B. (2020). Introduction: What are knowledge work practices in education? How can we study and promote them? *Research Papers in Education, 35*(1), 1–7.

Kılıç, A. O., Sari, E., Yucel, H., Oğuz, M. M., Polat, E., Acoglu, E. A., & Senel, S. (2019). Exposure to and use of mobile devices in children aged 1–60 months. *European Journal of Pediatrics, 178*, 221–227.

Kirsh, D. (1995). The intelligent use of space. *Artificial Intelligence, 73*(1–2), 31–68.

Klein, P. S., Nir-Gal, O., & Darom, E. (2000). The use of computers in kindergarten, with or without adult mediation; effects on children's cognitive performance and behavior. *Computers in Human Behavior, 16*(6), 591–608.

Krumm, J., Davies, N., & Narayanaswami, C. (2008). User-generated content. *Pervasive Computing EEE, 7*(4), 10–11.

Lakkala, M., Ilomäki, L., Paavola, S., Kosonen, K., & Muukkonen, H. (2012). Using trialogical design principles to assess pedagogical practices in two higher education courses. In *Collaborative knowledge creation: Practices, tools, concepts* (pp. 141–161).

Lazer, D. M., Baum, M. A., Benkler, Y., Berinsky, A. J., Greenhill, K. M., Menczer, F., et al. (2018). The science of fake news. *Science, 359*(6380), 1094–1096.

LeMoyne, R. (2016). *Advances for prosthetic technology*. Springer.

Leont'ev, A. N. (1981). *Problems of the development of the mind*. Progress.

Lévy, P. (1997). *Collective intelligence: Mankind's emerging world in cyberspace*. Perseus Books.

Libin, A., & Libin, E. (2005). Cyber-anthropology: A new study on human and technological co-evolution. In *Future of intelligent and extelligent health environment* (pp. 146–155). IOS Press.

Ligorio, M. B. (1997). Conflict management in a computer mediated interaction. In *Swiss workshop on collaborative and distributed systems*.

Ligorio, M. B. (2001). Integrating communication formats: Synchronous versus asynchronous and text-based versus visual. *Computers & Education, 37*(2), 103–125.

Ligorio, M. B. (2010). Dialogical relationship between identity and learning. *Culture & Psychology, 16*(1), 93–107.

Ligorio, M. B., Amenduni, F., Sansone, N., & McLay, K. (2020). Designing blended university courses for transaction from academic learning to professional competences. In *Cultural views on online learning in higher education: A seemingly borderless class* (pp. 67–86).

Ligorio, M. B., Barzanò, G., Amenduni, F., Cauchi, R., Turrisi, S., Raffio, L., et al. (2024). Active citizenship and participation through "dialogue in the square". In *Education and dialogue in polarized societies, dialogic perspectives in times of change* (pp. 96–120). Oxford University Press.

Ligorio, M. B., Cesareni, D., & Schwartz, N. (2008). Collaborative virtual environments as means to increase the level of intersubjectivity in a distributed cognition system. *Journal of Research on Technology in Education, 40*(3), 339–357.

Ligorio, M. B., Loperfido, F. F., & Sansone, N. (2013). Dialogical positions as a method of understanding identity trajectories in a collaborative blended university course. *International Journal of Computer-Supported Collaborative Learning, 8*, 351–367.
Ligorio, M. B., & Sansone, N. (2009). Structure of a blended university course: Applying constructivist principles to blended teaching. In *Information technology and constructivism in higher education: Progressive learning frameworks* (pp. 216–230). IGI Global.
Ligorio, M. B., & Van der Meijden, H. (2008). Teacher guidelines for cross-national virtual communities in primary education. *Journal of Computer Assisted Learning, 24*(1), 11–25.
Ligorio, M. B., & Van Veen, K. (2006). Constructing a successful cross-national virtual learning environment in primary and secondary education. *AACE Journal, 14*(2), 103–128.
Loperfido, F. F., Sansone, N., Ligorio, M. B., & Fujita, N. (2014). Understanding I/We positions in a blended university course. Polyphony and chronotopes as dialogical features. *QWERTY, 9*(2), 51–66.
Luria, A. R. (1928). The problem of the cultural development of the child. *Journal of Genetic Psychology, 35*, 493–506.
McCarthy, J., & Wright, P. (2005, September). Technology in place: Dialogics of technology, place and self. In *IFIP conference on human-computer interaction* (pp. 914–926). Springer.
McLuhan, M. (2017). The medium is the message. In *Communication theory* (pp. 390–402). Routledge.
Miller, D. (2002). Artefacts and the meaning of things. In *Companion encyclopedia of anthropology* (pp. 430–453). Routledge.
Mukhopadhyay, S. C., & Suryadevara, N. K. (2014). *Internet of things: Challenges and opportunities* (pp. 1–17). Springer.
Paavola, S., Engeström, R., & Hakkarainen, K. (2012). The trialogical approach as a new form of mediation. In *Collaborative knowledge creation: Practices, tools, concepts* (pp. 1–14). Sense Publishers.
Paavola, S., Lakkala, M., Muukkonen, H., Kosonen, K., & Karlgren, K. (2011). The roles and uses of design principles in a project on trialogical learning. *Research in Learning Technology, 19*(3), 233–246.
Papert, S. (1980). *Mindstroms: Children, computers, and powerful ideas*. Basic Book.
Perret-Clermont, A. N. (2004). Thinking spaces of the young. In *Joining society: Social interaction and learning in adolescence and youth* (pp. 3–10).
Piaget, J. (2003). Part I: Cognitive development in children--Piaget development and learning. *Journal of Research in Science Teaching, 40.*
Pinch, T. (2010). The invisible technologies of Goffman's sociology from the merry-go-round to the internet. *Technology and Culture, 51*(2), 409–424.
Pires, H., & Martinho, R. (2021). Technology and its use in Families with Children.
Ramalingam, D., & Chinnaiah, V. (2018). Fake profile detection techniques in large-scale online social networks: A comprehensive review. *Computers & Electrical Engineering, 65*, 165–177.
Ritella, G., Martinelli, M., Loperfido, F., & Ligorio, M. (2015). Tecnologie (in) visibili: appropriazione in un percorso di training professionale [(In)visible Technologies: Appropriation in a Professional Training Path]. *Italian Journal of Educational Technology, 23*(1), 19–25.
Riva, G., Baños, R. M., Botella, C., Wiederhold, B. K., & Gaggioli, A. (2012). Positive technology: Using interactive technologies to promote positive functioning. *Cyberpsychology, Behavior, and Social Networking, 15*(2), 69–77.
Rymaszewski, M. (2007). *Second life: The official guide*. Wiley.
Sansone, N., & Grion, V. (2022). The "trialogical learning & assessment approach": Design principles for higher education. *QWERTY, 17*(2), 10–28.
Sansone, N., Cesareni, D., & Ligorio, M. (2016). The trialogical learning approach to innovate teaching. *Italian Journal of Educational Technology, 24*(2), 82–82.
Sarbin, T. R. (1943). The concept of role-taking. *Sociometry, 6*(3), 273–285.
Skinner, B. F. (1968). *The technology of teaching*. Appleton-Century-Crofts.

Slator, B. M., Borchert, O., Brandt, L., Chaput, H., Erickson, K., Groesbeck, G., et al. (2007). From dungeons to classrooms: The evolution of MUDs as learning environments. In *Evolution of teaching and learning paradigms in intelligent environment* (pp. 119–159).
Stahl, G., Koschmann, T. D., & Suthers, D. D. (2006). CSCL: An historical perspective.
Stefanova, S., & Vasileva, T. (2014). Trialogical approach to knowledge practices in CAD education. *Annual Journal of Electronics, 8*, 150–153.
Stout, D. (2010). Possible relations between language and technology in human evolution. In *Stone tools and the evolution of human cognition* (pp. 159–184).
Talamo, A., & Ligorio, B. (2001). Strategic identities in cyberspace. *CyberPsychology & Behavior, 4*(1), 109–122.
Tarc, P. (2020). Education post-'Covid-19': Re-visioning the face-to-face classroom. *Current Issues in Comparative Education, 22*(1).
Usaka, T., Yura, S., Fujimori, K., Mori, H., & Sakamuram, K. (1998, July). A multimedia MUD system for the digital museum. In *Proceedings of Third Asia Pacific Computer Human Interaction (Cat No. 98EX110)* (pp. 32–37). IEEE.
Van Dijck, J. (2009). Users like you? Theorizing agency in user-generated content. *Media, Culture & Society, 31*(1), 41–58.
Van der Veen, C., Dobber, M., & van Oers, B. (2016). Implementing dynamic assessment of vocabulary development as a trialogical learning process: A practice of teacher support in primary education schools. *Language Assessment Quarterly, 13*(4), 329–340.
Vygotsky, L. S. (1978). Socio-cultural theory. *Mind in Society, 6*(3), 23–43.
Vygotsky, L. S. (2012). *Thought and language*. MIT press.
Ward, S. (Ed.). (2008). *Making a difference: A comparative view of the role of the Internet in election politics*. Lexington Books.
Wartofsky, M. W. (2012). *Models: Representation and the scientific understanding* (Vol. 48). Springer.
Wenger, E. (1999). *Communities of practice: Learning, meaning, and identity*. Cambridge University Press.
Wertsch, J. V., & Sohmer, R. (1995). Vygotsky on learning and development. *Human Development, 38*(6), 332–333.
Wegerif, R. (2013). *Dialogic: Education for the internet age*. Routledge.
Zhang, J., & Norman, D. A. (1994). Representations in distributed cognitive tasks. *Cognitive Science, 18*(1), 87–122.
Zittoun, T. (2006). *Transitions: Symbolic resources in development*. IAP.

Chapter 2
Mapping the Information Landscape of St Helena: The Interplay of History, Technology and Culture in a Remote Island Community

Andrew Whitworth

> *...we arrived at this small particle of earth, placed in the midst of an immense ocean, and so very removed from anything terrestrial...*
>
> *From "A Description of the Island of St Helena" in the London Chronicle, May 30th 1755.*

2.1 Introduction

On October 1st 2023 the British Overseas Territory of St Helena was fully connected to Google's Equiano undersea cable, a spur linking it with the main cable off the west coast of Africa. This link brought high-speed internet access to this remote Atlantic island for the first time. In the successful application to the European Development Fund to cover the 21.5 million euros cost of the project, the St Helena Government (2018) suggested that creating this link was essential if the island were to meet its ongoing development goals, particularly in the area of health, business and education. While it is still too early to judge the impact of this significant investment in the island's connectivity,[1] on the surface it seems to be an exemplar of "digital transformation for development" (e.g. AU, 2020; GIZ, 2023). A common position

[1] This chapter was finalised in February 2025. The author has been engaged on a longitudinal study of the impact of Equiano, beginning in 2021 and for which data collection will conclude later in 2025.

A. Whitworth (✉)
Manchester Institute of Education, University of Manchester, Manchester, UK
e-mail: Drew.Whitworth@manchester.ac.uk

M. B. Ligorio (ed.), *Technology as Cultural Mediator*, Culture in Policy Making: The Symbolic Universes of Social Action,
https://doi.org/10.1007/978-3-031-97673-5_2

is to view an investment of this kind, and the enhanced connectivity it has brought, as the latest, almost inevitable step in industrial, or post-industrial, development: an information and communication technology (ICT) that will deterministically produce these anticipated benefits.

Yet like all technologies, Equiano is not being installed in some neutral, inert space, but into an environment, and culture, that has been shaped by diverse forces over time. In this case (Hearl, 2005):

> St Helena's cultural climate is… determined by its isolation, its British colonial heritage, and by a lack of purposeful activity. At a deeper level, the legacy of the East India Company, the shadow of slavery, and the island's role as a prison still shape social assumptions.

Building on these observations, this chapter considers how flows of information, culture and technology have sustained and influenced culture and society in this very remote place. St Helena is around 1165 miles (1875 km) from the west coast of Africa, and for most of its history has required a voyage of at least 6 days to reach (though this changed when an airport was opened in 2017; see below). But while St Helena has always been, and must always be, separated from the rest of the world by this profound physical gulf, that does not mean it has always been inaccessible, or even peripheral.

In fact, St Helena offers a case study of how the impact of technology on culture and society is a more nuanced, less linear process than the determinist narrative suggests. The island's history provides evidence for a persistent and profound *separation* between technology and local culture. Several significant investments in 'connectivity' have been made in the past, but all have come and gone with little impact being felt by the island community. In addition, St Helena is a colony, and always has been: never home to an 'indigenous' population, it is now one of the 14 remaining British Overseas Territories.[2] As Hearl noted, this status is very significant for any analysis of the island's cultural development—and, I will suggest, its technological development also.

2.2 Sources

St Helena's population is presently around 4000, so it is a small community. Yet it is a thoroughly documented one, perhaps exceeded only by the Vatican in the scope and detail of its records *per capita*. These sources allow a detailed mapping of the island's information landscape (Lloyd, 2010; Whitworth, 2020), and how this landscape has 'sedimented' out of the practices that characterise this distinctive social and cultural site. Such landscapes are palimpsests, with many layers (Harvey, 1996,

[2] The full, official name of the Territory is Saint Helena, Ascension and Tristan da Cunha. Ascension Island lies 800 miles/1300 km to the northwest, and is discussed below. Tristan da Cunha is a small group of islands some 1500 miles (2400 km) to the south, the largest of which sustains a permanent population of around 230. With no airfield, it can be reached only by sea, and is considered the most remote inhabited place in the world.

p. 417); practices and architectures laid down in earlier periods continue to shape present activity.

The historical literature is extensive: the main general sources consulted were:

- Gosse (1938, republished 1990), still the 'standard' history of the island up to the date of its publication, though Schulenburg (1999, p. 139) notes that methodologically the work is weak;
- Schulenburg (1999), a comprehensive history of the discursive and textual development of the landscape of information about St Helena;
- Denholm's (1994) history of the island's communications technologies;
- Pearson et al. (2011) for the slave trade and its aftermath;
- and Kitching's brief histories of the island's records (1947) and printing presses (1936).

Archive sources consulted include:

- records of the East India Company (hereafter, EIC), available for consultation in London and at the Castle Archives on St Helena. In 1908, Banks compiled, annotated and published a selection of these records, and this volume was reissued as Teale (1980). Winterbottom (2010) and Grove (1995) make excellent use of these records in their own in-depth studies, both of which include St Helena in their scope while not being solely focused on the island.
- The UK National Archive, formerly the Public Records Office, in Kew, London; and also the online Hansard (hansard.parliament.uk), the record of proceedings in both houses, Lords and Commons, of the UK government (hereafter referred to for convenience as HMG, for His/Her Majesty's Government, its official name).
- The archive of the late Trevor W. Hearl, held at the Weston library in Oxford. Hearl's role as an agent in, and shaper of, St Helena's information landscape is worthy of a book chapter in itself: Schulenburg reviews his biography in his introduction to an edited collection of Hearl's writings (Hearl, 2013). All references to material from this archive are prefixed TWH.
- The private collection held by the owner of "Miles Apart", a book dealer specialising in the South Atlantic islands.[3]
- On St Helena, the Jamestown Museum and Plantation House (residence of the island's Governor) display many relevant artefacts and artworks.
- Back issues of the *St Helena Connection* and *Wirebird*, the two journals of the Friends of St Helena society (https://www.friendsofsthelena.com); also the online archive of the UK *Daily Telegraph* newspaper.
- The archive of Cable and Wireless (C&W) plc, housed at their former training centre (now the Museum of Global Communications) in Porthcurno, Cornwall.

The aim is not just to "mine" these sources for information but analyse the archive, as Winterbottom (2010, p. 6) does for the EIC. Any archive is a

---

[3] Thanks are due to the owner for providing access to this collection, particularly for trusting me for a time with some unique items, including the scrapbooks of Tony Cross, referred to below.

representation of the system that has enunciated it (Foucault, 1972, p. 146), and what we include in the archive, or exclude from it, is an indication of the underlying values of the societies and institutions which have produced and maintained the archive (Cook, 2011). Technologies are not natural phenomena, but the product of some kind of institutional decision-making process that has involved "the organisation of symbolic spaces… and the spatial organisation of symbolic systems" (Harvey, 1996, p. 112). The mapping and consequent definition of the features of these spaces and systems is a *discursive* activity, one that incorporates power (*ibid*, p. 111). These maps of the information landscape thereby serve as records of the practices, values, assumptions, that have shaped it, and the voices that are represented or unrepresented in an archive are an indication of whose voices have been heard, directly or indirectly, when decisions have been made that have laid down layers of this landscape (Whitworth, 2020, 2024).

In the list of sources there is an acknowledged absence of islanders (known as Saints). Hearl noted a lack of locally published literature in the past, though was more enthusiastic about what had come out recently (Hearl, 2005). There are exceptions in the academic sphere like Yon's work (2007). But this general exclusion of Saint voices—and, in earlier times, enslaved African voices—that speak either *through* the technology, or *about* it, is itself part of the core argument of this chapter: that technology, as deployed on St Helena, is a fundamental part of a "representational machine" (Salvatore, 2006, p. 665):

> a machine that produced, processed and disseminated texts and images in order to accommodate notions of self and other to the new conditions of capitalist accumulation…

Salvatore is writing about Latin America, but this chapter will show that his observations are also eminently applicable to St Helena. A palimpsest of overlapping technologies, texts and sociotechnical systems have maintained St Helena as a venue for colonisation and, mostly, separated themselves from local community knowledge and culture.

2.3 Travellers' Tales and the Imaginary

St Helena has no 'prehistory' nor indigenous human population. It was unknown—or, at least, unrecorded—until discovered by a Portuguese expedition led by João da Nova in the early sixteenth century.[4] For another century and a half there was no permanent population. Despite this, this early part of the island's history is not at all insignificant when it comes to understanding how discursive representations of the island took on particular forms (Schulenburg, 1999, pp. 134–5) that were connected as much to "imaginings" about the island as they were to its geographic reality.

[4] 1502 is the usually quoted year of discovery, although there are some contradictions in the evidence (Schulenburg, 1999, 136–9) and it may have been found slightly later than this.

Only at the point that da Nova and colleagues *recorded* St Helena did it become an informational concept, and *became known*. Its first appearance on maps came shortly afterwards, by around 1510 (Schulenburg, 1999, p. 166). But this embryonic informatisation and representation of the territory of St Helena—the first moves in turning it into a *place*, a locus of collective memory (Whitworth, 2020, pp. 28–31)—did not prevent the Portuguese mostly keeping the island to themselves. Although it appeared on many maps, its depiction, and location, were often inaccurate. For example, Schulenburg (1999, p. 166) includes a section of a chart drawn by Valentim de Moravia, dated between 1506 and 1510, where the shape of the island is so stylised it has been reduced to a mere symbol.

This lack of information about specifics, and the problem of fixing longitude (which meant that navigation, particularly in the deep ocean, was still an art rather than a science) meant that it was easy to miss the island. Nevertheless, St Helena's existence was known in English seafaring circles by the 1580s (Schulenburg, 1999, p. 145) and at some point before 1588, Sir Thomas Cavendish captured a Portuguese pilot (Gosse, 1990, p. 15) and thereby found the necessary information to penetrate (today we might say hack) this informational network and to become the first English captain to visit St Helena. On the homeward leg of his round-the-world voyage,[5] he stopped there for 12 days and "wrote a lucid description of the island", reproduced in Gosse (1990, pp. 15–9). By this time there was already a church and village: this lay empty much of the year but was used when ships called, and sometimes convalescent sailors rested up on St Helena for a time. That Cavendish was the *first* non-Portuguese to 'discover' the Island is a claim that Schulenburg (1999, p. 147) states is more likely a function of the "prominent status of the narrative of his voyage", and Gosse's telling of the story in this way. But he was the first person with any kind of prominent role in English seafaring society to know about it.

By means such as this, knowledge of the island spread, and St Helena changed from being a concept, a node, only in the tightly-connected information and transportation networks of the Portuguese, to also becoming a concept within the competing networks of the British, Dutch, and other seafaring and colonising powers. In 1598 (Gosse, 1990, p. 20) Dutchman Jan Huyghen van Linschoten wrote a detailed description of St Helena. And by the 1620s, Francis Godwin used it in his work of proto-science fiction, *Man in the Moone*, as a base for the protagonist's flight into space (Jeremiah, 2019).

Once the island was finally settled in 1659 by the East India Company (see the next section) and it could be somewhat more reliably and safely visited—in that services like food and lodging became locally available, it developed an administration and a fledgling economy—it also emerged as a potential destination for peripatetic members of wealthy society and a setting for their 'travellers' tales'. Gosse (1990, pp. 189–90) offers an account of an early tourist, who wrote an article for the *Gentleman's Magazine* in Nov. 1759 under the name 'Susannicus' that lauds St Helena's landscape, climate,

[5] After Sir Francis Drake, Cavendish was only the second English captain to complete a circumnavigation of the globe.

and people. The description related in the London Chronicle in 1766, and used as this chapter's epigraph, is another example of the genre.[6]

The dominant view of St Helena was thereby defined, in these early years of its human history, as (Schulenburg, 1999, pp. 91–2):

> a perception of the island and its society in terms of an enchanted, rural idyll, an Arcadia or Eden… these images too, like those of the Picturesque, have the potential to encourage colonisation in areas that have not been colonised already.

These projections of an *anticipated* St Helena (*ibid*, p. 138) are akin to idealised images of tropical islands displayed in modern brochures, or written up in the travel columns of Sunday newspapers. Following its discovery, St Helena came, fairly rapidly, to occupy a place in maps of information landscapes, but only those that were held by those with the power to reach it: that is, those with access to the information and transport technologies needed to both travel the distance, and navigate the route. This happened before the island even possessed a permanent human population, let alone before that population had developed any kind of indigenous 'culture' of its own.

2.4 The East India Company

Cavendish's communications about the island did not lead to its immediate colonisation by the English crown or HMG.[7] But colonisation was a commercial enterprise long before it was a military one, and it was the East India Company (EIC) that settled and fortified St Helena from 1659. They were briefly ousted by Dutch forces in 1673, but once the island was recaptured soon after, the EIC were in full control.

The decision to colonise the island was due to its strategic value as a way-station on the route home from India, via the Cape, and was provoked by ongoing conflicts, particularly with the VOC (Vereenigde Oostindische Compagnie), its Dutch competitor (Royle, 2007). St Helena was considered a valuable asset based on its positioning with respect to flows of capital, and hence information; which at that time, equated to *transportation*. It served as a refueling station, a rest stop, convalescent home and defensive fortress, all on behalf of the EIC. The logistical requirements of transport technologies therefore had the most profound influence over St Helena's history and information practices, and this meant more, culturally, than its being the seventeenth century equivalent of a transit airport or motorway service station. Rather, St Helena was one manifestation of the EIC's attempt to be more than "mere merchants", but to develop (Stern, 2007, pp. 3–4):

> a coherent, if composite, political ideology and economy, drawn from examples and experiences in Europe, the Atlantic and Asia. St Helena thus serves to introduce us to what was, in effect, a Company-State: a corporate body politic that competed for political power and

[6] TWH MSS. Atlan. s. 23/57.

[7] Cavendish died in 1592, while leading his second attempted circumnavigation.

> authority in an early modern world defined, from the pope to pirates, by fragmented, overlapping and rival forms of sovereignty…

Winterbottom concurs (2010, p. 197):

> The early East India Company's settlements were envisaged as spaces for the creation of ideal societies: however, this could only be achieved by 'governing' and 'improving' their wildlife and inhabitants.

Such an endeavor required reliable and consistent information, and 'travellers' tales', rumor and vagueness could no longer be considered adequate intelligence. Hence the active development, on St Helena itself and in the EIC more widely, of technologies of information collection, transmission, organisation and publication. Richards (1993, p. 4 cited in Schulenburg, 1999, p. 25) notes that: "The British may not have created the longest-lived empire in history, but it was certainly one of the most data intensive." The EIC *Records* of 27/10/1679 (Teale, 1980, p. 12) note that:

> Captain Anthony Beale who hath measured all the lands that hath bin distributed and disposed to the Inhabitants is desired to draw up and prepare as exact and punctual a draught Mapp of every man's land on the Island with their due and just Buttals and Boundary's as possibly he can to be transmitted to the Company.

This is just one early act in a detailed record-keeping endeavor that was sustained for more than two and a half centuries. Despite occasional complaints from EIC headquarters in London about sloppiness (and counter-complaints from Jamestown about the lack of staff and specialist expertise) (Schulenburg, 1999, p. 76), records are of high quality (Kitching, 1947) and almost complete throughout this time.[8]

The printing press arrived on the island in 1806 (Gosse, 1990, p. 262), first set up as the St Helena Press and then taken over by the EIC. A regular journal, the *St Helena Monthly Register*, began in 1809 and was used enthusiastically by Governor Beatson to promulgate his social and economic policies (Hearl, 1996, p. 20):

> In 1810, four years after its introduction by Saul Solomon for commercial work, Governor Beatson began to employ the press to promote schemes of economic and social development. For the next three years the first literary productions with a St. Helena imprint, periodicals and pamphlets running to hundreds of pages a year, poured from the Jamestown press.[9]

The library was opened in 1813 by Governor Wilks (Gosse, 1990, p. 263): reputedly, it is the oldest public library in the southern hemisphere.[10] Information technologies for maritime navigation were also emphasised. The Jamestown museum displays a range of devices, such as azimuths, chronometers and sextants, which were important in the historical information landscape due to voyagers' need—and

[8] In 2022–2023 the British Library's Endangered Archives Programme funded a project to digitise the Records: see https://doi.org/10.15130/EAP1364.

[9] Original copies of the *Register* from this time were acquired by the British Library, via a grant from the St Helena Government, in 1994 to prevent them being acquired by a private dealer in the USA.

[10] This claim is frequently made, including on the library's web site (https://www.sainthelena.gov.sh/public-services/library/), but, as yet, this author has found no confirmation of its accuracy.

commercial imperative—to find the island. An observatory was also set up on Ladder Hill, above the wharves of Jamestown. In the *Records* for 24/10/1823 (Teale, 1980, p. 221) it was noted that:

> It had been intended by the Governor that the studies of the Military Institution should embrace the knowledge of the Celestial bodies and that advantage should be taken of the favourable situation of the Island for Astronomical Observations. Capt. Hamilton of the ship Susan *suggested that the establishment of an Observatory on a small scale at Ladder Hill is very desirable, as it would afford an opportunity of correcting Chronometers, which there is frequently great difficulty in doing.*

As Denholm explains (1994, p. 9):

> It was then absolutely vital for a ship to have an accurate chronometer for its navigation… St Helena being such a tiny dot of land in a vast ocean, many ships missed it altogether, and quite a number found Ascension Island instead. Therefore, as ships were by far the Island's most vital means of communication and supply, the observatory was providing a valuable facility…

Astronomy was an important subject in the 'lifelong learning' of members of the garrison (Evans, 1994, pp. 42–3). As would be the case in a modern corporation, generating this kind of professional competency was a route to promotion within the global system of the EIC, hence a more lucrative posting. Winterbottom (2010, p. 15) notes how EIC officials could build expertise by undertaking work such as scientific observations, or compiling word books and local guides. This work helped them advance in the company, develop a private income and perhaps acquire a 'consultancy' job in Asia. An ironic application of this professional expertise came with Captain Richard Keigwin whose (Stern, 2007, p. 4):

> Remarkable success at leading a mutiny at Bombay in 1684 was doubtless influenced by having been the object of one himself as deputy governor at St Helena some years earlier.

An illustration of how, despite St Helena's remoteness, its officials could be advantageously positioned in networks of professional learning and information exchange comes with Governor Pyke's letter to the EIC Directors dated 19/2/1715, where he noted that "the fruitful Island called Mauritius that was lately left by the Dutch is yet uninhabited and has not had any dearth upon it but abounds plentifully…." He is passing on information from 'Capt. Litten' which he (Pyke) can corroborate, and he suggests the advantages of occupying Mauritius both for the EIC's and Britain's interest. In the notes included in his 1908 edition of the *Records* (Teale, 1980, p. 122) Grant observes that, seeing as Mauritius was not occupied by the French until 1721 (the Dutch left in 1710), the value of this commercial 'intelligence' was significant, albeit unappreciated by the EIC:

> The subsequent history of that century proved how important would have been its early occupation by England… its [eventual] capture became a necessity and was effected in 1810 by an expedition specially sent out by the British Government. How much would have been gained if Governor Pyke's hint had only reached the right ear at that time.

Thus, St Helena's position in transport and information flows was a commercial asset, and added value, for the island.

Winterbottom (2010, p. 8) argues that the EIC's settlements, employees and slaves constituted a global network for "the creation and distribution of knowledge".

The EIC sponsored scientific research of various kinds. While these projects were of benefit to science they were also firmly linked to what Grove (1995) calls "Green Imperialism", "directed more towards the aims of conquest than the amelioration of the conditions of life for the majority of people in the world" (Winterbottom, 2010, p. 12). Whatever the motivations, the work being undertaken was extensive during this period of the island's history. In the seventeenth and eighteenth centuries information derived from the island directly contributed to the advance of scientific knowledge, including a first understanding of the relationship between deforestation and reduced rainfall (Halley, 1694); and the first evidence of endemism, that is, that a species can be uniquely found in one particular place (Grove, 1995, p. 349). In the 1991 *St Helena: Document Prepared for Recognition of the Entire Island as an International Recognised Site of Nature Conservation Importance*,[11] this biodiversity is recognised alongside—and fully integrated with—the cultural and scientific heritage, the value of the island as a site for research throughout its history and the (p. 2) "earliest recorded plant species conservation measures anywhere in the world, in 1718". The document also states that (*ibid*, p. 20): "It is obvious from the roll of renowned scientists and explorers who have called at St Helena... that the island must have played an important part in the Global history of ideas."

There was also a network of British-run botanical gardens throughout the tropics, with (Grove, 1995, p. 340): "the main tropical axis running between Calcutta and St Vincent and having a central and essential transit point at St Helena". The facility could help reduce losses of plants that would die on longer voyages, and was intended to prepare the way for commercially valuable plants such as rubber or coffee to be transplanted elsewhere. Winterbottom (2010, p. 203) describes how:

> Colonial botanical or 'acclimatisation' gardens were important to the project of early colonialism: in them, plants might be planted and monitored to test whether they could be produced on a larger scale. In a sense, the small island of St Helena functioned like an extended botanical garden in which crops and techniques were tested before being exported to other settlements.

Stern (p. 15) concludes that by the late seventeenth century the EIC:

> Was now a corporate body politic and an early modern government, concerned with those things early modern governments took remarkably seriously: order, justice, religion, revenue and civic duty, among others. St Helena stood at the centre of efforts, stretching from London to Asia and back, which were deeply concerned with the settlement, growth and perfection of civil societies and the global network of people, goods and ideas that tied them together.

[11] TWH MSS. Atlan. s. 23/10.

2.5 Napoleon, Then the HMG Takeover

In 1815, St Helena's prominence in world affairs erupted, almost overnight, thanks to the decision to exile a defeated Napoleon Bonaparte to the island. The strategic value of the island's remoteness was never made more explicit.[12] Napoleon's captivity at Longwood House turned it into one of the most famous places in the world for a time (Gosse, 1990, p. 268), leading to an explosion in the availability of information about the island, though much of it was of dubious provenance, accuracy or ethics (Gosse, 1990, p. 244):

> When St Helena was chosen by the British Government as the best place to imprison Bonaparte, the London publishers were ready and eager to buy up any scrap of first-hand description of this little-known island, with, if possible, 'Views' [pictures, paintings] and print them to sell them to an eager public.

'Souvenirs' of this time, on display in the museum in Jamestown, include miniature copies of the Emperor's death mask. Many maps of the island were produced. One, dated 1815 and still on display in the Governor's residence, Plantation House, includes the error of labelling it as 'The Residence of Buonaparte [*sic*]'. As Plantation was never even considered as a home for Napoleon, this is speculation that cannot be based on first-hand knowledge. A series of prints by G. H. Bellasis, *Views of St Helena*, depicting landmarks such as Plantation, the rock pillar of Lot and Jamestown's Grand Parade[13] was published in similar haste on November 1st 1815. Though the images are broadly accurate, they remain idealised depictions of the (anticipated) imaginary, rather than reality: a representational stage onto which distant audiences could project their own images of the great Emperor in Exile. Bellasis dedicates the portfolio to the Duke of Wellington, noting that his actions in "restoring the peace and liberties of Europe" have made St Helena "an object of interest to the whole world". Too far away for most people to ever reach, these visual media could still position the island within European current affairs, and hence (colonising) culture and discourse.

Most records of this period pertaining to Napoleon himself, and the technical details of his captivity there, were subsequently removed from the island, or never kept there in the first place (Denholm, 1994, p. 8). In both ways, then—the imaginary, and the reality—a great deal of information was emanating from the island at this time; St Helena certainly did not lack 'connectivity' to global information flows. But the conduits that had been set up, whether prior to or during Napoleon's 6 years at Longwood, were less connected to the actuality of St Helena—the island as an environment, society and culture—and more to the imaginary, the colonial

[12] Space precludes detail, but St Helena's effectiveness as a penal colony has been actively exploited on at least three other occasions: the imprisonment of Boers from 1900; of the Zulu king Dinuzulu from 1890; and of three Bahraini dissidents from 1956 (Joyce, 2000). In the 1920s there were plans to intern Irish Republicans there, though this never came to fruition (Murray, 2003).

[13] Copies of these can also now be viewed in the dining room of Plantation House. See http://sainthelenaisland.info/bellasis1815sixviewsofsthelena.pdf

artefact. The information flows did not correspond to any boost to the community's ability to generate and retain information of value, and thus, capital.

The essential form of this 'colonial artefact' shifted dramatically in 1834 when the patience of HMG and other merchants, regarding the EIC's monopoly over the China tea trade (Fox & Baldwin, 2014, p. iii), finally ended. An Act of Parliament of August 1833 transferred sovereignty over St Helena to HMG, a transfer completed by February 1836. In the interim, HMG commissioned an in-depth mapping of their newly acquired colonial asset, using different domains of information. The geographic mapping of the island was undertaken by Robert Seales, and disseminated through his *Geognosy* of 1834 and map of 1835.[14] Seales's mapping is most detailed, down to individual Jamestown streets and landholdings, and communicating quantitative information including acres under cultivation and the population of particular settlements. The 1835 map includes a depiction of elements of the island's information networks, too, as it includes a list of telegraph stations, listing the extent of each station's line-of-sight and the compass bearings in view.

Alongside Seales's work was the detailed census taken by Brandreth and Walpole (republished as Fox & Baldwin, 2014), who surveyed local personnel via questionnaires and interviews (*ibid*, p. 1) between October and December 1834. This census was very comprehensive,[15] covering almost every aspect of life on the island including geography, infrastructure, religion, defense, education and more. Detailed financial accounts are presented: for instance, over the year previous the island's "expenses for relief of the poor" were £217 (*ibid*, p. 55) while £151-15s-3d was allocated "to afford officers and soldiers generally, the advantage of continuing the study of the scientific part of their education" (*ibid*, p. 27).

And yet despite all this surveying and mapping (Kitching, 1947, n.p.):

> The transfer of St Helena to the direct care of the Crown was an ill-conducted piece of business, much bitter feeling being aroused.

Winchester goes further (1985, p. 142):

> The Crown took over all the running of the island in 1834; of all the disasters attendant upon St. Helena's history, this was quite probably the worst. None of the islanders wanted the change; most were appalled at the cavalier way King William's men dismissed faithful Company servants, slashed budgets, reduced the status of the island to a mere cipher in the grand colonial roll.

These budget cuts were substantial (Fox & Baldwin, 2014, p. iv):

> In total the cuts proposed by the commissioners [Brandreth and Walpole] would reduce the cost of running the civil administration of the island from over £29K to under £10K and the military from nearly £61K to £23K.

The regime change, therefore, directly removed significant amounts of capital from St Helena. Additionally, a longer-term impact came with the island's separation

[14] National Archives CO 1069/757 (*Geognosy*) and National Archives CO 700/StHelena7 (map).

[15] Fox and Baldwin's modern edition runs to 216 pages and even then, several appendices and subsidiary reports have been omitted (2014, p. iv).

from EIC information flows (Winterbottom, 2010), and the decision-making expertise that was integrated with them. In the EIC's map of the landscape, St Helena was a valuable node in information and transportation networks, and thus worth subsidising even if they knew it would never make a profit in itself, due to remoteness and the lack of natural resources. HMG, on the other hand, saw St Helena as just one more colony, reluctantly managed by various departments and ministries.

It is not therefore lack of information (and subsequent poor decision making) that resulted in such negative outcomes for St Helenians, but the narratives that were already in place, and how these discursive maps shaped emerging practices. The incoming regime disparaged their predecessors as wasteful and indulgent, as part of the general political narrative of the time which justified the dissolution of the EIC (Schulenburg, 1999, p. 251):

> St Helena's first Crown governor, Middlemore, took a dim view of St Helenians from the start, stating that 'St Helena would undoubtedly become a very flourishing little Colony if we only possessed an industrious people but the present race have been too much indulged by their very munificent masters.'

This prejudiced view of Saints themselves has been a driver of the island's cultural subordination to Britain ever since, as the next section will discuss.

From this point on, the ultimate authority over island matters would be the Minister of whichever subdivision of HMG was in charge of Britain's colonial territories at the time (presently the Foreign, Commonwealth and Development Office) or, if military issues arose, the Admiralty or its successors. And, as noted in several Parliamentary debates,[16] no government Minister has ever visited the island. The government files in the National Archives illustrate a model of decision making which is invariably brought to a close by a statement from an authority figure (a Minister or Under-Secretary) who has no first-hand experience of the island at all. Thus, there has emerged a cognitive separation (Blaug, 2007): ultimate authority resting with a succession of figures who have never been to St Helena, and have no knowledge, or at best, only second-hand knowledge of it as a place.

This is a characteristic not of technology in a pure sense, but the establishment of a sociotechnical system that is profoundly separated from the culture of the society it purports to be serving. Symbols of this separated, remote authority remain very apparent on the island. The entrance hall of Plantation House displays portraits of every British monarch, and their consorts, from Victoria on, with portraits of every Governor since 1659 also hung on the walls [see Governor Gurr's introduction to Fox and Baldwin (2014)]. Images of Saints, however, are not to be seen: the local culture is invisible in this authoritative setting. Phippard (2023, p. 153) uses the term "colonial scarring" to describe the impact of HMG rule on the culture of the island.

[16] Hansard: see statements by Bob Russell MP on 23/4/2009 and again on 17/6/2009. It should be noted that several members of the British royal family have visited the island, most recently the Duke of Edinburgh (Prince Edward) in January 2024.

2.6 Peripheral Populations and Supporting Information Systems

This peripheralisation of a significant proportion of the local population has been a feature of St Helena's information landscape since the early days of the EIC. In the seventeenth and eighteenth centuries this was particularly pertinent when considering the institution of slavery. The movement of slaves was an integral part of the giant information system that was the EIC. Not just for 'labour', though it was partly that—but, as Winterbottom (2010, p. 195) shows, also to tap into knowledge about topics such as flora, agriculture and medicine. The EIC was engaged in experimentally "transferring skills and people between territories" (*ibid*), and this applied not just to the 'executives', that is, actors such as Gov Pyke, but with slaves too. They were a financial and informational asset, and recorded as such.

For instance, despite being compiled 2 years after the formal emancipation of slaves on St Helena Brandreth and Walpole could still conclude (Fox & Baldwin, 2014, p. 132) that the average value of a slave in late 1834 was £43-8s-0d. Slaves were profoundly, and formally, excluded from information flows: they were not allowed to give evidence in court (Schulenburg, 1999, p. 216). And as Cunningham (2024, p. 34) notes, there was cultural exclusion too, omission from the archive:

> Much of enslavement era documentation is heavily biased and written from the perspective of enslavers (e.g. plantation records, ship manifests, court records...). And even in the case of documents that centre enslaved people as their authors or subjects, such as autobiographies and portraiture, these documents were also often produced through a racialised lens, limiting the degree to which they provide genuine insight into enslaved persons' identities and ways of positioning themselves...

By the early nineteenth century the UK's system of slavery had been replaced, at least to some extent, with anti-slavery: but this value could only be operationalised by becoming the basis of a sociotechnical system comprising institutional structures such as laws, technologies and information networks. The "Liberated African Establishment" that was established in Rupert's Valley on St Helena was a nexus of practice settings (Hui et al., 2017), integrating the naval power that permitted the capture of suspected slave ships; the legal system through which to hear the case and pass judgment; the break-up of the ships; and the housing of the emancipated slaves. Strategic and logistically, St Helena was considered preferable to other possible African locations for this Establishment. Compared to Sierra Leone it had a moderate and healthy climate, and it was closer than the Cape. The Foreign Office thereby recognised St Helena as an "invaluable asset" for its anti-slavery agenda, and the Admiralty were also supportive (Pearson et al., 2011, p. 17). However, the Treasury objected, grumbling about the cost—a common theme throughout this history. In the House of Commons on 25/7/1848,[17] Sir William Molesworth went so far as to suggest abandoning the project altogether, calling the impediment of the slave trade a "most useless expenditure".

[17] Hansard.

Conditions on the slave ships were appalling and it is estimated that around 8000 slaves died either before or shortly after arrival on St Helena (Pearson et al., 2011, p. xviii), being buried in an institutional graveyard in Rupert's Valley. On the other hand, around 18,000 survived (*ibid*), but the Treasury would not countenance paying for their onward travel, nor maintain them on St Helena in perpetuity. Many of the "liberated" Africans thereby ended up as indentured labourers in the Caribbean, their circumstances little altered (*ibid*, pp. 35–7).

Once the slave trade was effectively suppressed and the Establishment closed in 1867: "public attention in England shifted to other subjects, whilst the topic rapidly disappeared from the official correspondence between St Helena and the Colonial Office" (*ibid*, p. 6). There was no need to continue to generate information about the slaves, their fate or that of their descendants. The graveyards in Ruperts' were *known*, depicted on maps in plain sight in the community (for example, in the museum: *ibid*, pp. 5–6), but they had still been *forgotten*. There was no technology, no information system, that required the maintenance of records about the graveyard, so they disappeared from that realm of knowledge though there was 'folk', local knowledge of the burial ground (*ibid*). Nor did this system, and all the information, capital and human life that flowed through it, ultimately bring long-term benefits to the island (*ibid*, pp. 37–8):

> The British (and later the American) Navy's use of the island for provisioning of their ships and resting of crews brought in considerable revenue to St Helena, revitalising an economy that was heading towards decline after its transition from East India Company possession to Crown Colony. These benefits did not outlast the closure of the Establishment and the withdrawal of the West Africa Squadron, however. Writing in 1875, J C Melliss summed up the bitterness felt by the island's inhabitants: they had played a major part in the suppression of the slave trade, but had not benefited.

Whether before or after their "liberation", slaves, as a group, are noticeably absent from St Helena's archives. This is a narrative of exclusion, driven by essentially racist cognitive schema, that has often extended to Saints themselves. The "representational machine" has long been a part of (Schulenburg, 1999, p. 65): "colonial praxis and of the continuous re-negotiation and re-constitution of particular colonial situations…." From the earliest 'imaginaries' (*ibid*, p. 95): "St Helena is seen as an earthly paradise of which its people are seemingly unworthy. If these people were not Englishmen themselves, this could be read as an explicit call for their displacement and colonisation." And (*ibid*, p. 241): "nineteenth century accounts of St Helena are distinctive for their engagement in the construction of a St Helenian 'native', a discourse which is indeed comparable to colonial discourses about an indigenous 'Other'."

Dominant discourses often stress the 'loyalty', 'Britishness' and 'friendliness' of the local population while at the same time depicting them as inferior, subservient, apathetic and unintelligent. The diverse genetic makeup of Saints means they are difficult to classify into neat racial categories, though this does not mean administrations down the years have not tried: usually the Saints are defined as 'mixed race', as in Sterndale (1895, p. 8):[18]

> The annual report for 1891 by the Governor, Mr W. Grey-Wilson C. M. G. states: 'The condition of the island in August was such as to excite very grave anxiety. Work was almost unobtainable...' This is a serious outlook even with a thrifty hard working people, but much worse with one combining much of the apathy of the Oriental with the improvidence peculiar to mixed races akin to the Eurasian in India. The question now is, What is to be done?

And this continues in the twentieth century... HMSO (1905, pp. 404–5):[19]

> The poorer population of the Island consists mainly of coloured people who are scarcely, as yet, sufficiently appreciative of the benefits of education, and therefore there is a somewhat serious irregularity of attendance [at school]....

In his preface to Grant's 1908 edition of the *Records*, Governor Gallwey—a person with an authoritative and custodial role on the island, remember—states that:

> St Helenians are, however, unfortunately as a whole apathetic by nature, nor do they possess any real power of initiative. On the other hand, they are wonderfully 'handy' people and very readily adapt themselves to any new idea or handicraft.

Contemporary utterances in the UK press continue to represent Saints as either unworthy recipients of largesse (see the discussion below of media representations of the island's airport project) or as servile and passive. A 2009 article in the *Daily Telegraph* provides an excellent example of this patronising view, as well as a geographic error that displays the source's ignorance of basic facts:[20]

> 'Housekeeping couples from St Helena in the Mediterranean—known as Saints—are considered the very best you can get', one upper-class insider tells me.

In the same newspaper on 27/9/2006, Adam Edwards, in another article about how hard it is for the English upper classes to employ reliable staff, notes that

> A live-in couple from St Helena has become the latest must-have accessory in the Cotswolds, after several islanders followed each other to settle in the area.

The people of the island have been reduced to 'accessories', a discursive move that supports Phippard's view that (2023, p. 166): "For St Helena, colonialism is not over: it is merely reworked." These ongoing utterances accumulate into the representational field.

2.7 Changes of the Nineteenth Century

In the second half of the nineteenth century, Melliss (1875, p. 41) could write that:

---

[18] TWH MSS. Atlan. s. 23/38.

[19] TWH MSS. Atlan. s. 23/14.

[20] 29/5/2009, p. 29: Gale Document Number GALE|APPJXO302092181. Even if the geographical error was made by the source she is quoting, the reporter makes no move to correct it.

> In internal telegraphic communications, St Helena is not behind the rest of the world, electric wires stretch from post to post, along the roads and up and down the hills throughout the island.

A telephone system was first installed in 1886, only 10 years after the technology had been invented. However, it was not islanders, but (Denholm, 1994, p. 36):

> military requirements [that] were top priority in the early system.… as stated by Governor Sterndale in his Annual report for 1898 the lines were kept up solely for military and official purposes.

Through the middle part of the nineteenth century, transportation flows around the Atlantic changed profoundly, first with the increasing use of steam power and other technologies, such as refrigeration, that allowed longer, non-stop voyages, and then, in 1869, the opening of the Suez Canal. Over 1000 ships called at St Helena in 1860, but 50 years later, in 1910, only 51 did so (Britt-Gallagher & Hayne, 2020, p. 19). This is not just a technological shift but an informational one, though it was by no means immediate. The exploitation of St Helena, for what informational capital it could provide, continued.

In 1899 the island was first connected to an undersea telegraph cable (Gosse, 1990, p. 337); its laying being a direct consequence of the Boer War and the demand this produced for more effective and more secure communications with South Africa, via routes over territory under British control. Correspondence, held in the Cable & Wireless archive, between General Sir James Edmonds and J. L. Young of C&W[21] recounts how the existing communications route to South Africa, via Aden and Durban, was perceived as "roundabout and not wholly British"; thus, a strategic vulnerability. A project proposed in 1897 by the Eastern Telegraph Company (ETC, which eventually became C&W) for a chain of communication cables linking Britain via Cape Town with Australia, including an Ascension—St Helena—Cape Town connection, was rapidly implemented. A House of Commons debate on "Imperial Telegraphic Communication" (22/5/1900)[22] mentions St Helena in passing and clearly shows how important the network of cables—and "keeping them British" (Winchester, 1985, p. 118)—was perceived to be, both to the military or commercial interests of the Empire (but not its peoples, insofar as they had the cables installed through their territories). Sir Charles Dilke, for example, stated that:

> My main object is to get the largest number [of cables] possible laid in different parts of the world between different portions of the British Empire, because I am so firmly persuaded that our naval supremacy, our superiority at sea, will be the more powerful in time of war the greater number of cables we possess.

The value of the cables is taken as a given: a technologically determinist view (Winchester, 1985, p. 118): "The ultimate purpose of the cables was, of course, the unity, and thus the unassailability, of the Empire…"

[21] C&W archive DOC/CW/12/109—"St Helena—Cape Town cable".

[22] Hansard.

Though essentially built to support the military campaign in South Africa, the building of St Helena's cable was completed by a private contractor, the ETC. The company profited greatly from this, both during the war and after its conclusion. Once the telegraph cable was laid (Denholm, 1994, p. 41): "the charge for transmitting telegrams was 4s. per word, but as this was far more than the Island folks could afford, a committee was formed to establish a fund which would help those who had urgent need..." Though the cost of this "was later considerably reduced", it does suggest how the infrastructure was certainly not defined as a public good. Nor did it attract inflows of capital. Despite the hope that the ability to exchange messages immediately with London might increase in the number of ships calling, thus benefiting the island's economy, in 1904 it was reported that only five vessels had availed themselves of this facility in the year.[23]

2.8 The Shift to Ascension Island

The early part of the twentieth century saw significant shifts in the relative positioning and importance of St Helena and Ascension Island. The latter was first occupied at the time of Napoleon's captivity, as an additional layer of defense against possible attempts to free the Emperor. When the Admiralty decided to withdraw the St Helena garrison and demilitarise that island in 1906 its economy took a significant turn for the worse, but the military retained a broader strategic interest in the South Atlantic region, as did commercial concerns. In 1907 the possibility of phosphate mining on Ascension, employing St Helenian labour to help relieve its economic woes, raised questions about the legal status of Ascension, its inhabitants and its relationship with St Helena. Hart-Davis (1972, p. 159) observes that: "Some research was put in hand to establish the position of civil law on Ascension. The answer was that there had never been any: everyone had always come under naval discipline."

The first wireless station was built on Ascension in 1915, during the First World War, as a military operation: a ship was sent out with all the men and equipment required, and in conditions of strictest secrecy (Hart-Davis, 1972, p. 164). Nevertheless (Hart-Davis, 1972, p. 163):

> although Ascension had become a vital link in a cable network which spanned the world, its own internal communications were still extremely poor. After almost exactly a century of occupation, there was still only one road.... A primitive telephone kept Georgetown, Cross Hill and the Mountain Settlement in touch with each other, but anyone on duty in other parts of the island had to rely for instructions on flags hoisted on top of Cross Hill.

In 1922 Ascension became a dependency of St Helena. But this designation made little change to the day-to-day operations of the ETC—which, after a series of

[23] Information display, Jamestown Museum.

mergers, became Cable & Wireless in 1934—or the lives of the people living on Ascension; the island was run as a corporate fief (Hart-Davis, 1972, p. 172):

> in every practical detail it belonged to, and was run by, the ETC. The company's Manager became the resident magistrate, the harbourmaster and the lay preacher rolled into one. The company took over Green Mountain Farm and the garrison hospital, and organised their own school.

Subsequently the island became home to Wideawake airfield (officially RAF (Royal Air Force) Ascension Island, jointly run with the United States Air Force), a NASA telescope used for tracking orbital debris, a BBC relay station and a ground station for the Global Positioning System (GPS). Despite its small population, therefore (the 2016 census reported around 800 inhabitants), Ascension has become a crucial node in the twenty-first century's global information network of flows.

Some economic benefits accrue to Saints through these operations. In 1937 Philippa Esdaile's report on St Helena[24] noted that (p. 1): "many families are dependent upon the wages of the hundred or so St Helenians who work for the Eastern Telegraph Station on Ascension." Sixty-five years later Hogenstijn and van Middelkoop (2002, pp. 132–4) made the same observation. Yet these are small, ancillary benefits, and not evidence of the islands' communities jointly generating capital by managing the assets of Ascension. The tenuous nature of the link between the islands was revealed in a draft of a speech from 1984, made in response to a question in the Lords,[25] which clearly states how the relative value of the two islands was perceived, and that Ascension was and is an independent, corporate fief:

> Ascension Island is a vital link between the United Kingdom and the Falkland Islands… [and] also plays a significant role in the free world's communication… St Helena does not have a similar role at present, nor offers serious prospects for such a role in future. I cannot therefore agree with the view expressed by the noble Lord… about the strategic importance of St Helena. It is *Ascension Island that is of strategic importance. May I remind your Lordship that although Ascension is a dependency of St Helena for administrative purposes it is in fact entirely separate from St Helena. The link is provided solely by the Governor.*

For all Ascension's critical importance to information flows, HMG have been reluctant to allow information about the island to enter them. Indeed, at times they have actively sought to keep it out of the public eye altogether. In 1964, comments from J S Bennett,[26] discussing a plan for a telephone cable linking South Africa with Europe, via Ascension, noted that:

> Ascension Island is important to HMG because of the British communications facilities now being installed there. Until recently, Ascension was remote from the public eye, and there was no serious criticism of its colonial status. The recent episode of the Belgian para-

[24] TWH MSS. Atlan. s. 23/16.

[25] National Archive FCO 44/4179: "Policy towards St Helena".

[26] National Archive CO 1024/565: "Proposed Telephone Cable Linking South Africa with Europe via Ascension Island".

troopers has, as an unfortunate product, drawn attention to Ascension's colonial status in circumstances which some African countries at least regard as hostile to their interests...[27]

In a 1970 file[28] discussing the "Transmission of Information on St Helena under Article 73e of the UN Charter" there is recorded a lengthy discussion about whether, under this article, HMG is obliged to provide the requested compilation of economic and social statistics for Ascension, as officially, it does not have a permanent population. Document #6 in this file, a letter from J. D. B. Shaw to the Foreign and Commonwealth Office, notes that:

... I think we could acquiesce in the inclusion in the body of our 73.e transmission of material about Ascension (as well as Tristan da Cunha) if it is appropriate. But it still seems to me that by including a reference to Tristan and Ascension in the title of the transmission we focus unnecessary attention on the island and also run the risk at some stage of adding two more to the number of our remaining territories (as reckoned in UN terms). We thus feel that it would be better if in future the title of the transmission were to refer to St Helena alone, and were to make no references to either of its dependencies.

When the report is eventually sent to the UN, its front page has been amended to omit reference to Ascension.

In an article for the *Independent* in 1997,[29] Andrew Marshall called Ascension a "James Bond Island". He reports how the various organisations with facilities on the island (that is, including HMG, the BBC and C&W), with additional contributions from the US Air Force, have "paid for all the niceties that keep the island from being just a barracks....". But as neoliberal government took hold through the 1980s, and technologies changed:

the equilibrium is breaking down. Technology has always shaped the island's history, and now it is partly responsible for the new problems. Submarine cables are old hat; you can see their twisted and rusty remains on some of the beaches. More to the point, [HMG]... no longer needs so many people to monitor the ether, and most of their people are going home this year. Money, too, is reshaping the island. The RAF privatised their less essential operations and removed most of their people, to replace them with contractors. The BBC's transmission operations have also been privatised, leading to a cut in staff. The net result is numbers on the island have fallen from 1,200 to nearer 900, and there are more private sector companies, with less appetite and less money for propping up the central services, the niceties of life.

This final point is significant. Cable and Wireless, just as with the EIC on St Helena, were a corporate entity but because of both the strategic, capital-generating location of Ascension, and the isolation of the community on which their operations depended, they had reason to act in more paternalistic ways. But in the twenty-first century, changes in technology and also the spread of neoliberalist values,

[27] The reference is to "Operation Dragon Rouge", in which Belgian troops, flying from the Wideawake air base, rescued hostages from what is now the Democratic Republic of the Congo.

[28] National Archive FCO 58/500.

[29] C&W archive DOC/CW/12/258—*The Independent*, 31/5/1997, p. 11: "Why James Bond island needs to find a new role model".

privatisation and the increased liquidity of capital (Bauman, 2000) all mean there is less motivation, or requirement, for companies to invest in the supporting infrastructure of specific and particular places. While there is, presently, a splinter population of Saints on Ascension, mostly employed in service work, they are connected to St Helena, for most of the year, by one flight a month.[30] In 2005 HMG withdrew plans to offer citizenship rights to those living on Ascension, and Saints must immediately leave the island if they no longer have a job there.

St Helena and Ascension are not partner communities, sharing information and capital, learning together about how to use the jointly held assets of the territory to mutual benefit. Instead, there are "stark indications that the two islands are 'drifting away' from each other" (Hogenstijn & van Middelkoop, 2002, p. 134). Or, rather, that there are two Ascension Islands, coinciding in the same geographical location but otherwise in "disequilibrium" (Smallman, 2003, p. 143) and kept separate from each other, economically, politically and culturally. One has, for a century at least, occupied a key node in global information flows—but its connections to St Helena have been largely absent. The other 'Ascension Island' is a splinter of the Saint community, feeding some financial capital back home, but historically, with very few opportunities to participate in the sharing of knowledge and the development of any kind of jointly-held community aspirations. Bringing Ascension Island into the analysis thereby highlights even more the essential *separation* of technology and local culture in this colonial setting.

2.9 The Diplomatic Wireless Service and Radio St Helena

In the 1960s the UK government ran the secretive "Diplomatic Wireless Service" (DWS) from premises in Longwood, monitoring communications to and from Africa. The DWS is another example of how St Helena's isolation and position have been considered valuable informational assets, but Rippich (1998, p. 12) agrees with Denholm (1994, p. 48) that records of the DWS are scant. Presently, the National Archive holds only a few relevant documents, dated 1964, in a file originally classified "Secret".[31] These reveal only that the proposal to develop a "DWS Relay Station" (also known as Piccolo Hill) on St Helena was quickly agreed, without objections raised at departmental level, nor debate in Lords or Commons. Most likely the station was built to monitor communications in West and South Africa. Even if this assumption is false, the fact that Piccolo Hill was built so quickly (2 years from proposal to operation) illustrates the station's value to its sponsors in Westminster: and, by extension, the ongoing informational value of the island.

[30] Ascension is far better connected to the UK and the Falkland Islands, with two flights a week to both destinations, flights that originate from the Royal Air Force base at Brize Norton. One needs official permission to embark, and the route cannot be used as a 'bridge' to St Helena: transfers between the two routes (UK—Ascension, and Ascension—St Helena) are not permitted.

[31] National Archive CAB 21/5416: "Relay Station on St Helena".

The possibility of locals getting access to the medium of radio had been the subject of communications between the Governor and the Colonial Office.[32] Both agreed that proposals for a local broadcasting service would only be countenanced if censorship (control over "religious and political propaganda") was asserted and that:

> Nothing should be broadcast without Government agreement being obtained in advance. There is no reason why the licensee should not be asked to provide details of programmes and even scripts and/or tapes of controversial subjects in advance of a broadcast for Government approval.

In the face of these restrictions, Radio St Helena first broadcast on Christmas Day 1967 and "was established as part of a ten-year plan for education, under the control of the Education Department."[33] The service took time to develop. In 1969 a letter from Hearl and Colin Roderick[34] noted that the station:

> Unfortunately has no producer able to get efficient programmes going, so that its 8 hours a week on the air is confined almost entirely to 'pop' record requests, although education gets in about 2½ hours now, with BBC recorded schools broadcasts and other features…. There is no local news service on it… [and] it needs the energy and imagination which seems so sadly lacking from the ever-changing UK personnel…

The signal lacked the strength to be heard off-island without being boosted through the Cable & Wireless transmitter, although this did happen once a year through the 1990s:[35]

> The station is owned and operated by the St Helena Government and transmits in the medium wave band on 1548 KHz, 194 metres. But of course, you heard us on 11.0925 MHz on 15th October 1993 and this would not have been possible without the co-operation of our local branch of Cable & Wireless, which received our medium wave broadcast and retransmitted it to you on shortwave using 1.5 KW.

These annual global transmissions focused on promoting St Helena, and were a success with 'radio hams' abroad (Rippich, 1998, p. 17): "hundreds of reception reports filled up the mail bags carried by the RMS [Royal Mail Ship] *St Helena* in November, December, even January after the actual event". But even these charitable, limited donations of transmitter time were not initially prompted by C&W itself, nor HMG or the St Helena Government, but by a Swedish radio enthusiast, John Eckwall, who had developed contacts at C&W after undertaking a similar exercise in the Gambia (*ibid*, pp. 16–7).

Nevertheless, radio has arguably become an exception to some general rules derived so far from this history, in that it is a technology which has developed a level of integration with Saint culture and local life. At present (early 2025) the island

---

[32] National Archive: Letters in CO 1017/484: Broadcasting—St Helena. See also Hearl (1996) for a history of censorship on St Helena.

[33] TWH MSS. Atlan. s. 23/41: St Helena Info Office (1976)—*Broadcasting*, typescript.

[34] TWH MSS. Atlan. s. 23/14. Letter to Nina Joachim, principal of St Hild's College, Durham, dated 29/9/1969.

[35] TWH MSS. Atlan. s. 23/41. Article from *Contact* magazine, dated February 1994.

sustains two radio stations, SAMS (South Atlantic Media Services) Radio 1 and the independent Saint FM, as well as rebroadcasting the BBC World Service. Saint FM is available on streaming web sites such as Soundgarden and Spotify,[36] giving Saints a way of speaking in the world with an immediacy unrivalled by their use of other broadcast media, at least until the advent of internet-carried social media.

But the story of Radio St Helena also serves as an example of a wider phenomenon, in that what is significant here is less a lack of available infrastructure, and more the lack of trained professionals, including information professionals. It was many years before anyone was paid for running the radio station,[37] a professional lacuna which applies in other fields of activity. Pearson et al. (2011, p. 8) note that their excavation of the Rupert's Valley graveyard was the island's first ever formal archaeological dig. Crallan (1974, p. 33) discusses the lack of architects, resulting in the very uniform style of much of the island's housing stock. The lack of trained teachers on the island has been a chronic problem throughout history (Evans, 1994): work done by Trevor Hearl to develop the 'St Helena Link' with teacher educators at Cheltenham College did alleviate the problem somewhat in the later part of the twentieth century but salaries remain low. Finally, Baker (1985)[38] notes how a particular type of information, land registration, had become chaotically organised through practices dating all the way back to the EIC. Recruitment of staff was a problem, as there was a lack of enough local people with qualifications, and a need to:

> Train staff not only to assist in establishing the new Land Register but also to maintain the system in the future and in turn to train their successors, and on this the ultimate success of the system will depend…

Emanuel's 1959 report for the Government summaries the overall situation:[39]

> One of the most difficult problems of the island is the shortage of persons with any kind of specialist skill. This arises partly from the difficulty of providing a very wide range of training on the island and partly from the constant temptation of persons with specialist skills to leave the island for employment overseas.

2.10 Bridging the Gulf

Accessibility is a different thing from remoteness, and the remoteness of the island will never change. As noted, this characteristic of St Helena has been seen as an asset for certain scientific and penological activities, but it is not a state of affairs deemed conducive to the growth of capital.

---

[36] Director of Saint FM, personal communication.

[37] TWH MSS. Atlan. s. 23/41, correspondence between TWH and John Ross, 17/10/1994.

[38] TWH MSS. Atlan. s. 23/29.

[39] Miles Apart collection: A. Emanuel (1959): *Report on a Visit to St Helena: March–April 1959*, paragraph 57.

Over the last few decades, efforts have been made to improve the island's accessibility, both for information and transportation, with the frequent argument that without these investments the viability of St Helena as a functioning community can no longer be guaranteed. Direct dial telephony arrived on the island in 1983 (Denholm, 1994, p. 38) and, 6 years later, a satellite link. Not long afterwards Bain (1993, p. 79) was moved to write that

> instant direct international telephone dialling and that great modern invention, the facsimile machine, have revolutionised life on St Helena and transformed the meaning of island isolation in a shrinking world.

Though video recorders had become widely used on the island beforehand, it was only in 1995 that broadcast television arrived, and a team led by Tony Charlton (see Charlton et al., 2002; Charlton & O'Bey, 1997) took the opportunity to conduct a longitudinal study of the impact of this new medium, focusing particularly whether there was evidence for a link to levels of violence. The conclusion of their study was that there was no such link; also that TV, while it did lead to some *initial* reduction in social interactions, over time came to have more positive effects on the island community, introducing them to more diverse sources, and more current, up-to-date information. But, once more, the wider discourse about this event presented the islanders as essentially naive and 'uncorrupted':

> It is startling to find a people still innocent of live television, with its insistent access to the rest of the world. The immediate communication, the daily reckoning, the impotence as violence is thrust into your face—these, the island of St Helena has never before had to face. They have had videos on the island for some years now, but never have the islanders had such current information—both trivial and mind-blowing—as they are receiving now...[40]

A satellite uplink had been installed by C&W in 1989, and through the 1990s, a space devoted to information about St Helena emerged online, one largely constructed and curated off-island as connections remained slow and expensive right through to 2023. These limitations dramatically slowed any growth in the online presence of Saints themselves, past a certain early point in time. In their 2002 study Hogenstijn & van Middelkoop (2002, p. 144) noted that "use of the internet on the island has grown quickly since its introduction, both in the number of St Helenian web pages and in the number of people connected to the 'world wide web'." But the quotes they present (*ibid*, pp. 144–5) from Saints who speculate about the potential impact of the internet state positions that are little different from those made in advance of Equiano (SHG, 2018); the hopes are for more use of online and distance learning, searching a broader spread of resources and accessing external expertise: but always, expressing concerns about the potential expense. Hogenstijn and van Middelkoop's correspondents note plans for selling the .sh domain name, but it was expensive, and there were few takers.

C&W had been nationalised after World War Two, but its re-privatisation began in the 1980s, and its breakup in 2010. In December 2012 the company's 'Monaco &

[40]TWH MSS. Atlan. s. 23/57, cutting of a *Guardian Weekend* article by Dina Rabinovitch, 24/12/94.

Islands' division, which included its operations on St Helena, was sold to Batelco, owned ultimately by the royal family of Bahrain. St Helena's present Internet Service Provider, Sure, is a subsidiary of Batelco and managed from a holding company in the Channel Islands, yet still holds a (private) monopoly over all the island's communications, one still enshrined in the first clause of the island's 1989 Telecommunications Ordinance.[41] In a press release[42] Tony Rice, Chief Executive Officer of C&W, could thereby comment that: "The Monaco & Islands portfolio is a premium telecoms business and we are pleased to have agreed a deal that achieves an attractive value for our shareholders"; while Sheik Mohamed bin Isa Al Khalifa, Batelco Group Chief Executive, observed how: "This acquisition supports our strategy by adding new cash generative business clusters to our existing operations across the Middle Eastern region."

The separation of technology from community is also evident in the dramatic change to the island's accessibility that was the opening of St Helena's airport in 2017. Until this time, reaching the island required a minimum of 6 days' voyage from Cape Town, or 2 weeks from the UK: the airport reduces the time to a few hours, from South Africa at least. The saga is a long one. In 1985 HMG was discussing (and dismissing as uneconomic) plans from a developer to construct an airfield on St Helena.[43] An infrastructural map dated 1988 and entitled "Major Land Use Zones"[44] marks the future position of the airport accurately, on Prosperous Bay Plain in the eastern part of the island, almost 30 years before it actually opened there. In Parliamentary debates the subject recurs sporadically, always with the declarations that the airport is "essential", and that:

> All the evidence points to the fact that the airport would quickly transform the island from being a net recipient of aid to being self-sufficient within a decade.[45]

"Access" is a key thematic trope, including in local voices speaking up in favour of the development. In a press release from 2001,[46] the incumbent Governor Hollamby stated that:

> Local employment opportunities, improved income and a reduction in poverty are reliant upon improved access.

While some local voices concurred:

[41] See page 5, clause 4 of https://www.sainthelena.gov.sh/wp-content/uploads/2019/04/Telecommunications-Ord-Updated-010419.pdf. A revision of this ordinance, giving the St Helena Government more powers to regulate the activities of the ISP, has been due for some time, but at the time of writing (February 2025) remains unpublished and in the hands of legal advisors.

[42] C&W archive DOC/CWC/8/46: "Agreement on Monaco & Islands Disposal", 3/12/2012.

[43] National Archive FCO 44/4757: "St Helena: Communications Link".

[44] Held in the Miles Apart collection.

[45] Hansard: Bob Russell MP in the Commons, 23/4/2009.

[46] TWH MSS. Atlan. s. 23/1, fol. 36, St Helena Government press release.

> This lovely Island has so much to offer, but if St Helena is ever to develop properly, prosper and become self-financing there must be quick ACCESS to and from the island. This can only be achieved if there is an air service to St Helena.[47]

That quote comes from a pamphlet produced by a pro-airport campaign, "Fly or Die", the name of which pulls no punches in its assessment of the importance of this investment. Yet even here there is ignorance, possibly even willful, about the island's rich history. In the Lords in 2017,[48] it was stated that "This service will end centuries of isolation for the island", which is blatantly a miss-statement. Donaldson and Forssman (2020) are somewhat guilty of this same discursive move when they claim to be studying the "opening up" of St Helena after the installation of the air link.

The island's previous shipping service, the RMS *St Helena*, in fact served as a point of access for several decades prior to 2018, and while clearly slower than the air link, the time it took meant that the ship became a transitional or liminal space, and could be defined as a technology of the island (including of Ascension Island in this case). In 1980, St Helena's former Education Officer, Tony Cross, revisited on the RMS and gathered materials from the voyage into two scrapbooks[49] in which he documents this process of transition, the adjustments that are made *en route*. Information sheets, handed out at breakfast each morning, advise passengers of social events (such as quizzes or exercise sessions) that will help them get to know both the island ahead of them, and the people with whom they will be arriving there. Passengers are also told how they can send radio messages forward to St Helena or Ascension.

Thus, when the RMS was running it was almost unavoidable that passengers would be engaging deeply with the cognitive schema of the place ahead, and encouraged to put aside, to forget, those from home. There was an informal, but definite, mapping going on through this mode of transport. Visitors were being introduced to possible routes through the information landscape that awaited them, so that by the time one arrived, aspects of it were already familiar. In a contemporary travel guide (Britt-Gallagher & Hayne, 2020, p. 59), Matt Joshua, remembering the RMS, writes:

> For many Saints, just seeing the yellow funnel could trigger an emotional reaction, such was the symbolic strength of the RMS. For those visiting the island, their St Helena experience started the minute they set foot on the gangway.

Air travel offers no similar opportunity to acclimatise, to adjust from what is seen as the hustle and bustle of the UK (or South Africa[50]) to the more relaxed pace of island life; and, thus, to cross the informational gulf at the same time as crossing the geographical gulf. Many Saints, most likely, will now never leave or arrive on their

[47] TWH MSS. Atlan. s. 23/1, fol. 55, pamphlet.

[48] Hansard: Lord Bates, 7/9/2017.

[49] Held in the Miles Apart collection.

[50] All current commercial flights to St Helena depart from either Cape Town or Johannesburg airports. That the island's main transport links, including for seaborne cargo, are all now with South Africa rather than the UK, is a change over time that has cultural implications, but the discussion is beyond the scope of this chapter.

island by sea. This is a profound cultural-technological shift, the long-term impact of which remains to be determined.

And yet, despite this shrinkage of its level of isolation (though not its remoteness), dominant representations of the island change little. The same travel guide suggests that (2020, p. ix):

> Prospero would have felt at home on St Helena.... this tiny vestige of the British Empire has all the feel of an enchanted isle.... Walk through Jamestown at any time of day and you will be greeted on all sides with a friendly nod, a quick 'good morning', a genuine smile that is of itself immensely welcoming. The shops may not have the latest goods, you may struggle to find apples, or green vegetables, or decent Wi-Fi, but somehow it doesn't matter on an island where people live in the here and now.

Thus, remoteness is still defined as a *cultural* asset in the twenty-first century: but only if it is *accessible* remoteness.

In the eyes of the UK media and antagonistic interests in HMG, the airport was given little if any time to get over its teething problems and recoup the investment made. Termed "essential" before the fact, immediately afterwards the development was "doomed" or "failed". In 2017 The Independent newspaper offered a positive report about the island but tagged it with the headline "Why you should visit St Helena, home to the 'world's most useless airport'".[51] In the Lords on 14/7/2021, in a debate about Overseas Development Assistance,[52] Lord Agnew of Oulton stated:

> We need to be much more stringent in our assessment of how the money is spent. We saw from the St Helena Airport incident, for instance, that money can be wasted.

Whatever the eventual impact of the airport may be on St Helena and Saints themselves, the dominant discursive powers—always external to the island—see the investment in its connectivity only in terms of deficiency.

2.11 Conclusion

Discussion of a number of important events and historical trends have had to be omitted from this chapter for reasons of space. These include the withdrawal of Saints' UK citizenship in 1981, and the battle to restore it, finally won in 2002; the nature and evolution of the island's education system (Evans, 1994); and its relationship with other UK Overseas Territories beyond Ascension, including the Falkland Islands. A great deal more detail could have been included regarding how St Helena is represented in HMG communications and the UK media, and the topic of slavery, and the story of the discovery and subsequent media discourse surrounding the graves in Rupert's Valley, is also under-treated here.

---

[51] https://www.independent.co.uk/travel/africa/st-helena-what-to-see-do-best-guide-island-distillery-tortoise-coffee-where-to-stay-consulate-hotel-a8132291.html

[52] Hansard.

What I have tried to do in this chapter is focus on some specific strands in St Helena's 520-year timeline, strands that display evidence for how the interrelated information and communication technologies (ICTs) of the island have historically emerged, and depended upon, dominant colonial discourses—and so are, in turn, separated from local culture and often irrelevant to it (as was the DWS, for instance). Reckwitz (in Hui et al., 2017, p. 115) notes that "social space... consists of the organisation of interrelated artefacts, interpreted by both participants and observers", and the ways in which St Helena and its ICTs have been discursively mapped, through centuries of history, has had a most significant impact on its cultural and economic development.

St Helena is, and always has been, a colony, being now one of the world's few remaining formal colonies. A distinctive local culture, that is, an indigenous 'representational field', is evident (Hearl, 2005; Yon, 2007; Phippard, 2023), but this is not the field of representations that is integrated with ICT. Rather, albeit on a much smaller scale, the mapping of St Helena has proceeded along similar lines to that of Latin America in the early twentieth century, conducted by a *representational machine*, as Salvatore (2006) puts it, comprised of overlapping technologies, discourses and ways of generating knowledge, all under the control of the colonial power. For Latin America these included scientific expeditions, particularly those which built on Hiram Bingham's rediscovery of Machu Picchu in 1911; commercial publications such as the *National Geographic*; cartographic mapping; museum exhibitions and more (Salvatore, 2006, p. 665). All emerged alongside the opening of the grand technological, transport innovation that was the Panama Canal—and, ultimately, justified that huge investment by constructing images of the 'Other' that supported their colonisation. In any "representational field" like this (Schulenburg, 1999, p. 150), the capacity to (Whitworth, 2020, p. 53): "define particular representations, or interpretations, as having 'meaning' or 'value' while alternative representations are effaced or concealed is a locus of power". These are not discourses that exist only in some abstract space, but which drive action and practice, and thus economic and political change (Schulenburg, 1999, p. 261).

In St Helena's case this representational field—the discursive map of the information landscape relevant to the island, that acts as the background, against which the relevance of decisions is judged (Whitworth, 2020)—has been largely created by an interplay between the accounts of travellers and official, colonial-administrative discourse. Both are external to the island's local culture: in the case of administration, this was less true prior to HMG's takeover in 1836 but it has certainly been true since. These are the fields that have continuously worked to define the island as a text, and thus, position it as an artefact in decision making processes. A series of technologically-supported information networks—the EIC, the penal system, the Liberated African Establishment, the 1899 undersea cable, the DWS—have exploited the island's position and remoteness, but all have done so for the benefit of colonising powers (mainly, though not entirely, the UK) with very little, if any, diffusion of benefits ('trickle down') to the local community.

Gallwey wrote in 1908 (preface to Grant): "that *sine qua non* to progress, namely capital, is almost entirely conspicuous by its absence on St Helena." This was not, and still is not, strictly true—the island is rich in many forms of capital including natural, human and social capital. But when it comes to financial capital, this may have flowed freely along the information and transport networks of which St Helena has often been a crucial node, but the flow has usually been *away from*, *past* or *through* the island, rather than *onto* it. The flows of capital can easily shift away from particular places that once depended on them (cf. Bauman, 2000), and this is certainly the case with St Helena. And this lack of capital, in turn, has led to those with expertise and skills leaving the island, or never basing themselves there.

Equiano could improve this situation—the St Helena Government (2018) certainly hope it will—but as of 2025, the population remains in long-term decline, and the interests of this population, the Saints, have only rarely been to the forefront of debates surrounding capital investments made into the island's ICTs. Most of these, and certainly all the significant ones, have been made for strategic, military or commercial reasons. The island and its people are more frequently presented as 'unworthy' of these developments. And even where such opinions do not explicitly emerge—there is, as yet, no evidence of Equiano being called a 'waste' or 'failed'—there is nevertheless a remaining undercurrent of colonial attitudes, only now, transmuted into the digital sphere and running the risk of subjecting St Helena to what Heeks (2022) calls "adverse digital incorporation". Once again, the island is, at least potentially, defined in the dominant discourse (now, that of Batelco) as a "cash generative business cluster": not as a community in charge of its own communications infrastructure, and able to exploit these technologies to generate capital on their own behalf.

Culturally, these new technologies have opened up the Saints to influences to which they may not previously have had much access. Yet to see the Saints as naive and innocent 'islanders' who have somehow not yet been corrupted by these influences, or by some new medium or form of entertainment, just perpetuates the narrative of technological determinism. St Helena is not an unspoiled idyll but a place of fluidity and flux, lying at the interstices of continents (Yon, 2007, p. 159), a transition point. It is precisely because Saints have always been positioned at a nexus of flows that this small community has the very rich informational and cultural heritage that it does (*ibid*). Yet the separation of this heritage from ICT, while never having been total, is evident in the relative absence of Saint voices from the archive, both historically and in more recent times.

St Helena's history therefore illustrates several trends relevant to understanding the impact of technology on culture. First, that the nature of this impact is in no sense guaranteed, or prefigured in a deterministic way. A dominant view about St Helena has long been that if only *this* or *that* innovation is deployed, then a local populace (cast as deficient in skills, will or attitude) will then deterministically move into the desired state of affairs, usually defined by its colonial rulers, HMG, as one of 'self-sufficiency' or 'paying its way'.[53] Yet there have been periods in history where the island has occupied a key node in information networks, and these have had only minimal impact on the development of the island's economy, society

[53] See the 2009 Parliamentary debate referred to above, for instance.

or culture whether in the short-, medium- or long-term. There has been very little evident diffusion or 'trickle-down' effect.

If Equiano, and its eventual effects on and for the Saint community, come to follow the same historical pattern, then this undersea cable will not be acting as a technological 'bridge' spanning the gulf that separates St Helena from the rest of the world—a bridge that has somehow never existed before, and which does not influence the nature of the traffic crossing it. Rather, the cable will have to be seen as another constituent node in a representational machine, comprised of many different layers of information and communication technologies; a machine that may already be rewriting the culture of this remote and distinctive place in its own image, for the benefit only of those who hold capital, power and authority in this technocratic world.

References

AU. (2020). *The digital transformation strategy for Africa (2020–2030)*. African Union.

Bain, K. (1993). *St Helena: The island, her people and their ship*. Wilton 65: Bishop Wilton.

Baker, L. G. (1985). *Notes on the history of cadastral survey and land registration in St Helena*. St Helena, Typescript.

Bauman, Z. (2000). *Liquid modernity*. Routledge.

Blaug, R. (2007). Cognition in a hierarchy. *Contemporary Political Theory, 6*(1), 24–44.

Britt-Gallagher, S., & Hayne, T. (2020). *St Helena, Ascension and Tristan da Cunha* (4th ed.). Bradt.

Charlton, T., & O'Bey, S. (1997). Links between television and behaviour: Students' perceptions of TV's impact in St Helena, South Atlantic. *Support for Learning, 12*(3), 130–136.

Charlton, T., Gunter, B., & Hannan, A. (Eds.). (2002). *Broadcast television effects in a remote community*. Routledge.

Cook, T. (2011). 'We are what we keep; We keep what we are': Archival appraisal past, present and future. *Journal of the Society of Archivists, 32*(2), 173–189.

Crallan, H. P. (1974). *Island of St. Helena: Listing and preservation of buildings of architectural and historic interest*. Typescript, Jamestown.

Cunningham, A. S. (2024). Rupert's valley and stories of biosociality. *Wirebird, 53*, 34–48.

Denholm, K. (1994). *From signal gun to satellite: A history of communications on the island of St Helena. Education Office, Jamestown.*

Donaldson, R., & Forssman, A. (2020). 'Opening up to the world': An exploration of residents' opinions on and perceptions of St Helena island's tourism development. *African Journal of Hospitality, Tourism and Leisure, 9*(6), 944–958.

Evans, D. (1994). *Schooling in the South Atlantic islands 1661–1992*. Anthony Nelson.

Foucault, M. (1972). *Archaeology of knowledge*. Tavistock Press.

Fox, C., & Baldwin, E. (2014). *A precarious livelihood: St Helena 1834—East India Company outpost to Crown Colony*. Friends of St Helena.

GIZ. (2023). *Digital transformation for sustainable development*. Deutsche Gesellschaft für Internationale Zusammenarbeit.

Gosse, P. (1990/1938). *St Helena 1502–1938*. Anthony Nelson.

Grove, R. H. (1995). *Green Imperialism: Colonial expansion, tropical island Edens and the origins of environmentalism 1600–1860*. Cambridge University Press.

Halley, E. (1694). An account of the circulation of watry vapours of the sea, and of the cause of springs. *Philosophical Transactions of the Royal Society, 192*(17), 468–473.

Hart-Davis, D. (1972). *Ascension: The story of a South Atlantic island*. Constable.

Harvey, D. (1996). *Justice, nature and the geography of difference*. Blackwell.

Hearl, T. W. (1996). Censorship, St Helena style. *Wirebird, 13*, 43–47.

Hearl, T. W. (2005). St Helena. In E. Benson & L. W. Conolly (Eds.), *Encyclopedia of post-colonial literatures in English* (Vol. 2, 2nd ed.). Routledge.

Hearl, T. W. (2013). In A. Schulenburg (Ed.), *St Helena Britannica: Studies in South Atlantic Island history*. Friends of St Helena.

Heeks, R. (2022). Digital inequality beyond the digital divide: Conceptualizing adverse digital incorporation in the global South. *Information Technology for Development, 28*(4), 688–704.

HMSO. (1905). *Board of education special report on educational subjects* (The system of education in St Helena) (Vol. 12, pp. 403–405). HMSO.

Hogenstijn, M., & van Middelkoop, D. (2002). *Saints: Spatial identities of the citizens of Saint Helena* (PhD thesis). University of Utrecht.

Hui, A., Schatzki, T., & Shove, E. (Eds.). (2017). *The nexus of practices: Connections, constellations, practitioners*. Routledge.

Jeremiah, D. J. (2019). *England's moon: Saint Helena's place in the history of modern science fiction*. Self-Published.

Joyce, M. (2000). The Bahraini three on St. Helena, 1956–1961. *Middle East Journal, 54*(4), 613–623.

Kitching, G. C. (1936). The St. Helena printing-presses. *Notes and Queries, 171*. https://doi.org/10.1093/nq/CLXXI.dec05.398

Kitching, G. C. (1947). Records of the island of St Helena Lat. 15° 55′ S. Long. 5° 42' W. *The American Archivist, 10*(2), 151–171.

Lloyd, A. (2010). *Information Literacy Landscapes*. Chandos.

Melliss, J. C. (1875). *St Helena: A physical, historical and topographical description of the island*. Reeve.

Murray, P. (2003). "'On Saint Helena's Bleak Shore": Free state plans to intern republican prisoners. *History Ireland, 11*(1), 10–11.

Pearson, A., Jeffs, B., Witkin, A., & MacQuarrie, H. (2011). *Infernal traffic: Excavation of a liberated African graveyard in Rupert's Valley, St Helena*. Council for British Archaeology.

Phippard, S. (2023). *Remote childhoods: Exploring what matters for children on St Helena island* (PhD thesis). University of Winchester.

Richards, T. (1993). *The imperial archive: Knowledge and fantasy of empire*. Verso.

Rippich, M. (1998). Radio St Helena. *Wirebird, 18*, 10–17.

Royle, S. (2007). *The company's island: St Helena, company colonies and the colonial endeavour*. I. B. Tauris.

Salvatore, R. (2006). Imperial mechanics: South America's hemispheric integration in the machine age. *American Quarterly, 58*(3), 662–691.

Schulenburg, A. H. (1999). *Transient observations: The textualizing of St Helena through five hundred years of colonial discourse* (PhD thesis). University of St Andrews.

Smallman, D. (2003). *Quincentenary: A story of St Helena 1502–2002*. Patten Press.

St Helena Government. (2018). *SHG signs financing agreement for the territorial allocation of 11th EDF*. Retrieved June 20, 2023, from https://www.sainthelena.gov.sh/2018/public-announcements/shg-signs-financing-agreement-for-the-territorial-allocation-of-11th-edf/

Stern, P. J. (2007). Politics and ideology in the early East India Company-state: The case of St Helena, 1673–1709. *The Journal of Imperial and Commonwealth History, 35*(1), 1–23.

Sterndale, R. A. (1895, January). St Helena: The Gibraltar of the South Atlantic. *Asiatic Quarterly Review, 9*(17), 99–116.

Teale, P. (Ed.). (1980). *St Helena records. Typescript, Jamestown.*

Whitworth, A. (2020). *Mapping information landscapes: New methods for exploring the development and teaching of information literacy*. Facet.

Whitworth, A. (2024). Archives as the prologues of information literacy. *Journal of Information Literacy, 18*(1). https://doi.org/10.11645/18.1.564

Winchester, S. (1985). *Outposts*. Hodder & Stoughton.

Winterbottom, A. E. (2010). *Company culture: Information, scholarship, and the East India Company settlements 1660–1720s* (PhD thesis). Queen Mary College London.

Yon, D. A. (2007). Race-making/race-mixing: St. Helena and the South Atlantic World. *Social Dynamics, 33*(2), 144–163.

Chapter 3
The Cultural Dimension of Space-Time in Technology-Mediated Learning

Giuseppe Ritella

3.1 Introduction

Over the past two decades, there has been a growing interest in addressing the significance of spatial and temporal relations for learning and education (Ritella et al., 2021). One crucial reason for such a growing relevance of space-time in educational research is that more and more the traditional spatial and temporal boundaries of learning are blurred as individuals engage in learning across multiple virtual and physical spacetimes. Indeed, in the current societal context, the usual organization of educational space-time is being questioned due to changing historical and social conditions, including those that have emerged with the forced adoption of distance learning during the pandemic (Ritella & Ligorio, 2023). The integration of digital technology in educational settings has been playing an important role in the transformation of the space-time of learning (Castells, 2010). Within the mainstream discourse addressing the impact of technology for learning, the prevailing argument emphasizes that technology allows to learn "anywhere" and "at any time", transcending the constraints imposed by physical learning environments (Goodyear, 2006). This argument is grounded in a conceptual framework that regards space and time as background variables against which learning processes unfold. This approach involves an analytical focus on physical space and "clock-time" (Hassan, 2003) as the background of learning.

Nevertheless, several authors argue for a conceptualization of space and time as socially negotiated constructions rather than physical realities, thus requesting a socio-cultural analysis (Fairclough, 2004; Ritella et al., 2021). One of the main

G. Ritella (✉)
University of Campania "Luigi Vanvitelli", Caserta, Italy
e-mail: giuseppe.ritella@unicampania.it

M. B. Ligorio (ed.), *Technology as Cultural Mediator*, Culture in Policy Making: The Symbolic Universes of Social Action,
https://doi.org/10.1007/978-3-031-97673-5_3

arguments for this theoretical switch is that the mere measurement of physical time and space is not appropriate nor sufficient for the examination of how students, teachers and other educational actors perceive, navigate and interact with learning environments. For example, the physical distance between two students in a classroom is not an appropriate measure for the examination of the spatial dimension of social interaction in current educational environments. Indeed, classroom interaction can be negotiated across several layers of space-time such as the iterative use of a mobile messaging application or the spatial organization of signs in the symbolic space of a table projected on a virtual whiteboard.

Interacting with these tools is not just a matter of overcoming physical distance. On the contrary, their use implies a transformation of the space-time relations of learning that is both the result and the trigger of social processes that are relevant for cultural analysis. How space and time are perceived and navigated by human beings is deeply affected by several socio-cultural processes that might span beyond educational settings but are still crucial for the field of education for several reasons.

First, the shared assumptions held within a society concerning where and when learning should take place become apparent in the organization of educational systems. Suffice to think of how the organization of space in the classrooms and the regulation of time by means of the bell marking the temporal boundaries of the lessons was established historically only in relatively recent times and it reflects shared assumptions and normative beliefs concerning learning (Foucault, 1977).

Second, the organization of space and time can have a profound impact on cognitive processes in many contexts and domains. As shown by Kirsh (1995), spatial organization can affect cognitive processes in various ways and an "intelligent use of space" can enhance cognitive capabilities of human beings at work and in everyday life. Social practices of using space and time "intelligently" can be considered as cultural tools that are shared within (professional) communities. For example, teachers can learn how to organize the learning environment according to the principles of a specific pedagogical approach and students can collaboratively develop productive arrangements of space-time during learning task that can be interiorized by each student and transferred to other contexts at later times. Previous research has explored how managing social interaction across multiple virtual and physical space-time frames is not a trivial task for teachers and learners (e.g. Ritella, 2010). In this sense, the management of space-time can be considered as a (culturally-mediated) higher psychological function, to use Vygotsky's term (1977). In other words, how to navigate the (learning) environments typical of a society can be conceptualized as a developmental achievement that is reached through the participation in cultural practices.

Third, human thinking often involves non-linear movements across space-times, creating bridges between past, present and future space-times (Cole, 2023). This is the case, for example, when future space-times are envisioned through a semiotic reworking of past events. These non-linear connections between different space-times are also extremely relevant for education. Suffice to think of the fact that learning about past events and scientific discoveries is considered necessary for taking informed decisions in the future. Furthermore, as learning processes usually transcend single educational settings, non-linear connections across different situations of learning emerge as learners make sense of the overall educational tasks (Ritella et al., 2019). In this way, the coordination of past, present and future space-times becomes an integral part of the learning process.

Fourth, space and time are fundamental categories that help people define coordinates and orientate within any kind of environment they experience, within and outside educational contexts. The conceptions of space-time through which the people use to orientate in the social world are not static, they develop historically. Suffice to think of the origin of the seven days' week that seem to be rooted in either the seven planets of ancient cosmology or the seven days of Creation in Jewish cosmology (Zerubavel, 1989). Major societal transformations require societies to rethink to some degree these fundamental categories (Holquist, 1982). For example, at the start of the twentieth century, the development of faster means of transportation triggered significant societal transformations that affected people's perception of space and movement. The development of digital technology has then generated further challenges for traditional conceptions of space and time, leading to a further transformation of the beliefs and the meaning that people in general, and students and teachers in particular, associated to time and space. The culturally negotiated conceptions of space-time shared within the larger communities and societies are then implicitly or explicitly used by students and teachers when they make sense of learning environments. In this sense, research shows that students' conceptions of the space-time of learning is strictly interconnected with their construction of a shared understanding of a learning task (Ritella et al., 2019).

When stating that conceptualizing space-time in terms of physical realities is not appropriate, I do not mean that the physical environment is irrelevant for learning processes. The claim here is that the object of interest for a sociocultural analysis of spacetime does not coincide with the conception of space-time developed in physics. What is interesting for sociocultural analysis is not what space-time is as a physical reality, but how people make sense of it, how they organize their activities, how recurrent patterns of space-time configurations are connected with expectations or assumptions about where and when learning takes place. From this perspective, when symbolic and virtual spaces are integrated in temporally layered practices, the physical space can be perceived and navigated differently by participants and thus we need a conception that is able to address also its cultural and social dimension:

> The more portable and pervasive that technology becomes, the more—as designers and analysts—we need to pay attention to relations between the digital and the physical. Digital technologies can change the way we experience physical space, and the physical properties of the spaces in which we find ourselves have implications for how—and even whether—we make use of digital devices. […] We need to be able to work with complex entanglements of physical, digital and hybrid tools and artefacts in physically anchored places. (Goodyear et al., 2017, p. 243)

Realistic 3d immersive virtual environments, as well as augmented reality tools that dynamically integrate virtual objects in a physical environment are clear examples of how the relationship between physical and virtual space-times is extremely relevant in contemporary society. In this sense, educational environments can be conceived as networks of interdependent physical-virtual space-time frames. The integration of virtual tools adds extra layers or dimensions to the space-time of learning, so that the physical world becomes only one layer interacting with the other ones as teachers and students move from one space to the other or coordinate across several space-times at the same time. Some previous studies have analysed how groups of learners involved in a collaborative task actively organize the space-time of learning across complex arrays of physical and virtual space-times according to the aims of the activity and considering local constraints (e.g. Ritella & Sansone, 2020).

According to this line of thinking, it is unfitting to conceptualize an educational space as either exclusively physical or exclusively virtual. It is theoretically and empirically more functional to consider the physical and the virtual as interdependent dimensions of any educational environment. On the one hand, digital tools are so pervasive worldwide that it is not anymore possible even to conceive a classroom that is alienated from any form of virtual space. On the other hand, even in the absence of digitally generated virtual space, it is possible to consider the symbolic space of blackboard or the page of a book as symbolic spaces that might establish distinctive socially negotiated spatial and temporal relations not understandable only in terms of physical realities. The unrealistic representation of the distance between astronomical objects that has been so common in typical handbook illustrations for several decades (see Engeström, 1991) is a clear example of how the examination of the symbolic space is not compatible with a conception based on a physical understanding of space-time.

From this perspective, how teachers and learners socially negotiate the space-time relations relevant for their learning across these interdependent layers (or dimensions) of learning environments can vary significantly depending on several cultural, historical, and material aspects, some of which constitute the focus of the chapter. To address this topic, the concept of chronotope (Bakhtin, 1981), which was specifically introduced as a heuristic concept for a social (dialogic) examination of space-time, is discussed and adopted for illustrative empirical analysis. Chronotope is thus considered as a conceptual and analytical tool that allows reaching a sociocultural and dialogical understanding of human action and interaction in space-time. Empirical illustrations from a case study that examines the use of Minecraft as a learning tool in primary schools during the COVID-19 pandemic are used to highlight the cultural dimension of space-time for technology-mediated learning. The excerpts from the case study, through a chronotopic analysis, allow to shed light on the dialogical construction of space-time, its socio-cultural dynamics, and its hybrid configurations.

3.2 Theoretical Framework

3.2.1 Space-Time in Technology-Mediated Learning

As mentioned above, the increasing integration of digital technologies in educational settings has profoundly affected the space and time in learning. Nevertheless, classrooms have been for a long time characterized by rigid spatial and temporal boundaries, and the widespread conception of space-time that is associated to school learning is still at times tied to the notion of traditional classroom learning. Accordingly, learning is often expected to occur mainly within those predetermined spatial and temporal configurations that were historically developed to enhance teachers' control over the activity of the students (see Foucault, 1977). More recent educational approaches, especially those advocating for the adoption of digital technology, often challenge the assumptions of such view of the space-time of learning. Blended learning (Ligorio et al., 2011; Amenduni & Ligorio, 2022), connected learning (Ito et al., 2013), networked learning (Carvalho et al., 2017) are all examples of approaches that challenge the idea that learning mainly takes place within the boundary of the classroom. These approaches, in different ways call for flexible and interconnected educational environments and consider learning as a process that transcend individual locations. In this sense, these approaches adopt an "expanded" view of the classroom, able to connect learning across formal and informal contexts (Rajala, 2019). One implication is that such interconnected learning environment are not as simple for teachers to oversee compared to the confined space of a traditional classroom (Ritella et al., 2016), especially if we consider that the traditional conception of learning taking place in the classroom still endures in many educational contexts. On the one hand, teachers spend several years within educational institutions organized according to the traditional conception of learning, firstly as learners and later as teachers. So, for them it might not easy to change old habits and beliefs consolidated across several decades of attendance within educational institutions. On the other hand, to change the space-time organization of complex organizations such as schools is not a trivial task. Even though there is a growing number of successful institutions that have reorganized radically the learning environments by creating desk-less or open-space schools characterized by a flexible physical learning environment (Reinius et al., 2021; Sigurðardóttir & Hjartarson, 2016), most of the schools worldwide still reflect the traditional conception of learning. The organisation of space-time imposed by the school systems, in this way, might confirm the teachers' beliefs and expectations that learning should take place within such a structured physical school environment.

As mentioned at the outset of the chapter, an important issue that needs to be addressed in this chapter is that the design of learning environments is not just a technical problem but involves complex cultural processes, and design decisions can be considered as the embodied enactment of cultural assumptions and normative ideas. For example, Hinton et al. (2017) shows how the design of physical, virtual and social spaces within educational institutions and the organization of tasks and social practices can be driven by a specific paradigm and in turn generate particular kinds of problems and opportunities for the students and staff using them. The authors discuss how design decisions that were grounded on a participatory approach deeply affected the emerging learning processes, enhancing the "participation in valued practices" and stimulating specific kinds of interactions (p. 223). The cultural processes involved in the design of educational environments and the ones through which the students experience and enact configurations of space-time during learning activities are therefore processes that require a specific analytic attention. Interestingly, when the students make sense of a learning activity and its space-time coordinates, they can transcend the learning environment designed by the teacher. For example, students might choose to interact using a different virtual space than the one intended by the teacher or they could move in a classroom in unexpected ways, generating patterns of space-time that conflict with the teachers' conceptions of where, when and how learning should take place. The socio-cultural conceptualization of space-time articulated in this chapter allows to examine how physical, virtual and symbolic spaces overlap and alternate during educational activities as teachers and learners negotiate the relevant space-times for educationally relevant interaction and self-organize their learning activities in space and time (Ritella & Loperfido, 2021). In addition, some recent research also shows that emotional processes might be involved in defining how digital technology is integrated in educational environments (Ritella et al. 2024). According to this literature, it is possible to state that the investigation of the transformations of the space-time of education that characterize contemporary education allows to highlight the importance to incorporate cultural factors in the conceptualization of space-time.

One of the first attempts to develop such a social and cultural conceptualization of space and time is attributed to Bakhtin (1981), who conceptualized the notion of chronotope to examine the space-time dimension of narrative genres. His pioneering insights revealed how different narrative forms are shaped by and reflect specific cultural ways to represent space and time. Bakhtin emphasizes that the interplay of time and space is not merely a backdrop but an integral part of meaning-making. In this sense, the chronotope is depicted as the gate that makes meaning making possible, thus emphasizing that space and time are crucial dimensions for social and cultural analysis. Applying this framework to educational research, learning environments are understood as spatiotemporal configurations that emerge through the interaction of cultural, institutional, and individual dynamics. Accordingly, chronotopic research invite us to consider how time and space are socially constructed, fluidly interwoven, and dynamically reimagined in educational contexts. In this view, time and space are not static entities; they are actively negotiated by participants. This dialogism foregrounds the collaborative ways in which teachers and students co-construct the boundaries of their learning environments.

At the same time, the concept of chronotope draws attention to the material and discursive aspects of education. Physical environments, such as classrooms or online platforms, are deeply intertwined with symbolic constructions, such as curricula, cultural narratives, and institutional norms. As will be clarified in the discussion of the empirical illustrations of this chapter, in the case of a virtual learning tool like Minecraft, the materiality of the game interface interacts with the discursive practices of students and teachers. The process of constructing virtual worlds can become a way of externalizing creative ideas, negotiating social roles, and engaging with the broader cultural context of learning. This dual focus on the material and discursive dimension allows the chronotope to capture the complexity of educational practices in ways that other frameworks might overlook (Ritella et al., 2021). As an analytical tool, the chronotope is particularly suited to understanding the fluid and hybrid configurations of contemporary learning environments. In educational environments where physical and digital spaces overlap, the chronotope provides insights into how students navigate these intersecting worlds. It highlights the ways in which learners construct continuity across contexts using digital tools, adaptat to new schedules, or negotiate cultural expectations of where and when learning takes place.

Many scholars have adopted this notion to examine how teachers, students and other educational actors socially negotiate and enact culturally-mediated configurations of space and time in educational settings. This line of research offers valuable insights into how space and time are socially constructed and dynamically negotiated in educational settings, also allowing to foreground the interplay between material, discursive, and cultural dimensions of learning environments (Ritella et al., 2021). For example, scholars have examined how students actively shape classroom interactions, creating hybrid time-space contexts that allow them to convey complex ideas and assert their agency (Brown & Renshaw, 2006); how they use discourse to co-construct the space-times of their learning (Leander, 2001; Silseth & Arnseth, 2022); and how they develop taken for granted views of where and when learning takes place as they make sense of novel learning environments (Ritella & Loperfido, 2021). In addition, some authors have used the concept of chronotope to explore the space-time configurations of students' technology-mediated creative learning practices (Kumpulainen et al., 2013). This framework helps illuminate how students' learning practices are organized across different spaces and times, highlighting the hybrid, poly-contextual, and inter-contextual nature of their activities. The study revealed that these chronotopes are developmental achievements emerging from collective efforts within the school community, supported by sociocultural practices and mediating artifacts. Finally, chronotope has been used as dialogical indicators to understand shifts in students' identity trajectories by analysing how time and space are represented in their discourse within the course context (Ligorio et al., 2013).

Since Minecraft-based projects involve students in interdisciplinary tasks that can transcend some social and cultural boundaries (Ritella & Marcone, 2024), they offer an interesting research context for chronotopic investigations. In particular, in this chapter, the focus is on the cultural processes that are connected with the students' dialogical co-construction of the space-times of learning as they iteratively negotiate and collaboratively re-configure the complex arrays of space-time constituting the educational environment. These are considered as crucial processes that contribute to define the experience of the students in educational settings. In this sense, Minecraft, can function as a boundary-crossing environment where students can engage in educational projects bridging the gap between formal education and the culture of gaming that is an important aspect of the life of many students (Ritella & Marcone, 2024).

3.2.2 A Case-Study: Using Minecraft to Build a Ziggurat

The project from which the illustrative examples discussed below are derived was a case study that explored the use of the virtual world Minecraft in primary school education during the COVID-19 pandemic. The study was conducted over two academic years (2019/2020 and 2020/2021) in two sections of a primary school in Italy corresponding to the fourth and fifth grade. It involved 50 students (aged 9–10) and their teacher in the design and implementation of educational activities using Minecraft: Education Edition. The study focused on how virtual worlds could serve as tools for fostering creativity, collaboration, and critical thinking among students (Ritella & Marcone, 2024). During the first phase of the project, the students were invited to create buildings with a high degree of freedom, as the aim was to familiarize themselves with the virtual environment. During the second phase, the tasks assigned were directly connected with the curriculum of history and geography and the students were invited to build a Ziggurat.

Spatial and temporal relations gained particular relevance for this project in the context of the pandemic, as distance and hybrid teaching adaptations became essential. During the periods of remote learning, Minecraft provided a virtual platform where students could engage in collaborative activities. The virtual environment allowed students to navigate and construct shared spaces, blurring the boundaries between formal, structured schoolwork and informal, creative play. Instead, during the school year 2020–2021, most school activities were conducted in a hybrid format, as each family could choose between distance learning or in-person attendance, depending on their preferences and circumstances. By integrating students' digital experiences into formal learning, the project fostered a range of dynamic space-time configurations where learning extended beyond both the physical and the virtual classrooms, highlighting the transformative possibilities of hybrid education during challenging times. At the end of the whole project, 37 students attended group interviews where the researchers asked the students to discuss their learning experience. All the excerpts that will be discussed are extracted from these interviews. The names of the participants are anonymised by means of pseudonyms.

In the next section, the major features of Minecraft, which are relevant for data interpretation, are presented. Indeed, the characteristics of game designs are significant aspects to be considered when discussing the educational use of digital games (Clark et al., 2016).

3.3 Minecraft

Minecraft is a popular sandbox video game that is accessible across an array of platforms and devices. In Minecraft, participants are situated within an environment made of blocks of various materials. In this digital landscape, players can utilize the wide range of block types to fabricate an extensive assortment of structures and designs, ranging from rudimentary houses to sophisticated machinery. The game is characterized by two principal modes: survival mode and creative mode. In survival mode, players are tasked with the accumulation of resources and the construction of a shelter to endure against adversities including hostile game characters and ecological threats. Conversely, in creative mode, players are endowed with boundless resources and are permitted to construct any desired structure without the concern of hostile entities or the necessity for sustenance.

Minecraft can be conceptualized as a "digital making platform" (Dezuanni, 2018) that empowers players to engage in a multitude of creative and collaborative endeavours. The open and flexible environment afforded by the game enables players to experiment with various (virtual) materials and tools. Furthermore, Minecraft can be perceived as a virtual social domain, wherein players are afforded the opportunity to interact with one another and derive insights from each other's creations. Finally, the Education Edition, which is specifically tailored to augment the educational experience, facilitates the adoption of the game in pedagogical contexts. For instance, this variant empowers educators to control the in-game environment and incorporates supplementary tools such as a virtual chemistry laboratory. Minecraft has been implemented within numerous educational frameworks and it has been shown that it can contribute to cultivate creativity, enhance problem-solving skills, and promote collaboration. It has been used to teach subjects such as math, science, and language arts, as well as to develop social and emotional skills.

3.4 Space-Time as Dialogically Constructed Learning Environments

In this section, some excerpts are analysed to discuss how the students participating in the project described above have perceived, socially negotiated and orchestrated the learning environment in which they have collaboratively engaged with educational activities. The analysis is not aimed at a comprehensive discussion of the project but at illustrating the potential of chronotopic analysis for examining the cultural dimension of space-time in technology mediated learning. The first excerpt allows us to illustrate the intricate entanglement between the features of the learning environment, the dialogic relationships between the participants, and the students' agency in negotiating joint configurations of space-time. In this excerpt, Ginevra expresses enthusiasm for being able to engage in educational activities in Minecraft. Nevertheless, she also reflects on a limitation that she faced, which is extremely relevant from a chronotopic perspective: she declares that, for reasons she did not specify, she has not been able to invite her classmates into her own virtual world. As will be clarified in the discussion following the excerpt, most likely such difficulty was generated by the interaction between the material features of the educational environment and her development of technological skills. Ginevra's narrative reflects a temporal-spatial tension, as her experience of the game is marked by a perceived imbalance in agency. Indeed, the movements across the virtual worlds created within her group of peers were possible for her only in one direction (she could visit other worlds but not host her classmates). On the contrary, her classmates perceived a higher sense of agency since they could both visit other worlds and host classmates in their own world.

Excerpt 1

Ginevra: I was always attracted by Minecraft, both the normal one and the other versions, because… anyway… one looked at the videos by the youtubers that played at this… Minecraft, so… ehm… let's say that when the teacher told us that she would give it to us, I was really happy because I'd never had Minecraft in my life. It was like a dream come true because I always wanted to try it, and I was always curious. So, it was like a dream come true… but I was the only one in the whole class who maybe didn't let people in… so that made me a little sad, well, just like Nunzio, who didn't let his friends into his worlds. It was always me having to go into their worlds… my friends' worlds, so I never got the chance to show my friends my own worlds. But when we met up, I would show them, and I'd ask them what they thought, even though they couldn't come in. So, I really liked this experience with Minecraft.

In Excerpt 1 Ginevra states that she was very happy for the possibility to use Minecraft at school. She motivates this positive emotional reaction based on the cultural practice of watching videos of Youtubers playing Minecraft, which is a quite widespread cultural phenomenon among youth (Dezuanni, 2020). This allows to discuss how larger societal processes, such as the development of a participatory culture in which children share online their experience with a game, might have an impact on their perception of the introduction of a virtual space in the educational environment. She also describes how during the project she was able to enter others' worlds but could not reciprocate. In her perception this difficulty generated some kind of social boundary that constrained to some degree her participation and generated a negative emotional reaction. From her perspective, the educational environment prevented her from accessing a specific social space that she tried to arrange—one where her classmates were co-present in a (virtual) environment that allowed them to see the buildings she had created in Minecraft. This reflects an imbalance in participation structures that can relate to the digital materiality of Minecraft, which affected her experience with the educational activity. Even though the virtual space of the game offered a range of possibilities to express the students' agency, somehow the software precluded some actions. Her virtual world—in Ginevra's perception—was not open to allow access to her peers, while the worlds of her classmates were accessible for her. In this way, the virtual space did not allow for reciprocity and symmetricity of interaction. In Pickering's terms (Pickering, 1993), the non-human actor (the technological tool) exerted a strong agency, resisting the students' attempts to create and maintain reciprocity in their relationships. In this sense, the materiality of Minecraft contributed to shape the cultural dynamics activated among the group of students, potentially limiting Ginevra's participation. The sharing of one's virtual creation appears a cultural practice that is pervasive within the community of her peers, and it is for her frustrating not being able to fully participate in this practice.

Since most of her peers were able to invite friends in their world, it is likely that Ginevra's difficulty was also due to her technological skills. Indeed, another student—Elvira—who was interviewed at the same time as Ginevra, mentioned how, through the activity in Minecraft, she had learned to create a server. This server was necessary for hosting classmates in her world (Ritella & Marcone, 2024). Nevertheless, despite feeling limited in her ability to share her virtual world online,

Ginevra found alternative ways to show her creations to classmates, asking for their feedback when they met in person. This process allows to highlight how the chronotope of the digital game does not exist in isolation but intersects with other spaces of participation. This reinforces the idea that learning occurs across multiple, interconnected spatiotemporal contexts and that the agency of the students is also expressed in their ability to manage the complexity of their interaction across multiple space-times, even when the materiality of the external world opposes resistance and precludes some lines of action.

Interestingly, Ginevra and Elvira address the resistance opposed by the virtual materiality of Minecraft in different ways, allowing to highlight how the two students engaged with the virtual space in different ways and thus constructed different chronotopes. While Elvira addressed the limitation by developing her technological skills, actively transforming the settings of the virtual space to accommodate her will to show her creations to her peers, Ginevra actively created connections between the virtual and the physical layers of the educational environment, generating a different chronotope of learning that involved coordination of several space-time dimensions. The result, although different in many respects, in both cases allowed to share the virtual creations with classmates, creating grounds for social interaction. This excerpt also allows to reflect on how the accessibility of the virtual space might contribute to processes of social exclusion. Fortunately, both for Ginevra and for Elvira, the potentiality for social exclusion could be overcome through alternative chronotopes, which in one case involved the negotiation of a hybrid virtual-physical space-time, and in the other case required the active transformation of the virtual space through the development of technological skills.

Overall, this excerpt shows how cultural processes are inextricably linked to the perception of the learning environment and to the social negotiation of the space-time arrangements that allow cultural practices to be enacted. On the one hand, the shared cultural practice of watching "Let's Play Videos" within her social group contributes to shape her perception of the integration of the virtual world of Minecraft in the educational context. On the other hand, the interplay between the features of the virtual space and the agency of the students gives rise to configurations of space-time (chronotopes) that make possible the enactment of the social practice of showcasing virtual constructions to her peers. Both the creation of a virtual space accessible for classmates (Elvira's case) or the arrangement of a space-time that combines the use of virtual tools in face to face situations (Ginevra's case) are chronotopes that allow the cultural practice to take place.

The next excerpt (Excerpt 2) allows to get additional insights on how the perception of the spatial and temporal relations relates to social and cultural processes. Indeed, Chiara provides a slightly different representation of the space-time of learning if compared with the previous excerpt. The excerpt starts with Chiara's explanation of why she preferred to attend school offline. As mentioned above, for some periods during the school year 2020–2021, attendance to the physical classroom was voluntary and parents could decide to opt for online or offline attendance. Chiara depicts the chronotope of distance learning as chaotic while the return to school after the lockdown was perceived as a relief, even though the hybrid nature of schooling in that period reduced the possibilities of social interaction with peers. Nevertheless, she communicates how the opportunity to spend time in the virtual world of Minecraft in that period has for her a very positive connotation.

Excerpt 2

> Chiara: during 4th grade we were all at a distance and there was no choice but in fifth grade, when there was a choice, I went to school because, anyway, well, not to complain… but it's really annoying to be in online classes. Many times, there was no connection, the microphone, presentations, it was all chaotic. So, for me, it was a kind of relief to go to school, and from the very beginning, like in October, I went with seven other kids. But, let's say it was still bad because you could see 17 other people on a screen, and even if you wanted to meet them, you couldn't. However, the advantage is that during this time, I spent 24 hours a day playing Minecraft; I was obsessed. And I became a bit smarter, in the sense that I didn't even know how to turn on a computer before, but now I can start meetings and do other things I didn't know how to do before.

The narrative of Excerpt 2 appears to some degree paradoxical: remote learning was perceived as frustrating, and going back to the physical classroom is perceived as a relief; however, the online engagement with Minecraft is described as an obsession (with a positive connotation). Chiara represents a complex array of space-times, each with a different connotation. Interestingly, for Chiara the space-time of social interaction with her classmates coincides with the physical classroom, while online communication has a negative connotation, mainly due to the perception of chaos and technical difficulties, such as unstable connections and malfunctioning microphones. In this sense, Excerpt 2 allows to address the difficulty that students (and teachers) might encounter when developing a new chronotope for learning. The relatively frequent complains concerning online teaching that the students made during the interviews are interpreted not only in terms of material constraints (such us unstable internet connection or malfunctioning devices), but also in terms of a difficulty that both teachers and students encountered in negotiating a satisfactory chronotope within the new learning environment that was forcefully imposed during the pandemic. When distance or hybrid teaching are implemented, it is difficult and possibly dysfunctional to try to preserve the space-time organization they usually implement during classroom teaching and a re-negotiation of the spatial and temporal negotiation of the activities is needed. The innovative nature of some online activities can disrupt learning experiences, necessitating strategies to maintain engagement and continuity, which are not needed in well-established face-to-face practices that teachers and students have been repeating for several years. For example, managing turn-taking in an online conversation requires adaptations that might challenge the temporal flow of speech typically experienced in face-to-face settings. Furthermore, distance teaching alters the organization of school routines, as students and teachers may struggle to establish clear boundaries between school time and personal time. In other words, the perception of a "chaotic" chronotope might not be related only to technical problems, but also to the difficulty of making sense of the transforming learning environment, which requires some adaptations in the cultural practices of schooling. This interpretation aligns well with Chiara's narrative when describing her social interaction in Minecraft, where the sense of chaos and the technical problems are not so central in the students' account.

A more detailed discussion of the need to socially co-construct a new chronotope of learning when switching to online teaching can be made based on the next excerpt (Excerpt 3). Indeed, in this excerpt, while discussing his perception of online teaching, Leonardo explicitly mentions how the virtual space of online classes did not offer sufficient opportunities for unsupervised social interaction among peers.

Excerpt 3

Leonardo: So, staying at home for online classes was bad because, in class, you can usually get close to a friend and talk, but in online classes, no, even though there was a chat, it was useless to use it because sometimes the teacher would see it (laughs)

At a first level of analysis, Leonardo's speech allows to reflect on how the features of the online classroom did not offer a private space where the students could interact without the teacher, which is instead perceived as a possibility in the physical classroom. This process seems to affect how classmates could engage in a type of social interaction that might often be unrelated with the school task but still constitutes a cultural practice usually performed in the physical classroom (and that is missed when moving online). At a deeper level of analysis, this excerpt also allows to illustrate how power relations are relevant for chronotopic analysis. Indeed, the fact that the chat is represented by Leonardo as a space of surveillance overseen by the teacher rather than as a free space for dialogical interaction is not due to the features of the virtual space alone. This perception of the chat emerges from the entanglement of the features of the technology, the dialogic relationships between the participants (the teacher and the students), and the cultural practices that are typical in the educational context. From a chronotopic perspective, in which space and time are considered social constructions, it is reasonable to postulate that a different perception of the teacher's surveillance of the chat, or the presence of a different cultural practice for students' peer interaction (for example, unsupervised breaks) might have led to a different perception of the virtual space of the chat, and in turn this might have promoted a different construction of the chronotope of distance learning. Based on the current analysis it is not possible to make claims on which teacher actions could have allowed a reframing of the chronotope of online classes described by Leonardo. Nevertheless, for the scope of this chapter, the excerpt allows to illustrate how the students can assign different meanings to the learning environment based on the cultural practices that in their experience can be enacted within it (get close to a friend and talk VS write in a chat supervised by the teacher). In this sense, this highlights the complexity of the processes that underlie the students' perceptions of the space-time of learning and of its affordances.

In some occasions, during the project the students have demonstrated high levels of agency as they collaboratively co-constructed complex configurations of space-time that were not planned by the teacher and that allowed them to overcome restrictions to social interaction. Already Excerpt 1 can be considered as an illustration of how Ginevra negotiated with her peers an alternative space-time for overcoming the technical problems that she encountered when trying to invite classmates in her virtual world. The next excerpt (Excerpt 4) offers an even more tangible illustration of this process. This excerpt allows to reflect on two dimensions that are relevant for the cultural analysis of space and time discussed in this article. First, Eleonora's speech allows to illustrate how the openness of the virtual space of Minecraft offered opportunities for students to creatively image a space of possibilities that seemed precluded in the traditional educational context. Second, the excerpt describes how the group of students, autonomously orchestrated complex configurations of space-time in order to engage in collaborative activities in Minecraft despite the restrictions in place during the pandemic.

Excerpt 4

> Eleonora: When the teacher told us to make ziggurats, I was very happy because I thought that with these ziggurats we could experiment with… our abilities to build things, and so it was… because we did some ziggurats, all very beautiful, and we continued to make the other constructions… and anyway, we never gave up. We continued… to arrive at a great result of many worlds. Then for me Minecraft was… during school… it was still a game that… it allowed me to do everything I wanted while in the real world we had to do… anyway we had to stick to some rules and everything, instead in the world of Minecraft we could see each other… we made video calls with the others… and we joined the other worlds… and so we kind of… did dinners with… with… Minecraft men [meaning avatars]… this couldn't be done in presence… so we had fun with rules that… in real life couldn't… couldn't be done… now can't be done…

Eleonora's reflections on her experiences with Minecraft reveal how she perceives a duality between the perceived structural limitations of the physical world during the pandemic and the boundless creativity that was possible within the virtual space during the educational activities in Minecraft. Minecraft is not only described as an environment that allowed to test and develop her abilities. For Eleonora, the virtual world opened up a space for creative engagement that allowed to overcome social restrictions. It is emphasized here that the usage of Minecraft described in this excerpt was not initially intended by teacher but was socially constructed by a group of students. In this sense, Eleonora's speech highlights how the students purposefully configured technology-mediated creative modalities of interaction that allowed to overcome the sense of social isolation associated with the pandemic and to create a fully functional shared space for social interaction. Such socially constructed space created the conditions for shifting the experience of the pandemic shared within Eleonora's social group. The practice of meeting for such online social gathering can be considered in itself a cultural practice developed within the classroom community, which had implications for the whole experience of schooling in that challenging historical period. The interweaving of (1) students' social negotiation of relevant spaces for social interaction, (2) the perception of institutionally imposed social restriction and (3) the possibilities offered by the virtual space, together generated opportunities for micro-cultural processes that affected both the meanings that students associated with the learning environment and the emerging socio-material configurations of participation. In Bakhtinian terms, the chronotope that is described in this excerpt defines at the same time the student's meaning making on schooling and the organization of the space-time in which their meaning making was embedded. By integrating video calls and virtual co-presence in Minecraft, they created a shared experience that fostered a sense of community and transcended social boundaries, which in turn led to the emergence of new viewpoints of what schooling is for the students. Engaging through avatars and enjoying "virtual dinners" exemplifies the collaborative emergence of a meaningful micro-cultural phenomenon that redefined both their shared experience of schooling during the pandemic and the social dynamics taking place within her group of peers. Interviews with other students during the same project allowed to discuss how, especially for some students, this kind of chronotopes emerging during the activities in Minecraft also became an opportunity to consolidate existing friendships or build new relationships with classmates (Ritella & Marcone, 2024). Moreover, this excerpt allows to illustrate how Minecraft became a dialogically constructed space for the students, diverging from the chronotope of "the real world" (and as discussed in Excerpt 3 it diverged also from the chronotope of regular online classes). The shared virtual worlds they built became a hybrid space that combined educational and recreational elements, supporting the notion that the use of open ended digital platforms such as Minecraft can foster meaningful processes of boundary crossing, with an impact on how the students co-costruct their lived experience of schooling.

The relevance of the meanings associated with schooling and the agency that the students can exert in reinterpreting the space-time of learning is well illustrated in Excerpt 5, where Gabriele imagines Minecraft as "a new way of distance teaching".

Excerpt 5

Gabriele: I wanted to say that, for me, Minecraft was like a lifesaver. I preferred to hear my friends' voices rather than being in online classes. Every afternoon, I would sit at the computer… because… well I had spent all my money on gaming setups to play Minecraft… I would rather listen to my friends' voices, and not only from school, but also from my friends outside of school. I preferred hearing their voices for hours and hours [while playing together in Minecraft] rather than just looking at their faces on a computer screen.

Researcher: What do you mean by this? Could you maybe…

Gabriele: Well, what I mean is that Minecraft could easily be the new way of doing online classes. It's a style of play that a kid has…. I don't have the exact words, but I want to say that Minecraft could very well be a new way of distance learning.

Gabriele's reflections on Minecraft as a potential new type of online education highlight a shift in how students might perceive learning environments. By stating that Minecraft could serve as a "new way of doing online classes," Gabriele is not merely suggesting an alternative platform for education; he seems to point to a transformation of the educational experience itself. Even though Gabriele finds it difficult to express his ideas ("I don't have the exact words"), when he mentions "a style of play that a kid has", he suggests that the activities in Minecraft were more aligned with his (and his peers) interests and their out of school experiences. Thus, his focus seems to be not only on the features of the virtual environment provided by Minecraft, but also on the types of activities (of "play" to use his term) that were involved in the project. Interestingly, in this excerpt Gabriele states that he prefers to hear his peers' voices rather than to see their faces during online classes. Most likely, this points to the importance of social interaction in learning. Several students, as Gabriele, missed the possibility to interact with their peers during online classes, when the students perceived themselves as having a more passive role. The immersive nature of the activities within Minecraft seem to facilitate students' social interaction in a manner that is more meaningful and more engaging, supporting social interaction in ways that are atypical if compared with the regular online classes conducted by teachers during the pandemic using videoconferencing applications.

A relevant research thread concerning the topic at hand is that of the so-called "sense of presence" (Waterworth et al., 2010) defined as the sensation of being situated in an external world existing around the person, which can be physical, virtual or a combination of the two. This aspect is crucial as it can impact both levels of participation and learning outcomes. For example, in a study aimed at evaluating the adoption of virtual reality for the development of procedural skills, it was found that the sense of presence was associated with a better level of learning (Grassini et al., 2020). This was observed in instances of training activities facilitated by virtual reality tools as well as in situations without the use of these tools. The sense of presence in the context of technology-mediated educational activities can be very complex to manage, as the boundaries between different virtual and physical spaces are often blurred: even if physically seated on the couch in their apartment, a student may be "present" in multiple virtual spaces such as a chat with a neighbour, an online game with friends from other parts of the city, or a video produced by peers in another continent (Leander et al., 2010). An element to consider when examining the sense of presence is the perception of one's actions. In fact, some authors argue that it provides feedback on the status of the undertaken activity (Riva, 2009). Therefore, the sense of presence appears to be connected to the virtual or physical environment in which one perceives the results of their actions. In other words, it seems that students—just like teachers—tends to perceive themselves as "present" in those virtual or physical spaces where they feel that their actions take place and where they perceive that those actions produce recognizable results. Thus, experiencing a sense of presence regarding the space-time in which educational activities are conducted—be it physical or virtual—seems to be intricately linked to the active participation of students and the feedback received in that specific context. For example, observing the effects of his actions in the virtual world of Minecraft and at the same time actively engaging in conversations with his peers, might have enhanced Gabriele's sense of presence in the educational environment, which was jeopardised by the passive nature of online lectures in which he could only observe his classmates' faces not being able to interact with them. In the same way, social presence, which denotes the perception of others in the same space, was enhanced when Gabriele could perceive the actions of his peers on the virtual world and their discursive actions through verbal interaction ("I would rather listen to my friends' voice"), rather than just looking at their still faces during classes. According to this analysis, the chronotope that emerged during the activities in Minecraft, for Gabriele, was more aligned with his interests and at the same time was characterized by a more interactive space that enhanced sense of presence and social presence. This phenomenon highlights the importance of interactive elements in educational environments, as they can significantly enhance engagement and foster a deeper connection to the learning experience. Finally, Gabriele's account shows that the engagement with Minecraft involved a boundary crossing phenomenon that permitted the connection of educational activities with his out of school community of peers, creating a bridge between school culture and gaming culture.

Finally, in Excerpt 6, Cinzia's speech provides insights on how shifts in space-time configurations can be part of the students' learning experience and significantly affect the students' participation. In this Excerpt, Cinzia discusses how initially she attended online classes from her parents' shop, an environment that was not ideal for her as it was filled with distractions. As she transitioned to studying from home, her experience of remote teaching radically changed.

Excerpt 6

> Cinzia: I've always liked school. At first, I used to go to my parents' shop to do lessons, but it wasn't very comfortable because customers would come in, and I'd get distracted. Then I started staying home, and I felt much calmer. I could follow the lessons better. And, um, the best part… I mean, one nice thing about the video lessons… was the silence because, with the microphones off, it was so quiet, and the teacher's voice ruled, you know… And then, as soon as Teacher Angela started talking about Minecraft, like when she explained that we had to build a house, the ziggurat, or the open-air garden… I'd always get this rush of excitement because I already knew I was about to start a project that I'd be proud of, you know.

The shift of learning environments described by Cinzia illustrates how space-time configurations can influence cognitive engagement. First, this excerpt shows how the perception of the features of the physical world can also affect the students' perception of the virtual space of online classes and their engagement with the online educational activities. This reinforces the claim made at the outset of the chapter that virtual and physical space-time are best conceptualized as interconnected dimensions of learning environments. Secondly, differently from other students, Cinzia did not perceive distance teaching as chaotic, emphasizing that microphones could be easily turned off to create a silent environment where the teacher voice could be clearly heard. This observation highlights an essential chronotopic shift. In a physical classroom (as well as in her parents' shop), noise and peer interactions are typically an element of the learning environment that might not be fully controlled by the teacher or by the individual student. Not being able to control the appearance of distracting stimuli can influence both the meanings that the student associate to that learning environment as well as her cognitive engagement with the activity. On the contrary, in online education, the soundscape can become more hierarchical, allowing the teacher to express his or her authority in assigning speech turns and silencing students when their participation is considered inappropriate. For Cinzia, this is described as an ideal chronotope that helps her focus on the content of the educational activity, thus enhancing the learning process. This is not to state that in absolute terms silent environments are always better for learning, but to remark that how students make sense of the environment matters for better understanding how they feel and act during educational activities. The difference between the perception described by Cinzia and the one expressed by Chiara in Excerpt 2, suggests that—as theoretically claimed above—chronotopic relations do not mechanically derive from the features of the environment, but involve complex socio-cultural phenomena of sensemaking and social construction of space-time, some of which have been discussed in this chapter. Finally, Excerpt 6 also illustrates how learning activities based on Minecraft can be perceived as personally meaningful by the students, as it offers a space where open ended tasks can foster a sense of ownership and pride, thus supporting active engagement with learning tasks.

To conclude, these excerpts allow us to illustrate how on the one hand each student perceived the space-time of learning differently based on his or her experience with the cultural practices enacted within the learning environment and on the other hand the students as a group socially negotiated spatial and temporal relations that allowed them to engage in educationally relevant interaction. In particular, some complex configurations of space-time that the students have jointly co-costructed allowed them to overcome limitations that could have negatively affected their learning experience. In addition, the chronotopic analysis of the excerpts foregrounded the relationship between the students' meaning making concerning educational activities, the dynamic co-costruction of the space-time of learning and the material conditions in which the activities took place.

3.5 Conclusions

In the present chapter the cultural dimension of space-time in technology-mediated learning has been explored by means of chronotopic analysis. The concept of chronotope as conceptualized by Bakhtin has been used to examine empirical illustrations from a case study involving fifth-grade students engaging with Minecraft Education during the COVID-19 pandemic. Consistently with the theoretical discussion, the analysis of the excerpts reveals that some cultural processes are intrinsically connected with the emerging chronotopes. In particular, the focus has been on micro-cultural processes that emerged within the group of students participating in the project. In particular, the analysis of the excerpts shows that the students actively orchestrated configurations of space-time (chronotopes) that allowed the emergence of specific cultural practices within the group of peers. For example, through the integration of video calls and joint virtual co-presence in Minecraft, the students created the conditions for the emergence of a chronotope that contributed to redefine their sense-making about the educational activities during the pandemic as well as the network of social relationships within the group of classmates. At the same time, larger cultural phenomena, such as the practice of watching "Let's play" videos, contribute to frame the social negotiation of space-time that the students performed during the project.

First, the process through which students make sense of the space-time of schooling was discussed, showing how the use of Minecraft supported the development of a conception of the space-time of learning more aligned with the students' out of school cultural practices. Second, the chapter illustrated how the students created configurations of space-time that crossed the fixed boundaries of the traditional classroom and creatively found ways to create their own learning environments mixing several tools and media across physical and virtual spaces, actively generating a shared space for the emergence of new cultural practices. Third, the analysis shows how the students interpreted in slightly different ways the same features of the learning spaces surrounding them, allowing for the illustration of some socio-cultural-material processes involved in the students' perception of the learning environment.

Overall, it has been highlighted how learning environments are not merely predetermined physical or virtual spaces but are dynamically constructed through social interactions and reflect cultural, social, and material processes. Rather than being passive recipients of predefined learning spaces, students socially co-construct the space-time of their learning through their interactions, which can be considered in itself as a cultural process of space (and time) co-construction. Indeed, this type of examination makes visible how the culturally-mediated norms and assumptions held by the students (and implicitly also the ones of the teacher) were involved in the creation of the configurations of space-time that the students enacted. In turn, the social interaction that took place within such socially negotiated chronotopes contributed to transform the classroom culture, allowing for the generation of new perspectives on distance teaching during the pandemic. It is also clear in the analysis of the excerpts that, as any cultural process, the making of space-time is not a linear and homogenizing process. Rather, it emerges from the interaction of a variety of perspectives (voices), that include the perspectives of the human participants (the students and the teachers) as well as the non-human participants (for example, the virtual materiality of Minecraft that opposed resistance to some actions). In this sense, the framework presented in this chapter adopts a socio-material view on learning, foregrounding the interaction between the social (and cultural) negotiation of space-time and the material elements of learning environments that display their own agency (Pickering, 2010). This also aligns with the argument that ICTs are not mere tools but rather environmental forces that contribute to reshape our self-conception, social interactions, and agency (Floridi, 2015).

The findings underscore that the blurring of traditional spatial and temporal boundaries in education necessitates a revaluation of how we understand and design learning experiences. As students navigated the complexities of online and hybrid learning, they engaged in dialogical processes that allowed them to redefine their educational experiences. The students' cultural background, shaped by their experiences with the social practices of their communities, serves both as the foundation for the negotiation of space and time in learning and as its outcome—manifesting in their socially co-constructed new perspectives and assumptions about where and when learning occurs. The chapter emphasizes the importance of recognizing the fluid interaction between meaning making and the emergence of a wide range of configurations of space-time in educational practices, advocating for pedagogical approaches that provide flexible learning environments and embrace the interconnected nature of learning in the digital age. Future research should continue to investigate these dynamics, considering the implications for pedagogy, institutional practices, and the evolving landscape of education in an increasingly digital world.

Acknowledgments The author wishes to thank Ivana Lorusso and Angela Ruotolo for their contribution to the data collection and to the initial phase of the data analysis. The author acknowledges ChatGPT's assistance in providing suggestions for structuring and refining the manuscript to enhance clarity. However, the final content and interpretations were made solely by the author.

References

Amenduni, F., & Ligorio, M. B. (2022). Blended learning and teaching in higher education: An international perspective. *Education Sciences, 12*(2), 129.

Bakhtin, M. (1981). *The dialogic imagination. Four essays by M. M. Bakhtin*. University of Texas Press.

Brown, R., & Renshaw, P. (2006). Positioning students as actors and authors: A chronotopic analysis of collaborative learning activities. *Mind, Culture, and Activity, 13*(3), 247–259.

Carvalho, L., Goodyear, P., & de Laat, M. (Eds.). (2017). *Place-based spaces for networked earning*. Routledge.

Castells, M. (2010). *The rise of the network society* (Vol. 12). Wiley.

Clark, D. B., Tanner-Smith, E. E., & Killingsworth, S. S. (2016). Digital games, design, and learning: A systematic review and meta-analysis. *Review of Educational Research, 86*(1), 79–122.

Cole, M. (2023). Prolepsis as a coordinating mechanism of semiotic mediation. *Constructivist Foundations, 18*(2), 235–236.

Dezuanni, M. (2018). Minecraft and children's digital making: Implications for media literacy education. *Learning, Media and Technology, 43*(3), 236–249.

Dezuanni, M. (2020). *Peer pedagogies on digital platforms: Learning with Minecraft Let's Play videos*. MIT Press.

Engeström, Y. (1991). Non scolae sed vitae discimus: Toward overcoming the encapsulation of school learning. *Learning and Instruction, 1*(3), 243–259.

Fairclough, N. (2004). *Analysing discourse: Textual analysis for social research*. Routledge.

Floridi, L. (2015). *The onlife manifesto: Being human in a hyperconnected era* (p. 264). Springer nature.

Foucault, M. (1977). *Discipline and punishment: The birth of the prison*. Vintage.

Goodyear, P. (2006). Technology and the articulation of vocational and academic interests: Reflections on time, space and e-learning. *Studies in Continuing Education, 28*(2), 83–98.

Goodyear, P., Carvalho, L., Hogdson, V., & de Laat, M. (2017). Conclusion—Place-based spaces for networked learning, Chapter 17. In L. Carvalho, P. Goodyear, & M. de Laat (Eds.), *Place-based spaces for networked earning* (pp. 242–260). Routledge.

Grassini, S., Laumann, K., & Skogstad, M. R. (2020). The use of virtual reality alone does not promote training performance (but sense of presence does). *Frontiers in Psychology, 11*. https://doi.org/10.3389/fpsyg.2020.01743

Hassan, R. (2003). *The chronoscopic society: Globalization, time, and knowledge in the network economy* (Vol. 17). Peter Lang.

Hinton, T., Yeoman, P., Ashor, L., & Poronnik, P. (2017). Spaces enabling change: X-lab and science education 2020, Chapter 1. In L. Carvalho, P. Goodyear, & M. de Laat (Eds.), *Place-based spaces for networked earning* (pp. 1–10). Routledge.

Holquist, M. (1982). Bakhtin and Rabelais: Theory as praxis. *Boundary, 2*, 5–19.

Ito, M., Gutiérrez, K., Livingstone, S., Penuel, B., Rhodes, J., Salen, K., Sefton-Green, J., Mahendran, D., Pascoe, C. J., Shresthova, S., Schor, J., & Watkins, S. C. (2013). *Connected learning: An agenda for research and design*. BookBaby.

Kirsh, D. (1995). The intelligent use of space. *Artificial Intelligence, 73*, 31–68.

Kumpulainen, K., Mikkola, A., & Jaatinen, A. (2013). The chronotopes of technology-mediated creative learning practices in an elementary school community. *Learning, Media and Technology, 39*, 53–74.

Leander, K. M. (2001). "This is our freedom bus going home right now": Producing and hybridizing space-time contexts in pedagogical discourse. *Journal of Literacy Research, 33*(4), 637–679.

Leander, K. M., Phillips, N. C., & Taylor, K. H. (2010). The changing social spaces of learning: Mapping new mobilities. *Review of Research in Education, 34*(1), 329–394.

Ligorio, M. B., Loperfido, F. F., Sansone, N., & Spadaro, P. F. (2011). Blending educational models to design blended activities. In *Techniques for fostering collaboration in online learning communities: Theoretical and practical perspectives* (pp. 64–81). IGI Global.

Ligorio, M. B., Loperfido, F. F., & Sansone, N. (2013). Dialogical positions as a method of understanding identity trajectories in a collaborative blended university course. *International Journal of Computer-Supported Collaborative Learning, 8*, 351–367.

Pickering, A. (1993). The mangle of practice: Agency and emergence in the sociology of science. *American journal of sociology, 99*(3), 559–589.

Pickering, A. (2010). *The mangle of practice: Time, agency, and science*. University of Chicago Press.

Rajala, A. (2019). Expanding the context of pedagogical activity to the surrounding communities. *Psychology and Society, 11*(1), 161–175.

Reinius, H., Korhonen, T., & Hakkarainen, K. (2021). The design of learning spaces matters: Perceived impact of the deskless school on learning and teaching. *Learning Environments Research, 24*(3), 339–354.

Ritella, G. (2010). Presence, social presence and heterotopia: The self and the others in a multispace. *Cultural-Historical Psychology, 6*(4), 39–46.

Ritella, G., & Ligorio, M. B. (2023). Re-conceptualising the space–time of teachers' professional development. In *Re-theorising learning and research methods in learning research* (pp. 264–279). Routledge.

Ritella, G., & Loperfido, F. F. (2021). Students' self-organization of the learning environment during a blended knowledge creation course. *Education Sciences, 11*(10), 580.

Ritella, G., & Marcone, R. (2024). Constructing in minecraft in primary school as a boundary-crossing practice. *Education Sciences, 14*(1), 85.

Ritella, G., & Sansone, N. (2020). Transforming the space-time of learning through interactive whiteboards: The case of a knowledge creation collaborative task. *QWERTY-Interdisciplinary Journal of Technology, Culture and Education, 15*(1), 12–30.

Ritella, G., Ligorio, M. B., & Hakkarainen, K. (2016). The role of context in a collaborative problem-solving task during professional development. *Technology, Pedagogy and Education, 25*(3), 395–412.

Ritella, G., Ligorio, M. B., & Hakkarainen, K. (2019). Interconnections between the discursive framing of space-time and the interpretation of a collaborative task. *Learning, Culture and Social Interaction, 20*, 45–57.

Ritella, G., Rajala, A., & Renshaw, P. (2021). Using chronotope to research the space-time relations of learning and education: Dimensions of the unit of analysis. *Learning, Culture and Social Interaction, 31*, 100381.

Ritella, G., Crescenzo, P., Bulut, S., Sansone, N., Annese, S., & Ligorio, M. B. (2024). Italian teachers' emotional styles and burnout when using educational technology. *QWERTY-Interdisciplinary Journal of Technology, Culture and Education, 19*(2), 42–58.

Riva, G. (2009). Is presence a technology issue? Some insights from cognitive sciences. *Virtual Reality, 13*(3), 159–169.

Sigurðardóttir, A. K., & Hjartarson, T. (2016). The idea and reality of an innovative school: From inventive design to established practice in a new school building. *Improving Schools, 19*(1), 62–79.

Silseth, K., & Arnseth, H. C. (2022). Weaving together the past, present and future in whole class conversations: Analyzing the emergence of a hybrid educational chronotope connecting every-day experiences and school science. *Mind, Culture, and Activity, 29*(1), 60–74.

Vygotsky, L. S. (1977). The development of higher psychological functions. *Soviet Psychology, 15*(3), 60–73.

Waterworth, J. A., Waterworth, E. L., Mantovani, F., & Riva, G. (2010). On feeling (the) present: An evolutionary account of the sense of presence in physical and electronically-mediated environments. *Journal of Consciousness Studies, 17*(1–2), 167–188.

Zerubavel, E. (1989). *The seven day circle: The history and meaning of the week.* University of Chicago Press.

Chapter 4
Reimagining Digital Technologies in Environmental Education: Relating with the More-than-Human World Through Augmented Storying

Kristiina Kumpulainen, Jenny Renlund, Chin Chin Wong, and Jenny Byman

4.1 Introduction

This chapter is set in the challenging era of the "Anthropocene," a term that underscores the harmful effects of human activity on the planet and its ecological systems (Wallenhorst & Wulf, 2023). It explores the complex relationships between humans and nonhumans—including living beings and materiality—highlighting the necessity to rethink digital technologies in environmental education. Specifically, our chapter focuses on how children of the Anthropocene are afforded opportunities to develop their relations with forests, trees, other plants, insects, and animals amid changing ecologies, societies, and technologies. If these relations are not carefully attended to by education, they are likely to lead to increased shifts in children's relations with their living environments, with negative consequences for their pro-environmental behaviours. Overall, our chapter addresses the socio-ecological challenges of our precarious times by considering how digital technologies can create educational opportunities for children to immerse in the more-than-human world, considering their relations with it.

Despite the growing interest in digital technologies in environmental education research, the focus has been mainly on anthropocentric approaches prioritizing human agency over the interconnected, more-than-human world (Kumpulainen, 2022). Most existing studies in this field focus on how digital technologies can

K. Kumpulainen (✉)
University of British Columbia, Vancouver, BC, Canada
e-mail: kristiina.kumpulainen@ubc.ca

J. Renlund · C. C. Wong · J. Byman
University of Helsinki, Helsinki, Finland
e-mail: jenny.renlund@helsinki.fi; Chin.wong@helsiki.fi; jenny.byman@helsinki.fi

M. B. Ligorio (ed.), *Technology as Cultural Mediator*, Culture in Policy Making: The Symbolic Universes of Social Action,
https://doi.org/10.1007/978-3-031-97673-5_4

advance children's conceptual learning and increasing children's interest in environmental issues through structured and pre-planned approaches. However, there is a lack of more holistic and open-ended approaches that address the emotional, ethical, imaginative, and even spiritual dimensions of relating to, learning from, and relating with the more-than-human world (Kumpulainen, 2022; Kumpulainen et al., 2023b). This is a significant limitation because increasing environmental knowledge alone does not necessarily attune children to consider humans' relations with the more-than-human world or promote an emotional connection (Renshaw et al., 2023). It is through holistic, enchanted and immersive experiences that children can develop an appreciation for, care about, and advocate for the environment (Giusti, 2019). Therefore, there is a pressing need for more research on how digital technologies might contribute to children's relational engagement with the more-than-human world. At the same time, many debated assumptions about digital technology in environmental education remain unexamined, particularly concerning whether and how digital technologies can immerse children in the more-than-human world, arousing their curiosity and sense of interconnectedness with it.

Integrating digital technologies into environmental education can offer numerous benefits, such as increased engagement and improved access to information; however, several concerns must also be addressed to ensure their meaningful, responsible, and sustainable use (Greenwood & Hougham, 2015; Kumpulainen, 2022). One key tension to recognize is the environmental impact of technology. It is widely accepted that the production and disposal of digital devices contribute to environmental degradation, creating a paradox in using digital technologies for environmental education that may harm the planet. Additionally, there is a risk that technology diminishes children's hands-on, embodied experiences with the world around them, thereby disconnecting them from the natural environment instead of connecting them. At the same time, it is acknowledged that excessive screen time is linked to adverse health outcomes, such as decreased physical activity and possible effects on mental well-being. Concerns regarding equity and access also arise, as not all children have equal access to digital devices and reliable internet, potentially exacerbating educational inequalities. A significant concern relates to privacy and surveillance, as the use of digital platforms can raise issues of data privacy and surveillance, particularly when technologies monitor student activities, potentially undermining trust and autonomy. To mitigate these concerns, a balanced approach is needed that combines digital tools with immersive, real-world environmental experiences, ensuring inclusivity, protecting children's privacy, and promoting overall well-being across both human and more-than-human worlds.

In this chapter, we address the necessity of reimagining digital technologies within environmental education by examining how digital engagement offers children opportunities to immerse themselves, explore, and wonder in the green spaces of their living environments, thereby nurturing their relational orientation to the world. Importantly, we attempt to move away from the anthropocentric approaches to learning and education that privilege human interests above those of nonhuman others. To these ends, we draw on post-human theorizing to explore the educational potential of stories, storytelling, and augmented technology as animated means to immerse children in the more-than-human world and encourage children to consider interconnections and interdependencies between humans and nonhumans. It is this interconnected world between humans and non-humans that we refer to in our chapter as the 'more-than-human world' (Kumpulainen et al., 2023a, 2023b; Rousell & Cutter-Mackenzie-Knowles, 2020). Our chapter holds that a post-human perspective offers less-researched opportunities for conceptualizing and researching digital technologies in environmental education, fostering new ways of thinking and acting, and helping us address the pressing ecological challenges of our time.

To illustrate our approach and its grounding in post-humanism, we will discuss our research conducted in a Finnish primary school where children utilized an augmented story-crafting application to explore their local urban forest and create and share their stories. Specifically, we investigated how trees became entangled with the children's augmented storying in the forest, as well as the educational opportunities of these encounters. Our inquiry shows how augmented storying invited the children to attend to their interconnectedness with the more-than-human world by considering *trees as kin*, *trees as dwellings*, *trees sustaining life*, and *trees as sources of wonder*. From a theoretical perspective, the chapter illustrates the potential of post-human theorizing to change how we think about digital technologies in environmental education.

4.2 A Post-Human Approach to Digital Technologies in Environmental Education

Building on post-human theories, our research explores how storytelling, augmented technology, and movement intersect and the opportunities these connections create for young children to relate to the more-than-human world. Post-human theorizing challenges a human-centred perspective by emphasizing the co-agency of both humans and nonhumans. It moves away from dualistic views and instead embraces relational ontologies, aiming to overcome anthropocentrism (Barad, 2003, 2007; Bennett, 2010). This perspective highlights the inseparability of nature and culture, human and non-human, body and mind, and subject and object, paying particular attention to the materiality through which meanings and actions emerge (Kumpulainen et al., 2023a, 2023b).

The post-human approach views digital technologies as relational and emergent, and as agentive co-participants in the unfolding of activities that, together with other actors, including humans and nonhuman entities, create a potential space for relating, learning and becoming with the more-than-human world (Barad, 2003, 2007; Bennett, 2010; Haraway, 2008, 2016). By conceptualizing technology this way, the post-human approach draws attention to the relationships and processes through which humans are irreducibly intertwined and co-evolving with technology (Hoel, 2018; Jukes et al., 2023). The post-human approach, hence, challenges the binary understanding of humans and technology as separate entities. Instead, it recognizes that humans and technology are deeply intertwined and mutually constitutive. Further, it disputes the idea of technology as either an enabler or disabler of human potential, viewing it as an integral aspect of human existence and development. In conclusion, a post-human approach to digital technology underscores the intricate, interrelated nature of human-technology relations. It promotes a more nuanced and critical engagement with digital technologies, moving beyond simple notions of human mastery or technological determinism.

Following the post-human theorizing, in our research we view children's augmented storying in the forest as 'material-discursive' that emerge through human–material–spatial-temporal intra-actions. For Barad (2003, 2007), intra-actions entail the complex co-productions of human and nonhuman matter, time, spaces, and their signification. The human is not seen as acting on matter, but rather, humans and nonhumans are viewed as agential actors in the world that come into being through their intra-actions (Fenwick & Landri, 2012; Tanggaard, 2013). Similarly, we underscore the unity of relations between human beings and the more-than-human world and approach these relations as a subject-subject relation (Barad, 2003, 2007; Bennett, 2010; Haraway, 2008, 2016; Lenz Taguchi, 2010, 2011). In doing so, we move beyond an anthropocentric view that approaches humans' relations with the world as a subject-object relation.

The post-human conceptualization approaches language and literacy from a non-representational perspective (Leander & Boldt, 2013). That is, rather than understanding language and literacy as representations of fixed meanings that are self-expressive, they are performative that emerge through enacted relations and connections across signs, objects, bodies, and socio-material and cultural contexts in often unexpected and improvisational ways. Therefore, the stories that children create and move with are not regarded "about" the world but rather they are actions texts through which meanings emerge (Wohlwend, 2011). From this perspective, children's augmented storying with the forest can be viewed as being about imagining, thinking, creating, communicating, and experiencing with the tools, contents, and contexts in situ and across space and time (Harwood & Collier, 2017). The post-human approach also views language and literacy practices as fuelled by affect, resulting in 'affective intensities' that are different from the rational control of meanings and forms (Burnett & Merchant, 2020; Leander & Boldt, 2013). On this basis, our research draws attention to the performative, affective and open-ended character of children's augmented storying with the more-than-human world.

The post-human approach has methodological implications for researching digital technologies in environmental education and learning. Firstly, while decentering the human and underscoring the relationality and intra-actions of human and nonhuman beings, it offers researchers an opportunity to consider the material-discursive forces that are present in a learning activity and that play into issues of sustainability and equity. Hence, the post-human approach asks researchers to use methodological means to address the complex human–material–spatial-temporal intra-actions that create opportunities for relating and learning (Barad, 2003, 2007). Secondly, it recognizes the need for multimodal inquiry that can address the non-representational, multisensory-experiential qualities of agential encounters that emerge across the human and nonhuman worlds embedded in the materiality, fluidity and messiness of entangled bodies and things (Leander & Boldt, 2013). Consequently, a post-human inquiry recognizes the need to attend to children's augmented storying as emergent that draws on a range of semiotic systems and multimodal resources.

Importantly, the post-human approach calls for creative methodologies to study the complex relational entanglements of human and nonhuman encounters that can shed light onto the contextual processes, events, and relationships that produce and shape one another (Le Grange, 2019). In our research, we have applied arts-based inquiry to address the material-discursive and multisensory-experiential aspects of the 'in-betweenness' of multiple agencies in an activity (Renlund et al., 2024). Further, by underscoring the 'unexpectedness and improvisation', we have focused on inquiring how different materiality, including augmented technology, turn into various kinds of things and serve different purposes when taken up in situated activities. Hence, our conceptual and methodological approach recognizes that what happens in situ is always more than what is designed or expected, with unpredictable outcomes and potentiality (Burnett & Merchant, 2020).

4.3 Researching Children's Augmented Storying with the Forest

We now discuss our empirical research on children's augmented storying with the forest. This research was conducted in a Finnish primary school and a local urban forest. Children aged 7–9 used an augmented story-crafting application to explore their local urban forest and create and share their stories.

Our pedagogical approach and designs for children's activities derive from our interdisciplinary research and development work with artists, designers, educators, and researchers (Erfving et al., 2017; Kumpulainen & Keso, 2019; Wong & Kumpulainen, 2020) motivated by the aim of encouraging children's storying and relating with the more-than-human world. Our pedagogy is inspired by old Finnish myths and folk tales about elves and forests, combined with children's use of augmented reality technology to support their mobile and multimodal storying activities outdoors in their local environments. Instead of presenting the forest to children as an object to learn about, the emphasis is on children's wonder, experiential and immersive engagement through folk tales on the forest, and crafting and communicating their own stories. Before children's augmented storying activities, they engage in learning about folk tales through multimodal, arts-based activities that will orient them to their explorations and immersive engagement in the forest. The augmented-story crafting app that the children use in their storying allows them to project an immersive rendering of an elf character, Julle, in the physical environment and to create their own stories around it. After children have created their augmented stories, they communicate and reflect on their stories and share what they have experienced and learned.

Our empirical data corpus comprises multimodal data including videos, observational field notes, children's narrations of their augmented stories, interview data and children's story artefacts, allowing us to make multiple inquiries in and with the data to attend to unexpected relationalities and entanglements in the data. Our reading and inquiry of these data have been inspired by ecological narrative inquiry (Moore, 2018) and visual and sensuous ethnography (Pink, 2014) that point to recognizing the multiple modes and means through which meanings and knowledge are constructed. We have also been affected by A/r/tography (Irwin, 2013; LeBlanc et al., 2015) that similarly underscores inquiring in the world through an ongoing process of art making, with interest in relational aesthetic inquiry grounded in embodied understandings and exchanges between art and text (see also Renlund et al., 2024).

The analytical reading of our multimodal data can be characterized as a recursive process guided by an attempt to acknowledge the full range of senses and modalities through which meanings and knowledge emerge in the children's storying in the forest. Our inquiry also focused on how different actors, such as people, augmented reality character Julle, animals, insects, and trees, entered the children's storying with the more-than-human world; how the stories unfolded across actors across space and time, whether physically co-present or on-screen, human or not; and the scope and diversity of the emerging stories. Our analysis involved individual and group readings of the data interspersed with reflective discussions during which we shared our interpretations with each other. We then revisited our data and interpretations in light of our collective discussions.

Our goal is to provide insight into children's augmented storytelling in the forest and how this activity created spaces for relating with the more-than-human world. We aim to transcend the limitations of viewing humans as isolated subjects, blurring the perceived boundaries between people and the world they are part of. By incorporating photos and videos, we hope to turn our reading beyond words and text—offering something more affective. Importantly, our goal is not to validate student learning in a positivist manner. Instead, we aim to explore onto-epistemological questions related to how children engage with the more-than-human world through their augmented storying in the forest.

4.4 Learnings from Our Research

Our post-human inquiry illustrates how augmented storying in the forest invited children to recognize interconnections and interdependencies between humans and nonhumans. In particular, trees emerged as a prominent element in the children's augmented storying in vivid and unexpected ways. The children's enchantment with trees piqued our curiosity as researchers, motivating us to read and analyze these stories in our data. Our analytical reading of the multimodal data revealed four relational encounters in the children's augmented storying with trees: *trees as kin*, *trees as dwellings*, *trees sustaining life*, and *trees as sources of wonder.* These encounters enhanced our understanding of augmented storying and its capacity to prompt children to reflect on their relationality with the more-than-human world.

We have summarized our findings in Fig. 4.1 through a combination of digital artwork and textual narration that illustrate the discursive-material entanglements, or, in other words, the "middle of things" in the children's augmented storying. The image-making, digital painting, and writing guided our inquiry into the multiple relationalities in the children's augmented storying across space and time. Importantly, our art-based, creative approach and its open-endedness allowed us to consider and include non-representational qualities of the children's encounters with trees and their affections in-between. Our post-human inquiry reveals tensions, confusions, and opportunities in children's augmented storying, thus creating a space for the unexpected. Thinking through image creation and writing also affects how we perceive ourselves as researchers in reading and learning with data situated at the intersection of art and text (Renlund et al., 2024).

Fig. 4.1 Immersing in and relating with the more-than-human world through augmented storying with the forest

4.4.1 Trees as Kin

Our research revealed that the children viewed trees as their kin in their augmented storying with the forest (see Fig. 4.2). This perspective illuminated the responsibilities, obligations, pleasures, and attachments that the children felt towards trees. They recognized the significance of trees in their lives as friends and beings they wished to care for. The children's augmented storying conveyed vivid experiences with specific trees from their early childhood. Additionally, they maintained a general awareness of the necessity of protecting trees.

The augmented stories the children wanted to share about their personal experiences, affection and care for trees pushed them to overcome language barriers through painting and drawing. For instance, a multilingual child Kazimir,[1] whose first language was Russian and who was learning Finnish, was eager to share an

Fig. 4.2 Trees as kin in the children's augmented storying with the forest

[1] All the names of children mentioned in this chapter are pseudonyms.

augmented story about how trees take a long time to grow. He explained how he had planted a sapling with his father and how this sapling had grown into a bigger tree in the same way as he had grown big. Kazimir's augmented storying about the tree became alive through his gesturing with his hand, illustrating how the tree had grown with him. Kazimir also shared how this tree was "his" tree and how it grew in "his" yard, which was surrounded and protected by a brick fence. In his yard, several trees were growing. During this conversation, Kazimir eagerly asked for help from his friend Daniela and a teacher so that they could translate his stories from Russian to Finnish. Daniela and Kazimir were gesturing to the teacher the word "fence", repeating it in Russian, and the teacher, who spoke some Russian, translated the word into Finnish. Kazimir was also eager to draw pictures explaining how humans need to nurture and care for growing trees. It was clear that trees were close to Kazimir's heart. Some children's kinship with trees became alive in embodied ways, as in the children's augmented storying; they were hugging trees in the forest with their family members.

Also, other children in our study felt very attached to woods, and trees were familiar to them. In their augmented storying, trees turned into agentive beings. Mary explained how "*I think that nature also needs humans. When a tree is a bit lonely in the woods and some people cut down these trees, it is a bit lonely, so then trees need friends. Then it can grow and grow, like a human as a baby, it grows to become an adult*". This example illustrates how the children's augmented storying with trees also included grieving the loss of trees to which they felt a strong kinship. The children's empathy for trees seemed to direct their attention to both their affective landscape and to relationality and ongoing storying that illuminated their efforts to transform local surroundings for the well-being of trees. These encounters with trees made visible and emerging through their engagement in augmented storying were also fuelled by tensions and moral consideration (see also Kumpulainen et al., 2021; Lenz Taguchi, 2010).

4.4.2 *Trees as Dwellings*

In the children's augmented storying, trees turned into sites for dwelling, making visible how physical movement and embodiment with trees mattered to the children (see Fig. 4.3). The children's augmented storying about their dwelling with trees not only reflected their personal lives but also their cultural and ecological worlds. The children would go to the forest to climb, jump and play in trees. They would also build treehouses to get together and play. At times, treehouses grew into bigger worlds in the children's augmented storying that inspired games and explorations in the forest.

Moosa's and Luca's augmented storying detailed how they built treehouses in the forest near their homes. Moosa storied how her father had once helped her build a treehouse and how she still visits the treehouse and has even spent a night there. The treehouse was near a pond where Moosa and her friends could feed ducks.

Fig. 4.3 Trees as dwellings in the children's augmented storying with the forest

Moosa also brought her dog Magic, to this place, and together with her father, they built a small house for the dog next to the treehouse. Moosa shared how, together with her dog Magic, they had painted the treehouse by using all the colours in their palette for making a rainbow: "*He (Magic) went and poked the colours he wanted, and he wanted all of them. There was red, yellow, green, black, white, blue and purple and then it became a rainbow...*". Moosa's augmented storytelling also detailed how she and her friends collected items they could find in the forest beneath the treehouse. This was a way for the children to pick up garbage from the forest, which Moosa and her friends found a problem.

Similar to Moosa, another child called Mauno storied with augmented technology how he spent time in the forest building treehouses with his friends. Mauno explained that he liked trees and talked about building huts and tree houses as something exciting and inspiring. Mauno's augmented storying illuminated his favourite game called 'tribe' that he played with his friends in the forest. During this game, the children built a treehouse where they often gathered to play the game. Mauno said, "*I like being in nature, especially in the summer, then the tribe game becomes very common. I can still remember how we came up with that game*". Sadly, Mauno shared how someone had recently destroyed their treehouse.

Through climbing in trees, building treehouses and gathering objects, the children left traces in the forest; thus, their dwelling with trees during augmented storying was a part of becoming with and transforming the forest. Ingold (2011) describes dwelling as a highly sensorial and embodied situatedness, which interweaves with the environment, changing both the dweller and the surroundings. In our inquiry, the children's dwelling with trees during their augmented storying emerged as a way to create special places that became familiar and cherished while opening up opportunities to imagine and experience adventures, play and be together. These relationships of mutual transformation with the forest seemed to develop children's attachment towards trees and the forest, in general.

4.4.3 *Trees Sustaining Life*

In their augmented storying, the children considered how trees and the forest were crucial for sustaining life (see Fig. 4.4). Many children emphasized that trees give oxygen for living creatures to breathe. When asked if nature can provide something good to humans, Nellie, one of the children in our study, explained that trees give oxygen and that nature also gives beauty. In her augmented storying, Nellie had previously described how the forest is a place of peacefulness and quiet, where she can go and calm herself. Nellie also pondered how important it is for humans to take care of forests and to plant more trees because of their essential role in sustaining life on earth: "...*If we would just have five trees left in the world, then if someone was so smart and would grow more trees and the trees would again give more oxygen for those people...*". Nellie continued to reflect on the reciprocal relationship

Fig. 4.4 Trees sustaining life in the children's augmented storying with the forest

between trees and humans, proposing that humans should provide trees with the resources they need to thrive, allowing the trees to produce oxygen for people.

Several children also described trees during their augmented storying as necessary for animals. For instance, Beata described how trees are essential for squirrels to climb and inhabit. A few children considered how trees can help prevent erosion. For example, Kazimir explained how trees are important for humans and all living creatures as their roots hold together soil and this keeps the earth's surface stable. Furthermore, some children had conflicting emotions and thoughts about humans using trees as resources to build houses, make paper and consume them as fuel. The children understood these actions as important for humans, but detrimental for trees and forests. For instance, in his augmented storying Kalevi, expressed strong opinions about the harmful effects of using wood charcoal to produce energy: "*We should avoid using charcoal, like from trees, as fuel*". Kalevi also expressed that he was upset about the extension construction in his school because this meant trees were being cut down. Trees emerged as essential agentive beings in the children's augmented stories. These stories were not only smooth encounters but also tension-laden, provoking the children's moral reflections about the interdependence between humans and trees.

4.4.4 Trees as Sources of Wonder

In the children's augmented storying, trees appeared as an infinite source of wonder and curiosity (see Fig. 4.5). When asked what the children would like to learn about nature, they expressed wanting to know more about trees, such as their names and habitats. One of the children, Tatu, explained how he enjoyed spending time in nature with his friends and family and how sometimes they picked mushrooms together in the forest. He showed curiosity about how trees grow and which trees and plants in the neighborhood were edible. Tatu explained that he had learned a little about trees and plants at school but would be curious to learn more. During the same conversation, Liam, another child in our study, extended his curiosity from trees to other plants in the neighborhood. Liam explained how he already knew a lot about trees, but he wished to learn about the names of all plants and how to grow and take care of them: "*I already know all about trees, but I would like to learn something about plants, how they grow*". Tatu also further elaborated his wonder for plants and explained how some plants can help humans to be happy and healthy as they can be used to cure wounds. In addition, Tatu expressed a sense of fascination with trees when wondering how the forest actually grows in his local neighborhood: "*Near to my home there is a very big forest*". Tatu also elaborated on how he especially enjoyed the sensory experience of calm and quietness when walking deep into a forest. Some other children expressed curiosity about learning how to navigate and get to know the local forest. Elsi explained, "*It would be fun to know a forest, so that you could wander there…skillfully*". She emphasized how getting to know a big forest would be especially exciting. Later, Elsi also expressed frustration about

Fig. 4.5 Trees as sources of wonder in the children's augmented storying with the forest

the degradation of their local forest. Tatu's, Liam's and Elsi's augmented storying in the forest set in motion their care and curiosity for trees and plants.

The children's wonder about trees and desire to learn their names, characteristics and connections to different trees and plants bear great pedagogical potential for exploring the complex and multifaceted relationalities and diversities of forests and landscapes (Carson, 2017; Gandy, 2019). Although embodied exploring and immersive engagement in the forest are essential to developing children's connections and caring attitudes toward the more-than-human world, scientific curiosity and knowledge are also vital to ecological awareness and sensitivity (Eaton, 1998). In our inquiry, trees aroused the children's wonder and curiosity in their augmented storying with the forest, creating pathways to discover and make new meanings and knowledge of human and nonhuman relations.

4.5 Beyond Screens: Augmented Storying in Environmental Education

In this chapter, we discuss our research on young children's augmented storying with the forest. Specifically, we highlight how trees became integral to the children's augmented storying and the educational opportunities arising from children becoming more aware of their relationality with the more-than-human world. The children's augmented storying challenged human exceptionalism and brought to light moral, aesthetic and political considerations regarding the co-existence of human and nonhuman actors, inviting children to consider human and nonhuman relations and our kinship with others on more equal grounds. Issues of environmental crises, sustainability and equity are, and should be, at the forefront of educational inquiry. To explore these complex matters, education scholars are shifting towards posthuman approaches that acknowledge the blurred relationships between social and material worlds and address the discursive-material forces in learning and education that actively contribute to issues of sustainability and equity (Barad, 2003). Our research supports these initiatives, deepening our understanding of how digital technologies can promote children's relational engagement with the more-than-human world.

Our research demonstrates how digital technologies, specifically storying activities in the forest supported by augmented technology, engaged the children in their natural environments and strengthened their sense of interconnectedness with the planet. Augmented storying inspired the children to create their own stories, nurturing creativity and a personal connection to the environment. Layering the AR character Julle over the real world and capturing personally significant moments in the forest captivated the children and enriched their experiences with the more-than-human world. Augmented storying during outdoor walks encouraged multisensory learning, where visual, auditory, and kinesthetic elements emerged to enrich storying and learning in the forest. It can be concluded that thoughtfully integrating digital technologies, such as augmented storytelling, into environmental education can enhance teaching and learning, and strengthen children's connection with the planet.

In formal education, most literacies typically occur indoors and mainly focus on text or the world from an anthropocentric perspective. Less attention has been given to how stories and storying, embedded in augmented reality technology, can transform into experiential and embodied 'openings' that invite and engage children to attend to and learn with the more-than-human world both inside and outside the classroom (Payne, 2010). In response, our pedagogical approach builds on stories, storytelling, art, and augmented technology as animated means to immerse children in exploring the interconnections and interdependencies between humans and nonhumans. Our approach emphasizes children's wonder and their experiential and immersive engagement in the forest, alongside crafting and sharing their (place) stories with the assistance of augmented reality technology. This pedagogical framework contributes to environmental education that is open to action, ambiguity, and imagination, harnessing new digital technologies in affective and sustainable ways (Greenwood & Hougham, 2015; Huang et al., 2016; Kumpulainen et al., 2021). Our approach also builds on research evidence suggesting that embodied, immersive, and emotional engagement and exploration in the forest and other ecologies can enhance children's respect and care towards the more-than-human world, recognizing childhood as an essential time to begin building these experiences and relations (Ampuero et al., 2015; Ives et al., 2018).

In more traditional environmental education, trees and plants are often investigated from the perspective of their ecological qualities. Our research shows how children's augmented storying with trees incorporates cultural, social, affective, moral, and sensuous aspects of trees, offering an essential means to attend to the relationality between humans and nonhumans (Kumpulainen et al., 2023b). Furthermore, our research not only sheds light on the children's relational encounters with trees but also helps give a greater sense of their lives beyond these direct encounters, challenging understandings of what it means to story with the more-than-human world. These discursive-material intensities emerged in the improvisational intra-actions across the children, technology, plants, animals, and other living and non-living systems and things, pointing to the importance of researching and understanding children's storying from a new materialist, post-human perspective.

The children's storying with the forest provides evidence of complex human-nature relations made visible through our post-human-inspired inquiry (Atkinson, 2015). The children's augmented storying mobilized care, concerns, and awareness of many tensions and challenges in human and nonhuman relations. In their augmented storying, the children lingered with and revisited difficult and upsetting topics instead of avoiding them. They also envisioned futures that called for change and action. In this way, the children not only accepted the world as it is but also engaged in imagining how the world could be. Overall, our inquiry demonstrates how augmented storying entered the children and us as researchers in 'considering and questioning relationships' while exploring differences with curiosity and enchantment (Byman et al., 2022; Kumpulainen et al., 2021).

Augmented storying with the forest created a space for children to immerse themselves in the spatio-temporal geographies of their narratives and to relate with the more-than-human world in holistic ways. The interrelations that sprang to life in the children's augmented storying, were intertwined with material relations, experiential relations, cognitive relations, emotional attachments, and affective responses, as well as philosophical and moral perspectives on humanity's relationality with the more-than-human world (Burnett et al., 2020; Ives et al., 2018; Kumpulainen et al., 2023b). The children's augmented storying with the forest provided a playful way for them to explore, imagine, and connect with their inner selves, social dynamics, and more-than-human environments (Payne, 2010). Importantly, the children's augmented storying set in motion the children's and our researchers' attentiveness to the intrinsic relationship between social and ecological phenomena, prompting us to rethink "social justice" in light of a relational ontology of human and nonhuman worlds (Yaka, 2019). Moreover, the augmented storytelling acted as a crucial catalyst for the children to transcend their rationally assumed roles as students or naive children. Altogether, our findings underscore the importance of recognizing that young children can engage in rich modes of storytelling across the human and more-than-human worlds when provided with appropriate opportunities, tools, and support.

Our research illustrates how children's relating with the forest addressed the interconnections and interdependence that exist among human and nonhuman beings. Augmented storying with the forest allowed the children to become experientially and holistically immersed in both the human and nonhuman worlds, enabling them to consider various perspectives and dimensions. The children narrated with and through the AR character Julle and envisioned the living world through "nature's eyes," such as those of bees and trees. Overall, our inquiry demonstrates how the augmented story-crafting method engaged both the children and us as researchers in "considering and questioning relationships" and exploring differences with a sense of curiosity (Haraway, 2008).

Our research demonstrates how augmented storying can draw children into imaginative dialogues about their relations with the more-than-human world. At the same time, our research offers novel insights into how stories, storytelling, art, and augmented technology can create spaces for children's encounters with the living world, while also considering ecocentric perspectives that decentre humans and position them as part of complex relationships. In doing so, we respond to calls for environmental education that embraces action, ambiguity, and imagination, while harnessing new digital technologies in affective, meaningful, and sustainable ways.

Acknowledgements This research was funded by the Australian Research Council (grant no. DP190102067), KONE foundation (grant no. 202008316) and Academy of Finland (grant no. 339458).

References

Ampuero, D., Miranda, C. E., Delgado, L. E., Goyen, S., & Weaver, S. (2015). Empathy and critical thinking: Primary students solving local environmental problems through outdoor learning. *Journal of Adventure Education and Outdoor Learning, 15*(1), 64–78. https://doi.org/10.1080/14729679.2013.848817

Atkinson, K. (2015). Wasps-bees-mushrooms-children: Reimagining multispecies relations in early childhood pedagogies. Special issue: Learning how to inherit colonized and ecologically challenged lifeworlds. *Canadian Children, 40*(2), 67–79.

Barad, K. (2003). Posthumanist performativity: Toward an understanding of how matter comes to matter. *Signs, 40*, 801–831.

Barad, K. (2007). *Meeting the universe halfway: Quantum physics and the entanglement of matter and meaning*. Duke University Press.

Bennett, J. (2010). *Vibrant matter: A political ecology of things*. Duke University Press.

Burnett, C., & Merchant, G. (2020). Literacy-as-event: Accounting for relationality in literacy research. *Discourse: Studies in the Cultural Politics of Education, 41*(1), 45–56. https://doi.org/10.1080/01596306.2018.1460318

Burnett, C., Parry, B., Merchant, G., & Storey, V. (2020). Treading softly in the enchanted forest: Exploring the integration of iPads in a participatory theatre education programme. *Pedagogies: An International Journal, 15*(3), 203–220. https://doi.org/10.1080/1554480X.2019.1696199

Byman, J., Kumpulainen, K., Wong, C., & Renlund, J. (2022). Children's emotional experiences in and about nature across temporal–spatial entanglements during digital storying. *Literacy, 56*(1), 18–28. https://doi.org/10.1111/lit.12265

Carson, R. (2017). *The sense of wonder*. Harper Collins.

Eaton, M. (1998). Fact and fiction in the aesthetic appreciation of nature. *The Journal of Aesthetics and Art Criticism, 56*(2), 149–156. https://doi.org/10.2307/432253

Erfving, E., Hintsa, A., Sintonen, S., Sairanen, H., & Kumpulainen, K. (2017). *Whisper of the spirit*. University of Helsinki, Playful Learning Center. https://helda.helsinki.fi/handle/10138/222483

Fenwick, T., & Landri, P. (2012). Materialities, textures and pedagogies: Socio-material assemblages in education. *Pedagogy, Culture and Society, 20*(1), 1–7. https://doi.org/10.1080/14681366.2012.649421

Gandy, M. (2019). The fly that tried to save the world: Saproxylic geographies and other-than-human ecologies. *Transactions—Institute of British Geographers (1965), 44*(2), 392–406. https://doi.org/10.1111/tran.12281

Giusti, M. (2019). Human-nature relationships in context. Experiential, psychological, and contextual dimensions that shape children's desire to protect nature. *PLoS One, 14*(12), e0225951. https://doi.org/10.1371/journal.pone.0225951

Greenwood, D. A., & Hougham, R. J. (2015). Mitigation and adaptation: Critical perspectives toward digital technologies in place-conscious environmental education. *Policy Futures in Education, 13*(1), 97–116. https://doi.org/10.1177/1478210314566732

Haraway, D. (2008). *When species meet*. University of Minnesota Press.

Haraway, D. (2016). *Staying with the trouble: Making kin in the Chthulucene*. Duke University Press. https://doi.org/10.1215/9780822373780

Harwood, D., & Collier, D. (2017). The matter of the stick: Storying/(re)storying children's literacies in the forest. *Journal of Early Childhood Literacy, 17*(3), 336–352. https://doi.org/10.1177/1468798417712340

Hoel, A. S. (2018). Technicity. In R. Braidotti & M. Hlavajova (Eds.), *Posthuman glossary* (pp. 420–423). Bloomsbury Academic.

Huang, T. C., Chen, C. C., & Chou, Y. W. (2016). Animating eco-education: To see, feel, and discover in an augmented reality-based experiential learning environment. *Computers and Education, 96*, 72–82. https://doi.org/10.1016/j.compedu.2016.02.008

Ingold, T. (2011). *Being alive: Essays on movement, knowledge and description*. Routledge.

Irwin, R. L. (2013). Becoming a/r/tography. *Studies in Art Education, 54*(3), 198–215. https://doi.org/10.1080/00393541.2013.11518894

Ives, C. D., Abson, D. J., Von Wehrden, H., Dorninger, C., Klaniecki, K., & Fischer, J. (2018). Reconnecting with nature for sustainability. *Sustainability Science, 13*(5), 1389–1397. https://doi.org/10.1007/s11625-018-0542-9

Jukes, S., Stewart, A., & Morse, M. (2023). Learning landscapes through technology and movement: Blurring boundaries for a more-than-human pedagogy. *Journal of Adventure Education and Outdoor Learning, 24*, 535–552. https://doi.org/10.1080/14729679.2023.2166543

Kumpulainen, K. (2022). Bridging dichotomies between children, nature and digital technologies. In K. Kumpulainen, A. Kajamaa, O. Erstad, Å. Mäkitalo, K. Drotner, & S. Jakobsdóttir (Eds.), *Nordic childhoods in the digital age: Insights into contemporary research on communication, learning and education* (pp. 41–50). Routledge. https://doi.org/10.4324/9781003145257-6

Kumpulainen, K., & Keso, M. (2019). *MyArJulle*. http://www.myar.community/julle/info-en.html

Kumpulainen, K., Renlund, J., Byman, J., & Wong, C. C. (2021). Empathetic encounters of children's augmented storying across the human and more-than-human worlds. *International Studies in Sociology of Education, 31*, 208–230. https://doi.org/10.1080/09620214.2021.1916400

Kumpulainen, K., Byman, J., Renlund, J., & Wong, C. C. (2023a). Dialogic learning with the 'more-than-human world': Insights from posthuman theorising. In C. Damsa, A. Rajala, G. Ritella, & J. Brouwer (Eds.), *Re-theorizing learning and research methods in learning research* (pp. 47–64). Routledge.

Kumpulainen, K., Wong, C.-C., Byman, J., Renlund, J., & Vadeboncoeur, J. A. (2023b). Fostering children's ecological imagination with augmented storying. *The Journal of Environmental Education, 54*(1), 33–45. https://doi.org/10.1080/00958964.2022.2152407

Le Grange, L. (2019). What is (post)qualitative research? *South African Journal of Higher Education, 32*(5), 1–14. https://doi.org/10.20853/32-5-3161

Leander, K., & Boldt, G. (2013). Rereading "A pedagogy of multiliteracies": Bodies, texts, and emergence. *Journal of Literacy Research, 45*(1), 22–46.

LeBlanc, N., Davidson, S. F., Ryu, J. Y., & Irwin, R. L. (2015). Becoming through a/r/tography, autobiography and stories in motion. *International Journal of Education through Art, 11*(3), 355–374. https://doi.org/10.1386/eta.11.3.355_1

Lenz Taguchi, H. (2010). *Going beyond the theory/practice divide in early childhood education: Introducing an intra-active pedagogy*. Routledge.

Lenz Taguchi, H. (2011). Investigating learning, participation and becoming in early childhood practices with a relational materialist approach. *Global Studies of Childhood, 1*(1), 36–50. https://doi.org/10.2304/gsch.2011.1.1.36

Moore, D. (2018). Children's maginative play environments and ecological narrative inquiry. In A. Cutter-Mackenzie, K. Malone, & E. Barratt Hacking (Eds.), *Research handbook on childhoodnature*. Springer International Handbooks of Education. Springer, Cham. https://doi.org/10.1007/978-3-319-51949-4_23-1

Payne, P. G. (2010). Remarkable-tracking, experiential education of the ecological imagination. *Environmental Education Research, 16*(3–4), 295–310. https://doi.org/10.1080/13504621003613160

Pink, S. (2014). Digital–visual–sensory-design anthropology: Ethnography, imagination and intervention. *Arts and Humanities in Higher Education, 13*(4), 412–427. https://doi.org/10.1177/1474022214542353

Renlund, J., Kumpulainen, K., Byman, J., Wong, C. C., & Sintonen, S. (2024). Aesthetic flux: Inquiring into the sensuous dynamics of children, matter and environments with a more-than-human lens. *Environmental Education Research, 30*, 1–17. https://doi.org/10.1080/13504622.2024.2350675

Renshaw, P., Jackson, K., Mortlock, H., & Tooth, R. (2023). Enchantment and digital technologies: Cultivating children's enchantment with the more-than-human through video-walks in local places. *The Journal of Environmental Education, 54*(1), 20–32. https://doi.org/10.1080/00958964.2022.2152408

Rousell, D., & Cutter-Mackenzie-Knowles, A. (2020). Uncommon Worlds: Toward an ecological aesthetics of childhood in the anthropocene. In A. Cutter-Mackenzie-Knowles, K. A. Malone, & E. B. Hacking (Eds.), *Research handbook on childhoodnature* (pp. 1657–1679). Springer International Publishing. https://doi.org/10.1007/978-3-319-67286-1_88

Tanggaard, L. (2013). The sociomateriality of creativity in everyday life. *Culture and Psychology, 19*(1), 20–32. https://doi.org/10.1177/1354067X12464987

Wallenhorst, N., & Wulf, C. (Eds.). (2023). *Handbook of the Anthropocene. Humans between heritage and future*. Springer.

Wohlwend, K. E. (2011). *Playing their way into literacies: Reading, writing, and belonging in the early childhood classroom*. Teachers College Press.

Wong, C. C., & Kumpulainen, K. (2020). Multiliteracies pedagogy promoting young children's ecological literacy on climate change. In K. Kumpulainen & J. Sefton-Green (Eds.), *Multiliteracies and early years innovation: Perspectives from Finland and beyond* (pp. 95–114). Routledge.

Yaka, Ö. (2019). Rethinking justice: Struggles for environmental commons and the notion of socio-ecological justice. *Antipode, 51*(1), 353–372. https://doi.org/10.1111/anti.12422

Chapter 5
Living and Learning with Techno-Cultural Mediatization

Ola Erstad

5.1 Introduction

One obvious characteristic of the human-technology relationship today is the increased complexity of our media culture and environment. Commercially driven technology companies have become powerful actors on a global scale that has an impact on everything from global economy, democratic elections to the ways we learn and interact with people and objects in our everyday lives (Pangrazio & Sefton Green, 2022; Erstad et al., 2024).

The appropriation of technologies into diverse institutions and social practices is always embedded with both affordances and challenges—possibilities and risks—for human social-emotional wellbeing and meaning making (Wertsch, 1998). However, this is not to be understood as technological determinism, but rather as a continuous interrelationship of human and technological development. Throughout history, there has been an interconnection between technological innovations and people's use of diverse technologies (Säljö, 1999). Some technologies come and disappear, while others stay with us over longer time periods.

The argument made in this chapter is that we have are now entering a new technological culture and environment with increased complexity and increasing worries about the intrusiveness of digital technologies in all aspects of human living and existence, and with implications for the ways we learn. The technological culture today is fundamentally different from just a few decades ago, and thereby also needs new analytical tools and concepts to fully understand how we interact with diverse

O. Erstad (✉)
Department of Education, University of Oslo, Oslo, Norway
e-mail: o.a.erstad@uv.uio.no

M. B. Ligorio (ed.), *Technology as Cultural Mediator*, Culture in Policy Making: The Symbolic Universes of Social Action,
https://doi.org/10.1007/978-3-031-97673-5_5

technologies embedded in our everyday lives and the implications this has for how we understand learning and literacy. In order to explore these issues, I will draw on concepts and perspectives from both socio-cultural learning theories and media studies. The main focus will be on aspects of the everyday lives of people, how we make meaning of cultural transformations where technologies increasingly play an important role, and the implications for ways of understanding learning, literacies and education of our times. Key questions will be; What characterizes the interrelationship between humans and technology in contemporary societies, and which implications does this have on conceptions of learning and literacy? In the discussion below and the examples I draw on the focus will be on the tension between experiences of intrusiveness versus affordances in using available technological resources.

5.2 Communicative Figurations: From Things We Live by to a Culture of Connectivity

Politicians, the public press and parents are increasingly expressing concerns about screen time use among young people, access to harmful content from an early age, hateful communication as well as bullying on social media and the impact of artificial intelligence and disinformation. At the same time school teachers and researchers report on the affordances provided by digital resources for teaching and learning in diverse subject domains, in ways that playing computer games can gain engagement among boys, virtual reality provides insight into human gene structures or ways that young people can develop communities with other young people from around the world. This polarization between pros and cons has a distinct focus on the technology per se.

In his book 'the Invention of Communication' (1996) Armand Mattelart argues for the need to explore the broader developments of communication technologies aligned with social development over time. By studying developments of communication in a broad sense, from city planning, infrastructures of transport to modern machines and technologies, linked to theoretical positions and understandings developed during specific periods, Mattelart manages to provide a fundamental understanding of the social framing of communication as part of human development. Similar arguments for broader conceptions of communication within societies and the implications of technologies can be found in writings by Jack Goody on literacies (Olson & Cole, 2006) and Vilhelm Flusser on the cultural embedding of media (Ströhl, 2002).

Within media studies the term 'communicative figurations' has been used to explore new technological assemblages in social practices, a term that points back to Norbert Elias (1897–1990). A key person in drawing out this perspective is Andreas Hepp. He has for several years been interested in developing "a new approach to research on transforming communications in times of deep mediatization" (Hepp et al., 2018, p. 6).

Also, within science and technology studies (STS) and historic accounts of how specific technologies and artefacts enter our societies, have provided accounts of how social practices change as a consequence, for example such as the refrigerator and the freezer and how this changed food conservation and practices surrounding meals in homes. From a psychological perspective Alan Costall and Ole Dreier (2006) have explored similar issues in the book '*Doing things with things. The design and use of everyday objects*'. This is written with the aim of documenting the importance of everyday objects in ways of meaning making from a psychological perspective. The main point in these studies is to highlight the importance of everyday objects as interactional means in our everyday lives, and how new objects constantly enter everyday practices with implications for how we make meaning and understand the world around us.

Within the field of literacy studies the implications of technological developments on reading and writing has been of great importance. Since the days of the printing press, technological and cultural transformations have been central to how we conceptualize literacy and how it changes over time. Some term this as 'artifactual literacies' (Pahl & Rowsell, 2010), in highlighting the role of artifacts themselves in ways of understanding literacy and transformation. Further, with writers such as Jack Goody, Brian Street, Shirley Brice-Heath and David Barton, the social representations and cultural contexts for studying literacy as part of techno-cultural transformations have brought further complexity to the field.

My main point with this short exploration is that the traditional perspective of studying things and artifacts as something exterior to humans has fundamentally changed in recent years with the development of a whole new media infrastructure and technological culture in our societies. This challenges us in the ways we study and conceptualize such transformations and developments and how we understand meaning making, literacy and learning.

Some talk even of a 'post-digital' society (Pettersen, 2023), expressing a concern with how humans relate to rapidly changed and changing relationships with digital technologies, shifting the focus from technologies towards what it means to be human. As digital technologies are all over it becomes more blurred what the distinct human represents.

With reference to the above the term 'Internet of Things' has emerged, as many objects and things are connected to the internet and can thereby be operated in new ways, like toys for children, home appliances and remote access to operating heating in houses. Everyday objects and things are networked and interconnected. And these things are becoming increasingly advanced, now also with artificial intelligence embedded. One example of such changes in the way we interact with objects and artefacts are 'smart speakers' such as Alexa or Google Home (Mascheroni, 2023).

One implication of media culture today is the pervasiveness of media in society and everyday life, especially because of the development of mobile technologies, datafication and platformisation of our societies (van Dijck et al., 2018; Sefton Green, 2021). These developments have also been described as a 'culture of connectivity' (van Dijck, 2013) and 'hyperconnectivity' (Brubaker, 2022), emphasising how our lives are connected to others and diverse online spaces throughout our everyday lives to a degree never experienced before.

'Hyperconnectivity' (Brubaker, 2022) is actually an interesting term for social analysis in the ways it points towards key transformations taking place in our societies and culture due to the ways technologies have developed in recent years and its implications for human living and our social institutions. Brubaker has described this as:

> Digital hyperconnectivity—a condition, to exaggerate only slightly, in which everyone and everything is connected to everyone and everything else, everywhere and all the time—is a defining fact of our time. Hyperconnectivity has colonized the self, reorganizing our attention and reshaping our ways of thinking, seeing, and feeling. It has recast social interactions, stretching them over space and time, gamifying them, and channeling them into platform-friendly, surveillance-enhancing forms and formats. It has converted the whole of human culture into an unending stream of digital content, served to us by personalized algorithms. (See https://brubaker.scholar.ss.ucla.edu/hyperconnectivity-and-its-discontents/)

With reference to these conceptions and developments within social theory, how can we define frameworks that can help us study and understand learning and social practices as human—technology dyads?

5.3 Mediation and Mediatization

As way of approaching the question above I will explore the intersection between two concepts and fields of study, that of socio-cultural learning theory and media studies. The term 'mediatization' has evolved as a key analytical concept within media studies (Hjarvard, 2008; Hepp, 2013), while the term 'mediation' has been used within socio-cultural learning theory, often with reference to Vygotsky. Both imply the role of mediational means within communication, but on different levels of analysis and with different implications. At the same time these concepts are overlapping and have much to offer each other for a deeper understanding of the interconnection between culture and technology.

5.3.1 Mediatization

The concept of 'mediatization' has a long tradition within media studies with a focus on how media become part of societies and cultural developments (Lundby, 2009). Within media studies this concept has been used to express ways of understanding the implications of media developments on society at large, as well as on social institutions such as education and schools. Indeed, the term mediatization has come to denote how increasingly global and technically convergent media catalyze transformations of organizations, systems and cultures (Krotz, 2009).

It is important to distinguish between the concept of 'technology', which refers to the tools and things we use in everyday life like the book, computer or phone, and the concept of 'media', which refers to the cultural processes and implications diverse technologies have, as forms of media that impact social practices and how we come to understand the world around us (Drotner & Erstad, 2014). Technologies and media change over time, providing new means of accessing information, content production and ways of communication. One way of dividing this is between mass-, personal- and data driven communication. In media studies the tradition has been to study the process of mass communication, with audience research and reception studies as specific areas of research. The object of study is the media themselves and how people interpret content. However, the whole media environment has now changed with the emergence of hyperconnectivity as expression of complex and problematic interactions between people and technologies, for example as shown by recent developments of artificial intelligence.

5.3.2 *Mediation*

The main objective of a socio-cultural approach to the mind is to explicate the relationships between human mental functioning, on the one hand, and the cultural, institutional, and historical situations in which this functioning occurs, on the other (Wertsch et al., 1995, p. 3). The central task is to understand how individual functioning is shaped by and related to the socio-cultural setting within which it exists (see Erstad & Wertsch, 2008).

In Vygotsky's writings the construct of mediation, especially semiotic mediation, played a central role, becoming increasingly important during the last years of his life and career (Wertsch et al., 1995, p. 20; Wertsch, 1985, p. 50). A year before his death he wrote that 'the central fact about our psychology is the fact of mediation' (Vygotsky, 1982, p. 166). He provided an outline of how mental functioning is situated in a cultural space. Vygotsky extended Engels's notion of instrumental mediation by applying it to 'psychological tools' as well as to the 'technical tools' of production (Wertsch, 1985, p. 77). He invoked the analogy between psychological tools, or what he termed 'signs', and technical tools, or simply 'tools', at several places in his writing. Language, which was Vygotsky's main interest, can then be seen as a cultural tool and speech as a form of mediated action.

The renewed interest in such issues, and the reinterpretation of the texts of Vygotsky in the 1970s, can be seen as a strong movement away from methodological individualism, where the focus of the research is targeting the individual in a cognitive sense rather than social relations and communication. The emphasis is on the complexity embedded in studying human psychological and communicative activities. Such a socio-cultural approach emphasises that human action is mediated through the semiotic means available in the culture (Mertz & Parmentier, 1985).

As Wertsch (1998) has argued, the natural unit of analysis in this approach will be 'mediated action', or 'agent-acting-with-mediational-means', in order to highlight the focus on the agent—technology relationship. In his book *Mind as Action* (1998), Wertsch outlines certain properties of mediated action (p. 25):

1. Mediated action is characterized by an irreducible tension between agent and mediational means,
2. Mediational means are material,
3. Mediated action typically has multiple simultaneous goals,
4. Mediated action is situated on one or more developmental paths,
5. Mediational means constrain as well as enable action,
6. New mediational means transform mediated action,
7. The relationship of agents toward mediational means can be characterized in terms of mastery,
8. The relationship of agents toward mediational means can be characterized in terms of appropriation,
9. Mediational means are often produced for reasons other than to facilitate mediated action,
10. Mediational means are associated with power and authority.

Mediated action as an analytic approach to the study of mind and technologies is thereby seen both on the microgenetic level of agents and instruments, and on broader issues of socio-cultural history and issues of cultural struggle as in power relationships. In a general sense the term 'mediation' can be associated with the objectification of symbolic meaning in time and space as part of socio-historic development.

There are two important properties of psychological tools that are relevant for the discussion here (Wertsch, 1985, pp. 79–80). The first is that by being included in the process of meaning making, a psychological tool alters the entire flow and structure of mental functions. There are different sets of tools and different forms of thinking that go with them. Vygotsky viewed the introduction of a psychological tool (for example language) into a mental function (such as memory) as causing a qualitative transformation of that function. Psychological tools are not viewed as auxiliary means that simply facilitate an existing mental function while leaving it qualitatively unaltered. Rather, the emphasis is on their capacity to transform mental functioning. Vygotsky did not view development as a steady stream of quantitative increments but in terms of fundamental qualitative transformations associated with changes in the psychological tools.

The second major property of mediation is that by their nature psychological tools are social, not organic or individual. The mediational means, or cultural tools, are inherently situated culturally, institutionally, and historically. There are two aspects in which Vygotsky considered psychological tools to be social. First, he considered psychological tools such as language, various systems for counting, mnemonic techniques, algebraic symbol systems, and so forth to be social in the sense that they are the products of socio-cultural evolution. Individuals have access to psychological tools by virtue of being part of a socio- cultural milieu. The cultural knowledge of our society is in a developmental sense built into our tools. The second aspect concerns the more 'localized' social phenomena of face-to-face communication and social interaction. Instead of examining forces that operate on a general socio-cultural level, the focus here was on the dynamics that characterize individual communicative events. Vygotsky said of language that 'the primary function of speech, both for the adult and for the child, is the function of communication, social contact, influencing surrounding individuals' (in Wertsch, 1985, p. 81).

Another point about mediation is that it involves constraints as well as empowerment (Wertsch et al., 1995, pp. 24–25). Any form of mediation involves some form of limitation. It frees us from some earlier limitations while at the same time introducing new ones of its own. Our emphasis, of course, is often on the new possibilities that new mediational means represent for empowerment and new actions. However, we need to keep a focus on the limitations at the same time, on how tools shape our action in an inherently limiting way which is evident in the power of algorithms in the ways digital platforms operate today (Pangrazio & Sefton Green, 2022).

The important point here, and again, a point that is often missed in sociological and psychological studies, is that when a new tool, a new medium, is introduced into the flow of action, it does not simply facilitate or make an existing form of action more efficient. The emphasis is on how it transforms the form of action, on the qualitative transformative, as opposed to facilitative role of cultural tools.

5.3.3 Terms Combined

Leading on from this we can define that mediatisation theories lack a fundamental understanding of the meaning-making processes between people and media in specific settings, while mediation theories lack a theoretical framing of the semiotic properties characterizing media (see also Drotner, 2008).

Hepp (2013) argues for combining different traditions in order to understand 'mediatization transmedially' and on different levels, from the everyday communication practices, towards social and institutional media structures. He proposes the term 'moulding forces' as a possible linking of the two concepts and as a way "... to capture the specificity of a medium in the process of communication" (p. 619).

Different media shape communication in different ways. This is further linked to 'mediatized worlds', which are the level at which mediatisation becomes concrete and can be analyzed empirically (Hepp, 2013, p. 621). 'Mediatized worlds' are activities or social worlds "which in their present form rely constitutionally on an articulation through media communication" (Hepp, 2013, p. 621) and the communicative networks of individuals ('figuration') using different media. By approaching mediatization and mediation in such a combined way, looking at different analytic levels, Hepp is also relevant for sociocultural learning theories as ways of understanding how we use a number of different media ('cultural tools') for meaning making in specific contexts and institutional framings and how this changes over time. As such, media literacies represent key communicative practices in our societies today as ways of relating to and understanding the 'mediatized worlds' in which we live (Drotner & Erstad, 2014).

My argument is that we need both these concepts and positions in order to understand the ways technologies and media play a key role in our societies today and the ways we live our lives. Andreas Hepp (2013) makes an interesting attempt to align the two terms. He starts out by asking the fundamental question: "How can we find a practical approach to mediatization research when the times we live in are shaped by the 'mediation of everything'?" (Hepp, 2013, p. 615).

5.4 Towards Increased Techno-Cultural Complexities

Looking back on developments during the last three decades, two parallel discourses on education and technology have surfaced (Drotner & Erstad, 2014). The first puts the technology at the center of attention. The technology is defined as a catalyst for change, with implications for ways of studying digital technologies within educational practices and the impact these technologies might have on institutional transformations. These developments go back to the 1980s when several visionary educationalists created scenarios of fundamental change due to the impact of the computer in schools (Papert, 1993). With the introduction of the Internet similar cyber manifestos with implications for education where presented (Haraway, 1991), and the diverse imaginaries of what the internet as a new cultural space represented, especially in a US context (Anderson, 2005). These were important in addressing the fundamental impact of a so-called digital revolution on our societies. Some of these scholars came from the research fields of informatics and information systems, others from the humanities. As related to learning, this perspective, from the 1990s until today, has had a general focus on what can be termed as technology-enhanced learning, often targeting the impact of digital technologies on learning activities in schools. The main perspective is on how well students are using and operating the technology as such.

The second discourse is understanding technology as embedded in people's social practices in different contexts, where school is only one of several contexts studied. This discourse has a different pathway within media studies and the learning sciences than the former. One frame of reference is to be found within the literacy turn during the 1980s, where literacy initiatives and research changed from seeing reading and writing as a set of predefined skills across different cultures, towards studying literacy as social practices with specific impact and implications within the settings that people operated. The term multi-literacies (Cope & Kalantzis, 2000) emerged to signal the different ways people use language and different systems and modalities of representation in social practices. As a consequence, the concept of literacy was opened up to include interaction with different forms of text and studying them in diverse social practices (Barton, 1994). Similar influences can be traced to studies of how children and youth use different media as part of social practices (Drotner & Livingstone, 2008). Another frame of reference for this discourse is the influence from cultural studies, emphasizing the social semiotics of different sub-cultures (Willis, 2000), including ways of using different media. This can be seen as a more open-ended approach to studying ways that young people take up and use different media in their everyday practices as connected learning (Ito et al., 2020).

The flow of everyday lives using diverse technologies has escalated during the last 10 years in ways that the developments of digital platforms, datafication and artificial intelligence has been driven by the algorithmic power of global technological companies like Google, Facebook/Meta, Amazon, and Twitter/X. These developments represent a change in the ways our 'digital footprints' have become commodities in the ecology of technologies that target us as both consumers and producers of content. Within Europe and the US, initiatives are being made to regulate and develop digital skills that target these developments.

5.5 Studying Inclusiveness and Affordances in Everyday Lives: Two Examples

In my own research I have tried to address the developments mentioned above and what they imply for people's everyday lives and ways of learning in contemporary societies. These approaches open up perspectives on how learning is experienced by young people and the implications of digital platforms on the everyday lives of different generations. Fundamentally, these are examples of tensions embedded in the ways technologies are experienced as intrusive or that they bring affordances for learning and educational practices.

5.5.1 Learning Lives

The effort to understand how young people move between different contexts has grown in importance (Bronkhorst & Akkerman, 2016), partly because of the developments of new technological infrastructures and platformisation. This development reflects the transformation that has taken place, from studying computers within specific contexts like computer labs in schools, to studying technologies as mobile and following learners over time and space and as part of interaction with diverse digital platforms such as social media platforms, streaming of entertainment or as used within educational systems.

In several of the projects I have been leading during the last 15 years, we have tried to study and understand young people's trajectories across diverse spaces for learning, in what we term 'learning lives'. Our primary interest has been to understand what different practices in specific settings represent for ways of positioning themselves as learners, as learning identities, and how these practices relate to each other. However, what became obvious was that technologies were embedded in almost everything they were doing and that media environments connect people in new ways.

The notion of 'trajectory' provides an analytical lense for understanding learning activities across time and space. Participation trajectories are closely linked to identity as a "capacity for particular forms of action and hence a capacity to interpret and use environmental affordances to support action" (Edwards & Mackenzie, 2008, p. 165). The notion of trajectory is used as a way of identifying the pathways of a person, or an object, within and across situations, over time. Edwards and Mackenzie (2005) argued for a detailed analysis of the formation, disruption, reformation and support of trajectories of participation in the opportunities for action provided (p. 287). We ought, then, to explore how participants are not merely situated in time and space, but also how they are actively networking learning resources across space-time (Leander et al., 2010, p. 8). If we merely point out that learning is situated in context, we will be missing the fact that people themselves actively establish contexts of meaningful action (Van Oers, 1998).

In one study with the title 'Local literacies and community spaces' (2009–2013) we did ethnographic fieldwork related to three different age cohorts: 5–6 years old, 15–16 years old, and 18–19 years old. The team of researchers followed children and teenagers in these cohorts as they went through important transitions as learners from one level of schooling to the next, and we investigated changes and transitions in and between their institutional and everyday lives. One of our aims was to analyze how children's identities are shaped in different settings over time. The data consisted of interviews, observations, field notes, video recordings of selected episodes and activities, participant-generated materials in the form of diaries and photos, and maps produced together with the participants (Erstad et al., 2016). In another study with the title 'Knowledge in Motion across Contexts of Learning' (2013–2016) we studied about 100 students in two schools through lower secondary school. In this study we analyzed students in and out of school settings, as well as studying teachers in classroom settings teaching different subject domains.

As pointed out by Leander et al. (2010), "following" learners across and between sites is complex. While we can understand a great deal about how people make connections between spaces and experiences, we still face the challenge of gaining knowledge on how these resources actually move between contexts, how people appropriate them in one set of circumstances and are enabled to use them in other contexts.

A number of examples of the interrelationship between intrusiveness and affordances have emerged as part of our data analysis. In one example, we see how schools as institutions try to handle the intrusiveness of technologies on formal learning activities. One 15-year-old girl from a data collection in 2014, where the instruction for writing the diary of one day was ways of using diverse technologies during that day, she wrote:

> First time I checked the mobile today was just after the bell rang on my phone. As usual I checked Facebook, Instagram, Snapchat and YR. I usually check YR every morning and every evening to check on the weather for today and tomorrow. I checked the same social media several times during the morning before school. I usually send snapchats with my friends. If there is anything I need to ask my friends about I use snapchat, facebook messenger, kik or just send a message.

> When I went to school I put away the mobile phone.
>
> After school today I checked the usual social media. I used the PC to watch some series before a friend of mine sent me a message and wondered if I wanted to come into town with her. In town we sat on the pier and enjoyed the sun while we ate an ice-cream. I took a photo of my friend and shared it on Instagram. Several people liked the photo. Later on I slept over with another friend, and several times I checked social media. The last time I was on the mobile today was just before I went to sleep.

We see that social media are embedded in her everyday activities from morning to evening. After waking up she checks several of her social media to see if there have been any updates during the night. She also checks the weather forecast (yr.no) for the day, so she knows how to dress.

However, her school prohibits mobile phone use, so the students must hand them in when they enter the school and pick them up at the end of the day. The main reason given by the principal and the teachers was to restrict the possibility of using social media as a distraction during the school day. More recently arguments against screens altogether on certain levels in schools are being discussed based on the same arguments of distraction. This is an example of how the intrusiveness of digital technologies have consequences on certain school levels with the answer being a ban of such technologies. What is then excluded are the possible affordances these technologies might represent for learning activities in schools.

5.5.2 Platformisation of Family Life Across Generations

What was described above as studying 'learning lives' and how technologies are integrated in diverse practices young people are involved in, often with smart phones as their prosthetic devise, has escalated even further in later years as social media and the universe of apps has developed. Especially, the growth of digital platforms as new infrastructures, datafication and the growth of applications have impacted our everyday lives in fundamental ways, from dealing with bank services, communicating through social media, using streaming platforms like Netflix or learning through platforms like Canvas.

Digital platforms mark a major transformation over the last decade in how we interact with digital—and social—environments. Digital platforms are defined as "*(re-)programmable digital architecture designed to organise interactions among users, corporate entities and public bodies, geared toward the systematic collection, algorithmic processing, monetisation, and circulation of user data*" (van Dijck et al., 2018, p. 4). By profiling everyday activities and social relations, platforms are experimenting with ways to structure our choices through algorithms and digital design, undermining our privacy, shaping our social relations and engagement with the world, as well as opening up new possibilities for participation and future imaginaries.

In a recent project (2022–2025), we try to look at this from the point of view of families across different European countries. The title is 'Platforming Families:

Tracing digital transformations in everyday life across generations' (PlatFAMs). The PlatFAMs project focuses distinctively on intergenerational experiences in relation to the platformisation of family life (teenagers, their parents and their grandparents). The core of the project is the study of up to hundred three-generation families in five European countries (Norway, Estonia, UK, Romania and Spain) over a 2-year period, across different spaces online and offline.

Despite growing research interest in the fundamental social, institutional and individual consequences of platformisation, we know less about how families are transforming with the everyday use of today's heavily commercialised and globally networked platforms and their algorithms.

The ambition of the project is to unpack the relational and temporal aspects of digital platforms' wide-ranging social transformation of everyday family practices and inter-generational relations in contemporary societies.

As part of the data collection we have interviewed family members about how they navigate across diverse platforms and applications in their everyday lives. As part of the interview we asked family members to look at diverse logos of diverse platforms and applications and pick the ones they use and explain how they use them. The photo below is a photo I took of the logos a grandmother explained she was using for different purposes. It was obvious that such platforms and applications was an integrated part of their everyday activities. Many of the parents and grandparents expressed surprise when they saw all the technological tools they used laid out like this. From the interviews it was clear that these tools represented both intrusiveness in the sense that they felt these platforms and applications took a large part of their lives, at the same time as they provided a lot of affordances they could not do without, from communication with grandchildren to managing a public life and services (Fig. 5.1).

Another example from this project is the ways family members used tracking apps, which caused both tensions and opportunities. This is from an interview with a mother with a 16-years old daughter.

> **Mom (opens her phone)**: Right now, I can't find her location. Sometimes she turns it off, or it drops out. But she can see where I am now. And I like being able to go into the map and see where she is. I can see for instance. "Oh, yes. She's there now, she'll be home in 15 min". And I can have the food ready. Or; "now she's there, but she said she was there. What's happening?"
>
> **Researcher**: So you use it often? Every day?
>
> **Mom**: No, no, no. Absolutely not. But there are situations, like, if I call her and she doesn't answer. I can go [to the app] if I, like... start to get *impatient*, and then I go and check. (...) She hasn't been very against me knowing where she is. (...) we have a very close relationship. So that allows for it to be that way. And the reason I want to track her isn't necessarily because I think she's doing something wrong, but in case something happens, right? (...) And she understands that. She's used to me ... I'm someone who looks out for her a lot, but she's entirely used to that.

Obviously such tools provide safety and comfort that earlier had been difficult to achieve, but at the same time they create new challenges of intrusiveness and surveillance.

Fig. 5.1 Photo of platforms and applications used by a Norwegian grandmother. (Photo taken by Erstad)

These snippets of data from two projects over time show the complex interactions people experience when using digital mediational means in their everyday lives. A fundamental challenge across these examples is the tension between intrusiveness and affordances, in the ways these technologies has become and integrated part of living and challenging institutional practices and how we organize everyday lives in families, at the same time as they represent opportunities for communication and practices mediation. Still, these developments also raise fundamental challenges of how we master and appropriate such technologies.

5.6 Digital Literacies for an Intrusive Media Culture

A major concern, leading on from what has been presented above, is how people deal with techno-cultural transformations. Since the 1980s there has been a growing attention and concern towards how the media and technological developments are used and interpreted by citizens of different ages. And also asking what role education and learning should have in developing skills and competences in ways of dealing with these transformations.

During the 1970s and 1980s approaches towards media education was about how audiences interpret different genres of media content from the mass media, especially television and movies. With the growth of the Internet in the 1990s, this changed towards more focus on the overload of information access that developed, but also with many prospects of how software and internet access created new possibilities for knowledge development and collaboration across online and offline spaces. The growth of social media from the 2000s onwards generated new ideas about networks and sharing of content production. And in recent years more towards how people handle increasing disinformation and the impact of global technology companies.

Within socio-cultural approaches to learning this is termed as mastery and appropriation of technologies (Wertsch, 1998, pp. 46–53). This refers to how we interact with technologies as a mutual influence of how technologies challenge us in ways of relating with the world and at the same time opens up new possibilities. That is how we take up new cultural tools and make them part of our everyday practices. However, the introduction of new cultural tools also create tensions between what has been and what might be. In the examples mentioned above this has been referred to as a tension between intrusiveness and affordances.

Within the educational sciences the common term for this has been media literacy and since around 2000 digital literacy and/or multiliteracies. Literacy in this sense is understood as how we relate to information access, as ‘reading’, and how we produce content through different modalities, as ‘writing’. Digital literacies have now become a common term for many initiatives that focus on how young people gain knowledge and skills in ways of living in a technology saturated world and how such initiatives might prepare them for the future (see for example Fraillon, 2024).

However, as outlined earlier in this chapter, the situation during the last 4–5 years indicate increasing complexity in how we use and interact with technologies today. Algorithms are more and more setting the parameters for how technology infrastructures work, and the development of terms like datafication, platformisation and artificial intelligence (AI) as techno-cultural processes. As a consequence, new terms like computational thinking, data literacies and AI literacies have emerged (Mertala, 2020; Palsa & Mertala, 2023). The interesting question linked to these developments is to what extent these new concepts really indicate a break from the former conceptions and frameworks of digital literacies—with new complexities and understandings of how we use and interact with available fast developing technologies in our culture. More important than focusing on skills in handling the technology, it might rather now be about broader issues of digital life appropriation and wellbeing and also digital citizenship for an intrusive media culture.

This points back to the research questions posted in the introduction to this chapter. My main point has been to show how the interrelationship between humans and technology in contemporary societies has become increasingly complex. By combining terms like mediatization and mediation I have attempted to initiate a perspective that address these complexities in this new techno-cultural landscape that we ‘walk’ in and leave ‘digital footprints’ that can be both used and misused in social practices and within education. As a consequence, we are part of what Brubaker (2022) has described as hyperconnectivity, with both social and personal implications for how we live our lives.

One aspect that I believe is of key interest today is to study how people experience these technological developments as both intrusive, in the sense that the technology is affecting us in negative ways and is influencing what we can and cannot do, and with affordances, in the sense that we have agency to use the technology for our own interest. As shown in the examples presented in this chapter, in practices where people use these technologies both these aspects are included. The implications for conceptions of learning and literacy is that these terms also have to address the complexities of human living within the technological environment today. I argue for a broader conception of learning, in what I term 'learning lives', and a new orientation towards what literacies really imply related to this environment and technological ecosystem we are part of.

5.7 Design of Social Futures

The role of education within our contemporary techno-culture is important for several reasons. Our formal institutions of education, like schools and universities, are the only arenas where all citizens participate, meet and relate to each other. As digital technologies have entered these places and spaces tensions have been created between established practices of learning and teaching and new possibilities created by diverse digital means. Also, what characterize public discourse and popular conceptions today is either increasingly viewing technologies as threat, within strong public claims of reducing or even banning technologies from locations like schools, or it is expressed as a fascination of the hyperconnected ways we live our lives. The fundamental difference is about seeing technologies as external objects we relate to and technologies as embedded and part of us as humans.

Education is, of course, also an important way of providing the knowledge, skills and qualifications among students for entering work life, which is increasingly being digitalized, in what has been discussed as digital literacies above (Fraillon, 2024). Still, it is unclear how our education systems might best support and develop such literacies today, where technologies are changing fast, as seen with the introduction of ChatGPT. These difficult questions tend to disappear in the background in the public discourse which is dominated by screen time use and ban of mobile phones in schools.

Maybe the most important issue and challenge today concerns inclusion and exclusion of groups in the population as a consequence of these techno-cultural transformations, and what the role of education is in creating equal possibilities and create equality in learning possibilities. Today, these issues are less about access and people's skills, but rather about agency in ways of dealing with technologies across formal and informal settings. However, this is more a Western way of approaching this, since technologies are so embedded in every aspect of human activities today, while this might be experienced in very different ways in other parts of the world (UNESCO, 2022). Awareness of how different groups of populations, often based on socio-economic differences, get excluded in ways of taking advantage of the possibilities provided by technologies, and experience more intrusiveness than affordances, is something that needs more attention (Fraillon, 2024).

In this chapter I have tried to address ongoing changes in our cultures due to the development of technologies, what some term as increased 'hyperconnectivity' (Brubaker, 2022). In order to address these issues, I have drawn on two different fields of research, that of socio-cultural approaches to learning and media studies, expressed with the terms mediatization and mediation.

Hence, multi-method, multi-sited and multi-dimensional research approaches would do well do follow anthropologists Elisabeth Mertz and Richard Parmentier (1985), who advocate a joint perspective on the material and the immaterial, or semiotic, aspects of (learning) tools; or to heed the advocacy of Swedish education researcher Roger Säljö who stresses the importance of discursive tools (Säljö, 1999). Such insights offer important common ground for conceptual and methodological developments that are needed to grasp the complexity of the current learning landscape.

This leads towards perspectives on how we deal with the future, as something we are drifting towards or, rather, something we can act on. With today's techno-culture this becomes a key question in ways of overcoming the intrusiveness of technologies today, towards creating affordances for human life and learning. I will end with the words of Bill Cope and Mary Kalantzis (2000), that edited the classic book on 'multiliteracies' with the subtitle 'design of social futures', that point towards how we all can participate in designing social futures for ourselves:

> Instead of a focus on stability and regularity, the focus is on change and transformations. The breadth, complexity and richness of the available meaning-making resources is such that representation is never simply a matter of reproduction. Rather, it is a matter of transformation; of reconstructing meaning in a way which always adds something to the range of available representational resources. (Cope & Kalantzis, 2000, p. 204)

References

Anderson, J. Q. (2005). *Imagining the Internet. Personalities, predictions, perspectives.* Rowman & Littlefield Publishers.

Barton, D. (1994). *Literacy. An introduction to the ecology of written language.* Blackwell.

Bronkhorst, L., & Akkerman, S. (2016). At the boundary of school: Continuity and discontinuity in learning across contexts. *Educational Research Review, 19*, 18–35.

Brubaker, R. (2022). *Hyperconnectivity and its discontents.* Polity Press.

Cope, B., & Kalantzis, M. (Eds.). (2000). *Multiliteracies. Literacy learning and the design of social futures.* Routledge.

Costall, A., & Dreier, O. (2006). *Doing things with things. The design and use of everyday objects.* Ashgate.

Drotner, K. (2008). Leisure is hard work: digital practices and future competences. In D. Buckingham (Eds.), *Youth, identity, and digital media (pp. 187–211). Cambridge, MA: MIT Press.*

Drotner, K., & Erstad, O. (2014). Inclusive Media Literacies: Interlacing media studies and education studies. *International Journal of Learning and Media,* 2(2), 19–31.

Drotner, K., & Livingstone, S. (Eds.). (2008). *The international handbook of children, media and culture.* Sage.

Edwards, A., & Mackenzie, L. (2005). Steps towards participation: The social support of learning trajectories. *International Journal of Lifelong Education, 24*(4), 287–302.

Edwards, A., & Mackenzie, L. (2008). Identity shifts in informal learning trajectories. In B. van Oers, W. Wardekker, E. Elbers, & R. van der Veer (Eds.), *The transformation of learning* (pp. 163–181). Cambridge University Press.

Erstad, O., & Wertsch, J. (2008). Tales of mediation: Narrative and digital media as cultural tools. In K. Lundby (Ed.), *Digital storytelling, mediatized stories: Self-representation in new media* (pp. 21–40). Peter Lang.

Erstad, O., Gilje, Ø., & Sefton Green, J. (2016). *Learning identities, education and community. Young lives in the cosmopolitan city*. Cambridge University Press.

Erstad, O., Hagtvet, B. E., & Wertsch, J. (Eds.). (2024). *Education and dialogue in polarized societies. Dialogic perspectives in times of change*. Oxford University Press.

Fraillon, J. (Ed.). (2024). *An international perspective on digital literacy. Results from ICILS 2023*. IEA.

Haraway, D. (1991). *Simians, cyborgs, and women. The reinvention of nature*. Routledge.

Hepp, A. (2013). The communicative figurations of mediatized worlds: Mediatization research in times of the 'mediation of everything'. *European Journal of Communication, 28*(6), 615–629. https://doi.org/10.1177/0267323113501148

Hepp, A., Breiter, A., & Hasebrink, U. (2018). *Communicative figurations. Transforming communications in times of deep mediatization*. Palgrave Macmillan.

Hjarvard, S. (2008). The mediatization of society a theory of the media as agents of social and cultural change. *Nordicom Review, 29*(2), 105–134.

Ito, M., Arum, R., Conley, D., Gutiérrez, K., Kirshner, B., Livingstone, S., Michalchik, V., Penuel, W., Peppler, K., Pinkard, N., Rhodes, J., Salen, K., Schor, J., Sefton-Green, J., & Watkins, S. C. (2020). *The connected learning research network: Reflections on a decade of engaged scholarship*. Connected Learning Alliance.

Krotz, F. (2009) Mediatization: A concept with which to grasp media and societal change. In K. Lundby (ed.), *Mediatization: Concept, Changes, Consequences. New York: Peter Lang.*

Leander, K., Phillips, N., & Taylor, K. H. (2010). The changing social spaces of learning: Mapping new mobilities. *Review of Research in Education, 34*, 329–394.

Lundby, K. (Ed.). (2009). *Digital storytelling, mediatized stories. Self-representation in new media*. Peter Lang.

Mascheroni, G. (2023). A new family member or just another digital interface? Smart speakers in the lives of families with young children. *Human-Machine Communication, 7*, 45–63. Special Edition. https://doi.org/10.30658/hmc.7.3

Mattelart, A. (1996). *The invention of communication*. University of Minnesota Press.

Mertala, P. (2020). Data (il)literacy as a hidden curriculum of the datafication of education. *Journal of Media Literacy Education, 12*(3), 30–42.

Mertz, E., & Parmentier, R. J. (Eds.). (1985). *Semiotic mediation. Sociocultural and psychological perspectives*. Academic Press.

Olson, D. R., & Cole, M. (Eds.). (2006). *Technology, literacy, and the evolution of society. Implications of the work of Jack Goody*. Lawrence Erlbaum associates.

Pahl, K., & Rowsell, J. (2010). *Artifactual literacies. Every object tells a story*. Teachers College Press.

Palsa, L., & Mertala, P. (2023). Contextualizing everyday data literacies: The case of recreational runners. *International Journal of Human-Computer Interaction, 40*, 5845–5856. Early online. https://doi.org/10.1080/10447318.2023.2241612

Pangrazio, L., & Sefton Green, J. (Eds.). (2022). *Learning to live with datafication. Educational case studies and initiatives from across the world*. Routledge.

Papert, S. (1993). *The children's machine: Rethinking school in the age of the computer*. BasicBooks.

Pettersen, K. (2023). *Early childhoods in the postdigital inquiry into the literacies of young children's contemporary play with new media technologies*. PhD dissertation. Department of Education, University of Oslo, Norway.

Säljö, R. (1999). Learning as the use of tools: A sociocultural perspective on the human-technology link. In K. Littleton & P. Light (Eds.), *Learning with computers. Analysing productive interaction*. Routledge.
Sefton Green, J. (2021). Towards platform pedagogies: Why thinking about digital platforms as pedagogic devices might be useful. *Discourse: Studies in the Cultural Politics of Education, 43*, 899–911. https://doi.org/10.1080/01596306.2021.1919999
Ströhl, A. (Ed.). (2002). *Vilem Flusser writings*. University of Minneapolis: Minnesota Press.
UNESCO. (2022). *Technology in education: A tool on whose terms? Global education monitoring report*. UNESCO.
van Dijck, J. (2013). *The culture of connectivity: A critical history of social media*. Oxford University Press.
van Dijck, J., Poell, T. & e Walal, M. (2018). *The platform society: Public values in a connective world. Oxford University Press.*
Van Oers, B. (1998). From context to contextualizing. *Learning and Instruction, 8*(6), 473–488.
Vygotsky, L. S. (1982). *Sobranie sochinenii. Tom pervyi: Problemy teorii istorii psikhologii* (Collected works: Vol. 1, Problems in the theory and history of general psychology). Izdatel'stvo Pedagogika.
Wertsch, J. (Ed.). (1985). *Culture, communication, and cognition: Vygotskian perspectives* (pp. 119–145). Cambridge University Press.
Wertsch, J. V. (1998). *Mind as action*. Oxford University Press.
Wertsch, J., del Rio, P., & Alvarez, A. (Eds.). (1995). *Sociocultural studies of mind*. Harvard University Press.
Willis, P. (2000). *The ethnographic imagination*. Wiley.

Chapter 6
Culture Is a Right: Designing Multisensory Experiences for an Accessible Cultural Heritage Beyond the Museum's Walls

Patrizia Marti and Annamaria Recupero

6.1 Introduction

In recent years, a new concept of "sensory museology" is growing to promote multisensory exploration of cultural heritage as a means to provide engaging and memorable experiences (Howes, 2014; Levent & Pascual-Leone, 2014; Howes et al., 2018). This engagement strategy is pivotal to address accessibility issues, considering the diverse and changing needs of the older adults with age-related, motor or perceptual impairments. Indeed, they represent a marginalised social group who face physical, sensory and cognitive barriers which prevent them from experiencing the cultural heritage in autonomy.

The spreading of the concept of sensory museology has coincided with advancements in digital fabrication and the emergence of embodied technologies that fundamentally transform the nature of human-computer interaction. The inherent qualities of technologies like tangible interfaces, multi-touch screens, sensors, and mobile devices create opportunities for a broad range of multisensory experiences compared to traditional desktop computing. These technologies primarily enable the exploration of physically grounded experiences in novel ways, such as through the manipulation of tangible objects connected to a variety of digital enhancements for multisensory stimulation.

In this chapter we discuss the potential of tangible technologies in fostering innovative forms of access to cultural heritage, to favour participation of marginalised groups of people with onset and age-related disability.

In fact, the Universal Declaration of Human Rights (United Nations, 1948) and the Framework Convention on the Value of Cultural Heritage for Society—Faro

P. Marti (✉) · A. Recupero
Department of Social Political and Cognitive Sciences, University of Siena, Siena, Italy
e-mail: patrizia.marti@unisi.it; annamaria.recupero@unisi.it

M. B. Ligorio (ed.), *Technology as Cultural Mediator*, Culture in Policy Making: The Symbolic Universes of Social Action,
https://doi.org/10.1007/978-3-031-97673-5_6

Convention (Council of Europe, 2005) highlighted the access to the heritage and the participation to the cultural life of the community as fundamental rights of all. In 2022, the International Council of Museums (ICOM) Proposed the following definition of museum "open to the public, accessible and inclusive, museums promote diversity and sustainability".

The path towards accessible and inclusive museums for different audiences is challenging, and it requires a long-term commitment to innovate the museum at different levels: from the expertise of the staff, to the exhibit design and the public engagement strategies.

The traditional museology is based on a concept of exhibition in which artworks are considered as artefacts of the "higher, aesthetic, distal, intellectual senses of sight" (Howes, 2014, p. 260), and the related information is conveyed through audio guides or written text. More recent museology tends to conceive the museum not only as a space of pure contemplation of artworks, rather as a place of dialogue and multimodal interaction where all senses are actively solicited (Levent & Pascual-Leone, 2014; Blundell, 2023; Luo et al., 2024). Language is no longer the primary mediation tool of the cultural experience, and the aesthetic experience is no more based only on the contemplative vision of the artwork. The meaning-making process is enabled by interaction in which the entire body, different sensory perceptions, gestures and movements are engaged.

Current experimentations with tangible and embodied technologies are relatively poorly explored and the solutions documented in the scientific literature are mostly related to science museums with a specific focus on children's learning (e.g., Okerlund et al., 2016; Shaby & Vedder-Weiss, 2021). Further exploration is necessary to extend the concept of enabling technologies for multisensory experiences to favour accessibility and engagement for older adults with disability, including people with early-onset disability and people with age-related disability (Verbrugge & Yang, 2002), building on key-enabling technologies and the multisensorial nature of knowledge (Rieger, 2023).

This chapter discusses the potential of multisensory museum experiences through the presentation of the EU project BeauCoup, funded by the Active Assisted Living Joint Programme. The project aims at developing new services integrating digital technologies, multimedia contents and multisensory stimulations to enable the experience of the cultural heritage in an accessible and engaging way, specifically tailored to older adults, including those with disability. The project aims to bring the cultural heritage outside the museum's walls with the ultimate objective to overcome current barriers in reaching the museums due to mobility or autonomy issues preventing a full accessibility of cultural spaces.

6.2 The Sensory Turn of the New Museology

For a long time in museology, vision was considered dominating over the other senses, and the museum experience relied mainly on visual perception to appreciate art (Beşevli et al., 2024). The predominance of the "visual art" and the need for preserving the artworks shaped the way we conceive art and museum visit, fostering the perpetuation of conventional mode of spectatorship in which the visitor is a passive "spectator".

This traditional approach is in contrast to what we know about human perception and cognition. Indeed, human senses (vision, hearing, touch, olfaction, and taste) do not function in isolation as separate and independent perceptual systems. Rather, when we perceive an object, our senses receive correlated information which are combined in a multisensory sensation (Spence, 2016). We acknowledge the role of all senses in influencing consumers' choices of products (Spence, 2020) and in the domain of marketing and product development the use of non-visual cues and the design of multisensory experience is already a consolidated practice. Unfortunately, in the museum domain the "sensory turn" is still poorly practised.

The sensory turn is pushed by the need for accessibility considering that people with sensory, motor or cognitive disabilities face several barriers which prevent them from visiting the museums and experiencing the cultural heritage (Howes, 2014; Levent & Pascual-Leone, 2014). This represents a limitation of the fundamental right of access to the heritage and participation in the cultural life of the community (Council of Europe, 2005), and a limitation of the mission of museums that should be accessible and inclusive, in which diversity and sustainability are key goals to achieve (ICOM, 2022).

Taking advantage of innovative technologies and building on the knowledge from museum studies, psychology, and neuroscience, the experimentations of multisensory modalities to experience the cultural heritage are slowly taking hold in recent years. They aim at providing inclusive experiences for diverse audience groups, widening the possibilities for perceiving and making sense of the cultural heritage. Some projects are focused on one specific sense (e.g., touch or smell), while other projects are challenged by the combination of multiple sensory stimuli.

6.2.1 Beyond the Ban of Touch

Accessing information through touch is a well-established convention for blind and low vision people through the use of Braille as well as three dimensional objects (Race et al., 2023). 3D printing technologies proved to be effective when the 3D models are of high quality, reflecting every detail which leads to a comprehensive examination of the artefacts (Bruns et al., 2023; Karaduman et al., 2023; Race et al., 2023).

In case of sculptures and objects, laser scanning and photogrammetry allow to obtain digital models with a high accuracy, and 3D printing gives the possibility to obtain replicas of the original items, while adjusting the size to increase the perception of the details (Balletti et al., 2017). In the case of photographs and painting, moving from the 2D image to the 3D model is challenging and it requires 3D modelling software to create reliefs, and then 3D printers or milling machines to produce the tactile reliefs.

When "accurate replicas"—those that best capture the essential aesthetic and physical characteristics of an artwork, in addition to the weight, feel and materiality of the original artwork—are not feasible because of their cost and expertise needed, 3D printing with high quality resin provides a suitable alternative (Wilson et al., 2017).

It is acknowledged that the tactile replicas should be accompanied by audio description to contextualise the object and guide the tactile exploration (e.g., Vaz et al., 2018, 2022; Reinhardt et al., 2024). To this end, smart objects can be designed with embedded electronics or hand tracking devices to "augment" the tangible stimulus with audio contents.

6.2.2 *Can a Painting Be Heard?*

The use of audio descriptions of the museum items has a long tradition since the first audio-guide was developed in 1961 (Tallon & Walker, 2008). The contents of the audio description can convey diverse information: they can guide the attention of the visitors to notice and understand details; they can "translate" visual information into verbal description for blind audiences; they can provide factual, historical or contextual information about the artwork (Eardley et al., 2017; Hutchinson & Eardley, 2023). This stands to promote a richer mode of access through stimulating thoughts, feelings and imagination going beyond the provision of visual information (Hutchinson & Eardley, 2023).

An innovative trend is related to the sonification of art for conveying information about the artwork through sounds or auditory cues, or to transform the visitors' movements into a soundscape, as an alternative forms of engagement especially for those visitors who rely on non-visual sensory modalities (e.g., Nadri et al., 2019; Kapsali, 2020). The sounds can be integrated in the museum experience for diverse purposes, such as recalling memories, eliciting emotions, and imagining the scene represented in the painting.

6.2.3 *Tasting Art and Culture*

While the integration of auditory and tactile stimulation to experience the museum collection is increasingly widespread, the ability of taste to serve a pedagogical role and to inspire critical thinking is overlooked in the museum domain.

> Taste is the ideal sense for an innovative participatory culture in museums because taste bridges the gap between personal experiences—each of us tastes food differently and intimately at a biological level—and collective meanings and values attached to certain regimes of taste. (Levent & Pascual-Leone, 2014, p. 198)

Tasting experiences in museums are still rare. Considering the state of the art, we can identify three main trends: (a) food as an exhibition topic, (b) taste as a way to "augment" the perception of the artwork, (c) and food as a means to convey abstract concepts.

In the first case, exhibitions about food systems (networks and practices to produce, transform, deliver and consume food products) aim at involving the visitors in the reflection on the impact of the food system on the environment and the health status. An example is the exhibition "FOOD: Bigger than the Plate" at the Victoria & Albert Museum (London, UK) in 2019: "This exhibition explores how innovative individuals, communities and organisations are radically re-inventing how we grow, distribute and experience food. Taking visitors on a sensory journey through the food cycle, from compost to table, it poses questions about how the collective choices we make can lead to a more sustainable, just and delicious food future in unexpected and playful ways" (Victoria & Albert Museum, 2019).

In the second case, the tasting of ingredients or food products related to an artwork is a way to translate the visual representation of food in the painting into a gustatory experience, as well as to complement the visual contemplation of artworks. An example is "Amuse-bouche. The Taste of Art" at Museum Tinguely (Basel, Switzerland) in 2020: "The exhibition presents artworks by some forty-five international artists from the baroque to the present that explore our sense of taste as a dimension of aesthetic perception. Breaking with the usual museum practice of appealing primarily to the sense of sight, the show offers art-historical and phenomenological encounters with our sense of taste. Some of the works offer a participatory experience—during special guided tours and performances, the works themselves can be tasted" (Museum Tinguely, 2020).

In the third case, experiments made in other domains can be used to design gustatory experiences to convey information, cultural values and meanings (e.g., Deng et al., 2021; Floyd Mueller et al., 2021; Obrist et al., 2024).

The design challenge is, on one hand, to translate artwork into gustatory experiences and, on the other hand, to use flavour as a medium of artistic expression and creativity. 3D printers of edible material can support the experimentation of new concepts and experiences by creating edible artefacts with specific sensory properties (not just flavour but also texture and colours).

6.2.4 Olfactory Interfaces

Olfactory stimulation has the potential to relive memories and elicit emotions, but the complexity of working with olfaction compared to other senses makes the smell-based interaction challenging and poorly explored (Beşevli et al., 2024). Indeed, the sense of smell varies from person to person, it is not uniform throughout the day, and everyone has a smell blindness to some odours. Thus, when designing an olfactory stimulus, it is important to be aware that individuals have a different personal experience, including the inability to perceive the odour. Therefore, the olfactory stimulus can produce unintended responses (Levent & Pascual-Leone, 2014).

In the cultural domain, the olfactory stimulations are experimented by artists to create artworks with olfactory aesthetics. "Besides variation in the act of reception, mutability could be said to characterise the very nature of olfactory aesthetics. Unlike the bounded, defined aspects of visual artworks in a gallery, with autonomous spectators separated from the objects on view, olfactory art engages visitors intimately. […] Inherent to an olfactory aesthetics is the gradation of scent as individuals move about a space. The intensity of scent waxes and wanes, especially if there is a specific source, or airflow to disperse and refresh it. In this way, olfactory installations are performative—they come and go, appear and subside, become present and then fade, with all of the vividness and ephemerality of an event" (Levent & Pascual-Leone, 2014, p. 190).

Due to the difficulty to control the scent, the use of the olfactory stimuli to "augment" the artwork experience it is still rarely investigated.

Miotto (2016) reported the design of an olfactory delivery device, developed to address the issue of smell diffusion and containment inside the museum space, to enrich two exhibitions at the National Museum of Singapore. The selection and preparation of the fragrances was made collaboratively by curators, designers and flavourists. The olfactory interactive device was designed considering ergonomic factors (e.g. the movable hose allows the person to adjust the position of the sniffing cup), the technical requirements to preserve the chemical components and easily refill the fragrances, as well as the aesthetics to integrate the device into the exhibition display.

The olfactory interface is also experimented to enrich Virtual Reality and Augmented Reality experiences in museums. For example, Bordegoni et al. (2019) designed a wearable device that delivers different odours related to the exhibition, remotely controlled to synchronise with the virtual-augmented contents. The goal is to stimulate specific emotions through the combination of visual and olfactory stimulation. To this end, the fragrances were specifically selected to prompt both positive and negative emotions: for example, sugar for happiness, sweat-like for fear, and moss for sadness.

Verbeek et al. (2022) discussed the initiatives at the Rijksmuseum (Amsterdam, Netherlands) to experiment with olfactory storytelling: they employed different methods to enable olfactory stimulation, ranging from ultrasonic scent diffuser, mobile containers of scented air, a wearable fragrance diffuser in the form of a necklace, or acid-free cardboard scented strips. The importance of such experimentations relies also on the selection of the scents that was based on historical research and on the creative interpretation of the artwork. Indeed, the research in olfactory heritage is growing in recent years to investigate fragrances and odours which are culturally meaningful because of their connection with significant places, practices, artefacts and traditions, of present and past times (Bembibre & Strlič, 2017, 2022).

These studies point out that the challenges of designing olfactory cultural experiences range from the choice of the fragrance (to evoke emotions, memories or for historical scent reconstruction), to the control over the diffusion and dispersion, the management of the intensity that waxes and wanes, and the prevention of the so-called olfactory fatigue (Levent & Pascual-Leone, 2014; Bembibre & Strlič, 2022). Because the olfactory interfaces are gaining more attention from technology experts, curators, artists, and designers, it is likely that in the next future it will be possible to successfully integrate the sense of smell into the cultural experience.

6.3 Case Study: The BeauCoup Project

The project BeauCoup aims to develop new services to promote the cultural heritage outside the museum contexts with the ultimate goal to improve the quality of the life of older people with onset or age-related disabilities.

The project envisions a museum that extends beyond its walls, overcoming the geographical distance to reach people where they live and spend time, providing engaging and accessible experiences which have the potential to stimulate memories, dialogue and social interaction.

In light of the new museology, the impact of the cultural experience is not merely a matter of learning in terms of gaining information and enriching the understanding of a specific subject matter. Rather, the exploration of the cultural heritage is a means to address diverse motivations for enjoyment, self-fulfilment and social interaction: seeing rare and uncommon artefacts, being moved by beauty, reflecting on the personal and cultural meanings of the heritage, recalling personal memories, imagining other times and places, being exposed to different cultures, socialise with peers, and intergenerational dialogue (Hooper-Greenhill, 2004; Pekarik & Schreiber, 2012; Sheng & Chen, 2012).

The BeauCoup project developed along several co-design activities to iteratively ideate, design, prototype, and evaluate innovative solutions with various stakeholders, from older adults to museum experts and decision makers (Marti et al., 2023; Recupero et al., 2023). The co-design workshops took place in five European countries (Austria, Italy, Slovenia, Portugal, Switzerland) involving the target beneficiaries of the project solutions. The primary users are older people with motor, cognitive or sensory disability who are at risk of isolation, depression and cognitive decline. Unfortunately, still today these people face several challenges that prevent them from experiencing the cultural heritage. Together with the older people, the project addresses the caregivers from the healthcare sector and the personnel of the cultural sector as relevant actors to implement the project solutions.

During the first phase of the project, the stakeholders were involved to frame the problem and to ideate possible solutions in the form of scenarios and service blueprints (Stickdorn & Schneider, 2012). In the second phase, some concepts were prototyped and iteratively evaluated with experts and target users, as described in the following paragraphs. The iterative evaluation was essential to question the proposed solutions according to the diverse users' goals, needs and preferences, and orient the re-design of the technologies and the cultural contents accordingly. Once the project solutions were consolidated, the third phase of the project was devoted to the demonstration of the prototypes to bring the solutions to the target beneficiaries in real-life contexts.

In the following paragraphs we describe one of the services developed by the project, which makes use of an interactive tool called "magic casket" to enable multisensory and storytelling laboratories with older people in nursing homes and day-care centres.

6.3.1 The Magic Casket

The magic casket is a customisable box containing physical and digital elements designed to experience the cultural heritage in a multisensory and engaging way. The casket is designed to sustain storytelling laboratories at day-care centres and nursing homes, during which older people explore the stimuli included in the magic casket and narrate stories, with the mediation of the museum educator.

The magic casket has a modular design: it is composed of pentagonal tiles made of wood and felt, which are arranged on the table through magnets to create a configuration. The resulting shape enables a small group of older people sitting around the table to interact with the magic casket and explore the stimuli contained in it (Fig. 6.1).

The multisensory stimuli contained in the magic casket are: 3D printed replicas of items from the museum collection, audio narrations, fragrances, songs, photographs of the museum items printed on canvas, and interactive images. Further details on the stimuli and their combinations are provided in the next paragraph.

When the magic casket is folded, it is easily transported in a small suitcase (Fig. 6.2). Indeed, the magic casket is a way to bring the cultural heritage outside the museums in places where people live and spend time. Thus, it should be easy and safe to store, transport and arrange.

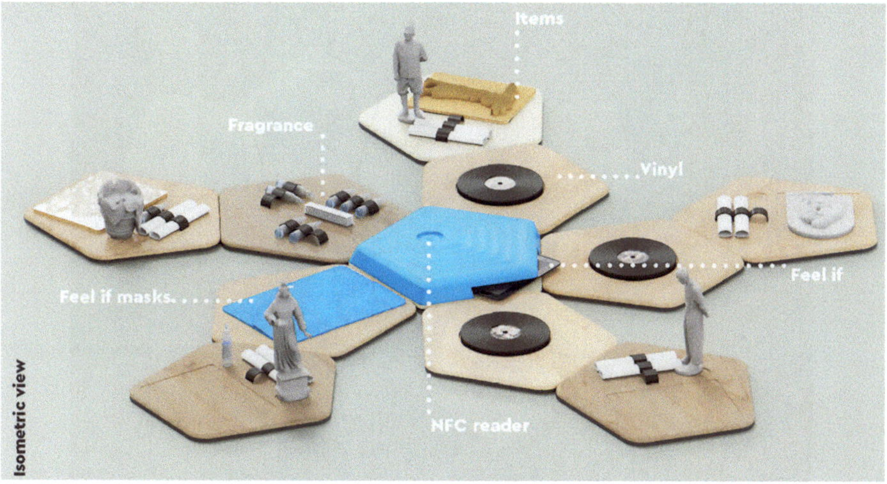

Fig. 6.1 The magic casket with the multisensory stimuli

Fig. 6.2 The magic casket stored in the suitcase to be easily transported

6.3.2 Themes, Stimuli and Technologies

The modular design of the magic casket allows the facilitator to customize the stimuli and the activity based on the museum collection and the characteristics of the participants to engage in the storytelling laboratory.

In this way, the different configurations of the magic casket enable different activities and narrations. The themes which currently connect the diverse multisensory stimuli through a narration are Protection, Rural life, Women and Motherhood (Fig. 6.3). However, many more can be easily added.

Fig. 6.3 Two possible configurations of the magic casket based on the theme "Women and motherhood" (*top*) and the theme "Protection" (*bottom*)

For example, the configuration for the theme of Rural life includes several stimuli, each of them related to the old traditions of the countryside in Tuscany (Italy) (Fig. 6.4).

- The olfactory stimulation includes: (a) three bottles of fragrance of flowers, linen and grass to spray on paper strips; (b) a scratch and sniff postcard made of wood, representing an old photograph of a woman who carries the bread to the communal oven, created through the application of a fragrant coating of baked bread so that the object releases a smell if you rub it.
- The 3D printed replicas are made of high quality resin and they represent four museum items: the "Game warden" and the "Farm worker" from the collection of Museo della Mezzadria Senese (Buonconvento, Italy); the relief "Madonna with the Child and two cherubs" from the collection of Museo d'Arte Sacra della Val d'Arbia (Buonconvento, Italy); the basin with the ash used for the laundry from the collection of Museo della Mezzadria Senese (Buonconvento, Italy).

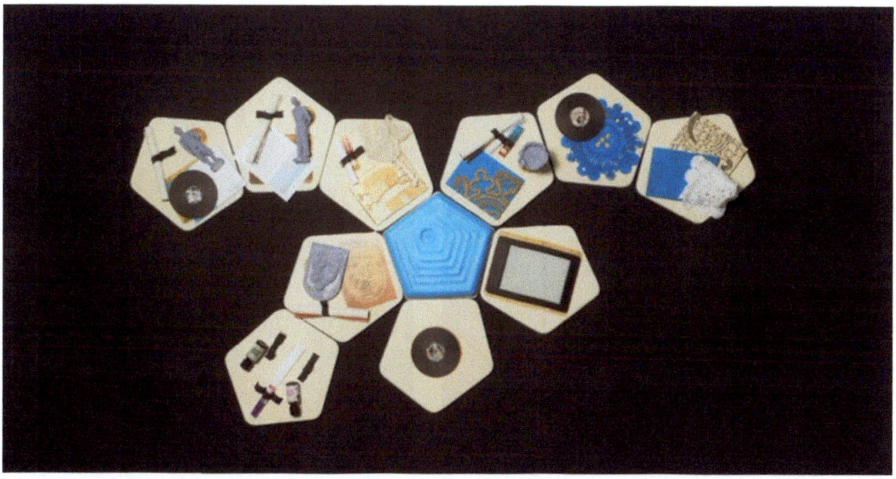

Fig. 6.4 Configuration of the magic casket based on the theme "Rural life"

Fig. 6.5 Tablet used to activate the audio content through the NFC reader and tag

- Photographs printed on canvas show the original museum items.
- Reproductions of a doily made of wood and felt, together with the original object from the collection of Museo della Mezzadria Senese (Buonconvento, Italy).
- Two vinyl disks to play Italian traditional songs related to rural life and seasons.

The 3D printed replicas and the small vinyl disks have the Near-Field Communication (NFC) tags to activate audio contents (narrations or songs) using the tablet contained in the magic casket (Fig. 6.5). To activate the audio contents, you just need to put the object on the NFC reader on the central part of the magic casket. The audio content is played automatically and it is paused when people remove the object from the NFC reader. In this way, the interaction with the magic casket is simple and easy (Fig. 6.6).

BEAUCOUP
Storytelling
laboratory

The magic casket

Audio description of the basin with ash for the laundry, from the collection of Museo della Mezzadria Senese (Buonconvento, Italy).

"Doing laundry used to be hard work, one day was not enough and several people had to be involved.
They used the basin where they arranged the clothes in layers, with the oldest and dirtiest ones at the bottom and then gradually the newer and more delicate ones.
Lastly, a thick, coarse cloth called 'cenerone' was spread out and the ashes recovered from the hearth were placed inside. Then they would start pouring boiled water on so that it would absorb the ash and pass through the cloths to make them clean and very white.
It was a long job, the water had to be boiled often, the basin had to be filled at least a couple of times, and the laundry had to be left to soak in the cloth all night so that it would turn out properly.
Then everything would be rinsed in the river water or at the springs and the laundry would be hung out on the hedges or in the field.
The air was filled with a unique perfume that I have never found again."

Fig. 6.6 Stimuli related to the basin with ash for the laundry in the form of photograph (*top left*), 3D printed replica (*top right*), and transcript of the audio description activated through the NFC (*bottom*)

The stimuli and the cultural contents were selected and developed through a collaborative process involving museum educators, curators, designers and some citizens who collaborate with the museums as volunteers, who were involved in interviews to collect their interpretation of the museum items.

In particular, the audio descriptions were designed not only to describe the original function of the artefacts but also to provide prompts for recalling memories and reflecting about local traditions.

The tablet inside the magic casket serves to enable two interactions. As described above, it is used to automatically activate the audio contents through the NFC reader when you place the object on the centre of the magic casket. In addition, the tablet is used to explore tactile interactive postcards of artworks thanks to the solution developed by the company Feelif d.o.o. (Fig. 6.7). The postcard of the painting is

Fig. 6.7 Tactile interactive postcard representing a painting (*top*), used with the tablet to explore audio contents by touch (*bottom*)

made of cardboard, it has a transparent 3D contour that outlines the elements of the painting. When you place the postcard on the tablet, the postcard becomes interactive and you can listen to the audio description and sound icons connected to each part of the painting which are activated by touch.

6.3.3 Workshops with Accessibility Experts

Once we prototyped the magic casket, we organised two workshops involving nine people who are blind or visually impaired, who collaborate with the non-profit association "Unione Italiana dei Ciechi e degli Ipovedenti" (in English, *Italian association for the blind and visually impaired people*), to evaluate the quality of the multisensory stimuli and the interaction with the magic casket for blind and visually impaired people. During the workshops, the facilitator described the scenario of the storytelling laboratory and invited the participants to explore the diverse stimuli included in the magic casket and provide their expert evaluation.

The material and size of the 3D printed replicas were considered appropriate to enable the person to perceive the details of the object. Some participants pointed out that the tactile exploration of the 3D replicas was not sufficient to appreciate the artwork since a narration is needed to understand what the replica represents, and to guide the tactile exploration of the objects (Vaz et al., 2018, 2022). In light of this, the participants appreciated the use of audio narrations, songs and sounds to complement the tactile exploration of the objects.

In particular, they evaluated positively not only the contents of the audio narration but also the quality of the voice. Even if the audio narration was developed with a voice synthesiser, the voice was perceived as flowing and warm. Moreover, as suggested by Hutchinson and Eardley (2023), the contents and the quality of voice of the audio narrations were designed to go beyond the provision of visual information, to stimulate feelings and imaginaries.

Regarding the tactile interactive postcards with the Feelif tablet, the participants consider this solution very useful for blind and visually impaired people because it transforms a 2D image of a painting into a 3D interactive image that people can explore using a personal mobile device like the tablet. In this way, the person does not need to get expensive special equipment.

During the workshops, the participants focused the attention on the micro-interactions with the tablet and provided relevant suggestions to improve the gestures to activate the contents using both hands. They also suggested reproducing images of artworks which do not contain too many details and to increase the thickness of the embossed contours of the images so as to better perceive the details of the painting.

6.3.4 The Magic Casket in Everyday Life Contexts

The magic casket was also evaluated with older people and caregivers in home cares and day-care centres. Two evaluation workshops involved one museum educator acting as facilitator, two caregivers, ten older people with more than 80 years old (eight female, two male) who suffer from age-related sensory and motor impairments. One workshop took place in a nursing home, and the other workshop took place in a day-care centre. During the workshops, the storytelling laboratory was carried out according to the following format.

1. Organisation of the lab activity and personalisation of the magic casket. The museum educator selected one of the themes available in the magic casket. Based on the theme, different stimuli were included in the magic casket as described in paragraph 3.2.
2. Set up of the lab activity. The museum educator brought the magic casket to the nursing home/day-care centre, and arranged it on the table. Then, the laboratory started with the introduction of the activities.
3. Presentation of the theme. The museum educator introduced the theme of the "Protection": "*Protection is a topic that concerns all of us, since we were children. Protection can have many meanings, it depends on the moment of our life, it depends on the people we live with. Let's start remembering the first kind of protection we experienced: the protection from our parents*".
4. Exploration of the stimuli and narration of the stories. Once the theme was introduced, the museum educator followed the configuration of the magic casket to stimulate the exploration of the stimuli and the narration of stories. In this phase, the competence and sensitivity of the museum educator were essential to mediate the exploration of the cultural contents, the interaction among the participants and the narration of the stories. In particular, to stimulate the memories and sharing of stories, the museum educator combined the exploration of an object with questions asked to the participants. For example, when showing the replica of "Madonna with the Child and two cherubs" (Anonymous author, collection of Museo dell'Arte Sacra della Val d'Arbia di Buonconvento, Italy), she asked: "*What do you remember about your mother?*".

In addition to the museum educator who played the role of facilitator of the storytelling laboratory, two members of the project team attended the workshops acting as onsite passive participant observers (Roller & Lavrakas, 2015; Ciesielska et al., 2018).

The data collected for the evaluation include the video recordings of the workshops, and observation grids with notes taken by the project team. Specifically, the observation grid was designed as a spreadsheet with a structure to note down how the participants reacted to and interacted with the stimuli, and how the stories were narrated (Fig. 6.8). The objective of the grid was to remind the observer of the key elements to observe and note down (Roller & Lavrakas, 2015). The grid also includes the blank spaces for free comments. We created one observation grid for

Stimulus: **3D printed replica of Saint Anthony**
Participant code: ________

Stimulus				
Identification	**Interaction**		**Dialogue**	**Emotions**
❑Spontaneously identify the stimulus ❑Identify the stimulus only once the facilitator presents it	Tactile exploration: ❑Not at all ❑A little ❑A lot Observation: ❑Not at all ❑A little ❑A lot	❑Spontaneously explore the stimulus ❑Explore the stimulus only when the facilitator invites to do it ❑Explore the stimulus alone ❑Explore the stimulus together with other participants	❑Ask questions to and dialogue with the facilitator ❑Ask questions to and dialogue with the caregiver ❑Ask questions to and dialogue with other participants	❑Curiosity and interest ❑Wonder ❑Joy ❑Melancholy and sadness ❑Boredom ❑Fear ❑Anger ❑Passive approach ❑Active approach
Comments				
Story				
Connection with the stimulus	**Initiation**	**Topic of the story**	**Dialogue**	**Emotions**
❑The topic of the story is connected with the stimulus ❑The story is «out of topic»	❑The story is initiated spontaneously ❑The story is stimulated by the facilitator	❑Personal experience ❑Historical events ❑Local traditions	❑The story is narrated individually by the person ❑The story is co-narrated by the participants ❑The other participants comment on the story	❑Curiosity and interest ❑Wonder ❑Joy ❑Melancholy and sadness ❑Boredom ❑Fear ❑Anger ❑Passive approach ❑Active approach
Comments				

Stimulus: **song "Madonna delle Grazie"**
Participant code: ________

Stimulus				
Identification	**Interaction**		**Dialogue**	**Emotions**
❑Spontaneously recognise the song ❑Recognizse the song only once the facilitator describes it	Listening: ❑Listen without interruptions ❑Interrupt the listening to comment ❑Listen while exploring another object (________) ❑Ask for listening the song again	Activation of the song: ❑Spontaneously activate the audio ❑Activate the audio only when the facilitator invites to do it Exploration of the vinyl disk: ❑Not at all ❑A little ❑A lot	❑Ask questions to and dialogue with the facilitator ❑Ask questions to and dialogue with the caregiver ❑Ask questions to and dialogue with other participants	❑Curiosity and interest ❑Wonder ❑Joy ❑Melancholy and sadness ❑Boredom ❑Fear ❑Anger ❑Passive approach ❑Active approach
Comments				
Story				
Connection with the stimulus	**Initiation**	**Topic of the story**	**Dialogue**	**Emotions**
❑The topic of the story is connected with the stimulus ❑The story is «out of topic»	❑The story is initiated spontaneously ❑The story is stimulated by the facilitator	❑Personal experience ❑Historical events ❑Local traditions	❑The story is narrated individually by the person ❑The story is co-narrated by the participants ❑The other participants comment on the story	❑Curiosity and interest ❑Wonder ❑Joy ❑Melancholy and sadness ❑Boredom ❑Fear ❑Anger ❑Passive approach ❑Active approach
Comments				

Fig. 6.8 Observation grids used to note down the interaction with the 3D printed replica (*top*) and song (*bottom*)

each type of stimulus included in the magic casket (3D printed replica, fragrance, song, audio narration, photograph on canvas, Feelif interactive images).

Given the complex dynamics of the workshops, the observation grids were further completed afterward using the video recordings of the workshops. In this way, the grids were completed for each stimulus and for each participant. Then, the grids were integrated into a digital spreadsheet to facilitate the data analysis.

6.4 Results

The results described hereafter emerged from the analysis of the observation grids and the video recordings of the workshops. They provide insights about the participants' interaction with the multisensory stimuli, and the way the stories were stimulated during the storytelling laboratory. A final reflection is included below and is related to the role of the facilitator and the caregiver involved in the activity.

6.4.1 Effects of the Multisensory Stimuli

The magic casket with its multisensory stimuli was an effective prompt to reflect on the personal and cultural meanings of the heritage, recalling personal memories, older times and places related to the personal experience and historical events, all within a collective experience among peers (Hooper-Greenhill, 2004; Pekarik & Schreiber, 2012; Sheng & Chen, 2012).

From the observation grids it is evident that some stimuli were more effective in attracting the attention and interest of the participants compared to others, but the value of the experience relies on the combined use of diverse stimuli connected to the theme and the narration proposed by the museum educator.

Specifically, all participants spent time looking and touching the 3D printed replicas. The photographs of the artworks printed on canvas were used in combination with the replicas to show the colours and decorations of the original items (Fig. 6.9).

Fig. 6.9 One participant explores the 3D printed replica and the photograph of the original museum item at the same time

The audio descriptions activated by the NFC provided the prompt for both the facilitator and the participants to reflect and discuss together.

The songs activated by the vinyl attracted the attention so that the participants listened to the songs without interruptions, and then they spontaneously started singing songs all together.

From the observation grids we noticed that the fragrances played a major role in attracting the attention of participants and stimulating the dialogue. The fragrances were specifically selected to be familiar and to recall memories (baked bread, grass, linen). The scratch and sniff postcard with the fragrance of the baked bread passed from hand to hand among the participants, and once one person recognised the smell of the baked bread the participants spontaneously started to remember old traditions and personal experience. An excerpt of the dialogue is reported in paragraph 3.4.2. This finding supports the need for further investigations about the use of olfactory stimulation as a means to experience and narrate the cultural heritage (Levent & Pascual-Leone; Bembibre & Strlič, 2017, 2022).

Regarding the tablet with the tactile interactive postcards, the accessibility experts considered this solution very useful to explore the artworks by blind and visually impaired people. However, older participants with no sight impairments tended to use the tablet just as a screen to see an image, and the support of the facilitator was essential to properly use the tablet application. This highlights a preference for physical objects compared to digital tools.

6.4.2 Recalling Memories and Telling Stories

The scientific literature provides some evidence about the use of objects to stimulate reminiscence and dialogue among older people, especially those who live in nursing homes, with a positive effect on the short-term mood, cognitive process and socialisation. These psychosocial outcomes are generated when the cultural contents are aligned with the topical interests of the participants (e.g., Smiraglia, 2015, 2016). This is the case of the workshops of BeauCoup since most of the participants (eight out of ten) share the same cultural background having spent their entire life living in the same village. In this context, the themes of "Protection" and "Rural life" resonated with their memories and personal experiences resulting in a particularly engaging experience.

Overall, the stimuli included in the magic casket not only attracted the interest of the participants for the sensorial exploration, but some of them acted as triggers to recall memories of personal experiences and historical events. The replicas, the songs and the smells were the most effective stimuli to prompt memories and the dialogue among the participants.

In most of the cases, the sharing of personal stories happened spontaneously while only in a few cases the museum educator asked questions to directly stimulate the dialogue.

Fig. 6.10 Participant looking at a photograph representing a woman who carries the bread to the communal oven

By analysing how the stories were produced based on the video recordings of the workshops, it is evident that the stories were co-constructed as a choral process: when exploring an object by touch and listening to the description, a person starts sharing a memory and other participants comment and contribute to the collective narration. The following table reports an excerpt that exemplifies the way the stories are stimulated by the facilitator (F) and shared by the participants (P1, P2, etc.) during the workshops. Even if the dialogue is fragmented, with comments that interrupted and diverged the attention, overall the participants were spontaneous in initiating the dialogue and contributing to it.

Moreover, this excerpt serves to highlight that the value of the multisensory stimulation relies on the combination of diverse, connected objects: the original photograph of a woman who carries the bread to the communal oven (Fig. 6.10), its representation in the form of a scratch and sniff postcard with the fragrance of baked bread.

The facilitator shows the old photograph of a woman who carries the bread to the communal oven. The facilitator introduces the object.

F: This image comes from Museo della Mezzadria Senese (Sharecropping museum) in Buonconvento.

Before concluding the sentence, the facilitator is interrupted by P1 who initiates the dialogue about local traditions.

P1: My mother used to make the bread at home.

P2: Yes, the bread was homemade.

P1: And in the village there were the communal ovens. My father brought the bread to the communal oven. My father and my mother used to wake up at five in the morning to knead the bread. [...] And when there was stale bread, my mother used to boil it with tomato, celery and carrot.

P2: I made the bread for 18 people, we were two women, the bread must be enough for eight days. So, we needed to make a lot of bread, but it was tiring. I was very young but my mother was sick and she couldn't make any more effort, so I made the bread for my mother.

F: Who taught you how to make bread?

P2: Who taught me? I saw them and I did it like them.

P5: In the evening we added the yeast, and in the morning everything was ready to knead.

P1: There was a big kneading trough.

P5: Yes, yes, it was a kneading trough to close at night.

P2: And there was the woman who lit the fire in the wood oven. The oven should be red, otherwise the bread wouldn't bake.

The subject of the discussion changes (recipes for food preparations, cooking expertise) for a few minutes until the facilitator invites the participants to smell the *fragrance of the baked bread*. F: I brought something to smell.

The smelling object is passed from hand to hand among the participants.

P4: I can perceive it.

F: Does it remind you of something?

P5: I cannot perceive anything.

P4: It is something I know but I cannot say.

P2: I cannot perceive anything.

P1: It is the smell of the baked bread!

P5: Now I perceive the smell of the bread, but look at the effect it has on me! The bread had a delicious smell. But at that time people suffered from hunger, I suffered from hunger, we were 23 people in the family.

The dialogue proceeds on the topic of post war living conditions.

The stories narvrated during the workshops are related to personal experiences (e.g., the protection of the family during childhood), other places and traditions experienced during travels in the past, and local cultural traditions (e.g., the practice of homemade bread and communal ovens).

Since the participants were more than 80 years old, they remembered how it was to live during the Second World War and the socio-economic conditions in the post war period in the rural context. This was a recurrent topic of the stories that generated negative emotions such as sadness. Even if the memory of that time was sad and painful, the participants demonstrated the wish to share their experience. This is in line with the ultimate goal of the storytelling laboratory proposed by BeauCoup: to engage the older generations in the narration of stories with cultural and historical relevance, since they are custodians of meaningful memories which are at risk of being lost over time.

6.4.3 The Role of the Facilitator(s)

The museum educator involved in the project to facilitate the storytelling laboratory is expert in mediating the exploration of the cultural heritage in museums. She was engaged to employ such expertise outside the museum context. Indeed, in the case of outreach programs when the cultural heritage is brought to the local communities, the function of the museum educator might change while some capacities and dynamics remain fundamental both inside and outside the museums.

By analysing the evaluation workshops, we found that the museum educator adapted the activities, the presentation of the stimuli and the narration according to the characteristics of the participants and their reaction. This ability of the museum educator was essential to make the experience personalised and engaging. When planning the storytelling laboratory, the museum educator selected the theme, the configuration of the magic casket and the multisensory stimuli. According to this, she prepared a script to use as a guideline to link the diverse stimuli and describe the museum items. The script served only as a starting point rather than a restriction. Her deep knowledge of the cultural contents included in the magic casket enabled her to adapt the narration by pointing out details based on the interest manifested by the participants, and to use the dialogue with the participants to connect the diverse stimuli and cultural contents.

As investigated by Ash and Lombana (2012), the reflective practice of the museum educators is based on "noticing" what happens in the situation, and flexibly "responding" to what they notice. This highlights the need for training the museum educators not just to properly use the technologies (e.g., arrange the magic casket, activate the audio contents etc.), but also to understand the situation and dynamically adjust the activity. In light of this, the modular design of the magic casket guides the activity with flexibility: it supports the facilitator to orchestrate the exploration of the stimuli based on a theme, while leaving the freedom to both the facilitator and the participants to freely explore the inside objects.

When the participants are older people with age-related disabilities in day-care centres and nursing homes, the caregivers play a pivotal role in mediating between the museum educator and the participants. Since the caregivers know the participants very well, they should be involved from the beginning to plan the activities, select the theme and the multisensory stimuli to include in the magic casket. During the laboratory, the caregivers should also be involved to "read the room" and help the educator in adapting the activity.

In conclusion, this kind of activity requires combining the curatorial perspective with the psycho-social perspective.

6.5 Conclusions and Future Directions

A major challenge for contemporary museum services is related to accessibility and active participation of visitors in educational activities, personal enjoyment, reflection and knowledge sharing (ICOM, 2022). While museums are institutions in the service of society, there are still marginalised social groups who are excluded from the full participation in the cultural life of the community. Older people with onset or age-related disabilities fall into this category, especially those who live in nursing homes.

The pathway towards the inclusion of diverse audiences can take different directions. The project BeauCoup described in this chapter is focused on two strategies: the design of multisensory experiences to make the cultural artefacts and contents accessible, and the organisation of outreach programs to bring the cultural heritage outside the museums' walls where the people live and spend time.

The design of the activities and tools was based on the integration of diverse perspectives and needs, from the curators to the older people and their caregivers. Through the analysis of the state of the art and the results of the workshops with the stakeholders, we identified relevant opportunities and challenges to employ the multisensory experience as a means to stimulate memories and dialogue within an engaging leisure experience.

The use of multisensory stimuli, including physical objects and digital tools, can be employed to support object-based reminiscence programmes for older adults in nursing homes for sensory exploration, cognitive and emotional responses, memory-sharing, and socialisation (e.g., Chatterjee & Noble, 2009; Smiraglia, 2015, 2016). Taking advantage of digital fabrication tools like 3D printing it is possible to reproduce artworks enriched by audio descriptions and smells to be explored in a multisensory way by people with different cognitive, perceptual and motor abilities.

The diverse sensory stimuli are effective when they are combined, reinforcing each other in combination with an engaging narrative. Moreover, the prompts for recalling memories and telling stories were generated by the group discussion, so that the memory and narration of one person provides the trigger for the other people (Smiraglia, 2016). This happened because the different stimuli were designed and combined together, to orchestrate a narration around a theme that is relevant for the workshop participants. The modular design of the magic casket proved to be effective in supporting such orchestration while providing flexibility when planning the activities (to select the theme, the museum items, and the stimuli based on the participants to involve), as well as when conducting the activity to adjust the exploration of the cultural heritage according to the interest of the participants.

While the workshops of BeauCoup offered the occasion to experiment with a new concept for the exploration of the cultural heritage, the results point out the need to advance the knowledge about the combination of multiple senses, new technologies to employ to enable an engaging experience, and to shed light on the outcomes of such cultural leisure activities addressed to older people.

Acknowledgement The project BeauCoup has received funding from Active Assisted Living Joint Programme under grant agreement No AAL-2021-8-156-CP. The authors thank the partners of the project: AIT - Austrian Institute of Technology, Feelif d.o.o., Fondazione Musei Senesi, Hilfsgemeinschaft der Blinden und Sehschwachen Österreichs, NOUSdigital, Santa Casa da Miericòrdia de Lisboa, Sign Time, terzStiftung, VRVis, Moritz Neumüller (ArteConTacto). Further information about BeauCoup project are available on the web site: https://beaucoup-project.eu/

Appendix: Observation Grids

This appendix includes the six observation grids created to note down the most relevant observable elements during the interaction with the multisensory stimuli included in the magic casket. Each grid is focused on a specific type of stimulus: 3D printed replica, audio narration, fragrance, song, photograph printed on canvas, Feelif interactive images.

Observation Grid for the 3D Printed Replica

Observation grid
Stimulus: **3D printed replica**
Participant code: __________

Stimulus				
Identification	**Interaction**		**Dialogue**	**Emotions**
☐ Spontaneously identify the stimulus ☐ Identify the stimulus only once the facilitator presents it	Tactile exploration: ☐ Not at all ☐ A little ☐ A lot Observation: ☐ Not at all ☐ A little ☐ A lot	☐ Spontaneously explore the stimulus ☐ Explore the stimulus only when the facilitator invites to do it ☐ Explore the stimulus alone ☐ Explore the stimulus together with other participants	☐ Ask questions to and dialogue with the facilitator ☐ Ask questions to and dialogue with the caregiver ☐ Ask questions to and dialogue with other participants	☐ Curiosity and interest ☐ Wonder ☐ Joy ☐ Melancholy and sadness ☐ Boredom ☐ Fear ☐ Anger ☐ Passive approach ☐ Active approach
Comments				

Story				
Connection with the stimulus	**Initiation**	**Topic of the story**	**Dialogue**	**Emotions**
☐ The topic of the story is connected with the stimulus ☐ The story is «out of topic»	☐ The story is initiated spontaneously ☐ The story is stimulated by the facilitator	☐ Personal experience ☐ Historical events ☐ Local traditions	☐ The story is narrated individually by the person ☐ The story is co-narrated by the participants ☐ The other participants comment on the story	☐ Curiosity and interest ☐ Wonder ☐ Joy ☐ Melancholy and sadness ☐ Boredom ☐ Fear ☐ Anger ☐ Passive approach ☐ Active approach
Comments				

Observation Grid for the Audio Narration

Observation grid
Stimulus: **audio narration**
Participant code: __________

Stimulus				
Understanding	**Interaction**		**Dialogue**	**Emotions**
❑ Understand the content of the narration ❑ Ask for listening again to understand the audio narration	Listening: ❑ Listen without interruptions ❑ Interrupt the listening to comment ❑ Listen while exploring another object (____________)	Activation of the audio narration: ❑ Spontaneously activate the audio ❑ Activate the audio only when the facilitator invites to do it	❑ Ask questions to and dialogue with the facilitator ❑ Ask questions to and dialogue with the caregiver ❑ Ask questions to and dialogue with other participants	❑ Curiosity and interest ❑ Wonder ❑ Joy ❑ Melancholy and sadness ❑ Boredom ❑ Fear ❑ Anger ❑ Passive approach ❑ Active approach
Comments				

Story				
Connection with the stimulus	**Initiation**	**Topic of the story**	**Dialogue**	**Emotions**
❑ The topic of the story is connected with the stimulus ❑ The story is «out of topic»	❑ The story is initiated spontaneously ❑ The story is stimulated by the facilitator	❑ Personal experience ❑ Historical events ❑ Local traditions	❑ The story is narrated individually by the person ❑ The story is co-narrated by the participants ❑ The other participants comment on the story	❑ Curiosity and interest ❑ Wonder ❑ Joy ❑ Melancholy and sadness ❑ Boredom ❑ Fear ❑ Anger ❑ Passive approach ❑ Active approach
Comments				

Observation Grid for the Fragrance

Observation grid
Stimulus: **fragrance**
Participant code: __________

Stimulus				
Identification	**Interaction**		**Dialogue**	**Emotions**
❑ Spontaneously identify the stimulus ❑ Identify the stimulus only once the facilitator presents it	Olfactory exploration: ❑ Not at all ❑ A little ❑ A lot	❑ Spontaneously explore the stimulus ❑ Explore the stimulus only when the facilitator invites to do it ❑ Explore the stimulus alone ❑ Explore the stimulus together with other participants	❑ Ask questions to and dialogue with the facilitator ❑ Ask questions to and dialogue with the caregiver ❑ Ask questions to and dialogue with other participants	❑ Curiosity and interest ❑ Wonder ❑ Joy ❑ Melancholy and sadness ❑ Boredom ❑ Fear ❑ Anger ❑ Passive approach ❑ Active approach
Comments				

Story				
Connection with the stimulus	**Initiation**	**Topic of the story**	**Dialogue**	**Emotions**
❑ The topic of the story is connected with the stimulus ❑ The story is «out of topic»	❑ The story is initiated spontaneously ❑ The story is stimulated by the facilitator	❑ Personal experience ❑ Historical events ❑ Local traditions	❑ The story is narrated individually by the person ❑ The story is co-narrated by the participants ❑ The other participants comment on the story	❑ Curiosity and interest ❑ Wonder ❑ Joy ❑ Melancholy and sadness ❑ Boredom ❑ Fear ❑ Anger ❑ Passive approach ❑ Active approach
Comments				

Observation Grid for the Song

Observation grid
Stimulus: **song**
Participant code: ________

Stimulus				
Identification	**Interaction**		**Dialogue**	**Emotions**
❑ Spontaneously recognise the song ❑ Recognizse the song only once the facilitator describes it	Listening: ❑ Listen without interruptions ❑ Interrupt the listening to comment ❑ Listen while exploring another object (____________) ❑ Ask for listening the song again	Activation of the song: ❑ Spontaneously activate the audio ❑ Activate the audio only when the facilitator invites to do it Exploration of the vinyl disk: ❑ Not at all ❑ A little ❑ A lot	❑ Ask questions to and dialogue with the facilitator ❑ Ask questions to and dialogue with the caregiver ❑ Ask questions to and dialogue with other participants	❑ Curiosity and interest ❑ Wonder ❑ Joy ❑ Melancholy and sadness ❑ Boredom ❑ Fear ❑ Anger ❑ Passive approach ❑ Active approach
Comments				

Story				
Connection with the stimulus	**Initiation**	**Topic of the story**	**Dialogue**	**Emotions**
❑ The topic of the story is connected with the stimulus ❑ The story is «out of topic»	❑ The story is initiated spontaneously ❑ The story is stimulated by the facilitator	❑ Personal experience ❑ Historical events ❑ Local traditions	❑ The story is narrated individually by the person ❑ The story is co-narrated by the participants ❑ The other participants comment on the story	❑ Curiosity and interest ❑ Wonder ❑ Joy ❑ Melancholy and sadness ❑ Boredom ❑ Fear ❑ Anger ❑ Passive approach ❑ Active approach
Comments				

Observation Grid for the Photograph

Observation grid
Stimulus: **photograph**
Participant code: ________

Stimulus				
Identification	**Interaction**		**Dialogue**	**Emotions**
❑ Spontaneously identify the object represented in the photo ❑ Identify the object represented in the photo only once the facilitator presents it	Tactile exploration: ❑ Not at all ❑ A little ❑ A lot Observation: ❑ Not at all ❑ A little ❑ A lot	❑ Spontaneously explore the stimulus ❑ Explore the stimulus only when the facilitator invites to do it ❑ Explore the stimulus alone ❑ Explore the stimulus together with other participants	❑ Ask questions to and dialogue with the facilitator ❑ Ask questions to and dialogue with the caregiver ❑ Ask questions to and dialogue with other participants	❑ Curiosity and interest ❑ Wonder ❑ Joy ❑ Melancholy and sadness ❑ Boredom ❑ Fear ❑ Anger ❑ Passive approach ❑ Active approach
Comments				

Story				
Connection with the stimulus	**Initiation**	**Topic of the story**	**Dialogue**	**Emotions**
❑ The topic of the story is connected with the stimulus ❑ The story is «out of topic»	❑ The story is initiated spontaneously ❑ The story is stimulated by the facilitator	❑ Personal experience ❑ Historical events ❑ Local traditions	❑ The story is narrated individually by the person ❑ The story is co-narrated by the participants ❑ The other participants comment on the story	❑ Curiosity and interest ❑ Wonder ❑ Joy ❑ Melancholy and sadness ❑ Boredom ❑ Fear ❑ Anger ❑ Passive approach ❑ Active approach
Comments				

Observation Grid for the Feelif Tactile Interactive Postcard

Observation grid
Stimulus: **interactive tactile postcard with tablet**
Participant code: _________

Stimulus					
Identification		**Interaction**		**Dialogue**	**Emotions**
❑ Spontaneously identify the image ❑ Identify the image only once the facilitator presents it		Tactile exploration: ❑ Not at all ❑ A little ❑ A lot Observation: ❑ Not at all ❑ A little ❑ A lot Listening: ❑ Not at all ❑ A little ❑ A lot	❑ Interact with the tablet autonomously ❑ Need the support of the facilitator to interact with the tablet ❑ Spontaneously explore the stimulus ❑ Explore the stimulus only when the facilitator invites to do it ❑ Explore the stimulus alone ❑ Explore the stimulus together with other participants	❑ Ask questions to and dialogue with the facilitator ❑ Ask questions to and dialogue with the caregiver ❑ Ask questions to and dialogue with other participants	❑ Curiosity and interest ❑ Wonder ❑ Joy ❑ Melancholy and sadness ❑ Boredom ❑ Fear ❑ Anger ❑ Passive approach ❑ Active approach
Comments					

Story					
Connection with the stimulus		**Initiation**	**Topic of the story**	**Dialogue**	**Emotions**
❑ The topic of the story is connected with the stimulus ❑ The story is «out of topic»		❑ The story is initiated spontaneously ❑ The story is stimulated by the facilitator	❑ Personal experience ❑ Historical events ❑ Local traditions	❑ The story is narrated individually by the person ❑ The story is co-narrated by the participants ❑ The other participants comment on the story	❑ Curiosity and interest ❑ Wonder ❑ Joy ❑ Melancholy and sadness ❑ Boredom ❑ Fear ❑ Anger ❑ Passive approach ❑ Active approach
Comments					

References

Ash, D. B., & Lombana, J. (2012). Methodologies for reflective practice and Museum Educator research: The role of "noticing" and responding. In *Putting theory into practice* (pp. 29–52). Brill.

Balletti, C., Ballarin, M., & Guerra, F. (2017). 3D printing: State of the art and future perspectives. *Journal of Cultural Heritage, 26*, 172–182. https://doi.org/10.1016/j.culher.2017.02.010

Bembibre, C., & Strlič, M. (2017). Smell of heritage: A framework for the identification, analysis and archival of historic odours. *Heritage Science, 5*, 1–11. https://doi.org/10.1186/s40494-016-0114-1

Bembibre, C., & Strlič, M. (2022). From smelly buildings to the scented past: An overview of olfactory heritage. *Frontiers in Psychology, 12*, 718287. https://doi.org/10.3389/fpsyg.2021.718287

Beşevli, C., Brianza, G., Dawes, C., Shabanova, N., Mathur, S., Lechner, M., & Obrist, M. (2024, July). Smell Above all: Envisioning smell-centred future worlds. In *Proceedings of the 2024 ACM designing interactive systems conference* (pp. 2530–2544). https://doi.org/10.1145/3643834.3660699

Blundell, E. W. (2023). Multisensory visitor engagement: An analysis of three case studies. In *Museums and technologies of presence* (pp. 93–111). Routledge.

Bordegoni, M., Carulli, M., & Bader, S. (2019, May). Wearable olfactory display for museum exhibitions. In *2019 IEEE international symposium on olfaction and electronic nose (ISOEN)* (pp. 1–3). IEEE. https://doi.org/10.1109/ISOEN.2019.8823224

Bruns, A., Spiesberger, A. A., Triantafyllopoulos, A., Müller, P., & Schuller, B. W. (2023, November). "Do touch!"—3D scanning and printing technologies for the haptic representation of cultural assets: A study with blind target users. In *Proceedings of the 5th workshop on analysis, understanding and promotion of heritage contents* (pp. 21–28). https://doi.org/10.1145/3607542.3617351

Chatterjee, H. J., & Noble, G. (2009). Object therapy: A student-selected component exploring the potential of museum object handling as an enrichment activity for patients in hospital. *Global Journal of Health Science, 1*(2), 42.

Ciesielska, M., Boström, K. W., & Öhlander, M. (2018). Observation methods. In *Qualitative methodologies in organization studies: Volume II: Methods and possibilities* (pp. 33–52). Palgrave. https://doi.org/10.5539/gjhs.v1n2p42

Council of Europe. (2005). *Council of Europe framework convention on the value of cultural heritage for society (CETS No. 199)*. Retrieved October 19, 2024, from https://www.coe.int/en/web/conventions/full-list?module=treaty-detail&treatynum=199

Deng, J., Olivier, P., & Floyd Mueller, F. (2021, May). Design of cyber food: Beginning to understand food as computational artifact. In *Extended abstracts of the 2021 CHI conference on human factors in computing systems* (pp. 1–6). https://doi.org/10.1145/3411763.3451687

Eardley, A. F., Fryer, L., Hutchinson, R., Cock, M., Ride, P., & Neves, J. (2017). Enriched audio description: Working towards an inclusive museum experience. In *Inclusion, disability and culture: An ethnographic perspective traversing abilities and challenges* (pp. 195–207). Springer. https://doi.org/10.1007/978-3-319-55224-8_13

Floyd Mueller, F., Dwyer, T., Goodwin, S., Marriott, K., Deng, J., Phan, H. D., & Ashok Khot, R. (2021, May). Data as delight: Eating data. In *Proceedings of the 2021 CHI conference on human factors in computing systems* (pp. 1–14). https://doi.org/10.1145/3411764.3445218

Hooper-Greenhill, E. (2004). Measuring learning outcomes in museums, archives and libraries: The Learning Impact Research Project (LIRP). *International Journal of Heritage Studies, 10*(2), 151–174. https://doi.org/10.1080/13527250410001692877

Howes, D. (2014). Introduction to sensory museology. *The Senses and Society, 9*(3), 259–267. https://doi.org/10.2752/174589314X14023847039917

Howes, D., Clarke, E., Macpherson, F., Best, B., & Cox, R. (2018). Sensing art and artifacts: Explorations in sensory museology. *The Senses and Society, 13*(3), 317–334. https://doi.org/10.1080/17458927.2018.1516024

Hutchinson, R., & Eardley, A. F. (2023). 'I felt I was right there with them': The impact of sound-enriched audio description on experiencing and remembering artworks, for blind and sighted museum audiences. *Museum Management and Curatorship, 39*, 1–18. https://doi.org/10.1080/09647775.2023.2188482

International Council of Museums. (2022). *ICOM approves a new definition of museum*. Retrieved October 19, 2024, from https://icom.museum/en/news/icom-approves-a-new-museum-definition/

Kapsali, M. (2020). Sonic bodies: Sonification and the hybridization of aesthetic experience. *Performance Research, 25*(4), 45–53. https://doi.org/10.1080/13528165.2020.1842029

Karaduman, H., Alan, Ü., & Yiğit, E. Ö. (2023). Beyond "do not touch": The experience of a three-dimensional printed artifacts museum as an alternative to traditional museums for visitors who are blind and partially sighted. *Universal Access in the Information Society, 22*(3), 811–824. https://doi.org/10.1007/s10209-022-00880-0

Levent, N., & Pascual-Leone, A. (Eds.). (2014). *The multisensory museum: Cross-disciplinary perspectives on touch, sound, smell, memory, and space*. Rowman & Littlefield.

Luo, D., Doucé, L., & Nys, K. (2024). Multisensory museum experience: An integrative view and future research directions. *Museum Management and Curatorship*, 1–28. https://doi.org/10.1080/09647775.2024.2357071

Marti, P., Recupero, A., Regal, G., & Sackl, A. (2023). Bringing culture to people: A co-design method for redefining the role of the museum. *Diid Disegno Industriale Industrial Design*, (81). https://doi.org/10.30682/diid8123j

Miotto, L. (2016, October). Using scents to connect to intangible heritage: Engaging the visitor olfactory dimension: Three museum exhibition case studies. In *2016 22nd international conference on virtual system & multimedia (VSMM)* (pp. 1–5). IEEE. https://doi.org/10.1109/VSMM.2016.7863208

Museum Tinguely. (2020). *Amuse-bouche*. Retrieved October 19, 2024, from https://www.tinguely.ch/en/exhibitions/exhibitions/2020/amuse-bouche.html

Nadri, C., Anaya, C., Yuan, S., & Jeon, M. (2019, June). Preliminary guidelines on the sonification of visual artworks: Linking music, sonification & visual arts. In *Proceedings of the 25th international conference on auditory display (ICAD 2019)*. Georgia Institute of Technology.

Obrist, M., Bertran, F. A., Makam, N., Kim, S., Dawes, C., Marti, P., & Wang, Y. (2024). Grand challenges in human-food interaction. *International Journal of Human-Computer Studies, 183*, 103197. https://doi.org/10.1016/j.ijhcs.2023.103197

Okerlund, J., Segreto, E., Grote, C., Westendorf, L., Scholze, A., Littrell, R., & Shaer, O. (2016, February). Synflo: A tangible museum exhibit for exploring bio-design. In *Proceedings of the TEI'16: Tenth international conference on tangible, embedded, and embodied interaction* (pp. 141–149). https://doi.org/10.1145/2839462.2839488

Pekarik, A. J., & Schreiber, J. B. (2012). The power of expectation. *Curator: The Museum Journal, 55*(4), 487–496. https://doi.org/10.1111/j.2151-6952.2012.00171.x

Race, L., D'Souza, S., Flouty, R., Igoe, T., & Hurst, A. (2023). Understanding accessible interpretation through touch object practices in museums. *The International Journal of the Inclusive Museum, 16*(1), 75. https://doi.org/10.18848/1835-2014/CGP/v16i01/75-98

Recupero, A., Marti, P., Regal, G., & Sackl, A. (2023). Service co-design to envision the transformation of museums. In D. De Sainz Molestina, L. Galluzzo, F. Rizzo, & D. Spallazzo (Eds.), *IASDR 2023: Life-changing design*. Design Research Society. https://doi.org/10.21606/iasdr.2023.426. 9–13 October.

Reinhardt, D., Holloway, L., Thogersen, J., Guerry, E., Diaz, C. A. C., Havellas, W., & Poronnik, P. (2024). The museum of touch: Tangible models for blind and low vision audiences in museums. In *Multimodality in architecture: Collaboration, technology and education* (pp. 135–155). Springer Nature Switzerland.

Rieger, J. (2023). *Design, disability and embodiment: Spatial justice and perspectives of power*. Taylor & Francis.

Roller, M. R., & Lavrakas, P. J. (2015). *Applied qualitative research design: A total quality framework approach*. Guilford Publications.

Shaby, N., & Vedder-Weiss, D. (2021). Embodied interactions in a science museum. *Science Education, 105*(5), 938–960. https://doi.org/10.1002/sce.21666

Sheng, C. W., & Chen, M. C. (2012). A study of experience expectations of museum visitors. *Tourism Management, 33*(1), 53–60. https://doi.org/10.1016/j.tourman.2011.01.023

Smiraglia, C. (2015). Museum programming and mood: Participant responses to an object-based reminiscence outreach program in retirement communities. *Arts and Health, 7*(3), 187–201. https://doi.org/10.1080/17533015.2015.1010443

Smiraglia, C. (2016). Targeted museum programs for older adults: A research and program review. *Curator: The Museum Journal, 59*(1), 39–54. https://doi.org/10.1111/cura.12144

Spence, C. (2016). Making sense of touch: A multisensory approach to the perception of objects. In *The power of touch* (pp. 45–61). Routledge.

Spence, C. (2020). Shitsukan—The multisensory perception of quality. *Multisensory Research, 33*(7), 737–775.

Stickdorn, M., & Schneider, J. (2012). *This is service design thinking: Basics, tools, cases*. Wiley.

Tallon, C., & Walker, K. (Eds.). (2008). *Digital technologies and the museum experience: Handheld guides and other media*. Altamira Press.

United Nations. (1948). *Universal declaration of human rights*. Retrieved October 19, 2024, from https://www.un.org/en/about-us/universal-declaration-of-human-rights

Vaz, R., Fernandes, P. O., & Veiga, A. C. R. (2018). Designing an interactive exhibitor for assisting blind and visually impaired visitors in tactile exploration of original museum pieces. *Procedia Computer Science, 138*, 561–570. https://doi.org/10.1016/j.procs.2018.10.076

Vaz, R., Freitas, D., & Coelho, A. (2022, June). Enhancing the blind and partially sighted visitors' experience in museums through integrating assistive technologies, multisensory and interactive approaches. In *International conference on human-computer interaction* (pp. 521–540). Springer International Publishing. https://doi.org/10.1007/978-3-031-05039-8_38

Verbeek, C., Leemans, I., & Fleming, B. (2022). How can scents enhance the impact of guided museum tours? Towards an impact approach for olfactory museology. *The Senses and Society, 17*(3), 315–342. https://doi.org/10.1080/17458927.2022.2142012

Verbrugge, L. M., & Yang, L. S. (2002). Aging with disability and disability with aging. *Journal of Disability Policy Studies, 12*(4), 253–267. https://doi.org/10.1177/104420730201200405

Victoria & Albert Museum. (2019). *FOOD: Bigger than the Plate*. Retrieved October 19, 2024, from https://www.vam.ac.uk/articles/about-the-exhibition-food-bigger-than-the-plate?srsltid=AfmBOoprXNk4hgRSatjRvmvPcxMGm5xDg8QU0-RsP2FwWR3FQoog2fQ4

Wilson, P. F., Stott, J., Warnett, J. M., Attridge, A., Smith, M. P., & Williams, M. A. (2017). Evaluation of touchable 3D-printed replicas in museums. *Curator, 60*, 445–465. https://doi.org/10.1111/cura.12244

Chapter 7
Building Peace in a World at Conflict: The Role of Educational Technologies

Roger Austin and William Hunter

7.1 Introduction

Previous research on the role of technology in peacebuilding in schools (Hunter & Austin, 2021) has provided a baseline regarding efforts across the globe to harness the power of the internet to connect teachers and classrooms in promoting local and global citizenship. This chapter builds on that work by examining more closely the role of virtual reality and Artificial Intelligence in schools and underlining how technology can occupy the liminal space between what was and what might be when projects use technology linked to powerful theories of contact.

The need for this work is even more pressing now than it was 4 years ago. In the last two decades, multiple international organizations have reported increases in violent conflict between nations as well as within nations. While the ongoing war between Ukraine and Russia and the escalating violence in the middle east are the foci of public media, the data indicate that these conflicts are part of an increase in violence and a decrease in peacefulness around the globe. In this chapter, we will review some of these reports and indicate ways in which educational technologies have been used to support efforts to reduce conflict and build peace, why it is being used and the impacts it is having.

R. Austin (✉)
Ulster University, Coleraine, Northern Ireland
e-mail: rsp.austin@ulster.ac.uk

W. Hunter
The University of Ontario Institute of Technology, Oshawa, ON, Canada
e-mail: Bill.Hunter@ontariotechu.ca

M. B. Ligorio (ed.), *Technology as Cultural Mediator*, Culture in Policy Making: The Symbolic Universes of Social Action,
https://doi.org/10.1007/978-3-031-97673-5_7

7.2 The Growth of Conflict

We will argue that blended and online learning afford educators new and better tools for addressing the growth of conflict in the world, but first we need to substantiate the claim that conflict is on the rise.

The Global Peace Index (GPI), a project of the Institute for Economics and Peace[1] (IEP), is a (free) annual report on global conflict based on an aggregate of 18 indicators of peace and conflict (e.g., peace and conflict, ongoing conflict, militarisation, homicide rates.[2]) Among the key findings in the GPI 2024 report:

- 2024 was the fifth consecutive year in which global peacefulness deteriorated;
- The year had the largest number of countries to deteriorate in a single year since the inception of the GPI in 2008;
- Conflicts in Gaza and Ukraine were the main contributors to the decline in peacefulness.
- Canada and the US recorded large falls in peacefulness due to increases in violent crime and perceptions of criminality;
- The Middle East and North Africa remained the least peaceful regions with four of the world's ten least peaceful countries;
- Eighty-six countries increased their relative military expenditure, compared to just 50 where it decreased (Global Peace Index, 2024).

The GPI report also has a full section devoted to the analysis of trends in its indicators over time. We do not have the space to discuss these analyses in detail but pages 27–33 of the report are filled with dramatic graphs that plot the changes over time in such indicators as safety and security, ongoing conflict, and militarisation. IEP provides a similar measure, the Positive Peace Index, The World Justice Project (WJP) promotes accountability, just law, open government, and accessible and impartial justice as the means to developing justice internationally. According to its website, WJP gathers data annually on indices of policies and practices pertaining to the rule of law in 142 countries. The data are published in highly interactive tables in the *WJP Rule of Law Inde*x which "… relies on more than 214,000 household and expert surveys to measure how the rule of law is experienced and perceived in practical, everyday situations by the general public around the world".[3]

The World Justice Project Rule of Law Index 2024 Insights lists the following key observations regarding the data reported in the index:

- For seven straight years, the rule of law has declined in more countries than it improved;
- Indicators for the Absence of Corruption, Regulatory Enforcement, and Criminal Justice factors improved in a majority of the countries surveyed from 2023 to 2024;

[1] https://www.economicsandpeace.org

[2] GPI research methodology is detailed in Appendix of the GPI report. The full list of indicators, their definitions, and the measures used to score them can be found in Appendix B of the GPI report.

[3] https://worldjusticeproject.org/rule-of-law-index/

- The five other factors of the Rule of Law (Constraints on Government Powers, Open Government, Fundamental Rights, Order and Security, and Civil Justice) declined in a majority of countries from 2023 to 2024;
- Where rule of law is stronger, people are often voting for change; where the rule of law is weaker, autocratic governments remain in power (World Justice Project, 2024).

WJP's data and observations regarding the rule of law seem to align with IEP's data and observations about conflict, violence, and peacefulness.

The United Nations is, of course, also a leading source of information on matters related to conflict within and between nations particularly with respect to its reports of its own activities in the service of peacemaking and peacekeeping. While UN documents provide further broad support for the arguments above, we want to call particular attention to comments in the secretary-general's annual report (United Nations, 2024a), regarding violence against children.

> In 2023, violence against children continued expanding at levels never seen before, due to the effects of multifaceted and overlapping crises worldwide. To prevent and protect children effectively from violence, the continuum of violence before, after and during conflict must be addressed comprehensively. To better understand prevention actions, we facilitated intergenerational dialogues between displaced, refugee and migrant children and policy-makers…. Of the 117.3 million people displaced globally, 40 per cent are estimated to be children. (United Nations, 2024a, p.48)

Such widespread disruptions in the lives of children create enormous challenges for the world's educators. However, there are also organizations working to improve the basic infrastructure and improve the delivery of schooling for children living in societies in conflict, for example, the Global Partnership for Education[4] (GPE) has focused heavily on maintaining access to education for children in conflict-affected countries. It has raised billions of dollars and developed frameworks to ensure continuous education, including rapid funding mechanisms for essential educational resources (e.g., temporary shelters and school supplies) in places that face acute needs due to ongoing conflict and displacement.

Programs like these which seek to provide resources that directly address the impact of conflict are clearly a critical element of how we need to respond to these international crises.

Developing a stable educational infrastructure, funding educational programs, and hiring teachers are necessary steps in improving the quality of schooling for children, however, they are not sufficient. An appropriate educational response should be grounded in a strong theoretical rationale and include attention to the curricula, to the use of technology, and to teacher professional development.

However, before we examine the positive benefits of the use of technology in peacebuilding, we need to take account of the views that it can also be a force for ill. Research by Firchow et al. (2017) is a salutary reminder about the role of technology in peacebuilding. Their work challenges the easy assumption that technology

[4] https://www.globalpartnership.org

deepens inclusivity and widens participation, two of the claims that suggest it is a force for good. They refer to the ways that mobile phone technology and social media can be used to promote and organise violence; a recent example of this was the spreading of fake information online that triggered anti-migrant demonstrations in the United Kingdom in the summer of 2024 (Horwood, 2024).

Firchow et al. (2017) summarise the situation as follows:

> It remains a challenge to identify mechanisms that support the peaceful use of technology, whether as a tool used by citizens and governments to support peace and security or a mechanism to enhance peace research and data collection in violence-affected communities (2017, pp. 6–7).

They remind us that "technology is only an 'amplifier of human intent' (Toyama, 2011, p. 75)." We want to make the case in this chapter that technology can have a powerful impact in particular settings, where there is little or no contact between groups. This is especially true in places where the concept of liminality can be used to create a framework for bringing people together. Firchow et al. (2017) define liminality as "a series of actions to achieve the reconstruction of identity in such a way that the new identity is meaningful for society." (p. 5). We will argue that our analysis of the ways that technology is being used in Northern Ireland and Israel to connect young people from separate schools is an exercise in liminality—assisting teachers and students to find new ways to think about themselves, their relations with one another, and their place in a future society.

7.3 Contexts of the Issue: Northern Ireland and Israel

In addition to addressing the need to find ways to reduce the risk of conflict globally, technology is also being used within countries where history, politics, religion, and ethnicity have resulted in children growing up leading separate but parallel lives. In the two cases we examine below, these differences have in one case led to continuing violence and in the other to a more settled political situation which might be described as post-conflict.

One striking feature of the school systems in both Israel and Northern Ireland is that nearly all the children from different faiths and cultural backgrounds are educated in separate schools. In Northern Ireland, for example, only 7% of the school population attend integrated schools where children of all faiths or none are educated together. The remaining 93% of pupils attend schools that are either Catholic in ethos or nominally Protestant. In Israel, nearly all children go to either Orthodox Jewish schools, secular Jewish schools or Arab-Israeli schools (Ganayem et al., 2021).

Given that the first integrated school opened in Northern Ireland in the mid 1980s, during a period of intense inter-communal violence euphemistically called "The Troubles" (1966–1998), recent research has examined why there has been relatively slow growth in this sector when the benefits to society might seem obvious. According to Austin et al. (2025), the British government, which was the de facto administration for Northern Ireland during the conflict, chose not to make this a priority partly because it was focused on security issues but also because it felt that support for integrated schools would alienate the churches, especially the Catholic Church. Since the Catholic Church represented a broad swath of the "nationalist" population that included people who were sympathetic to the idea of a United Ireland, the British government did not wish to pursue policies that might nudge moderate nationalist opinion towards support for the Irish Republican Army's violent campaign for a United Ireland.

After the Peace Agreement of 1998, when power was restored to locally elected political parties, neither of the two main parties, the Democratic Unionist Party or Sinn Fein, favoured integrated education. Analysts have suggested that the two parties believed that separate schools were more likely to shore up their respective voter base. However, these two parties and the representatives of the other political parties recognised that stability in Northern Ireland required steps to strengthen community cohesion. The result was all-party support for Shared Education, based on the principle of schools working together on a cross-community basis. The Shared Education Act of 2016 formalised this and provided both a legal basis and ongoing financial support to enable this policy to reach as many schools as possible (Austin et al., 2021). By 2024, some two thirds of all schools were working together with plans for the remaining schools to be included between 2024 and 2028 (McCormick et al., 2024).

Previous research has noted that the initial focus on pupils meeting face to face rather than online has retained considerable traction (Austin et al., 2021) but from 2017, courses were provided on how blended learning might enrich face to face work. Schools already had the ICT infrastructure to make this a realistic approach and evaluation of work teachers carried out showed an extensive range of benefits, including not only better use of ICT by teachers and pupils but positive outcomes in terms of pupil attitudes to their peers (Austin & Turner, 2020). In summary, the use of technology to help build better cross-community relationships between pupils, teachers and communities was one element in a broader policy to capitalise on the peacebuilding achievements of the Good Friday Agreement of 1998 which had brought an end to the conflict in Northern Ireland.

In the same way that conflict in Northern Ireland led to the use of technology to create links between schools, a similar process has been at work in Israel. Research by Shonfeld and Gibson (2018) provides an extensive overview of a wide range of educational technology projects that involve Israeli educators both within Israel and with partners in other countries. In almost all of the case studies the underlying rationale is the promotion of collaborative learning through technology to encourage intercultural learning.

Ganayem et al. (2021) have provided a very clear analysis of the tensions in Israeli society around faith, identity, land, language and economic opportunity and how this is reflected in the schooling system which essentially means that the vast majority of children attend schools that are largely mono-cultural. Orthodox or religious Jewish children attend their own schools, while the same is true for "secular"

Jewish children who have their own schools as do Arab-Israeli children. While the curriculum is broadly the same, the language of instruction is either Hebrew or Arabic. As Ganayem et al. (2021) summarise:

> For the most part, then, students grow and learn in schools and neighbourhoods where they have no interaction with people from other cultures and where they do not get unbiased knowledge about them. They are massively exposed to the stigmas and cultural stereotypes commonly present in the media (p. 62).

Furthermore, while it is compulsory for Arab-Israeli children to learn Hebrew in school, it is not a requirement for Jewish children to learn Arabic; this further restricts opportunities for cross-community communication and dialogue. In spite of attempts by the Israeli Ministry of Education to encourage contacts among the three main types of school, ongoing distrust between them has severely limited face to face contact. However, the Technology, Education and Cultural (TEC) diversity programme, based in the Mofet Institute in Tel Aviv since 2005 has steadily developed online links between the three main sectors as the principal channel for collaborative work both in teacher education and in schools. The focus of the work is on the acquisition of digital competence and intercultural communication, and an avoidance of "political" content, so that trust can be gradually built around the process of learning together. The increasingly sophisticated use of digital assets, such as avatars and gaming have been developed by the TEC not only because of their vocational value but because of their potential to reduce prejudice by encouraging empathy.

In summary, when we ask why technology can be used to promote peace-building, we can discern two key factors. At a global level, the continued scale of violence and the threat to the environment demand that we find ways to promote the sort of global citizenship which will help young people to use technology not only to communicate to get to know each other better but also to start to explore ways they can address the United Nations' Sustainable Development Goals. Although the penetration of the Internet is still uneven across the globe, it still represents one of the most cost-effective ways to enable large sections of the population to work together to find solutions to collective problems.

Secondly, in Israel and Northern Ireland, the use of technology in schools is an important part of the very slow process of building and rebuilding trust between young people whose separate lives place them at risk of getting caught up in a cycle where ignorance of the other breeds suspicion and prejudice.

7.4 An Educational Response

Our research interests have focused thus far on discussing WHY technology can play a part in creating cross-community partnerships. In this section we analyse HOW the potential of technology is being implemented in school-based projects. While such partnerships might well be part of local citizenship education, we explore the ways in which schools use educational technologies to manage learning in collaborative partnerships based on common curriculum goals. However, we want to emphasise that in this process, the technologies should not take the forefront; rather, they should be built on an underlying theoretical rationale that lays out principles for developing effective programs for working to counteract the divisive and distrustful environments in which conflicts take place.

7.4.1 A Theoretical Rationale

A central part of our argument is that there is a long-standing body of empirical research that has explored a rather simple assertion about how people's ideas about "the other" change. That assertion is called the contact hypothesis, arguably one of the most influential bodies of work in social psychology. Gordon Allport (1954) defined the contact hypothesis which posits that intergroup contact is more likely to be successful if that contact is:

- between people who have equal status
- between groups rather than individuals
- is long-term rather than short term, and
- has institutional support (Pettigrew, 1998; Pettigrew & Tropp, 2006).

Research on exactly how this works has been ongoing for seven decades and has been the focus of systematic reviews and meta-analyses (e.g., Paluck et al., 2019; Zhou et al., 2019). Some of that research has pointed to the ways in which successful contact can include online as well as face to face contact (Hasler & Amichai-Hamburger, 2013). We have explored the implications of the contact hypothesis for blended and online learning in contexts of building community cohesion (Austin & Hunter, 2013) and fostering intercultural education (Hunter & Austin, 2021).

This is particularly important because online contact can increase the frequency of contact, seen as vital in the growth of trust (Kuh, 2003) and minimise some of the challenges of face-to-face contact such as the distance between the participants, the cost of travel, and the existence of a history of conflict.

Research in Northern Ireland and in Israel has made explicit use of the contact hypothesis to help shape the design of programmes which bring young people together in schools. Among these, one of the largest was the Dissolving Boundaries Programme which linked children from the ages of 9 to 18 in Northern Ireland and the Republic of Ireland between 1999 and 2014 and involved over 5000 children, 500 schools, and 2500 teachers (Austin & Hunter, 2013). Similar work has been carried out in Israel by the Technology, Education, and Cultural diversity programme (Ganayem et al., 2021). Current work in Northern Ireland through the Shared Education programme which started in 2014 and is designed to offer every school the chance to develop collaborative cross-community partnerships has also been influenced by the contact hypothesis. In one example reported by McCormick et al. (2024) where children from two primary schools in the same town used Lego bricks to build their town of the future, the key ideas of the contact hypothesis (equal status, group based, etc.) were an explicit part of the project design which involved both online and face-to-face contact.

7.4.2 Curriculum

If we take the view that peacebuilding requires a combination of knowledge, skills and values, it follows that we would expect to find this combination in the curriculum of the schools taking part in education for peacebuilding. In some countries this is explicit. As we noted in the previous section, the vast majority of children in Northern Ireland, some 93%, attend schools that are either predominantly Catholic in ethos or nominally Protestant. To mitigate the effects of children growing up leading separate but parallel lives, Shared Education programme is anchored in the curriculum and promotes cross-community links between schools. To support this policy, the Curriculum Council for Examinations and Assessment (CCEA), the government agency responsible for the design of the curriculum, offers advice to teachers on how to embed shared education work in their everyday practice.

> The development of effective collaborative skills and practice is a core component of Shared Education. However, Shared Education should go further than a demonstration of collaboration in the classroom. The key difference is the requirement to engage in collaborative activities between learners from different religious and socio-economic backgrounds (CCEA, 2024a, p. 2).

In practice, when teachers in a shared education partnership plan work together, almost any part of the curriculum can be the focus for collaborative work. As Pollack (2011) noted about the Dissolving Boundaries Programme which linked schools in Northern Ireland with schools across the border in the Republic of Ireland, topics for joint study

> … range from land and sea creatures of China to the Irish famine; from healthy eating to learning together through poetry; from fairy tales and monsters to learning numeracy through card making; from observing and recording the weather to collaborative storytelling; from recycling and the environment to exploring similarities and differences (Pollack, 2011, p. 1).

In all these cases, the work carried out with a partner school was not an addition to the curriculum but simply an enrichment of what was already expected. Across all the projects the need to work in mixed teams developed pupils' communication and presentation skills and their use of technology. In short, even when the curriculum does not include a subject area like citizenship, it is the *process* of researching, summarising and working towards an end product like a PowerPoint presentation or google slides that helps children start to form relationships (Austin & Hunter, 2013).

In general, the use of Information and Communication Technologies (ICT) is either embedded in the curriculum or in some distinctive space. In Northern Ireland, for example, all schools are required to use ICT for pupils aged 5–14 and to show examples of this. One of the required areas is called "Exchange." Guidance from CCEA states that

> Exchange relates to communicating with others online to share and develop ideas. It can include sending and receiving emails, videoconferencing, contributing to online discussions or collaborating with digital tools (CCEA, 2024b, p. 3).

In effect, the way that ICT is expected to be used means that when teachers take part in collaborative partnerships with other schools, in Northern Ireland or anywhere else, they are also meeting the ICT requirements of the curriculum. This is an important part of the alignment between the desire to promote peace and the need for curriculum and technology to work closely together.

7.4.3 Technology

For technology to contribute positively to school programmes, it is critical that teachers have access to appropriate hardware, software that serves their needs, and reliable Internet connectivity to ensure that links with other schools can be developed confidently. The specific context in which work like this takes place also plays a part in how digital tools are used. In Israel, for example, where the Technology, Education and Cultural diversity programme (TEC) has been working for over 30 years to forge links between schools within the state of Israel, the design of the partnerships takes account of the visible differences between the children by insuring that interactions among Orthodox Jewish pupils, Secular Jewish children and Arab-Israeli children generally reduce tensions by starting with text interactions before progressing to audio and then video or face to face contact.

Age-appropriate uses of technology in the Dissolving Boundaries programme were evident when teachers reported greater use of real-time videoconferencing with children at primary school than with learners in secondary schools. One of the teachers commented on the motivational impact of videoconferencing for younger pupils as follows:

> …from the word go they realised that they could see themselves and others on video and see them responding on screen… that in itself was exciting and they wanted to be involved in that (Austin & Hunter, 2013, p. 35).

Videoconferencing worked well as a tool for communication not only because it didn't rely on extended written communication but because primary school teachers normally had a single class for full days for the whole of the school year and could therefore arrange real-time link ups more easily than teachers in secondary schools. Developments in the design of real-time communication platforms like the breakout rooms in Google or Microsoft Teams are making synchronous work in small groups much easier to set up and simultaneous editing of documents (e.g., Microsoft 365 or Google Docs) clearly provide new ways that teachers can make use of real-time learning activities. In the secondary school sector, with the timetable normally split into discreet subject areas with different teachers, it is often more manageable for links between classrooms to make greater use of asynchronous learning. The facility for teachers to be able to set up virtual classrooms on a shared platform like Padlet, Google Classroom or Microsoft Office, with folders for relevant resources, and for small groups to share ideas on their part of the project, is a key part of making collaborative learning possible. In short, the "communicative" dimension of technology continues to play a critical part in bringing disparate groups together. However, since technology is evolving rapidly we need to explore other roles new technologies play in peacebuilding.

Virtual reality (VR) technologies (sometimes called immersive or augmentative technologies) provide unique opportunities for engaging learners through participation in digital simulations of learning environments. Gossett (2023) summarised VR uses in many areas of education, including virtual field trips, art education, and virtual labs. In a market analysis that showed growing public acceptance of VR technologies, Navaratnam-Blair et al. (2022) regard the growing acceptance of VR in gaming and entertainment as likely to increase acceptance even further and that "VR—by broadening our horizons, exposing us to new cultures, and connecting us more directly to other people—has the potential to reintroduce some of that lost empathy back into society" (Navaratnam-Blair et al., 2022, p. 22).

The United Nations has also explored VR in peacebuilding and reported that its Verification Mission in Columbia has found that

> VR has a similar effect in terms of memory recall as other traditional multimedia interventions, in comparison to pure text-based communication products. However, much more than two-dimensional documentaries, virtual reality gives the opportunity to virtually walk through each other's journeys, helping build empathy with others (United Nations, 2024b, Measuring Impact).

We have also seen that VR can help participants develop a sense of empathy in Northern Ireland, using simulations of both past and current events. For example, Taggart et al. (2021) used VR with a group of teacher-trainees to help them get a fuller understanding of a controversial event called "Bloody Sunday" which took place in 1972 in the city of Derry/Londonderry when British soldiers, claiming that they had come under fire, shot a number of unarmed civilians. The students came from both Catholic and Protestant backgrounds and were given VR headsets to give them an immersive experience of how the event unfolded from a number of perspectives. The location of this event, in an area that is still identified as being more Republican/Nationalist/Catholic than Protestant, prompted many of the trainee student teachers to comment that they would be uncomfortable bringing pupils in uniform to visit the site in person, especially if they were from a Protestant background and wearing their school uniform. One local student, who had attended a Catholic school in the city expressed concerns about visiting the area.

> The people who live in this area would be seen as strongly republican [sic]. I would be worried about the students' safety and also the strong possibility of people shouting sectarian abuse at them which even I have heard people do within these areas (Taggart et al., 2021, p. 229).

The research showed that some places in Northern Ireland are still strongly associated with one side of the community or the other and outsiders are sometimes made to feel unwelcome. VR can offer a safe way in to explore and start to understand moments in the past that are deeply divisive and in places where ownership by one side of the community is still problematic.

In a similar way, research around the use of Virtual Reality reported by Hoter (2020) brought together trainee student teachers from both Israeli and Arab backgrounds to work collaboratively online in a virtual world. Unlike the previous examples in this chapter where the Internet was used to bring young people together from their own environment, "in virtual worlds we are all together in the same setting and therefore can collaborate in the same space. This type of environment is termed an immersive environment" (Hoter, 2020, p. 66). Hoter makes it clear that while the technology is important, the design of the task that the students are given is critical.

> ...from the outset students collaborate on tasks in small multicultural groups of six; throughout the semester they only meet their group members through the virtual world and not face to face. Students get to know one another gradually, through activities designed for building rapport, empathy and understanding, as well as trust (p. 70).

Evaluation of this work with the students showed that the gradual process of working together towards a common goal with others that were different, started to make some of the class reassess their prior negative views of the other students. One of the students put it like this:

> I realized that as we progressed individually in the course and accumulated joint experiences, the stigma I had about people who are different from me and had no past connection to them was wrong. I realized that it is not right to look only at these external elements, and we need to see what a person has inside. Often those who seem so different from me culturally are the people who have most in common with me (Hoter, 2020, p. 73).

In addition to the use of VR, the most recent and potentially far-reaching instance of new technology is Artificial Intelligence (AI). Literature on the applications of generative AI in education has been emerging since the introduction of ChatGPT in late 2022. Much of that work has focused on ethical concerns and on the attitudes of school leaders, teachers and learners regarding the use of AI, but there is also research that proposes instructional uses of AI as well as some reports of applications in school settings, including some attention to the possibilities of using AI in the context of education for peace.

In a report for the Alliance for Peacebuilding, Zuroski et al. (2023) make the case that "the peacebuilding field needs to raise awareness and educate how AI technology can positively and negatively impact global peace and security..." (p. 1). Although the report notes that education is an area of application for AI, it does not address the ways in which that might occur.

Following a careful situational analysis and interviews with peace and conflict experts, Mäki (2020) proposed three potential areas for the use of AI in support of peacebuilding:

- AI-assisted conflict analysis could produce larger, more complete, open access datasets that might serve to provide bases for developing agreements between parties;
- AI-supported early warning systems might be developed that could provide up-to-date identification of potential outbreaks of conflict based on locally relevant predictors;
- AI-based studies of human communication during flow of peace negotiations could help to build respect negotiating parties and might reinforce the commitment participants have to finding a positive outcome.

Some specific examples of research that fits nicely with Maki's analysis were described in a literature review focused on "measuring the impact of artificial intelligence (AI) on the peace and security agenda" (Giovanardi, 2024, p. 6, e-41-1). That analysis also suggests other possibilities like using AI to support and extend the analyses of the Global Peace Index (2024) and the Positive Peace Report (2024) done by the Institute for Economics and Peace.

AI technologies offer a wealth of opportunities and possibilities for having impact on programs designed to have school-age learners engaged in cross-community cooperative learning activities intended to reduce prejudice and conflict, but research to demonstrate how (and how well) such programs might work is not yet available. Nevertheless, we thought it worthwhile to consider what some specific possibilities for using AI in this way might be. It struck us that a useful source for speculating on these possibilities would be an AI programme, so we asked Microsoft CoPilot to address the question. Its response is reported verbatim in the appendix.

CoPilot's response was more helpful than we expected it might be. For example, for each of its suggested activities, CoPilot provided a link to a program that could be used to support the intended teacher in carrying out the activity. It suggested that MonkeyLearn[5] might be used to look for any consistent themes or sentiments in a body of text like blog posts or other social media. Such an activity would not be useful for elementary age children, but high school teachers might find the tool useful in social science or communication courses. Choosing a set of texts generated by a different group would have the potential to help students see alternative ways of thinking about the issues discussed and possibly give them a better basis for understanding others' perspectives. CoPilot's suggestion of Peacemaker,[6] which engages players as decision makers in a peace process centered on the Middle East conflict, also seems appropriate only for older students, possibly in courses in history or contemporary social issues. Since we were unfamiliar with the game, we asked CoPilot if there had been research on this game. In its reply, it cited two academic research sources, Nicolaidou and Kampf (2024), Gonzalez and Czlonka (2010), and one software review published on a blog that serves two university courses. The research does suggest that the game is an effective way to engage learners in

[5] https://help.monkeylearn.com/en/

[6] http://peacemakergame.com

simulated discussion and decision making, but it was not clear to us the extent to which the game actually uses AI since it was developed in 2005. Time and space considerations prevent us from a fuller discussion of CoPilot's suggestions, but interested readers will find the information needed to pursue the topic further in the appendix.

However, this initial indication of AI's potential, developed by an AI tool, suggests that there is certainly room for constructive and instructive exploration of the potential this technology may have for peacebuilding education. We would add that, beyond Co-Piolot's suggestions, there is ample room in AI environments for teachers and learners to construct their own AI explorations—i.e., users can direct most AI software to respond from any particular perspective (e.g., "in answering, include positions that would reflect the cultural perspectives of indigenous North American and New Zealand peoples.")

In short, technology offers two vital elements that are highly pertinent to peacebuilding; the first is its capacity to enable communication both synchronously and asynchronously at low cost and with tools that enable young people to genuinely collaborate on common problems. The second is in the way that tools like VR make it possible for participants to get a richer and deeper understanding of others; the ability to widen perspectives is a critical part in the growth of empathy, a core element in understanding differences. AI may offer a third element as it provides not only options to improve communication quality and data analysis, but also new means of understanding others' points of view.

7.4.4 Accessibility

In any analysis about what can be done with technology, issues around accessibility are vital if we contend that all children should be included in work of this sort. Teachers need to have sufficient digital devices and reliable Internet connectivity to feel confident that inter-school projects can run smoothly in very busy classrooms. According to a recent study in Northern Ireland (Passey, 2024), the pupil-computer ratio across all schools in Northern Ireland is 1:5 with many schools supplementing this state-funded core provision. All schools are part of a managed service which provides a core ICT service of hardware, software and Internet connectivity. In other words, decisions are taken centrally rather than at school level to try to ensure that every child has access to a minimum level of connectivity. The 1000 schools in Northern Ireland all have the same software such as Google Classroom and Office 365 and hardware that is refreshed every 5 years. If hardware breaks down, the service agreement means that it has to be fixed quickly to allow teachers to focus on the pedagogy of using ICT rather than sorting out technical problems. We can see in this further evidence of an alignment between the educational goals of the curriculum and the provision of technology to deliver the goals in the classroom.

Northern Ireland's approach is one example of ways to increase affordable accessibility; the Internet Society (2017) provided a broad analysis of inequities in access to educational technologies globally and suggested some priorities and means of addressing the issue. In summarizing their analyses, they say that achieving the affordances of technology of education requires

> …first and foremost, affordable access to the Internet. A legal and regulatory framework that encourages investment in connectivity and services, lowers costs and fosters creativity is critical to enabling access and unlocking the Internet's value for education (Internet Society, 2017, Summary).

7.4.5 Professional Development of Teachers

Research on the use of technology to build community cohesion frequently underlines the importance of the professional development of teachers (Austin et al., 2021). Indeed, Hunter and Austin (2021) in their summary of success factors in this kind of work argue that teacher professional development is critical. In both Northern Ireland and Israel, teachers from partner schools chose to take part in 2-day face to face intensive professional development where they learned not only about what software they could use together but had time to create a plan for joint work which involved both online and face to face contact. Plans included which children from each school would work together in groups, how "ice-breaking" activities would be used to help the pupils get to know each other, what the learning outcomes would be, and how each stage of the learning would be managed. The process of learning about the technology, thinking about how to make use of the contact hypothesis and planning together was seen as a very important part in the development of a professional partnership between the teachers (Austin & Turner, 2020).

Recent research on how teachers in Israel and Northern Ireland are finding ways to embed technology in their peacebuilding schoolwork, throws light on three key factors (McCormick et al., 2024). First, the data showed that teachers in both settings were clearly committed to the importance of building bridges between children in their respective communities. Over 80% of those who replied stressed their personal commitment for this type of work, even though they stated that the level of support from politicians or local officials was less than 50% (p. 358). Second, in Israel 87% of the teachers viewed the professional development they experienced as critical to the success of their collaboration. Seventy-five percent of teachers in Northern Ireland shared that view. The third finding, on whether the provision of hardware, software and Internet connectivity was good enough to enable the project to run smoothly, revealed differences between Israel and Northern Ireland—88% of teachers in Israel indicated that provision; only 66% of teachers in Northern Ireland shared that view. These figures can be explained partly by the fact that in Israel, technology is deemed the number one priority in this type of work whereas in Northern Ireland, much greater emphasis has been placed on face-to-face contact.

Teacher professional learning is also a core part of the European Union's ETwinning programme, one of the largest online learning projects in the world (Austin & Hunter, 2013) linking more than 60,000 teachers, 4,500,000 students and 200,000 schools in 2021 (Galvin et al., 2021). The focus of the professional development is not just how to use technology to link with partner schools within the EU but to do this within a policy framework that underlines creativity, communication skills and an inclusive approach to education. In effect, the educational work is seen as part of making young people in the EU have essential skills in a knowledge-based society which, as a result of recent migration trends, is becoming much more diverse. For the professional development of teachers, it means much more than simply learning about technology; rather e-Twinning projects provide:

> An invaluable tool for teachers to gain management competencies such as endurance, flexibility, time management and evaluation skills. They learn how to integrate new media and ideas into their enquiry-based learning lessons (Heindl, 2018, p. 138).

Teachers in the programme have commented on how eTwinning professional development helped them develop cross-curricular and transversal skills such as teamwork, creativity, problem solving and decision-making (Galvin et al., 2021). In other words, while the starting point for technology-enabled links between schools might be about building intercultural understanding, ETwinning has become the vehicle for "pedagogical, technological and organisational characteristics that favour innovation" (Bocconi et al., 2012, p. 8).

Other international projects which use online or blended links also place a high premium on teacher professional development, some of it delivered online. Different projects have emerged with distinctive characteristics. For example, the Connecting Classrooms through Global Learning (CCGL), a United Kingdom initiative, links schools in the UK with schools in developing countries (Hunter & Austin, 2021, p. 135). One of the teachers involved described how the link between pupils in his school in Northern Ireland with a school in Nepal made his children "see themselves as part of a bigger picture." In this case, reciprocal visits between staff from the two schools helped to establish a relationship of equality where learning how to use technology was a shared and common goal with all staff learning from each other (Hunter & Austin, 2021, p. 136). To help educators engage in virtual projects with their students, the International Education and Resource Network project (iEARN) offers two courses (available online or face-to-face) about global project-based learning.

7.5 Conclusion

From their origins in correspondence schooling more than a century ago (Azzioui, 2024) to the COVID-19 and post-COVID-19 surge in participation rates internationally (Wood, 2022; Cheung et al., 2023), online learning has grown to be a powerful influence on teaching and learning.

However, it is likely clear to most readers that technology is not a panacea. In the context of technology's role in peacebuilding education, we would note the following limitations:

- **Technology may aggravate conflicts**. The use of social media to spreading misinformation, disinformation and hate speech to incite violence and amplify social divisions has been reported in diverse locations around the world (Esberg & Mikulaschek, 2021);
- **The digital divide can lead to unequal benefits** from technological interventions which may intensify existing inequalities and tensions (e.g., Vassilakopoulou & Hustad, 2023);
- **Technologies often have unintended outcomes** as Baltay (2020) has noted with respect to automobiles and airplanes;
- **Technology may exacerbate issues of sustainability and scalability.** Many technological initiatives in peacebuilding are small-scale and pilot projects. Scaling these initiatives to have a broader impact requires significant resources, coordination, and long-term commitment (e.g., Eain et al., 2019).

It is important, therefore that we think about technology in the context of such educational developments as active learning, social constructivist and constructionist theories of learning, and the contact hypothesis. That is, it matters *how* we use technology in peacebuilding education and that we attend to the kinds of interactions that the technologies support. The contact hypothesis, in particular, has provided us with solidly grounded guidance for the conditions under which our uses of technology may be structured to connect young people in ways that that encourage them to work and learn together.

Appendix: Microsoft CoPilot Response to Question About Uses of AI in Peacebuilding in Education

On December 10, 2024, we asked the Microsoft AI CoPilot for specific suggestions about how AI could be used to assist teachers help children learn about peacebuilding and ways to reduce conflict in their own communities. The following is CoPilot's verbatim response (with some formatting changes for readability).

Reducing Conflict in Communities

AI-Powered Sentiment Analysis Project

- **Activity**: Students can use AI tools to analyze social media posts or local news articles to identify and understand community sentiments. This can help them recognize areas of tension and discuss ways to address these issues constructively.

- **Example Tool**: Tools like MonkeyLearn or IBM Watson can be used for sentiment analysis.[7]

Conflict Mapping with AI

- **Activity**: Students can create conflict maps using AI to visualize areas of conflict within their community. They can then brainstorm and propose solutions to mitigate these conflicts.
- **Example Tool**: Platforms like Ushahidi allow users to crowdsource and map conflict data.[8]

Learning About Global Conflict Resolution

Peacebuilding Games

- **Activity**: Engage students with AI-driven educational games that simulate global conflict scenarios. These games can teach negotiation, empathy, and conflict resolution skills.
- **Example Game**: "PeaceMaker" is a game where players take on the role of a leader in the Israeli-Palestinian conflict, making decisions to achieve peace.[9]

Virtual Reality (VR) Experiences

- **Activity**: Use VR to immerse students in conflict zones around the world, helping them understand the complexities of global conflicts and the importance of peacebuilding.
- **Example Tool**: VR experiences like "The Enemy" allow students to hear stories from both sides of a conflict.[10]

---

[7] Real-time conflict monitoring using artificial intelligence for peace …

[8] Designing AI for Conflict Prevention & Peacebuilding

[9] AI for Peace: Opportunities and Challenges for Conflict Resolution and …

[10] The Role of AI in Conflict Resolution Strategies and Practices

AI-Driven Role-Playing Simulations

- **Activity**: AI can facilitate role-playing simulations where students act as diplomats or peacekeepers in international conflicts. AI can provide real-time feedback and adapt scenarios based on student decisions.
- **Example Tool**: Platforms like Mursion offer AI-driven simulations for educational purposes.[11]

These activities not only make learning about conflict resolution engaging but also equip students with practical skills to address conflicts in their communities and understand global peacebuilding efforts.

Which of these activities do you think would be most effective for your students?

References

Allport, G. W. (1954). *The nature of prejudice*. Perseus Books/Addison-Wesley.

Austin, R., & Hunter, B. (2013). *Online learning and community cohesion: Linking schools*. Routledge. https://www.amazon.co.uk/s?k=hunter+austin+online+learning+community&ref=nb_sb_noss

Austin, R., & Turner, R. (2020). The role of blended learning for community cohesion; Lessons from Northern Ireland. *Technology, Pedagogy and Education, 29*(4), 361–376.

Austin, R., Roulston, S., Skinner, B., & Taggart, S. (2021). *Repurposing education through blended learning (REBEL): A case study of the impact and legacy of COVID-19 on schools in Northern Ireland.* https://pure.ulster.ac.uk/ws/portalfiles/portal/100679752/Rebel_Case_Study_20_Aug_21.pdf

Austin, R., Galway, G., & Hunter, W. (2025). The end of denominational schooling in Newfoundland and Labrador: Lessons for Northern Ireland? Global Comparative Education. https://www.worldcces.org/_files/ugd/a95ba5_d00c91411fc5411a8015f767f97d24c2.pdf?index=true

Azzioui, A. (2024). Innovations in education: Theoretical insights into online collaborative learning. *Journal of Studies in Language, Culture and Society (JSLCS), 7*(2), 68–84.

Baltay, C. (2020, January 9). Friend or foe? The role of modern technology in conflict and peace. *Organization for World Peace*. https://theowp.org

Bocconi, S., Kampylis, P. G., & Punie, Y. (2012). *Innovating learning: Key elements for developing creative classrooms in Europe*. Publications Office of the European Union.

CCEA. (2024a). *Shared education and the Northern Ireland curriculum*. https://ccea.org.uk/downloads/docs/ccea-asset/Curriculum/Shared%20Education%20and%20the%20Northern%20Ireland%20Curriculum%3A%20Post-Primary.pdf

CCEA. (2024b). *Using ICT in the curriculum*. https://ccea.org.uk/key-stages-1-2/curriculum/using-ict#section-2281

Cheung, S., Wang, F. L., & Kwok, L. F. (2023). Online learning and blended learning: New practices derived from the pandemic-driven disruption. *Journal of Computing in Higher Education, 35*, 1–5. https://doi.org/10.1007/s12528-023-09350-9

Eain, L., Yoni, N., & Adhikari, M. (2019, July 13). *Rethinking peace and transition processes in a changing conflict landscape*. PeaceRep (University of Edinburgh).

[11] Artificial Intelligence in International Negotiations and Conflict …

Esberg, J., & Mikulaschek, C. (2021). Digital technologies, peace and security: Challenges and opportunities for United Nations peace operations. *United Nations Peacekeeping, 7*. https://peacekeeping.un.org

Firchow, O., Martin-Shields, M., Omer, A., & MacGinty, R. (2017). PeaceTech: The liminal spaces of digital technology in peacebuilding. *International Studies Perspectives, 18*, 4–42. https://bpb-us-e1.wpmucdn.com/blogs.gwu.edu/dist/8/846/files/2017/11/ekw007-1y3cfw7.pdf

Galvin, C., Austin, R., Revyakina, E., & McMorrough, A. (2021). Building cultural awareness and understanding in Europe's schools: Insights from the European Commission's eTwinning programme. In W. Hunter & R. Austin (Eds.), *Blended and online learning for global citizenship* (pp. 92–121). Routledge.

Ganayem, A., Hoter, E., & Shonfeld, M. (2021). Lessons learned from 15 years of multicultural online collaborative learning in Israel. In W. Hunter & R. Austin (Eds.), *Blended and online learning for global citizenship* (pp. 59–91). Routledge.

Giovanardi, M. (2024). AI for peace: Mitigating the risks and enhancing opportunities. *Data & Policy, 6*, e41. https://doi.org/10.1017/S2632324924000373

Global Peace Index. (2024). *Institute for economics and peace*. https://www.economicsandpeace.org/wp-content/uploads/2024/06/GPI-2024-web.pdf

Gonzalez, C., & Czlonka, L. (2010). Games for peace: Empirical investigations with PeaceMaker. In *Serious game design and development: Technologies for training and learning* (pp. 134–149). IGI Global. https://citeseerx.ist.psu.edu/document?repid=rep1&type=pdf&doi=00bf593aa308fa4c7c4645f8d285a096fdf5762b

Gossett, S. (2023). Virtual reality in education: Benefits, uses and examples. *Built In*. https://builtin.com/articles/virtual-reality-in-education

Hasler, B. S., & Amichai-Hamburger, Y. (2013). Online intergroup contact. In Y. Amichai-Hamburger (Ed.), *The social net: Understanding our online behavior* (pp. 220–252). Oxford University Press.

Heindl, M. (2018). Determining factors in the European classroom with eTwinning when inquiry-based learning. *International Journal of Teaching and Case Studies, 9*(2), 131–141.

Horwood, C. (2024). *Fake news-driven anti-migrant riots and protests in the UK*. Mixed Migration Centre. https://mixedmigration.org/fake-news-populist-violence-uk-anti-migrant-riots/

Hoter, E. (2020). Collaboration in the virtual world. *Journal of Community Guidance & Research, 37*(3), 63–76.

Hunter, W. J., & Austin, R. (2021). *Blended and online learning for global citizenship: New technologies and opportunities for intercultural education*. Routledge.

Internet Society. (2017). *Internet access and education. Summary*. https://www.internetsociety.org/resources/doc/2017/Internet-access-and-education/

Kuh, G. D. (2003). What we're learning about student engagement from NSSE: Benchmarks for effective educational practices. *Change: The Magazine of Higher Learning, 35*(2), 24–32.

Mäki, N. (2020). *Between peace and technology: A case study on opportunities and responsible design of artificial intelligence in peace technology*. https://www.theseus.fi

McCormick, B., Austin, R., Turner, R. N., Hoter, E., & Shonfeld, M. (2024). Blended learning and the contact hypothesis: Insights from Israel and Northern Ireland. *Journal of Technology and Teacher Education, 32*(3), 347–382. https://www.learntechlib.org

Navaratnam-Blair, F., Wagstaff, K., Miller, G., Cumberbatch, M., & Rethore, C. (2022). *Beyond reality is the long-awaited VR revolution finally on the horizon*. National Research Group.

Nicolaidou, I., & Kampf, R. (2024). Serious games, knowledge acquisition, and conflict resolution: The case of PeaceMaker as a peace education tool. *Social Science Computer Review, 43*. https://ktisis.cut.ac.cy/bitstream/20.500.14279/33213/1/nicolaidou-kampf-2024-serious-games-knowledge-acquisition-and-conflict-resolution-the-case-of-peacemaker-as-a-peace.pdf

Paluck, E. L., Green, S. A., & Green, D. P. (2019). The contact hypothesis re-evaluated. *Behavioural Public Policy, 3*(2), 129–158. https://doi.org/10.1017/bpp.2018.25

Passey, D. (2024). Sustaining relevant digital inclusive education for young people (5–18 years of age): *Northern Ireland Case Study. IFIP*.

Pettigrew, T. (1998). Intergroup contact theory. *Annual Review of Psychology, 49*, 65–85.

Pettigrew, T. F., & Tropp, L. R. (2006). A meta-analytic test of intergroup contact theory. *Journal of Personality and Social Psychology, 90*, 751–783.

Pollack, A. (2011). *Bringing schools together in Ireland through ICT*. https://sluggerotoole.com/2011/06/30/bringing-schools-together-in-ireland-through-ict/

Positive Peace Report. (2024). *Institute for Economics and Peace*. https://www.visionofhumanity.org/wp-content/uploads/2024/04/PPR-2024-web.pdf

Shonfeld, M., & Gibson, D. (Eds.). (2018). *Collaborative learning in a global world*. Information Age Publishing.

Taggart, S., Roulston, S., & McAuley, C. (2021). From virtual peace with virtual reality: Exploring the contested narratives of spaces and places in Northern Ireland. *Glencree Journal, 1, 221–237.* https://www.glencree.ie/wp-content/uploads/2021/04/83639-essay-18-Sammy-Taggart-Stephen-Roulston-Clare-McAuley-1.pdf

Toyama, K. (2011). Technology as amplifier in international development. In *Proceedings of the 2011 ACM iConference* (pp. 75–82). https://www.kentarotoyama.org/papers/Toyama%202011%20iConference%20-%20Technology%20as%20Amplifier.pdf

United Nations. (2024a). *Resolve: Report of the secretary-general on the work of the organization, 2024*. https://www.un.org/sites/un2.un.org/files/sg_annual_report_2024_en.pdf

United Nations. (2024b). *Shifting mindsets: Integrating virtual reality in conflict mediation and peacebuilding*. https://dppa.un.org/en/shifting-mindsets-integrating-virtual-reality-conflict-mediation-and-peacebuilding

Vassilakopoulou, P., & Hustad, E. (2023). Bridging digital divides: A literature review and research agenda for information systems research. *Information Systems Frontiers, 25*, 955–969. https://doi.org/10.1007/s10796-020-10096-3

Wood, J. (2022, January). *These 3 charts show the global growth in online learning*. World Economic Forum.

World Justice Project (WJP). (2024). *Rule of Law Index 2024 insights*. https://worldjusticeproject.org/rule-of-law-index/downloads/WJPInsights2024.pdf

Zhou, S., Page-Gould, E., Aron, A., Moyer, A., & Hewstone, M. (2019). The extended contact hypothesis: A meta-analysis on 20 years of research. *Personality and Social Psychology Review, 23*(2), 132–160. https://doi.org/10.1177/1088868318762647

Zuroski, N., Corrado, M., & Hume, L. (2023). *Designing AI for conflict prevention & peacebuilding*. Alliance for Peacebuilding. Designing+AI+for+Conflict+Prevention+&+Peacebuilding.pdf (squarespace.com)

Chapter 8
Playful Cultural Technology

Henrik Hautop Lund

8.1 Introduction

Play is a free, voluntary activity pursued for its own sake, not to achieve a specific outcome or product. The primary motivation behind play is the pleasure and enjoyment derived from the act itself. While play may lead to various outcomes—such as educational achievements, enhanced motor skills, or cognitive and physical rehabilitation—these are merely secondary, or *collateral effects* of play (Lund, 2015). Importantly, these effects are not the reason one engages in play. Play is a self-sustaining phenomenon, with its value and purpose residing within the act itself. Unlike other human activities, in its pure form, play does not aim to produce anything tangible or functional; it exists solely as an end in itself.

As noted by play theorists, play is a creative yet unproductive activity, isolated from the routine demands of daily life. Johan Huizinga emphasized that play exists as a separate sphere of life, and its legitimacy should not depend on external purposes (Huizinga, 1938). Similarly, Roger Caillois describes play as free, separate in space and time, unproductive, and governed by rules that foster imagination and make-believe (Caillois, 2001).

Philosopher Hans-Georg Gadamer (1989) takes this further, suggesting that when humans engage in play, an *ontological shift* occurs. The player, while acting as a subject, becomes part of the act of playing and, in a sense, is "played" by the game itself. In this way, play draws us into a deeper, purposeless motion akin to the

H. H. Lund (✉)
Entertainment Robotics, Virum, Denmark
e-mail: info@e-robot.dk

M. B. Ligorio (ed.), *Technology as Cultural Mediator*, Culture in Policy Making: The Symbolic Universes of Social Action,
https://doi.org/10.1007/978-3-031-97673-5_8

natural flow of the universe. This separation from rationality and immersion in play allows us to forget about time and place, a phenomenon many of us recognize from our own experiences of deeply engaging in play activities, similar to flow (Csikszentmihalyi, 1990).

Despite societal perceptions that often equate play with childhood or triviality, play spans the entirety of human life. Adults, too, engage in activities that evoke a similar ontological shift—whether in sports, games, art, or even scientific research—where they lose track of time and place for the sheer pleasure and fulfillment of the activity itself. Friedrich Schiller eloquently captured this in his famous statement that humans are most complete when they play, as play allows us to experience life in its fullest and most joyful form (Schiller, 1795).

In this chapter, we will focus specifically on playful cultural technology and how the design of such playful technology, particularly in the form of *playware,* facilitates playful interaction. This interaction not only sustains the joy of play but also results in significant collateral effects that positively impact the health, well-being and quality of life.

8.2 Designing Play and Playware

The pursuit of play involves a wide range of strategies and techniques, and understanding these methods is essential for creating truly engaging play experiences. As psychologist Michael J. Apter (1991) notes, one of the most fascinating aspects of play is the diversity of tools and approaches people use to experience its joys. It's equally striking how much people are willing to invest—financially and otherwise—to access these moments of playful pleasure.

Some methods of play are well-known, such as games, which we learn from others or purchase, like video games. Other methods are built into physical equipment like swings or roller coasters. Both games and play equipment serve as "tools" designed to foster and regulate the mental and physical states we associate with play. These tools, whether physical or digital, work by triggering a series of reactions—what we refer to as *play dynamics*—that pull the user into a state of playful engagement.

Play dynamics can be defined as the forces that push individuals from their rational, everyday state into a playful mindset. This force might come from a physical movement, a competitive challenge, an element of risk, or even humor. The result is a shift in mental and emotional states that allow for play to emerge.

When designing play products or facilities, understanding these play dynamics is crucial. Not all games or tools will successfully induce play, and a deeper knowledge of what makes them effective is necessary. This is where the concept of *playware* comes into play. *Playware* (Lund et al., 2005) refers to intelligent hardware and software designed to create play and playful experiences for users of all ages. Playware tools interact with users, generating the "play force" needed to bring them into a play dynamic. These tools are capable of adapting to various play styles, making them versatile for different contexts, including rehabilitation, playgrounds, education, art, and sports.

In particular, *modular playware* offers a unique advantage. Its flexibility allows for easy assembly and customization, which makes it suitable for a wide range of users, including older adults who might otherwise struggle with modern technology. Modular playware is designed with key features that encourage engagement: tangible interaction, immediate feedback, flexibility, and adaptability (Lund & Marti, 2009). These qualities allow users of all ability levels to experiment, move, and explore play freely, benefiting from both the pleasure of play and its collateral effects, such as improved health and skills (Lund, 2022).

When people engage in play, they often transcend their usual fears and limitations, enabling them to accomplish more than they typically would. This can lead to significant secondary effects, the aforementioned *collateral effects of play*, especially in areas like education and health. In the context of children's play, this phenomenon has been keenly observed by Vygotsky, who noted that "Play creates a zone of proximal development in the child. In play, the child always behaves beyond his average age, above his daily behavior; in play, it is as though he were a head taller than himself. As in the focus of a magnifying glass, play contains all developmental tendencies in a condensed form and is itself a major source of development." (Vygotsky, 1978).

We believe that this transformative quality of play extends beyond children and can be applied to people of all ages. By integrating insights from artificial life robotics with the dynamics of play, we have developed a concept designed to harness these principles and create practical, user-friendly applications for society. We call this concept Playware ABC (Lund, 2017a, 2017b).

Playware ABC is built around three key components:

A. Anybody, Anywhere, Anytime
B. Building Bodies and Brains
C. Construct, Combine, Create

The Playware ABC concept enables the creation of technology solutions that are accessible to A: anyone, anywhere, at any time. Through embodied artificial intelligence that focuses on B: building bodies and brains, users are empowered to manipulate these technologies, allowing them to C: construct, combine, and create personalized solutions. This modular approach emphasizes usability and fosters an environment that encourages users to engage their own creativity, making the development process more inclusive and participatory.

Ultimately, the goal is to create playware that invites everyone—regardless of physical or cognitive ability—to participate in a joyful, dynamic, and fulfilling play experience. By focusing on modularity, flexibility, and user-centered design, we can ensure that the benefits of play are accessible to all. A suitable research method is needed to reach such goal of creating playful technology that has an impact in society.

8.3 Mixed Research Method

Traditionally, engineering has followed natural science research methods focused on controlled experimental approaches, such as the waterfall model, with distinct stages like project definition, design, and evaluation. This method is grounded in a reductionist view, assuming that systems can be fully understood by breaking them into components and isolating variables in a fixed environment. However, engineering often aims to develop technologies that address societal needs, such as in this chapter, where real-world conditions are less controllable than in laboratory settings.

To address this, we propose a cyclic action research method that blends participatory and experimental approaches. In 1946, Lewin originally pointed to a spiral of steps in action research, and the research method has been known as cyclic action research (Lewin, 1946), and Susman and Evered developed the action research cycle to include the five stages of diagnosing, action planning, action taking, evaluating, and specifying learning, which are then iterated (Susman & Evered, 1978). Hence, the method draws inspiration from interdisciplinary technology development and involves rapid prototyping cycles. By iterating technology development directly with end-users in their natural environments, the approach allows for continual adjustment and refinement, ensuring that the technology fits real-world contexts.

In certain fields, such as healthcare technology, merging positivistic and interpretivistic approaches is essential. Healthcare solutions for hospitals, rehabilitation centers, and home care require both technical rigor, user-centered design, and clinical evidence of effect. The mixed action research method is particularly suitable here, balancing participatory development with controlled experimental validation.

While participatory methods ensure that users can integrate new technology into their lives, rigorous experiments, such as randomized controlled trials, are necessary to demonstrate efficacy and gain acceptance from health authorities. Therefore, a mixed research approach allows for iterative user engagement while including controlled experiments to meet societal and regulatory standards. This combination is crucial for advancing health technology that can be adopted and trusted by the public.

Other fields, such as information technology training or community-based rehabilitation, also benefit from mixed research methods. While participatory methods are critical in these areas, experimental studies remain necessary to assess educational outcomes or therapeutic effectiveness.

In playware research, for example, the mixed research method is applied to integrate modular technology development with studies on user interaction and play dynamics. This research combines insights from artificial intelligence, modular robotics, and tangible interaction with an understanding of play culture and motivation. The process starts with fundamental engineering research, followed by the development of prototypes tested directly with users in real-world environments.

Each cycle involves both experimental and interpretivist approaches. For instance, the technical feasibility of modular playware systems is tested through experimental research, while human interaction and playfulness are assessed through participatory methods. The combination of results from both approaches informs subsequent cycles of development, refining the technology for broader application. This iterative method ensures that both the technological and social dimensions of playware systems are continuously improved.

In each cycle, the interdisciplinary collaboration and shared understanding between the different research areas are critical for synthesizing the findings and guiding further prototype development.

Rapid prototyping plays a key role in these iterations, enabling quick development of prototypes for testing in real-world environments. Unlike the waterfall model, which predefines requirements, rapid prototyping evolves systems through ongoing user feedback and small, incremental improvements. This method helps align the technology with real-world needs, allowing both users and developers to collaboratively learn and refine the system design.

By providing hands-on interaction with prototypes, rapid prototyping fosters a shared understanding among participants, facilitating interdisciplinary collaboration. This iterative process ensures flexibility, allowing researchers to adapt the research design to meet emerging needs and refine hypotheses based on real-time results.

8.4 Modularity

The rapid prototype development and the versatility of use scenarios can benefit from modularity. Modular systems can be described as those that are composed of multiple components, which can be mixed and matched in various configurations (Schilling, 2000; Baldwin & Clark, 2000). These components are designed to connect, interact, or exchange resources such as energy or data. In this context, modularity is a property that measures the degree to which closely connected compartments within a system can be decoupled into distinct communities or clusters that interact more intensively within themselves than with other parts of the system. This property is often associated with increased system stability and robustness, as it helps limit the spread of perturbations across the system (Thébault & Fontaine, 2010).

Modular systems, because they can be broken down into smaller components, share similarities with parallel and distributed processing systems from computer science (Pagliarini & Lund, 2012). In distributed computing, individual computational elements (or "atoms") are autonomous, yet insufficient on their own to achieve a complete solution. A process is termed distributed when two or more computers collaborate via a network, each contributing to the overall task by fulfilling different roles in a computational problem or process. Parallel computing, on the other hand, involves dividing large problems into smaller subproblems that can be solved simultaneously, or "in parallel."

Our approach to artificial life robotics leverages this modular design, incorporating both physical and functional modularity. This enables distributed and parallel processing, allowing for flexible construction of different morphologies and functionalities. In this way, users can build both the "bodies" (physical form) and "brains" (functionality) of their systems.

A well-known example of modularity in practice is the LEGO block system, which illustrates the power of modular building. With a limited set of LEGO blocks, users can construct a wide range of physical forms—such as towers, bridges, houses, and animals—by configuring the blocks in different ways. The shape, size, and connection points of the blocks define the number of possible configurations. For example, with just six LEGO blocks, it is possible to create roughly 100 million different combinations, depending on block size.

While LEGO blocks are effective for building physical structures (morphologies), they originally lacked the capability to build different functionalities (brains). To address this, we collaborated with LEGO to introduce the LEGO Mindstorms control unit, which allowed users to program their LEGO constructions. This unit enabled the attachment of sensors and actuators, and the centralized control unit could be programmed via a visual interface to control the functionality of LEGO builds. This made it easier to experiment with different morphological designs.

However, the LEGO Mindstorms system relies on a large, centralized control unit, which limits its modularity. A truly modular approach would eliminate this central control and distribute processing across all modules. This can be achieved through a system of intelligent building blocks, each with its own processing power and communication capability (Lund, 2003). When two blocks are connected, they can communicate and process information from neighboring blocks. These intelligent blocks can take various forms and be constructed from different materials. This concept was even applied to LEGO blocks, enabling a form of 'programming by building' (Lund, 2003).

In a distributed processing system, processing is spread across multiple modules, and the overall system behavior emerges from the interactions between these modules. Similarly, the physical characteristics of the system are distributed, and the overall physical expression results from the interactions between the physical modules. This is the essence of a modular robotic system: each module contributes both physical and functional characteristics, and the system as a whole emerges from their combined interactions (Lund, 2014).

The interaction between modules can be driven by either self-reconfiguration or user-configuration. Self-reconfigurable systems can autonomously modify both their physical form ("body") and processing capabilities ("brain"), as demonstrated in various works in the field of self-reconfigurable robotics (e.g., Fukuda & Nakagawa, 1988). One example is the ATRON modular self-reconfigurable robotic system (Jorgensen et al., 2004), see Fig. 8.1.

For contemporary applications, especially in areas like play, health, and green technology, our focus is on user-configurable modular systems. In these systems, users control the configuration of modules, enabling exploration of new solutions tailored to societal needs.

Fig. 8.1 The ATRON modular self-reconfigurable robotic system

8.5 User-Configurable Modular Systems

In many application areas, it is often beneficial to allow end-users to modify and adapt a system to better suit their personal needs, preferences, and capabilities. The user-configurable modular robotic approach enables users to easily and quickly adjust the technology, provided that the modules are designed with this flexibility in mind. We hypothesize that inspiration from modular robotics can lead to highly adaptable and user-friendly systems. In modular robotics, each module possesses both a physical form and the capability to process information and communicate with its environment. This communication can occur between neighboring modules or through interaction with external sensors and actuators.

The user-configurable modular approach draws upon the principles of behavior-based robotics (Brooks, 1986), extending these principles to include not only the coordination of primitive behaviors at the software level, but also the coordination of physical components. In this framework, we conceptualize each physical module as representing a "primitive behavior." The overall behavior of the system emerges from the physical arrangement and interaction of these primitive behavior modules, combined with their environmental interactions.

Just as behavior-based robots are controlled by coordinating primitive behaviors, we can envision the behavior of a robotic or interactive system emerging from the coordination of multiple physical modules, each representing a specific behavior. In user-configurable modular robotics, the user plays a central role in organizing and coordinating these modules—typically by physically arranging them (Lund & Nielsen, 2011). We have explored this approach across a variety of application domains, demonstrating its versatility and effectiveness.

8.6 Learning

We have developed educational applications based on Piaget's theories of cognitive development, using physical, modular robotic systems as teaching tools. Through simple assembly kits, students of all ages can design and construct functional robotic systems. This hands-on process helps students grasp complex concepts, particularly how global behaviors emerge from local dynamics (Miglino et al., 1999). By engaging in this construction process, students modify both the "brain" and "body" of artificial organisms, such as with the intelligent LEGO blocks, I-BLOCKS (Lund, 2003). These intelligent building blocks enable "programming by building," allowing students to explore the relationship between structure and behavior through tangible manipulation.

The use of these intelligent building blocks has significant potential in both developmental and educational settings. Trials involving children of different abilities (fully able, physically impaired, cognitively delayed) across diverse cultural contexts (Denmark, Tanzania, Italy) and varying levels of literacy have provided valuable insights into the creation of tangible media for collaborative and distributed edutainment environments. Feedback from children with learning difficulties and their therapists highlighted the importance of immediate, explicit feedback from physical constructions, which facilitated the solving and learning of complex cognitive tasks (Lund & Marti, 2005).

For example, when using I-BLOCKS in linguistic scenarios for children with dyslexia and aphasia, mapping the components of a sentence to physical, interactive blocks helped enhance cognition. By manipulating the blocks, children could immediately see the results of their actions and receive feedback on how they combined the blocks (Marti & Lund, 2004). Similarly, I-BLOCKS were used for secondary school and university students in Tanzania for subjects like mathematics, emotion construction, and language grammar training. In each case, the blocks represented different elements of the subject. For language training, the blocks might represent nouns, verbs, or prepositions, differentiated by color or size, while in mathematical training, they represented arithmetic operators and values (Fig. 8.2).

Building on these explorations, the development of modular playware technology continued, leading to innovations such as the Fable system (Pacheco et al., 2013). Fable is a chain-based, heterogeneous modular robot system featuring a scalable and reliable connector design. Its purpose is to allow non-technical users to create interactive robotic constructions. Fable includes various types of modules—joints, branching units, and terminations—and each module is equipped with sensors and actuators. Users can quickly assemble a variety of robots within seconds (see Fig. 8.3), and the system can be programmed at multiple levels, from simple

Fig. 8.2 Secondary school students in rural Tanzania using I-BLOCKS for mathematical training

Fig. 8.3 Early prototype of the Fable modular robot system

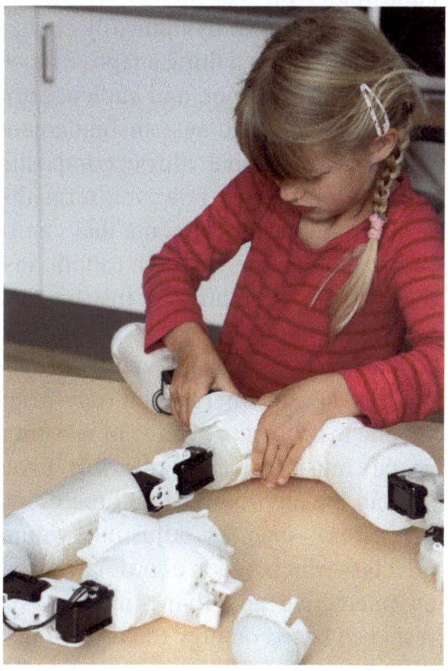

visual programming to advanced conventional languages. This flexibility makes the Fable system accessible to young children and it is now widely implemented in educational settings across the globe.

This modular, artificial-life robotics approach in the learning domain is directly inspired by the Playware ABC concept. Systems like I-BLOCKS and Fable embody the Playware principles of "Anybody, Anywhere, Anytime," empowering users to build both "bodies" and "brains." These systems allow learners to construct, combine, and create their own solutions, making them an essential part of the learning process.

8.7 RoboMusic: A New Paradigm in Interactive Music Performance

Another example of the use of Playware ABC is found in RoboMusic. RoboMusic (Lund & Ottesen, 2008) is a groundbreaking concept that redefines how music is created, performed, and experienced through the use of robotic instruments. First introduced in 2007 during a live concert with Funkstar De Luxe, RoboMusic integrates physical, intelligent objects—such as modular tiles, cylinders, and rolling pins—allowing users to interact with music in real-time. These robotic instruments, embedded with sensors and actuators, are programmable to autonomously generate sound but can also dynamically change their performance based on human interaction. The result is a fluid, adaptive musical experience where the boundaries between composer, performer, and audience are blurred.

The RoboMusic system fundamentally transforms the role of the music composer. In traditional music composition, an artist creates fixed, static pieces of music. RoboMusic, however, turns this on its head by introducing programmable, behavior-based instruments that can respond to user input. Composers design the baseline behaviors of these robotic instruments, which can play autonomously, but they also program how the instruments will react when triggered by human or environmental interaction.

This shift changes the nature of music from a static composition into a dynamic process. Music emerges not only from pre-recorded notes but also from how these robotic instruments behave in real-time, influenced by user interactions. The "composed" music becomes a flexible, evolving piece shaped by the interaction patterns of both the environment and the users. These robotic instruments trigger *primitive behaviors*—such as adjusting volume, altering tone sequences, or modifying effects—which, when coordinated, form the musical piece. This makes RoboMusic an interactive and living musical system, where the composition is constantly reshaped based on how the robotic instruments are engaged.

8.7.1 User Interaction and Intelligent Sampling

RoboMusic's core innovation lies in making music accessible and interactive for non-expert users, turning them from passive listeners into active participants. The design challenge for RoboMusic composers is to ensure that these robotic instruments are simple and intuitive enough for anyone to manipulate, yet sophisticated enough to produce meaningful musical outputs. By interacting with the physical objects, users can activate, deactivate, or modify the sounds in real-time, thus becoming part of the performance itself.

This interactive framework introduces a new level of *intelligent sampling* (Lund et al., 2014a, 2014b). Unlike traditional DJ sampling, where pre-recorded audio is remixed in predictable ways, intelligent sampling allows for dynamic manipulation of sound samples. In RoboMusic, the samples are designed to be flexible and adaptable, ensuring that users can combine them in various ways to create aesthetically coherent results. These samples become "intelligent" because they respond in real-time to user actions, creating a more immersive and creative experience for participants.

For example, during a RoboMusic performance, a rolling pin or modular tile may control a specific instrument, like drums or guitar. The sound produced by these instruments depends on the way users physically interact with them, creating countless possibilities for unique remixes. The intuitive nature of this interaction allows anyone—regardless of musical expertise—to engage with the system and produce original compositions.

8.7.2 The MusicTiles App: Virtual Sampling and Personal Remixing

The concept of RoboMusic was further expanded with the development of the *MusicTiles app*, launched in collaboration with Peter Gabriel for the *So* album. This app takes the idea of intelligent sampling into the virtual realm, allowing users to remix songs using digital modular tiles on a smartphone or tablet. Each tile represents an instrument or a musical stem (such as vocals, guitar, or drums), and users can manipulate the sound by arranging and connecting these tiles on a grid.

Each connection produces a different variation of the instrument's sound, depending on the direction and the number of connected tiles. For example, connecting a vocal tile with a guitar tile may produce a different sound based on how they are arranged (north, south, east, west). Users can explore the sounds by rearranging the tiles, discovering new combinations and remixing the song in their own creative way. This flexibility transforms music listening into an interactive, playful process where users are empowered to personalize the music according to their tastes.

By offering this interactive platform, MusicTiles enables a shift in the traditional music industry model. Instead of releasing fixed-format songs, artists can now provide their music in a format that users can endlessly remix, turning each listening experience into a creative act. Fans are no longer passive consumers but active performers, reshaping and personalizing the music.

8.7.3 *MusicTiles MagicCubes: Physical Sampling for Live Performance*

Building on the virtual concept of MusicTiles, the *MusicTiles MagicCubes* introduce a physical dimension to the RoboMusic experience. These robotic cubes, used in events like the Roskilde Festival and Peter Gabriel's *Back-to-Front* tour, allow users to remix music through tactile, physical interaction. Each MagicCube represents a particular instrument or musical stem, and users can activate or change the samples by physically turning the cubes. This introduces a hands-on, social aspect to music remixing, as multiple users can collaborate in real-time to create a new version of a song.

The MagicCubes are equipped with sensors and Bluetooth technology that allow them to communicate with a connected app, enabling seamless control of music samples. Each side of the cube represents a different musical variation, and by rotating the cubes, users can trigger different sounds. This physical interaction with the music adds a performative aspect to live remixing, as users must coordinate their movements with one another to shape the song.

At live events, such as Peter Gabriel's concerts, the MagicCubes took the form of large dice used on stage (see Fig. 8.4a, b). Each band member had a cube representing their instrument, and the song's structure emerged from the coordinated manipulation of the cubes, making the remixing process itself a central part of the performance.

8.7.4 *Extending the Boundaries of Music and Interaction*

RoboMusic, along with the MusicTiles app and MagicCubes, represents a significant leap in how music is both created and experienced. By integrating intelligent robotic instruments and user-driven interaction, RoboMusic transforms music composition into a dynamic, collaborative, and evolving process. It not only empowers users to actively engage with music but also pushes the boundaries of traditional performance, offering new possibilities for live interaction and creativity.

As the concept of *intelligent sampling* evolves, the potential to blend virtual and physical interaction becomes increasingly compelling. With tools like the MusicTiles app and MagicCubes, the line between musician and audience is blurred, creating a shared space for collective creativity. Whether through virtual remixing on a smartphone or physical collaboration in a live setting, RoboMusic reimagines the way music is produced, performed, and enjoyed, making it a truly interactive art form for the modern age.

Fig. 8.4 (**a**) Peter Gabriel playing with MagicCubes. (**b**) The band playing with MagicCubes at a live concert

8.8 Health Applications of the Playware ABC for Physical and Cognitive Rehabilitation

The Playware ABC framework, leveraging advanced modular robotics principles, plays an essential role also in modern physical and cognitive rehabilitation. By transforming traditional therapeutic exercises into engaging, gamified experiences, this system addresses the need for more effective and enjoyable rehabilitation tools.

A flagship example of this is *Moto Tiles* (2025), which integrates interactive, sensor-embedded tiles into personalized rehabilitation programs. Moto Tiles, part of the broader Playware ABC ecosystem, has proven particularly effective in rehabilitating patients with a range of conditions, from post-surgical recovery to cognitive impairment caused by aging and neurodegenerative diseases.

8.9 Technical Overview of the Moto Tiles System

At the heart of the Moto Tiles system are the individual, modular, interactive tiles, each measuring 30 cm × 30 cm. These tiles are wirelessly connected via the ANT protocol, a robust multicast wireless network operating at 2.4 GHz, which ensures minimal latency and reliable performance. Each tile is equipped with binary pressure sensors capable of detecting foot pressure when a user steps on it, and eight RGB LEDs that can display a wide spectrum of colors in real-time. The tiles function autonomously, yet they communicate wirelessly with one another and with a central control unit, typically an Android tablet, allowing for quick reconfiguration of exercises.

The modularity of the system enables a high degree of flexibility, allowing healthcare professionals to modify the arrangement of tiles to match the specific physical capabilities and rehabilitation needs of each patient. For example, in patients recovering from stroke or traumatic brain injury, who often struggle with gait imbalance or impaired motor coordination, the tiles can be arranged in a pattern that challenges both cognitive and physical skills. Similarly, for patients undergoing cardiac rehabilitation, where progressive exercise intensity is crucial for recovery, tiles can be spaced differently to gradually increase exercise demands as the patient regains strength.

This results from the Moto Tiles system offering significant flexibility in both its layout and gameplay due to its modularity with wireless connection to a controlling tablet, meaning the tiles do not need to be physically linked to one another. This modularity allows for an endless variety of layouts, enabling users to arrange the tiles in numerous configurations. The tiles' LED lights, which display different colors and patterns, further enhance this versatility by enabling a wide range of games in different modes, such as single-player or multiplayer, with customizable levels and time limits.

Over 40 distinct games have been developed for the Moto Tiles, catering to various therapeutic and recreational purposes. One key application has been in physiotherapeutic rehabilitation, particularly for cardiac patients recovering from surgery. These patients often need to engage in rehabilitation exercises that help them gradually increase their physical exertion, typically to a set pulse level, as they recover. Among the games designed for this purpose are Color Race, Lunges, Stepper, and Disco.

In the game Color Race, the user can select the number of participants (1–4). For each participant, a distinct color is assigned, which will light up on random tiles. For instance, if three players are selected, there will be tiles lit in red, blue, and green, each corresponding to a player. When a player presses their assigned color tile, it turns off and reappears at a new random location. The game continues until a player hits their color ten times, at which point all tiles light up with that player's color, signaling their victory. This game can be played in various ways: with multiple participants competing simultaneously, or with a single player aiming to hit their color as quickly as possible, or within a timed challenge, such as 2 min. In every scenario, players chase their assigned colors, racing to hit the most tiles or complete the task fastest. This multiplayer dynamic creates a competitive yet fun environment, encouraging participants to navigate around each other while walking, running, or jumping on the tiles to hit their colors with their feet.

Other games target cognitive development through play. For instance, there are memory games where participants must find two matching tiles hidden among others, and games like Special One, in which users search for the single tile that displays a different color from the rest. These cognitive tasks add another dimension to the training, requiring not only physical agility but also mental acuity.

The appeal of these games lies in their ability to transform rehabilitation into a joyful, playful experience. Most users don't perceive the activities as formal training but as an enjoyable interaction. Particularly in group settings, the social element further enhances the fun, as participants engage in friendly competition or collaboration (Jessen, 2016). The immersive nature of the games allows users to forget about their limitations or fears, enabling them to move more freely and with less hesitation than they might in traditional therapy settings. The intrinsic motivation to play leads to greater engagement, which is reflected in the smiles and enthusiasm seen during sessions. This phenomenon has been observed across all kinds of users—from young children to seniors, from athletes to cardiac, stroke, and multiple sclerosis patients, as well as individuals with cognitive impairments such as dementia. These positive effects have been consistently seen across diverse cultures and regions, including Asia, Europe, the Americas, the Middle East, and Africa (e.g. Lund, 2017a, 2017b, 2022).

The effectiveness of Moto Tiles can be attributed to the Playware ABC concept, emphasizing creating technology that is accessible to anyone, anywhere, and at any time (A). The modular design of the Moto Tiles reflects this by offering adaptability for various settings and abilities. The tiles serve as both the "body" and "brain" (B) of the system, facilitating diverse and responsive gameplay. Finally, this modular setup allows healthcare professionals—doctors, therapists, nurses, and caregivers—to easily configure, customize, and modify the game environment (C) to suit the specific needs, moods, and energy levels of the patients. This flexibility ensures that the technology remains patient-centered, enabling real-time adjustments for optimal therapeutic outcomes.

8.10 Moto Tiles for Children's Therapy in Rural Sub-Saharan Africa: Interventions and Outcomes

The use of modular interactive technology, such as Moto Tiles, offers an innovative and accessible solution for rehabilitation in resource-limited settings, since the system is designed to be used by anyone, anywhere, anytime, without requiring specialized knowledge or extensive infrastructure. This makes it particularly suitable for providing playful rehabilitation for children with disabilities, including cerebral palsy and intellectual impairments, in remote areas of sub-Saharan Africa (Lund et al., 2014a, 2014b).

The Playware ABC framework with the focus on highly mobile, modular, and energy-efficient technology, underpins the successful deployment of Moto Tiles in rural healthcare contexts. In Tanzania, a national partnership has been established to ensure sustainable implementation, including collaborations between government representatives, national hospitals, regional health facilities, universities, and NGOs. These stakeholders work together to incorporate Moto Tiles into community-based rehabilitation programs, addressing the unique challenges faced in these regions, such as limited access to electricity and healthcare infrastructure (Lund et al., 2015).

For example, in Iringa Regional Hospital in Tanzania, Moto Tiles have been integrated into therapeutic interventions for children affected by meningitis and other neurological conditions (Fig. 8.5). The system's portability and battery-powered operation enable health workers to easily set up and adapt the tiles to suit each patient's rehabilitation needs (Lund et al., 2014a, 2014b). This versatility is key in rural areas, where healthcare professionals are often required to manage a wide range of medical conditions with minimal resources.

Fig. 8.5 A meningitis affected child at Iringa Regional Hospital playing with Moto Tiles

Moto Tiles' modular nature allows for a wide range of co-designed interventions, providing significant flexibility in rehabilitation programs. Doctors and community health workers can quickly and easily configure the tiles to create personalized therapy sessions. These sessions are designed to improve motor function, cognitive abilities, and social interaction, using games that engage the child in a playful, motivating manner.

In Tanzania, for example, therapists have reported improved outcomes in children with cerebral palsy and cognitive delays following regular sessions with the Moto Tiles (Lund, 2017a, 2017b). The engaging, game-like nature of the system encourages participation and increases compliance with therapy, which is critical in the long-term rehabilitation process. The tiles support exercises that promote balance, coordination, and cognitive stimulation, all of which are crucial for children with developmental disabilities.

8.11 Addressing Broader Health Challenges in Low-Income Settings

Sub-Saharan Africa faces a high prevalence of disabilities, stroke, and coronary heart disease, yet the healthcare infrastructure in these regions often lacks the resources found in high-income countries. Moto Tiles provide a solution that addresses these gaps by enabling healthcare workers to administer therapeutic interventions without the need for advanced technical skills or costly equipment.

The flexibility of the Moto Tiles system also ensures that it can be adapted to treat a variety of conditions beyond children's therapy. Its modular approach allows health professionals to tailor the tiles to address both physical and cognitive rehabilitation needs in stroke survivors, elderly patients with mobility issues, and individuals recovering from cardiac conditions. Importantly, the system's ease of use empowers community health workers to deliver these interventions even in remote areas, where specialized healthcare professionals are scarce.

Initial interventions in rural Tanzania have demonstrated promising results, with children showing notable improvements in both physical and cognitive function after engaging in therapeutic activities with Moto Tiles. Health workers report that the playful and interactive nature of the system reduces the children's resistance to therapy, increases their enthusiasm, and encourages more sustained participation (Lund et al., 2014a, 2014b, 2015). This is particularly important in regions where rehabilitation services are limited and patients may have fewer opportunities for regular therapeutic sessions.

The broader impact of this technology is significant, particularly in settings where healthcare resources are limited, and a single health worker must often address a variety of conditions. The ability of Moto Tiles to accommodate different levels of patient ability and offer a scalable, easy-to-use intervention means it has the potential to transform rehabilitation in low-income and rural communities.

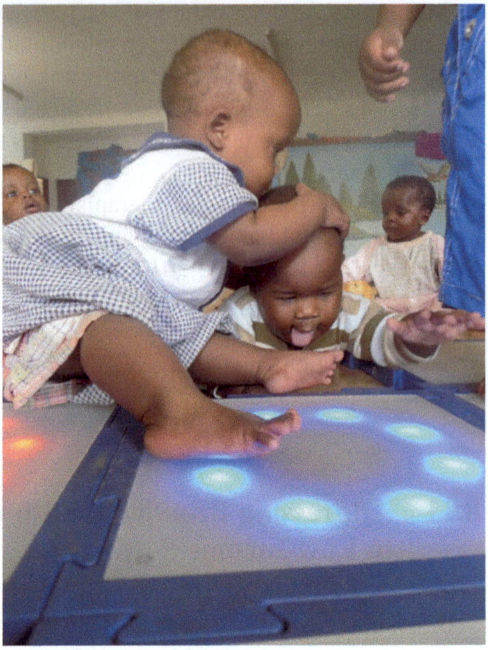

Fig. 8.6 Moto Tiles used at an orphanage in rural Tanzania

Moreover, the system's adaptability and its reliance on minimal infrastructure make it an ideal solution for widespread use in developing regions (such as in Fig. 8.6).

This deployment of Moto Tiles in rural sub-Saharan Africa represents a breakthrough in providing accessible, effective rehabilitation for children with disabilities. By leveraging the Playware ABC framework, Moto Tiles offer a sustainable, adaptable, and playful solution that addresses both cognitive and motor rehabilitation needs. The success of this system in contexts such as Tanzania suggests that it could serve as a model for expanding therapeutic interventions in other low-resource settings, where there is a pressing need for versatile and scalable healthcare solutions.

8.12 Clinical Applications in Physical and Cognitive Rehabilitation

The adaptability of Moto Tiles is crucial for rehabilitating not only a wide range of intervention areas for child patients as seen in Sub-Saharan Africa, but in general for a wide range of patient populations. By integrating into both physical therapy and cognitive training protocols, the system offers an innovative approach to rehabilitation, particularly for individuals recovering from neurological injuries or undergoing geriatric therapy.

8.13 Stroke Rehabilitation and Motor Recovery

Stroke survivors often experience hemiparesis or reduced motor control on one side of the body, necessitating targeted rehabilitation to restore function and coordination. Traditional stroke rehabilitation relies on repetitive motor tasks to improve movement in the affected limbs, but patient adherence and motivation can be a significant barrier due to the tedious nature of these exercises. Moto Tiles address this challenge by transforming these monotonous tasks into dynamic, interactive games, encouraging greater patient participation (see Fig. 8.7).

One game designed specifically for stroke rehabilitation is the Show the Pattern Game, in which the patient is required to step on tiles as they light up in a sequence. This activity promotes motor planning, coordination, and dynamic balance, key components in post-stroke recovery. The asymmetric tile arrangement encourages users to engage both the unaffected and affected sides of their body, thereby targeting motor recovery in a more balanced manner.

Patients recovering from cardiac events, such as myocardial infarction or heart surgery, require a gradual reintroduction to physical activity to rebuild

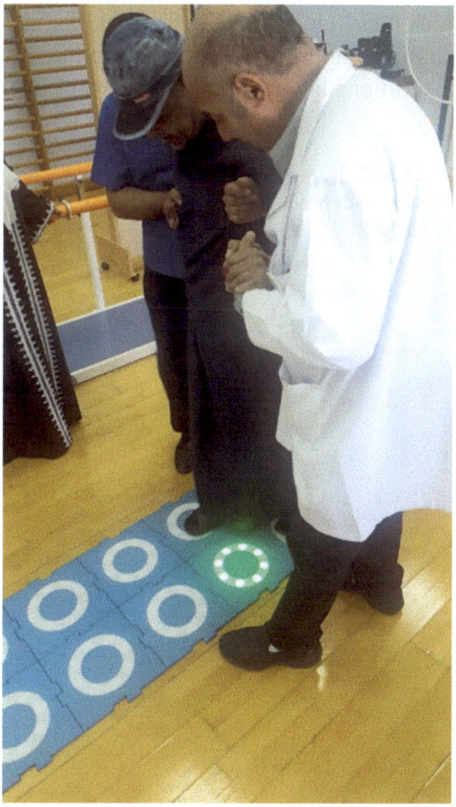

Fig. 8.7 Stroke patient rehabilitation at Al Qassimi Hospital, UAE

cardiovascular strength. Moto Tiles facilitate this process through controlled exercise programs that adjust in intensity based on real-time patient performance. The modular design enables healthcare providers to increase the complexity and difficulty of exercises as the patient progresses, minimizing the risk of overexertion while optimizing cardiovascular gains. In the Color Race Game, patients are tasked with stepping on tiles that light up randomly within a preconfigured grid. Initially, tiles may be arranged close together to minimize physical strain, but over time, they are spaced further apart to encourage more vigorous movement.

8.14 Balance and Fall Prevention in Older Adults

For elderly patients, maintaining mobility and preventing falls is a key aspect of rehabilitation. With age, both muscular strength and balance deteriorate, increasing the risk of falls, which can have devastating consequences, including fractures and loss of independence. Moto Tiles are particularly effective in addressing this issue by offering balance training games that are both enjoyable and effective (see Fig. 8.8).

The Color Race, Final Countdown and Reach Games require users to step on tiles that light up in specific patterns, necessitating quick changes in position and challenging the body's proprioceptive and vestibular systems. This task requires the user to engage their core and lower body muscles while continuously adjusting to

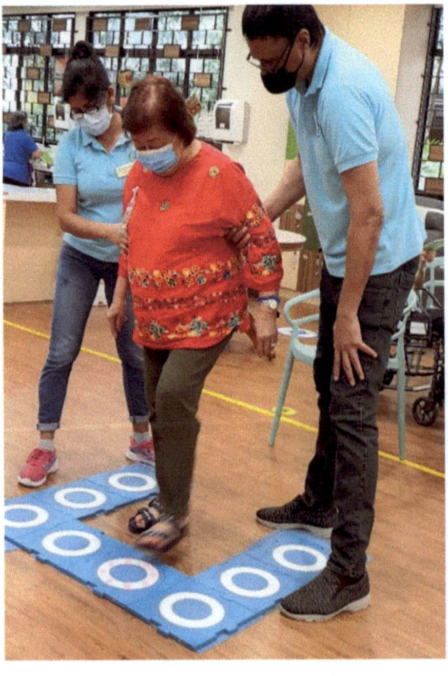

Fig. 8.8 Falls prevention training with Moto Tiles in Singapore

the shifting tile light patterns, thus improving postural control. Studies have demonstrated that such interactive balance games can significantly reduce fall risk among older adults.

Lund and Jessen (2013, 2014) conducted a pilot study involving 16 seniors aged 63–95. The participants underwent 13 group training sessions over a 16-week period, with each session lasting 12–13 min. The study assessed participants using the Senior Fitness Test, Timed-Up-and-Go (TUG), and other balance and endurance measures. The results showed significant improvements in functional fitness, including a 24% improvement in the Chair-Stand Test, a 21% improvement in the TUG, and a 66% improvement in the Line Walk Test. These improvements were associated with better lower body strength, endurance, and balance, key factors in reducing fall risk.

A larger study by Jessen and Lund (2017) involved 60 seniors average aged 83 years old, randomly assigned to either an intervention group (using Moto Tiles) or a control group (receiving standard care). Over a 12-week period, participants in the intervention group trained twice weekly for 13 min per session. At the end of the trial, the intervention group exhibited statistically significant improvements in leg strength, as measured by the Chair-Stand Test, and in balance, as measured by the Line Walk Test. Specifically, the intervention group showed a 148% increase in balance performance compared to the control group. This study demonstrated not only the effectiveness of Moto Tiles in improving physical health but also their feasibility for routine use in community settings.

Regarding balancing, the effect study in Japan by Kofuku et al. (2022) found statistically significant effects on numerous physical tests, and concludes that "exercise using Moto Tiles is effective for independent elderly people living in the community. It is recommended as one of the exercises for improving balance ability" (Kofuku et al., 2022, pp. 116).

8.15 Cognitive Rehabilitation: Enhancing Mental Agility

Beyond physical rehabilitation, Moto Tiles also play a crucial role in cognitive rehabilitation, particularly for patients with dementia, mild cognitive impairment (MCI), or traumatic brain injury (TBI). The incorporation of both physical tasks and cognitive challenges in many Moto Tiles games offers a dual-task training approach, which has been shown to enhance cognitive performance through neuroplasticity mechanisms.

For example, the Color Memory Game and Simon Says Game challenge patients to remember the locations and sequences of colored lights across various tiles, promoting working memory, spatial navigation, and cognitive flexibility. This dual-task scenario engages both the prefrontal cortex and the motor cortex, resulting in improvements in cognitive functions while simultaneously enhancing physical endurance.

Several studies have been conducted to evaluate the impact of Moto Tiles on cognitive abilities, particularly in older adults. One small randomized controlled trial (RCT) by Liu and Lund (2018) investigated the effects of a brief, 30-min training session using Moto Tiles on cognitive performance. Participants were assessed using four cognitive tests: Visual Search, Choice Reaction Time, and Sternberg Scanning. Statistical analysis of the data revealed significant improvements in reaction times for these tests in the intervention group, highlighting the positive cognitive effects of even short-term Moto Tile training.

Further research includes a randomized controlled trial involving 19 older adults with mild dementia, conducted at the iZhaohu facility in Shanghai, China (Liu et al., 2018). In this study, participants underwent ten sessions of 30-min playful training on Moto Tiles. Results showed a marked improvement in reaction time on the Visual Search task, indicating enhanced attention, scanning, and visualization abilities in participants after the intervention. This provides evidence of the potential cognitive benefits of playful interaction with the tiles, particularly for dementia patients.

Building on the insights gained from these studies, a novel, playful method for screening individuals for potential physical and cognitive impairments was developed (Liu et al., 2019). This method generates a comprehensive body and brain performance map for each individual, using Big Data analysis to automatically detect areas of underperformance. Based on these assessments, the system can create personalized training protocols by selecting appropriate Moto Tile games to target and improve the individual's weaker abilities.

The efficacy of this screening and personalized training approach was tested in a small pilot study with seniors (average age of 80) suffering from mild dementia at senior care centers in Roskilde, Denmark (Lund et al., 2020). Participants engaged in individualized training over 3 weeks, completing an average of nine sessions, each lasting around 7 min. Pre- and post-test measures included tasks correlated with the Timed-Up-and-Go (TUG), chair-to-stand (CS), and four squares step tests (FSST). Remarkably, the seniors demonstrated significant improvements across four Moto Tile test games, with performance increases of 41%, 31%, 42%, and 3%, respectively. Before the intervention, the seniors were classified as high-risk for falls; however, post-intervention results showed a substantial reduction in fall risk. These findings suggest that even brief training sessions (totaling just 1 h over 3 weeks) on Moto Tiles can significantly lower the fall risk in older adults, enhancing their mobility and safety.

Another study by Okada et al. (2020) in Japan involved 36 seniors (average age of 75) who played Moto Tiles twice a week for 12 weeks. Participants completed a dual-task exercise, combining Moto Tile play with functional assessments. Pre- and post-test evaluations showed significant improvements in functional fitness and cognitive control. Specifically, improvements were observed in TUG, stepping, the five-repetition sit-to-stand test (CS), toe grip strength, as well as cognitive tasks such as the Flanker and Stroop tests. The authors concluded that "Moto Tiles dual-task exercise programs appear to be effective in improving lower body function and cognition in frail older adults," reinforcing the positive impact of the tiles on both physical and cognitive health.

Similarly, a study by Kofuku et al. (2021) tested the effects of Moto Tiles on 21 seniors, also aged around 75, who participated in training sessions twice a week for 12 weeks. The results echoed previous findings, showing significant improvements in TUG, chair-to-stand, and functional reach tests. Additionally, there were statistically significant improvements in the Kihon Check List (KCL), a reliable tool for predicting vulnerability and risk of long-term care dependency. A KCL score of ≥ 7 points indicates increased risk of needing long-term care services. In this study, the average KCL score of participants dropped from 7.67 to 3.22, suggesting that regular, playful training on Moto Tiles can reduce the risk of long-term care needs. This reduction in risk has important implications for improving the quality of life (QOL) and activities of daily living (ADL) for seniors, highlighting the potential for Moto Tiles to enhance both physical and cognitive well-being in older populations.

An important clinical trial was performed with seniors with mild to moderate dementia in Shanghai by Wang et al. (2021). In the clinical trial, 93 seniors with mild to moderate cognitive impairment from a care home in Shanghai participated, with the intervention group (N = 48, Age: 78.43 ± 6.27) and control group (N = 45, Age: 76.80 ± 7.97). The intervention consisted of three times weekly Moto Tiles training (30 min) for 4 weeks, while control was normal activity and care. There were no significant differences between intervention group and control group at baseline. Pre- and posttests were performed with MoCA (Montreal Cognitive Assessment), DST (Digit Span Test), BBS (Berg Balance Test), TUG (Timed Up-and-Go), and FTSST (5 * Chair-to-Stand). The cognitive tests for the seniors with mild to moderate cognitive impairments like MoCA tests short-term memory recall tasks, visuospatial abilities tasks, executive function tasks, attention, concentration, and working memory tasks, language tasks, abstract reasoning task, orientation to time and place task, and DST tests verbal short term and working memory tasks. In comparison between the intervention group and the control group, the results showed statistically significant effect on MoCA, DST (Digit Span Test forward/backward), BBS (Berg Balance Test), TUG, and FTSST (5 * CS). It is an important result that the seniors with mild to moderate dementia increase their scores on the cognitive tests improving their cognitive skills after merely 6 h play on the Moto Tiles over the 4-week period. At the same time, they significantly improve their physical functional abilities.

8.16 Psychosocial Impact and Patient Engagement

Patient motivation and adherence are pivotal in any rehabilitation program. A common issue in traditional physical therapy is that patients often find exercises repetitive, tedious, and demotivating, particularly as they progress through long recovery phases. Moto Tiles directly addresses these concerns by incorporating elements of gamification into rehabilitation, turning exercises into interactive, competitive, and often socially engaging games (see Fig. 8.9). This approach has been shown to

Fig. 8.9 Social engagement of seniors in social play with the Moto Tiles in Taiwan

improve intrinsic motivation and sustain high levels of engagement, which are crucial for long-term rehabilitation success.

In a qualitative survey conducted by Jessen (2016; Jessen & Lund, 2017) high adherence was confirmed with adherence to training with the Moto Tiles in the intervention group of 93%. 90% of participants responded that they were happy with the training, and 85% responded that they wanted to continue this training with the Moto Tiles. 75% of participants self-evaluated that they had become better physically, and 60% that they could do more in their daily life after the intervention. The social aspect of group sessions using Moto Tiles, particularly in settings like elderly care homes, fostered a sense of camaraderie and support, further contributing to patient adherence.

8.17 Broader Implications and Future Directions

The success of Moto Tiles in clinical rehabilitation underscores the broader potential of the Playware ABC framework in various healthcare domains. The modularity and adaptability of the system make it suitable for a wide range of chronic conditions, including Parkinson's disease, multiple sclerosis, and even post-surgical recovery in orthopedic patients. Ongoing developments are enhancing the system's ability to provide personalized feedback, track patient progress with greater accuracy, and adjust exercise difficulty levels in real-time based on individual performance.

Interestingly, in all the clinical trials reported above, there is statistically significant effect after 4–6 h of playful training on the Moto Tiles, both on the cognitive abilities and the physical abilities. This is tenfold faster than with traditional training methods, for which systematic reviews show that a high dose of training is needed, for physical >50 h (Sherrington et al., 2008) and for cognitive: >52 h (Gomes-Osman et al., 2018). The training on the Moto Tiles is ten times faster to provide significant results since the users play and have fun, forgetting about their fears and limitations when in play, and therefore perform better and more freely in this type of training with the Moto Tiles.

Despite these promising developments, there are challenges to widespread adoption. The cost of implementing such technology in smaller clinics, concerns about technological literacy among older populations, and ensuring long-term sustainability of engagement all require careful consideration. However, as further studies continue to validate the efficacy of playful systems like Moto Tiles, the potential for these tools to become integral parts of mainstream rehabilitation practice becomes increasingly likely.

The integration of the Playware ABC framework through the Moto Tiles system marks a significant advancement in physical and cognitive rehabilitation. By transforming mundane, repetitive tasks into engaging, interactive, and highly customizable games, Moto Tiles significantly improves patient adherence, motivation, and outcomes. With clinical evidence supporting its effectiveness in improving balance, strength, cardiovascular health, and cognitive function, Moto Tiles offers a solution to modern rehabilitation challenges. As healthcare providers seek more effective ways to motivate patients through their recovery journeys, tools like Moto Tiles based on the Playware ABC framework may soon become essential in the field of rehabilitative care.

8.18 Discussion

The integration of playful cultural technology into various domains—education, music, and healthcare—highlights the transformative potential of play in promoting learning, creativity, and well-being. Play, a fundamental human activity, is deeply embedded in social and cultural practices. Its inherent flexibility and engagement make it a powerful tool in fields where motivation and interactivity are crucial. Through systems like playware, and particularly Playware ABC, this concept has been further evolved, transforming not only how people engage with technology but also how technology can meaningfully impact their lives.

Playware technology, as articulated through the Playware ABC framework, exemplifies how the principles of play can be applied to create systems that encourage active participation, creativity, and personal agency. By enabling users to construct, combine, and co-create, Playware ABC fosters environments where learning, problem-solving, and physical rehabilitation occur naturally through engagement and interaction.

Unlike conventional technologies, which often demand specific instructions or skills, playware is intuitive and user-friendly. The playful interaction engages users in a way that reduces barriers to participation, regardless of age, ability, or background. This democratization of technology is evident in multiple fields, such as learning and health, where complex tasks and goals can be reframed as playful challenges. Moreover, Playware's inherent modularity allows for personalized and adaptive experiences, making it versatile across different contexts.

One of the most prominent applications of playware is in education, where it enhances learning experiences through gamification and interactive problem-solving. In traditional educational environments, learning is often rigid and linear. However, playware introduces a dynamic element that encourages exploration, collaboration, and innovation. For example, interactive games and robotic systems can teach children fundamental principles of mathematics, physics, or coding without explicit instruction, engaging them through curiosity and fun.

The flexibility of the Playware ABC system ensures that it can be adapted to various learning contexts. From early childhood education to advanced robotics workshops, playware offers a scaffolded experience that adapts to the learner's progress, providing the right level of challenge. The active engagement inherent in play also nurtures intrinsic motivation, which is essential for long-term learning. As users interact with playware, they experience learning as a playful journey rather than a chore, increasing their commitment and reducing anxiety related to performance or failure.

In the realm of music, playware has similarly opened new avenues for creativity and expression. RoboMusic, a playware-based system, exemplifies how technology can transform music education and performance. RoboMusic systems, through their playful interfaces and real-time interaction, enable users to explore musical composition, rhythm, and harmony in a non-linear, experimental way. This system shifts music from a traditionally performance-based discipline to one that fosters improvisation and creative exploration.

RoboMusic also enables people with little or no formal musical training to engage meaningfully in the creation of music. The playful and interactive design removes the intimidation often associated with learning an instrument, making music accessible to a wider demographic. The system's adaptability means that it can be used both in educational settings and in rehabilitation contexts, where music therapy is known to enhance cognitive and emotional well-being.

Perhaps the most profound application of playware is in healthcare, where it is used for physical and cognitive rehabilitation. Moto Tiles, a modular interactive technology, have been employed in a variety of settings to help individuals with physical or cognitive impairments recover and improve their functional abilities. By integrating playful elements into rehabilitation, Moto Tiles encourage patients to engage in their own recovery process, which can often be tedious or painful in traditional therapy settings.

Studies have shown that Moto Tiles can significantly improve balance, coordination, and reaction time, particularly in elderly populations or individuals with conditions such as stroke, dementia, or cerebral palsy. The system's playful nature makes repetitive exercises more enjoyable, which increases patient compliance and engagement. Moreover, the cognitive challenges embedded in the games—such as memory tasks or visual search tasks—stimulate brain activity, potentially improving cognitive functions alongside physical recovery.

The adaptability of Moto Tiles also allows them to be used in various environments, from hospitals and rehabilitation centers to rural settings with limited resources. For example, in low-income regions like sub-Saharan Africa, Moto Tiles have been successfully implemented in community-based rehabilitation programs, where infrastructure and healthcare resources are scarce. The portability and modularity of the system make it highly adaptable to different patient needs and environments, offering a sustainable solution for regions with minimal healthcare technology.

Playful technology, as manifested through playware, has profound cultural and social implications. In educational contexts, it encourages collaborative learning and breaks down barriers of access to knowledge and skill-building. In health, it redefines rehabilitation as an enjoyable and patient-centered experience, empowering individuals to take an active role in their recovery. And in creative fields such as music, it democratizes artistic expression, making it accessible to people of all skill levels and backgrounds.

Moreover, playful technology enhances social connectivity by encouraging group activities and collaborative problem-solving. Whether in classrooms, rehabilitation centers, or even homes, playware fosters environments where individuals interact meaningfully with both technology and each other. This creates new opportunities for social learning, communal support, and shared experiences.

8.19 Conclusion

Playful cultural technology, driven by the principles of play and embodied through the Playware ABC framework, offers a transformative approach to education, health, and creativity. The key strength of this technology lies in its ability to simplify complex tasks, making them accessible, enjoyable, and personalized for users of all backgrounds and abilities. Whether through enhancing learning experiences in schools, enabling musical creativity, or improving physical and cognitive rehabilitation, playware systems such as RoboMusic and Moto Tiles demonstrate the potential of playful interaction to improve human outcomes in profound ways.

The flexible, modular design of these technologies ensures that they can be adapted to a wide variety of contexts—from well-resourced urban hospitals to rural community centers in low-income regions. Their success in diverse environments, such as schools in Europe and healthcare settings in sub-Saharan Africa, underscores their global relevance and scalability.

Moving forward, further exploration into the customization and deployment of playful cultural technologies in different cultural contexts will be essential. Continued research and development could explore how these systems can be optimized for specific populations and integrated into existing infrastructure, particularly in underserved communities. Ultimately, playful cultural technology represents not just a novel approach to interaction, but a powerful tool for improving quality of life, fostering creativity, and building inclusive systems of learning and rehabilitation.

References

Apter, M. J. (1991). In J. K. Kerr & M. J. Apter (Eds.) *A structural phenomenology of play*. Adult Play.

Baldwin, C. Y., & Clark, K. B. (2000). *Design rules, Vol. 1: The power of modularity*. MIT Press.

Brooks, R. (1986). A robust layered control system for a mobile robot. *IEEE Journal on Robotics and Automation, 2*(1), 14–23.

Caillois, R. (2001). *Man, play and games, 1958*. University of Illinois Press.

Csikszentmihalyi, M. (1990). *Flow: The psychology of optimal experience*. Harper & Row.

Fukuda, T., & Nakagawa, S. (1988). Dynamically reconfigurable robotic system. In *Proceedings. 1988 IEEE International Conference on Robotics and Automation* (pp. 1581–1586). IEEE.

Gadamer, H.-G. (1989). *Truth and method*. Crossroad.

Gomes-Osman, J., Cabral, D. F., Morris, T. P., McInerney, K., Cahalin, L. P., Rundek, T., Oliveira, A., & Pascual-Leone, A. (2018, June). Exercise for cognitive brain health in aging: A systematic review for an evaluation of dose. *Neurology Clinical Practice, 8*(3), 257–265.

Huizinga, J. (1938). *Homo Ludens*.

Jessen, J. D. (2016). *Evaluation and understanding of Playware Technology—Trials with playful balance training*. Ph.D. thesis. Technical University of Denmark, Department of Electrical Engineering.

Jessen, J. D., & Lund, H. H. (2017). Study protocol: Effect of playful training on functional abilities of older adults—A randomized controlled trial. *BMC Geriatrics, 17*(1), 1–6.

Jorgensen, M. W., Ostergaard, E. H., & Lund, H. H. (2004). Modular ATRON: Modules for a self-reconfigurable robot. In *2004 IEEE/RSJ International Conference on Intelligent Robots and Systems (IROS) (IEEE Cat. No. 04CH37566)* (Vol. 2, pp. 2068–2073). IEEE.

Kofuku, K., Fujita, E., Nakamoto, H., Takeshima, N., & Nakagaichi, M. (2021). Effects of dual-task exercises using Moto tiles on the functional fitness and cognitive function of older adults living in the community. *Research Journal of Sports Performance, 13*, 195–208.

Kofuku, K., Fujita, E., Kubo, S., Kohama, T., Kusunoki, M., Takeshima, N., & Nakagaichi, M. (2022). Effects of community-based Moto tiles exercise on balance ability in older adults. *Research Journal of Sports Performance, 14*, 109–117.

Lewin, K. (1946). Action research and minority problems. *Journal of Social Issues, 2*, 34–46.

Liu, Y. X., & Lund, H. H. (2018). Effect of playful physical interactive tiles on cognition. In *2018 International Conference on Information and Communication Technology Robotics (ICT-ROBOT)* (pp. 1–4). IEEE. https://doi.org/10.1109/ICT-ROBOT.2018.8549886

Liu, Y. X., Lund, H. H., & Wu, L. (2018). Playful cognitive training with physical interactive tiles for elderly. In *2018 International Conference on Information and Communication Technology Robotics (ICT-ROBOT)* (pp. 1–4). IEEE. https://doi.org/10.1109/ICT-ROBOT.2018.8549898

Liu, Y. X., Leggieri, M., & Lund, H. H. (2019). Playful body and brain test with the Moto tiles. In *Proceedings of the 2019 International Conference on Artificial Life and Robotics* (Vol. 24, pp. 648–651).

Lund, H. H. (2003). Intelligent artefacts. In *Proceedings of the 8th International Symposium on Artificial Life and Robotics, ISAROB* (pp. I11–I14).

Lund, H. H. (2014). Building bodies and brains. *Adaptive Behavior, 22*, 392–395.

Lund, H. H. (2015). Play for the elderly—Effect studies of playful technology. In J. Zhou & G. Salvendy (Eds.), *Human aspects of IT for the aged population. Design for everyday life. ITAP 2015. Lecture notes in computer science* (Vol. 9194). Springer. https://doi.org/10.1007/978-3-319-20913-5_46

Lund, H. H. (2017a). Playware ABC: Engineering play for everybody. *Journal of Robotics Networks and Artificial Life, 3*(4), 283–286.

Lund, H. H. (2017b). Playware ABC 2: A disruptive technology for global development. *Journal of Robotics Networks and Artificial Life, 3*(4), 287–290.

Lund, H. H. (2022). An artificial life robotics inspired modular approach for real life applications. *Sistemi Intelligenti, 34*(3), 653–672.

Lund, H. H., & Jessen, J. D. (2013). Effect of playful balancing training—A pilot randomized controlled trial. In *2013 ISAROB.*

Lund, H. H., & Jessen, J. D. (2014). Effects of short-term training of community-dwelling elderly with modular interactive tiles. *Games for Health: Research, Development, and Clinical Applications, 3*, 277–283.

Lund, H. H., & Marti, P. (2005). Designing manipulative technologies for children with different abilities. *Artificial Life and Robotics, 9*(4), 175–187.

Lund, H. H., & Marti, P. (2009). Designing modular robotic playware. In *Proc. of 18th IEEE International Symposium on Robot and Human Interactive Communication (Ro-Man 2009)* (pp. 115–121). IEEE Press.

Lund, H. H., & Nielsen, C. B. (2011). Modularity for modulating exercises and levels-observations from cardiac, stroke, and COLD patients therapy. In *2011 8th International Conference on Ubiquitous Robots and Ambient Intelligence (URAI)* (pp. 253–258). IEEE.

Lund, H. H., & Ottesen, M. (2008). RoboMusic—A behavior-based approach. *Artificial Life and Robotics Journal, 12*(1–2), 18–23.

Lund, H. H., Klitbo, T., & Jessen, C. (2005). Playware technology for physically activating play. *Artificial Life and Robotics, 9*, 165–174.

Lund, H. H., Jensen, L. S. D., Ssessanga, Y., & Abdalahman, R. (2014a). Implementing modular interactive tiles for rehabilitation in Tanzania—A pilot study. In P. Cunningham & M. Cunningham (Eds.), *IST Africa 2014 Conference Proceedings*. IIMC International Information Management Corporation. ISBN: 978-1-905824 43-4.

Lund, H. H., Marti, P., & Tittarelli, M. (2014b). Remixing playware. In *The 23rd IEEE International Symposium on Robot and Human Interactive Communication* (pp. 49–55). IEEE.

Lund, H. H., Jensen, L. S. D., Ssessanga, Y., Cataldo, S., & Yahya-Malima, K. I. (2015). An approach for a National eHealth implementation—The case of modular interactive tiles for rehabilitation. In P. Cunningham & M. Cunningham (Eds.), *IST-Africa 2015 Conference Proceedings*. https://doi.org/10.1109/istafrica.2015.7190552

Lund, H. H., Liu, Y. X., & Leggieri, M. (2020). Big data and AI approach for body and brain test for seniors. *Journal of Robotics, Networking and Artificial Life, 6*(4), 270–273.

Marti, P., & Lund, H. H. (2004). Novel tangible interfaces for physical manipulation, conceptual constructions and action composition. In *Proceedings of Intelligent Manipulation and Grasping (IMG04).*

Miglino, O., Lund, H. H., & Cardaci, M. (1999). Robotics as an educational tool. *Journal of Interactive Learning Research, 10*(1), 25–47.

Moto Tiles. (2025). Retrieved February 4, 2025, from www.moto-tiles.com

Okada, S., Ogayu, T., Nakamoto, H., Ikudome, S., & Takeshima, N. (2020). Effects of dual task exercise on functional fitness and activation of cognitive control in frail older adults. *Physiotherapy Science (Japan), 35*(3), 387–395.

Pacheco, M., Moghadam, M., Magnusson, A., Silverman, B., Lund, H. H., & Christensen, D. J. (2013). Fable: Design of a modular robotic playware platform. In *2013 IEEE International Conference on Robotics and Automation* (pp. 544–550). IEEE.

Pagliarini, L., & Lund, H. H. (2012). An educational tool for interactive parallel and distributed processing. *Artificial Life and Robotics, 16*(4), 441–447.

Schiller, F. (1795). *Letters upon the aesthetic education of man.*

Schilling, M. A. (2000). Towards a general modular systems theory and its application to inter-firm product modularity. *Academy of Management Review, 25*, 312–334.

Sherrington, C., Whitney, J. C., Lord, S. R., Herbert, R. D., Cumming, R. G., & Close, J. C. T. (2008). Effective exercise for the prevention of falls: A systematic review and meta-analysis. *Journal of the American Geriatrics Society, 56*(12), 2234–2243.

Susman, G. I., & Evered, R. D. (1978). An assessment of the scientific merits of action research. *Administrative Science Quarterly, 23*, 582–603.

Thébault, E., & Fontaine, C. (2010). Stability of ecological communities and the architecture of mutualistic and trophic networks. *Science, 329*(5993), 853–856.

Vygotsky, L. S. (1978). *Mind in society: The development of higher mental processes* (pp. 1930–1935). Harvard University Press.

Wang, J., Fang, Y., Zhang, S., Qiu, Q., Wu, L., Yang, Y. L. X., & Li, X. (2021, March). Effects of MOTO tiles on cognitive and motor functions in the elderly with mild to moderate cognitive impairment. *Practice of Geriatrics, 35*(3), 261–264.

Chapter 9
Human-Centred Robotics and AI for Trustworthy Human-Robot Interaction

Angelo Cangelosi, Manith Adikari, Rahul Singh Maharjan, Luca Raggioli, Francesco Semeraro, Radu Stoican, Federico Tavella, Hongbo Zhu, and Marta Romeo

9.1 Introduction

The latest impressive advancements in Artificial Intelligence (AI) and robotics can help progress on the development of digital AI technologies and social robot companions, which in turn can support people in everyday life, in education, at work, in health and social care. However, it is imperative that such technologies are developed following ethical principles, supporting transparent and trustworthy interaction between people and robots. Moreover, they must follow an ethical, human-centred robotics and AI vision.

Social and assistive robots are an emerging technology which is increasingly being investigated for real-world applications, from healthcare as socially assistive robots (Abdi et al., 2018) to education as robot tutors (Belpaeme et al., 2018). The definition of a 'Social Robot' has varied in the literature, however, current studies tend to define it as a robot whose social interaction plays a key role in Human Robot-Interaction (HRI)—as opposed to robots which have 'conventional' HRI like teleoperated industrial robots (Fong et al., 2003).

A. Cangelosi (✉) · M. Adikari · R. S. Maharjan · F. Semeraro · R. Stoican · F. Tavella · H. Zhu
Manchester Centre for Robotics and AI, University of Manchester, Manchester, UK
e-mail: angelo.cangelosi@manchester.ac.uk; manith.adikari@postgrad.manchester.ac.uk; rahulsingh.maharjan@manchester.ac.uk; francesco.semeraro@manchester.ac.uk; radu.stoican@student.manchester.ac.uk; federico.tavella@manchester.ac.uk; hongbo.zhu@manchester.ac.uk

L. Raggioli
University of Naples Federico II, Naples, Italy
e-mail: luca.raggioli@unina.it

M. Romeo
Heriot Watt University, Edinburgh, UK
e-mail: M.Romeo@hw.ac.uk

M. B. Ligorio (ed.), *Technology as Cultural Mediator*, Culture in Policy Making: The Symbolic Universes of Social Action,
https://doi.org/10.1007/978-3-031-97673-5_9

This chapter gives an overview of recent robotics and AI models in the application areas of healthcare, manufacturing and education, showing the use of AI and machine learning methods to help design social and cognitive skills in these robots, and discussing their evaluation with human-robot interaction experiments.

We first look at the use of assistive robotics, i.e., robots for health and social care. Two use cases are briefly presented: social robots as companions supporting older people, and robots and AI systems for people with communication needs. The first use case on assistive robots for health and social care is part of the MoveCare project, combining robots and other healthcare technologies to support older people in their homes. The robot is integrated within an intelligent ambient system combining Internet of Things (IoT) sensors and AI. This permits the integrated monitoring of the older people's health and needs. The second use case looks at social robots for people using sign language for communication. This employs the method of imitation learning, using algorithms to mimic human actions and gestures by leveraging data extracted from sign language videos.

In the field of social robots for education, robots can be used as tutors to support teachers and children, and as social mediators in group-based activities. This includes the use of the robot as a technology to support cross-cultural collaboration. Related models look at handling emotion, for a successful and adaptive interaction between people and robot assistants. These emotion recognition models also include research on Continual Learning—i.e., the gradual update and growth of the training dataset—as continual and developmental learning has been shown to improve performance and quality of the robot's skills.

Another important role of social robots is human-robot collaboration on joint tasks for flexible manufacturing scenarios, for example in situations where one or more users interact with a robot. This type of robots is called cobots (collaborative robots). In one example focussing on triadic human-human-robot interaction, we propose an alternative way of gathering data regarding multi-user activity and deep learning models to recognise the joint activities of the pairs of people.

Finally, the chapter will discuss issues related to trustworthy robots, looking at important ethical aspects of AI and robotics. These focus on trust and explainable AI. We examine examples on Explainable AI (XAI) for human-robot interaction, to support ethical transparent interaction for the design of human-centred robot systems.

9.2 Assistive Robots in Health and Social Care

In the realm of human-centred robotics and AI, assistive robots hold great potential for transforming social care. By integrating advanced AI computational techniques and machine learning algorithms, these robots can effectively support individuals with daily activities, thereby improving their quality of life and fostering greater independence. This section examines some key examples of projects and contributions on the development of assistive robots designed for health and social care, and robotics for sign language communication.

9.2.1 Socially Assistive Robots for Older People Care

Europe, as many other countries and regions, is experiencing a societal shift. The expected proportion of adults above 65 years old is projected to rise from 20% to 30% from 2019 to 2070, changing the way healthcare sectors across all countries will have to deliver care (European Commission, 2021). Promoting independent living offers several advantages, including cost savings, effectively addressing the needs of older adults, and postponing the need for nursing home care (Davey, 2006). Socially Assistive Robots (SARs) can be valuable assets in helping "ageing in place", as they can offer both companionship and health monitoring to their users through social interactions. The integration of SARs into Ambient Assisted Living (AAL) frameworks has proved to be a useful help to older adults living independently in many projects, such as Robot-Era (Cavallo et al., 2018), GiraffPlus (Coradeschi et al., 2014), and MoveCare (Luperto et al., 2024). Most of these works however, struggle with evaluating the benefits of such systems in a long-term evaluation in the field. For this reason, MoveCare aimed at demonstrating the potential of such systems in monitoring, supporting, and assisting pre-frail older adults, together with the open challenges that still need to be addressed by the community, through a comprehensive pilot field experiment conducted deploying the system to operate autonomously in older adults' homes for a minimum of 10 consecutive weeks.

MoveCare seamlessly integrated different technologies and equipped them to be deployed in the houses of its users in the most unobtrusive way possible. The full system comprised of: an Internet-of-Things (IoT) sub-system; smart objects; a Community-Based Activity Centre (CBAC); an intelligent Virtual Caregiver (VC) coordinating all the other components and embodied in a socially assistive robot (i.e., Giraff). The main functionalities of MoveCare are depicted in Fig. 9.1. MoveCare key components interact to: (1) provide a safety network to the users who could call for help and trigger an object search thanks to the integration of environmental sensors and the SAR through the VC; (2) monitor the physical and cognitive health of its users to detect early signs of possible decline though gamification and the delivery of cognitive tests by the robot; (3) offer a socialisation platform through the CBAC.

Carers and clinicians were involved from the start of the designing phases and had decisive say in the functionalities and in the design of the whole MoveCare system. Of particular interest, for both clinical and technical partners involved in MoveCare, was the monitoring functionality. Cognitive decline is a significant concern in healthy ageing due to its substantial impact on the quality of life for older adults and its potential progression into dementia (Johansson et al., 2015). Although there is no cure for dementia, early detection and intervention during the Mild Cognitive Impairment (MCI) stage can effectively slow its progression. Currently, neuropsychological assessments, typically performed through standardized cognitive tests in a controlled clinical setting under expert supervision, are the most effective tools for identifying MCI (Budd et al., 2011). Examples of such tests are the Bells Test (BT) (Gauthier et al., 1989) and the Trail Making Test (TMT) (Reitan,

Fig. 9.1 A participant of the experimental campaign completing the tests under the guidance of the SAR (from Luperto et al., 2024)

(a) The robot asks a user to perform the tests.

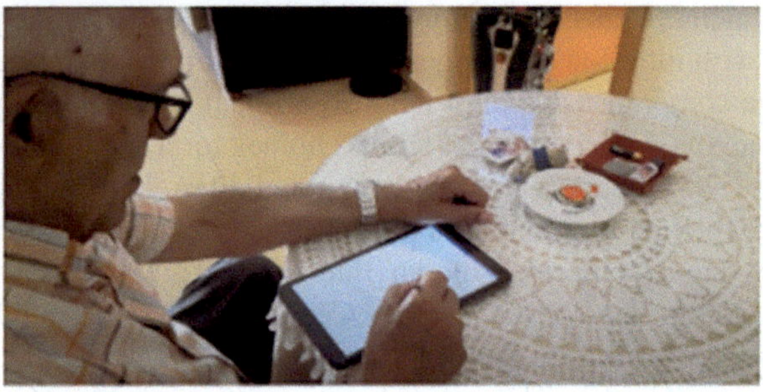

(b) The user performs the test on the tablet under the supervision of the robot

1958). The first one consists in finding all the bells in a canvas, among many distractors, while the TMT consists in connecting numbers (TMT-A) and numbers and letters (TMT-B) in order. To make cognitive monitoring quickly accessible and less reliant on older adults going to clinics to perform such tests, MoveCare digitised and integrated BT and TMT within the functionalities of the system. To deliver cognitive monitoring, the VC triggered the SAR to start the intervention. The SAR would then look for its user in their apartment, make sure they have the necessary time and tools to perform the tests (the tablet where the CBAC was integrated) and guide them through the completion of the two tests (Fig. 9.2 shows a participant carrying out the tests). This intervention was triggered twice during the long experimental campaign, once at the very beginning, used to establish a baseline for the participants, and once at the end (Luperto et al., 2024), and it was interleaved with all the other interventions that the robot was carrying out as part as the other MoveCare functionalities.

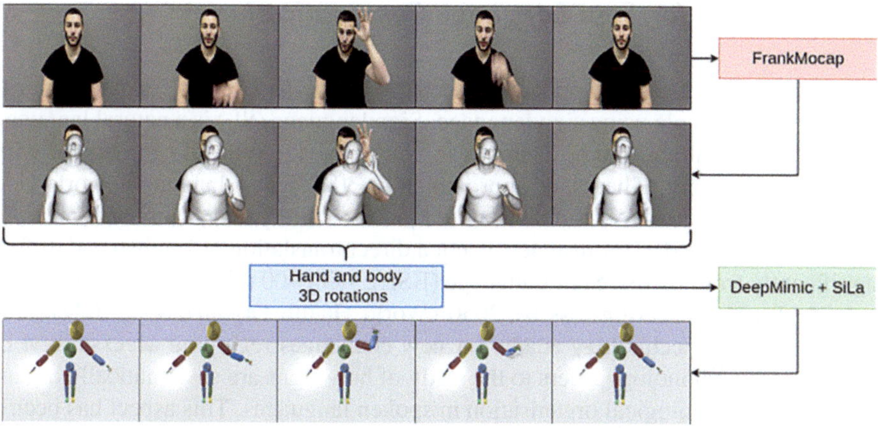

Fig. 9.2 The sign language acquisition pipeline (Tavella et al., 2024a)

A total of 13 older adults—all over 65, not suffering from any cognitive impairment, and living independently—used MoveCare for at least 10 weeks. Being an international project, participants were equally recruited between Italy and Spain. The evaluation of the acceptability and feasibility of MoveCare was performed using structured questionnaires and by analysing the data collected by the VC throughout the deployment (in depth details of all tools and results can be found in Luperto et al. (2024) (Fig. 9.1). Generally, although the system was not perfect and incurred in many technical problems during the campaign, participants reported feeling safe and comfortable using MoveCare, finding it easy to use with clear instructions. Despite some users finding the robot too large and slow, and preferring more direct control, the SAR was well-received, and boosted users' confidence, making them feel safer around the house, and was seen as a significant advancement. The robot also enhanced social interactions for the users, with participants reporting enjoying demonstrating the robot to friends and family. Overall, participants positively evaluated all interventions where they had to interact with the robot. In particular, open questions answered by participants showed that they enjoyed partaking in performing the digital neuropsychological tests with the robot, which could pave the way for widespread deployment of screening tests to foster early detection of MCI.

The main result of MoveCare was providing strong empirical evidence that SARs could be successfully integrated in AAL settings for long-term assistance of older adults, who accepted the system and its developed functionalities, proving both the feasibility and the acceptability of these assistive technologies. A critical aspect for the success of assistive technologies is making sure to include perspective users and carers in all technological design and deployment phases. Only by taking into consideration the views and needs of the users, SAR will improve and become real assets for healthy ageing and healthcare.

9.2.2 Robots for Sign Language Communication

Another important SARs application scenario concerns support for communication—e.g., for people using sign language. Sign language (SL) is a natural language which uses visual and motor elements to communicate, typically for people with hearing impairment. There are approximately 300 signed languages worldwide (United Nations, 2022), each featuring unique vocabulary and grammar. American Sign Language (ASL), for instance, is not a direct translation of English and differs significantly from British Sign Language (BSL). With 700 million people estimated to have disabling hearing loss by 2050 (World Health Organization, 2024), it is fundamental that technology adapts for new challenges regarding accessibility. In sign language, phonology refers to the study of how signs are systematically organised, akin to phonological organisation in spoken languages. This aspect has been a significant focus in recent research, comparing the articulatory systems of spoken and signed languages. For example, Sandler (2017) emphasises the distinctiveness of the visible articulatory system in sign language compared to the typically hidden system in spoken languages.

The intersection of computational methods and sign language has gained traction, with studies focusing on extracting properties and data to enhance understanding of sign language. However, a significant limitation in the development of SARs for sign language acquisition is the scarcity of comprehensive datasets that cover the wide variety of signs and gestures used in different sign languages. This lack of data hampers the ability of machine learning models to accurately learn and replicate sign language movements.

To address this challenge, Tavella et al. (2022a, 2022b) explored alternative approaches such as extracting phonological properties of sign language. These properties describe the fine-grained and low-level movements that constitute signs, including handshapes, locations, movements, and orientations. By focusing on these phonological elements, which are more granular and detailed than considering the whole sign, it becomes possible to generate more accurate and versatile models for sign language imitation, even with limited ground truth data. Initially, large datasets of sign language videos (Caselli et al., 2017; Li et al., 2020a, 2020b) are collected and processed using computer vision algorithms (Kanazawa et al., 2019; Rong et al., 2021; Wang et al., 2021) to track hand and body movements. Pose estimation algorithms play a crucial role, utilising machine learning models to detect and represent the positions and orientations of the body, hands and fingers. These components are then fed into classification models that have been trained to recognise specific phonological features. By focusing on these low-level movements, the models can accurately interpret and replicate the nuanced gestures of sign language. This methodological approach ensures that the quality of the data extracted from videos is sufficient to recognise the distinctive properties of each sign.

In addition to understanding sign language, a critical aspect of SARs is their ability to communicate using sign language. Imitation learning, a subset of machine learning, has shown promise in teaching complex motor skills (Peng et al., 2018b). This approach involves training algorithms to mimic human actions by leveraging data extracted from videos. The process begins with capturing precise body movements using motion capture technology, which serves as a reference for training simulated agents. By utilising frameworks like Human Mesh Recovery (Kanazawa et al., 2018) for pose extraction and DeepMimic (Peng et al., 2018a) for imitation learning, researchers have successfully trained humanoid characters to perform acrobatic skills. In a similar fashion, Tavella et al. (2023, 2024a) experimented with simulated robotic hands and agents trained to fingerspell six different letters and five different signs. They use a sign language acquisition pipeline (Fig. 9.2) (Tavella et al., 2024a) composed of multiple steps. Firstly, video frames of people performing signs are analysed one by one using FrankMocap (Rong et al., 2021), extracting body meshes, keypoints and rotations. Then, the 3D rotations of body and hands are fed to the imitation learning algorithm—a combination of DeepMimic (Peng et al., 2018a) and SiLa (Tavella et al., 2023) so that the simulated agent can learn to replicate the signs.

Despite the intricate nature of these tasks, the robots achieved high accuracy in replicating the required movements. This was accomplished by fine-tuning hyperparameters and iteratively testing the models to ensure robust performance. For more complex sign language lemmas, the researchers extended imitation learning to include whole-body motions (Tavella et al., 2024a). This broader approach addressed the challenges posed by dynamic and varied gestures. By leveraging advanced pose estimation and motion capture techniques, the simulated agents were able to learn and replicate these signs with a reasonable degree of accuracy.

The integration of these advanced capabilities into assistive robots offers numerous benefits for health and social care. One is enhanced communication, where robots capable of recognising and imitating sign language can bridge communication gaps between deaf individuals and those who do not understand sign language, facilitating better social integration and support. The second benefit is increased independence. By performing tasks that require manual dexterity, such as fingerspelling and signing, assistive robots enable users to communicate more independently, reducing reliance on human caregivers who can focus on other tasks.

9.3 Social Robots in Education and Affective Behaviour

Education is a major area which can greatly benefit from social robots, as these offer personalised tutoring, enhanced learning experiences and other pedagogical advantages (Belpaeme et al., 2018). A key benefit of a social robot is the factor of 'physical embodiment', which refers to its physical presence capable of enhancing interactions, compared to computer tablets and Conversational Agents (Deng et al., 2019).

In this chapter we will look at two examples of social robots use in education. One considers the potential role of robots as social mediators in educational content. The second example uses robot for early language learning in children, where a child interacts with robots playing different educational roles.

9.3.1 Social Robot as Tutors for Education

The strategy by which a robot interacts with a learned plays a crucial role in successful interaction and learning processes. In social robotics for education, there are three main roles that the system can assume:

- Robot as a Tutor: The system delivers key elements of frontal lessons, overseeing students, providing explanatory examples, and offering suggestions to facilitate concept learning.
- Robot as a Peer: The robot positions itself at the student's level, acting as a classmate and collaboratively supporting the learning process. This approach can be beneficial as it might be less intimidating than interacting with a teacher.
- Novice Robot: The robot takes on the role of a student in need of help, while the student becomes the tutor. This strategy can be effective in building the student's confidence and awareness, leading to improved learning outcomes.

The peer robot is the most widely used strategy in the literature. In the review by Belpaeme et al. (2018) it was shown that children tend to treat a robot as a peer in educational interactions. The physical limitations of the robot may be seen as more acceptable in a peer, rather than an adult-like figure like a tutor. Moreover, it has been argued that for difficult tasks children perform better when collaborating with a peer robot (Diyas et al., 2016; Zaga et al., 2015). The choice of the peer role could also be driven by the expectations one may have about the robot. While the tutor robot is usually expected to make less mistakes and display a seamless behaviour, for the peer robot less accurate performance may lead to increased confidence in the child (Baxter et al., 2017). In most works present in the literature, a more sociable and personalised behaviour of the robot has been proved to lead to higher learning performance.

While different types of applications of the various roles showed how robots can become a useful tool to complement teachers efforts in learning activities, it is also worth noting how these strategies present limitations that usually complement the benefits: for instance in STEM-oriented settings, like teaching time tables or learning prime numbers, a more social behaviour led to worse performance as compared to a more neutral characterization of the robot (Kennedy et al., 2015; Konijn & Hoorn, 2020).

While it is clear that in selected scenarios a specific role for the robot might be more suitable than others, we must also note how comparisons are often carried out using the same robot with different behavioural characteristics. This is reasonable and sound, but we also argue that it is important to account for different physical characterisation, mirroring the real-life difference between a human tutor and a human peer, in the same scenario. Moreover, one could wonder if combining two different roles together in the same session might improve the learning and the interaction, by leveraging on best practices from both strategies.

To answer to these experimental questions, we stipulate a study targeting early language learning in which a child interacts with (a) a tutor robot, (b) a novice peer robot, or (c) a tutor and a novice peer robots together, in which the research aims are to investigate if (H1) how two different robots, characterised with two distinct behaviours in the same scenario are perceived by a child during a learning task, and if (H2) by combining them together impacts significantly the child's behaviour towards the robots.

With the objective of pursuing these aims, we need a task where all the words naming occurs in the context of a story that can be narrated by the robot, while being realistic: it is necessary, in fact, that the objects fit well in the narrative so that it does not become confusing. The story used for our task is based on the material provided in a storytelling study (Piazza et al., 2021), where novel words and objects are embedded in an unfolding story. Our story revolves around an alien friend of the robot, who lost some of his toys, which are needed to fix the spaceship and go home. The objects chosen for this study are based on the NOUN dataset[1] and are presented in three distinct phases:

1. First word exposure: where the object is found and presented in context.
2. Isolated word exposure: where the object is shown on a black background and named again.
3. Function word exposure: where the object is presented again describing how it could be used in the context of the story.

The first two exposures are part of the training phase, while the last one forms the testing phase.

Based on the how the robots' behaviours are characterised in the literature, the robots' roles to be deployed in a language learning scenario could be formalised as follows (see also Fig. 9.3):

- The Tutor Robot. The interaction is led by a Pepper robot assuming the role of the tutor. In this case, the robot is operated as if it knew all the correct word-object pairings and the feedback to the child are delivered acknowledging correct answers or reassuring the participants if the answer is wrong or they do not wish to respond.

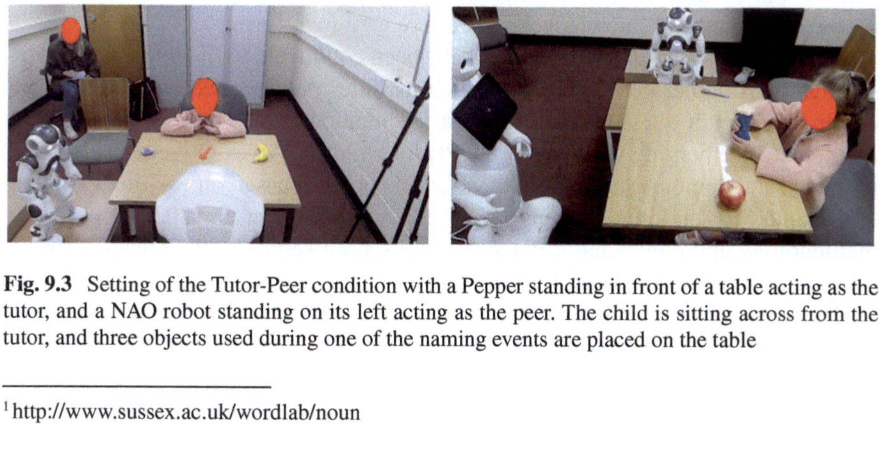

Fig. 9.3 Setting of the Tutor-Peer condition with a Pepper standing in front of a table acting as the tutor, and a NAO robot standing on its left acting as the peer. The child is sitting across from the tutor, and three objects used during one of the naming events are placed on the table

[1] http://www.sussex.ac.uk/wordlab/noun

- The Peer Robot. The robot is characterised as a novice peer, whereas not all the matchings are treated as known to the robot. Acknowledgements are delivered in a less resolute and confident way.
- Tutor and peer robots together: A robot is used as a tutor leading the interaction, while a second robot acts as novice peer being occasionally questioned by the tutor.

9.3.2 Social Robot as Mediators

A promising direction in fields such as education is to use a social robot to promote human-human interactions, as 'social mediators'. A social mediator robot—in this field—is defined as a robot capable of promoting positive human-human interactions (Weisswange et al., 2023). Current research has shown the effectiveness of social robot mediators in improving task participation, fostering inclusion, and positively impacting group dynamics of both adults and children (Adikari et al., 2023). A key motivation to develop robot mediators is due to the limitations of human mediators, who may have intrinsic biases and be logistically infeasible in many scenarios. Robot mediators could be designed to address these issues, by being neutral, always available, and patient (Neuhaus et al., 2022). This signifies the necessity and value of using a social robot mediator, for example in educational settings, as a tool to mediate groups of school children (Gillet et al., 2020).

To effectively develop social robots for real-world scenarios, it is essential to incorporate the needs of the target users. This calls for human-centred design and research practices, which have been implemented across numerous fields. To address this challenge in the field of HRI, a promising approach is to conduct a Participatory Design (PD) study. PD refers to encouraging participants to co-design, where they can actively join in the decision-making processes to shape the direction of the robot design (Winkle et al., 2021). This process of 'mutual learning', where there is communication between researchers and target users, has shown to enable better robot co-design. This is often conducted by engaging the participants in a two-way exchange of knowledge and ideas (e.g., a focus group).

In the current literature, PD studies have been conducted for a wide range of HRI settings with numerous target users, such as older people (Lee et al., 2017) and children (Gillet et al., 2020). Since most PD methodologies focus on adult target users, there is emerging work exploring PD for children. Alves-Oliveira et al. (2021) proposed and demonstrated a child-centred PD process based on existing PD methods adapted for children's development stages. Bjorling et al. (2020) presented a methodology and conducted a PD study in a school setting with teenagers for co-designing a social robot to address stress.

These previously mentioned studies, however, do not explore PD with children in group HRI settings. This research gap needs to be addressed to enable the use of robots, such as social robot mediators, for real-world applications—particularly in educational settings where groups of children frequently interact. Gillet et al. (2022)

presented a PD study to investigate how teenagers envision a social robot "group assistant", by engaging participants in focus groups, interviews, and conducting group interaction sessions. The transcribed audio data collected from the study was analysed qualitatively. The results indicated that each group of participants moved along a spectrum regarding their needs for the robot: broadly, for ice-breaking, turn-taking, and fun-making. This approach has been recently used in a study with teenagers to explore how a social robot mediator could be used for group collaborative scenarios, which are ubiquitous in educational settings. A PD workshop and focus group were conducted with different social robots for multiple stages of discussions, interviews, and co-design. The transcribed audio data collected can be analysed with a qualitative analysis (Thematic Analysis) to reveal recurring themes to address the research question. For example, the overall results only provided a general insight into how the students envision social robots helping them when engaging in collaborative group settings. The students demonstrated a wide range of understanding and experiences with robots, as well as how the challenges in collaborative group settings could be addressed with various social robot behaviours but did not reveal a critical insight.

9.3.3 Emotion and Affective Behaviour in Robots

Social robots are being developed with the aims of providing assistance, mediation, and even companionship to humans. Communication through verbal and non-verbal methods is crucial for interaction with humans in a social ecosystem. In a social ecosystem, human communication and social interaction often include the affective facet (Breazeal et al., 2016). As such, a crucial desideratum faculty in social robots is the ability to understand and recognise affective cues. Consequently, recognition of affective cues through facial expressions (Li & Deng, 2020), speech (El Ayadi et al., 2011), vocal bursts (Maharjan et al., 2024a, 2024b; Simon-Thomas et al., 2009), and body language (Santhoshkumar & Geetha, 2019) have been explored for social robotics and artificial agents.

Among the various affective cues, facial expressions serve as a critical nonverbal signal, conveying a wide range of emotions and intentions without the need for verbal communication. Humans can communicate their internal emotions through facial expressions (Ekman & Oster, 1979). As such Facial Expression Recognition (FER) has garnered considerable attention due to its wide-ranging applications across various domains. More recently, the focus has shifted towards developing deep learning (DL) methods to improve its reliability and performance (Li & Deng, 2020). Although the existing DL models show promising results in facial expression recognition on benchmark datasets (Kollias & Zafeiriou, 2019; Mollahosseini et al., 2017), they often struggle to translating that performance to where the models need to continuously interact with unseen humans, such as in human-robot interactions. While facial expressions have long been considered a universal language for conveying internal emotional states, each person reflects their emotional states through facial expressions unique to another person influenced by their personality traits (Calvo & Nummenmaa, 2016) and complexities of their cultural background (Gendron et al., 2014). This leads to inter-class similarities and, consequently, domain distribution shift occurs. The diverse nature of facial expressions, shaped by varying cultural and individual factors, presents significant challenges for DL models in FER, especially when applied beyond benchmark datasets. Despite these challenges, many existing DL models adopt a *"train-once-test-everywhere"* approach. Existing DL models often fail to address individual variations and depends heavily on balanced datasets, which may not efficiently perform on real-world conditions.

To address these issues, recent works (Churamani et al., 2020; Maharjan, 2022) have proposed exploring continual learning (CL) for FER. Churamani et al. (2020) emphasised the relevance of CL in real-world social robots, redefining and reformulating it as personalised affective perception. They put forward personalised affective perception as a form of task and/or class incremental learning. This approach requires a social robot to adapt its ability to new expression classes or adapt its learned expression classes to new social environments. Differently, Maharjan et al. (2023) addressed the FER from domain-incremental learning perspective. They argued that one individual's facial expressions are different from another, i.e. every individual's facial expression represent different domain distribution as shown in Fig. 9.4. Furthermore, Maharjan et al. (2023) visualised the features space of model for three different FER datasets and provided insights on how training facial expression may not share same features space with testing facial expression if both are not sampled from same domain distribution.

Churamani and Gunes (2020) presented CL method for FER designed to continually adapt to new facial expressions while still recognising previously seen expressions in contextual situations. Differently from Churamani and Gunes (2020) that addresses training of one facial expression class at a time, Maharjan et al.

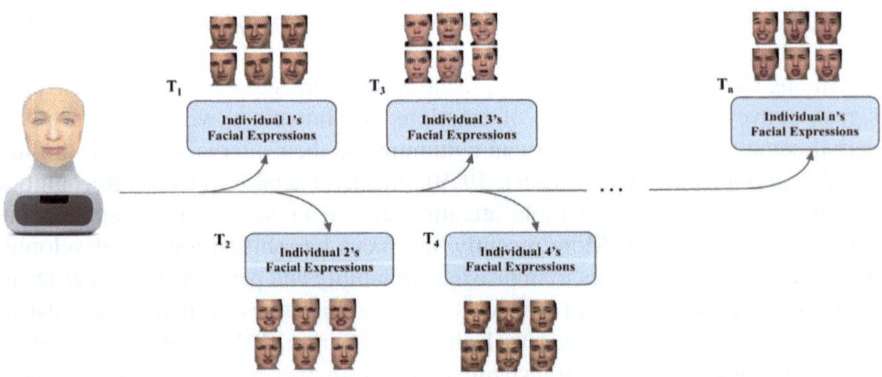

Fig. 9.4 A social robot (https://furhat.io/) in real-world conditions is expected to interact with human and leverage newly acquired facial expressions of individuals to adapt and improve it's facial expression recognition ability

(2023) introduced FIXR, a CL model tasked to continuously learn facial expressions from new individuals while adapting to shifts in domain distribution. FIXR leverages the strengths of EfficientNet with the concept of dark experience replay (Buzzega et al., 2020), enhancing learning through knowledge distillation from past experiences and the regularisation of previously observed human facial expressions. During the training stage, data containing basic facial expressions of individual is provided to FIXR incrementally and very small amount of the current individual's facial expressions are stored in memory buffer. As the new individual's facial expressions are available, FIXR combines previously stored the individual's facial expressions to continually learn without forgetting. Drawing inspiration from this approach, Maharjan et al. (2024a, 2024b) proposed continual facial feature transfers to address learning from heterogenous facial expression data, i.e., when all six facial expressions of the individual are not available. They leveraged teacher-student model to continuously provide facial feature information from teacher model to student model to learn new facial expressions in "in-the-wild" datasets. Comprehensively, integrating continual learning with affective communication in social robots holds significant potential, as further explored by Churamani et al. (2022).

9.4 Cobots: Collaborative Robots for Human-Robot Collaboration

Besides social mediation, elderly care and education, robots can also be employed as collaborative robots (cobots) in joint-work and manufacturing scenarios. In these contexts, robots abandon their human-like appearance in exchange for greater capability of physically affecting the environment. Most of the time, they assume the shape of a robotic arm; this allows them to reach a targeted location in multiple ways, so they can choose the most proper one for the specific task at hand. Besides, they are equipped with motors capable of exerting great and precise forces and torques and interacting with their target objects in different ways. If they are designed so that they can work at closer proximity with humans while ensuring safety of the human operator by sensing the users' presence in the environment, these robots gain the denomination of cobots (Guertler et al., 2023). Robotic architectures of this kind can sense the presence of a human worker at direct vicinity and stop if needed. Humans can also easily move the robot by dragging its joints by hand and without the cobot resisting the induced displacement. Furthermore, to prevent harmful situations, these robots are programmed to have tailored velocities according to predefined areas and have their capability of exerting forces preemptively limited.

The sector of human-robot interaction that explores the physical and cognitive interplay of cobots and humans while achieving a common goal together is called human-robot collaboration (HRC) (Ajoudani et al., 2018). This sector encompasses all possible cases of collaborative interactions, from coexistence, where a human and a robot share the workspace without actually working together, to proper collaboration, where they perform a task together, directly influencing each other in the interaction (Matheson et al., 2019). Applications of this field mainly involve manufacturing settings. In here, both the user and the cobot assemble and/or handle an object under different settings to come up with a final produce (Semeraro et al., 2023a, 2023b). The investigations carried out in HRC involve both the human and the robotic side of the interaction. Participants involved in user studies are probed regarding qualitative aspects—such as their trust in the robotic system (Romeo et al., 2022; Semeraro et al., 2024) and/or the perceived cognitive workload required for the collaboration (Story et al., 2022)—and quantitative aspects, such as their ergonomics (Tassi et al., 2022) and fluency of the collaboration (Hoffman, 2019). On the robotic side, research has frequently investigated the efficiency of the robot in fulfilling the task and its accuracy in identifying the ongoing state of the interaction.

For the collaboration to take place, the cobot needs to be able to sense information regarding the user to adjust itself accordingly. Besides this, to make collaborations seamless, cobots also need to infer high-level information regarding the ongoing interaction with the user. The robot can then use it to change its own behaviour at a higher level, to go beyond reactive routines and take into account the bigger picture, that is the completion of the task. One way to achieve this is by means of machine learning (ML), which is being progressively used more in HRC (Semeraro et al., 2023a, Semeraro et al. 2022). In ML, previously labelled data can be used to train a machine to recognise such labels when new unlabelled data is fed into the system. For instance, one could record users' movements, associate them with the possible activities carried out by them, so that for later instances the robot can understand which activities the user is carrying out and change its own behaviour accordingly. Other possible methodologies can involve the exposure of the machine to unlabelled data, to figure out on its own the activities that are relevant to the task (Chi et al., 2018). In other instances, the robot can use the observations from the environment to learn directly the policy to adopt without passing through a labelling phase (Deng et al., 2017).

A recent research line in HRC involves the investigation of scenarios that go beyond the classic dyad of one human and one robot. Indeed, research in human-robot interaction also considers settings with more than one person present in the scenario and interacting with a robot at the same time. There have been dozens of works in human-robot interaction in this topic (Schneiders et al., 2022, Semeraro et al. 2025). However, very few works tackle these scenarios in the specific context of HRC. The main reason for this is that the main applications of HRC deal with manufacturing in serial chain production, in which one operator at a time handles the manufacturing target before handing the object to the next operator. In this context, the cobot is usually deployed to assist the human in their own manufacturing operations; for instance, the cobot can detect when the user is switching to a different operation and pass the right tools to the worker. However, a cobot could be used to enable two workers to operate at the same time. In this case, the cobot could act as mediator between the two users (Semeraro et al., 2023b). Indeed, with the two workers operating on the same target at the same time, mutual disturbances are likely to occur. The inclusion of the robot as a third agent in the collaboration would allow the users to not interfere with each other while working on the target simultaneously. This would allow manufacturing operations to be parallelised, increasing the efficiency of the production process. Moreover, this would also favour the scalability of HRC technologies in industrial scenarios, as the same robot could be used to assist more than one user at the same time.

In using ML for recognising the users' activities in these triadic HRC scenarios, a first issue arises in finding data that are representative of these settings. There is very little data in robotics applications (Cabi et al., 2019), and even less for non-dyadic HRC. Moreover, gathering data for triadic settings is more demanding than dyadic ones, as it requires double the number of participants to produce the same amount of data (Briggs et al., 2015). As a possible solution to these issues, Semeraro et al. (2023a, 2023b, 2024) proposed to use data regarding activity of single persons to train deep neural networks to infer multi-user activity. For this purpose, it was assumed that the activities of the single users could be combined to high-level activities, which is the case in the triadic scenario specified. To validate the proposal, video recordings of single people performing three different activities were collected. At this point, their 3D body joints were extracted and combined later in post-processing to generate nine different multi-user activities, given by all their possible pairings. Such a dataset was used to train two different types of neural networks, namely a variational autoencoder (Kingma, 2013) and a cascade of long-short term memory networks (Hochreiter & Schmidhuber, 1997) to recognise the joint activity of pairs of people (Figs. 9.5 and 9.6). Then, during the testing phase, the networks were exposed to recordings of settings in which both users were present at the same time performing the same nine activities. The results successfully showed that the performance of the neural networks was comparable to when they were trained directly with the data coming from recordings of pairs of people. This consequently implies that it is possible to get training data regarding multi-party activities starting from data related to single individuals. This is a more viable way of gathering data that does not compromise the performance of the multi-user activity recognition.

This work on multi-party HRC has considered two humans with the same roles. More precisely, the workers are given different tasks in the experimental setting but the hierarchy of them is very similar. In other industrial settings, humans in a medium-sized or large-sized team will likely each have different roles. The type of human-robot interaction could depend on the human's role. This gives rise to some new interesting dynamics. The study proposed by Stoican et al. (2022, 2023) focused on human-human-robot collaboration. That is, a pair of humans interacting with a single cobot. Even a single additional human can give rise to new interesting interactions. Let us consider an industrial setting in which the first human has the role of a "worker". The worker's role is to directly interact with the cobot—i.e., by working together to solve a collaborative task. This is usually the role of the human in many single-human HRC studies. However, in real industrial teams, not every human would interact with every other team member, especially in large teams. It is

Fig. 9.5 Enabling two workers to operate on the same target object at the same time through the mediation of the robot increases the efficiency of the production process by parallelising manufacturing operations. In this user study, under the experimenter's supervision, two people experience a joint collaborative task with a UR5e robot. They need to perform different operations at the same time on a shared target object. The robot observes the task through a depth camera and adjusts position and orientation of the object to accommodate their needs

not far-fetched to assume that this translates to human-robot teams. That is, not every human would interact with the cobot. In Stoican et al. (2022, 2023), the second human had the role of "supervisor". The supervisor would still be interested in the cobot's behaviour, or more exactly, in the output generated by the worker-cobot team. This output could be obtained through a worker-supervisor interaction that does not involve the cobot. The complexity added by introducing a supervisor comes from the supervisor still being (indirectly) affected by the cobot's behaviour, even without any interaction between the two. For example, an inefficient cobot would still affect the supervisor, indirectly, through the output (e.g., by receiving a late or bad output). The worker, on the other hand, would be directly affected (e.g., solving the collaborative task becomes more difficult or error-prone). To summarise, the supervisor is affected by their interaction with the human worker, which in turn depends on the interaction between the worker and the cobot.

Additionally, there is another, subtler way in which the cobot affects the supervisor. This indirect supervisor-cobot interaction can lead to a new interesting dynamic between the two humans. The supervisor has to assign blame. That is, given an output, they have to decide how much credit the worker receives and how much credit the cobot receives. This gives the cobot a new important role: its behaviour affects the relationship between the two humans, potentially improving it. The cobot takes the role of a mediator, or more generally, an interaction-shaping robot (Gillet

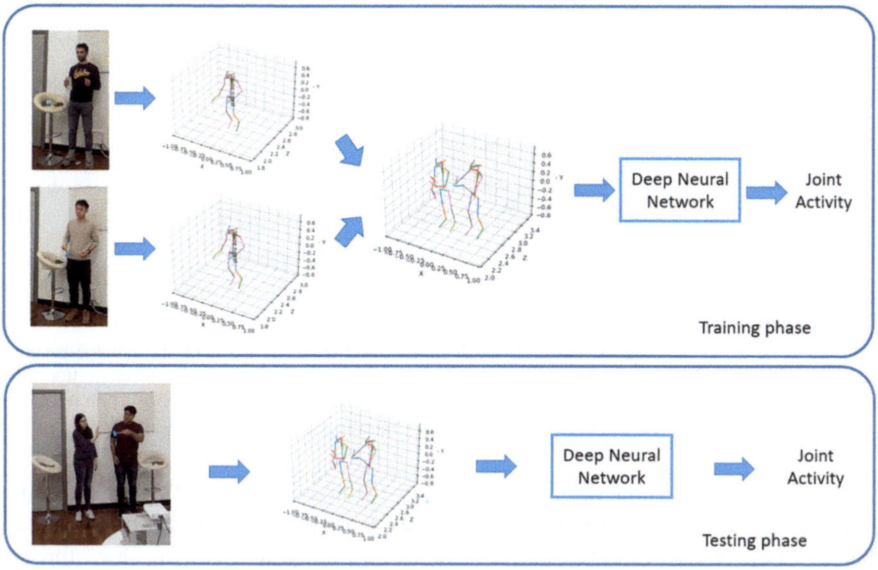

Fig. 9.6 Data pipeline of the joint activity recognition system. Starting from recordings of single individuals, group activity data are produced in post-processing to train a deep learning network to recognise the joint activity of a pair of people. The testing is then carried out using data coming from real pair recordings

et al., 2024). An overview of the two ways the cobot can indirectly affect a human is shown in Fig. 9.7.

Finally, it is worth discussing what the cobot's influence might consist of. In many cases in the HRI and HRC literature, robots are used to build trust (Khavas et al., 2020; Hancock et al., 2021; Vinanzi et al., 2021; Sanders et al., 2019; Xu & Dudek, 2016; Charalambous et al., 2016; Freedy et al., 2007). According to Fig. 9.7, this could be both cobot-human trust and human-human trust. However, other important characteristics might be influenced during an interaction like this. One example is wellbeing. In the field of human-computer interaction, wellbeing is the central characteristic studied in positive computing. Generally, technology is not designed to intentionally decrease the users' wellbeing. However, positive computing goes beyond that and focuses on technologies that explicitly improve the users' wellbeing (Sander, 2010; Calvo & Peters, 2014). Software built on this theoretical framework encourages positive emotions. Positive computing technologies have been used for self-help (Botella et al., 2016), stress management (Gaggioli et al., 2014), or for encouraging socialisation (Baños et al., 2012). An extension from positive computing to "positive HRI" or "positive HRC" seems natural, and could lead to similar benefits. Despite this, only a few studies choose to focus on wellbeing (Colim et al., 2021; Chang et al., 2012; Sauer et al., 2019; Tripathi et al., 2024; Simões et al., 2022). In the real world, integrating a cobot into a team of humans can affect the humans' wellbeing. For example, a cobot that considers its human

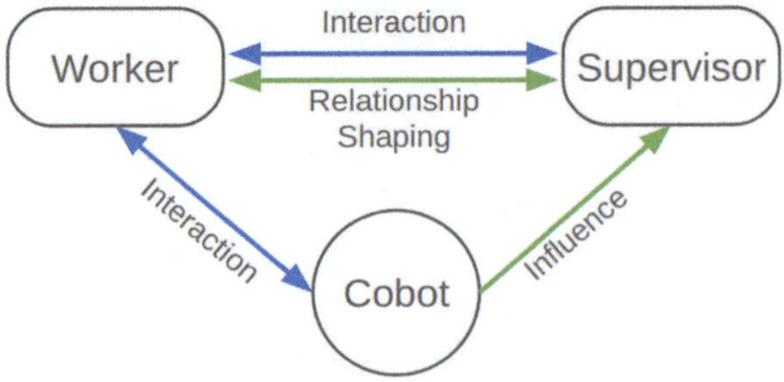

Fig. 9.7 The human-human-robot collaboration setup, adapted from Stoican et al. (2022). For each of the three agents, blue arrows show which other agents it interacts with. Green arrows show how the cobot affects the supervisor, in two different ways. First, through the worker-supervisor relationship, which is shaped by the cobot. Second, through the influence the cobot's behaviour has on the supervisor, even when there is a lack of direct interaction

teammates' safety could improve wellbeing (Simões et al., 2022). On the other hand, workers could be afraid that their cobot teammate would eventually replace them. Cobots should then be designed to actively mitigate this fear—e.g., through positive reinforcement. A good starting point for future positive HRI studies could be hedonic wellbeing, as it studies day-to-day emotions (Steptoe et al., 2015; Fisher, 2014). They are relatively simpler to influence and measure, compared to other types of wellbeing.

9.5 Trustworthy Robots

Trust is an essential aspect of human-human relationships generally defined as the willingness of the trustor to be vulnerable to the actions of the trustee (Mayer et al., 1995). This definition highlights that, for trust to be formed, vulnerability is an important precursor and that the trustor has some mental models of how worthy of trust the trustee is (Gambetta, 1988), which influence their decision to trust them or not. Trust is fundamental to all social interactions, crucial for building successful relationships, ensuring personal safety, and promoting team cooperation (Jones & George, 1998). Misplaced trust, due to incorrect judgments of someone's trustworthiness, can result in significant financial, emotional, or physical harm.

As we have seen in the previous sections, robots are starting to be used as social and personal assistants to help people with a wide range of tasks, including tasks in which people might experience a sense of vulnerability. Therefore, understanding how trust is built and maintained in HRI is fundamental. In HRI, trust is classically defined as the "Attitude that an agent will help achieve an individual's goals in a situation characterised by uncertainty and vulnerability" (Lee & See, 2004), and it is understood to be a multifaceted construct. In fact, trust has been broken down into two different categories: performance-based trust—i.e., trust in an agent's ability to complete a task consistently—and relation-based trust—i.e., trust that an agent will comply with social norms (Law et al., 2021). This distinction is reflected in HRI in state-of-the art measures for trust, such as the Multi-Dimensional Measure of Trust (MDMT) scale assessing capacity trust (composed of reliability and capability factors) and moral trust (composed of ethics and sincerity factors) (Ullman & Malle, 2019).

Being such a multifaceted and complex construct, there have been attempts in providing standards to individuate what could be the factors that influence trust in HRI when the human is the trustor and the robot the trustee. The framework that has been at the basis of HRI trust research for many years categorizes them into three groups: human-related factors (such as attitudes towards robots and engagement); robot-related factors (like dependability and adaptability); and environmental factors (including team communication and the physical environment). A substantial body of research has been carried out analysing each of the factors (Hancock et al., 2021). Recently, researchers have explored how robots' social skills influence human perceptions and how these abilities might impact or predict human-robot interactions (Salem et al., 2015). One of these abilities is Theory of Mind (ToM), the ability to attribute mental states (such as beliefs, intentions and desires) to others that may differ from one's own (Leslie, 1987) and that is considered crucial to build trustworthy human-human relations (Vanderbilt et al., 2011).

9.5.1 Trust in Human-Robot Interaction

Effective human-robot collaboration is essential for the successful integration of robots and autonomous systems in our homes and workplaces. Users would normally anticipate that information and suggestions from robots help reduce uncertainty in decision-making, therefore making the collaboration more efficient and effective. Given the importance of ToM on trust development in human-human interactions, recent works in HRI have started to look at the effect of ToM on human-robot trust and collaboration.

In Mou et al. (2020), a Pepper robot was equipped with ToM abilities, and it was programmed to play the Price Game (Rau et al., 2009) with a human user. In the game, participants had to choose the price of several objects, and Pepper could express its agreement or not. In case Pepper disagreed, participants faced the chance of aligning with the robot judgement or keeping their own choice. The hypothesis of the study was that a robot introduced as possessing a higher level of ToM would inspire higher trust over the robot presented with lower level of ToM abilities, making participants more willing to align to the suggestion of the robot with the higher level of ToM. The way participants were exposed to the two different ToM levels were through the use of priming videos shown to them prior to the game where they would see Pepper either passing (higher ToM) or failing (lower ToM) the Sally-Anne test, commonly used to verify whether children have developed a ToM (Baron-Cohen et al., 1985). Otherwise, during the game, the behaviour of the robot was exactly the same, independently on its ToM abilities. Through their between-subject user study with 32 participants, Mou et al. (2020) found that there was a statistically significant difference between the two groups: participants changed their decision more often over the price of an object when the robot with higher ToM abilities was giving its suggestion compared to the robot with lower ToM. This finding indicates that the ToM abilities demonstrated by the robot in the videos influenced participants' trust in the robot. Specifically, it showed that when the robot exhibited higher levels of ToM, human trust increased.

The results from Mou et al. (2020) confirmed that the role of ToM in trust building is equally important in human-human and human-robot interactions. To further the investigation of this claim, Romeo et al. (2022) bring the investigation a step forward, exploring whether a robot mimicking ToM capabilities during a collaborative game would influence the choices made by the humans collaborating with the robot. To do so, they examined the significance of ToM through an online video-based between-subjects study (N = 706). In the study, three groups of participants were tasked with escaping a large maze by correctly solving 10 mini-mazes with the assistance of the robot Pepper. In each mini-maze, participants could see where their starting point was and where two possible exits were. In each mini-maze, participants chose which exit (P1 or P2) to aim for, then the robot provided advice on which exit path it thought they should follow, and then participants could choose whether to follow the robot's suggestion or remain loyal to their initial decision. The three groups of participants were completing the task with three different robot personas that conveyed their different capabilities through the utterances they used to give advice: a Baseline robot, a Sensor robot and a ToM robot. Therefore, the ToM manipulation was carried out in two ways: (1) prior to the start of the actual game, participants were primed with the same videos used in Mou et al. (2020), which proved successful in manipulating participants' perceptions of the robot, and they would see Pepper either failing (Baseline and Sensor) or passing (ToM) the Sally-Anne test; and (2) the different robot personas used different language to convey their ability. In case the correct exit was P2 (see Fig. 9.8) the Baseline robot would say: "Go towards P2"; the Sensor robot would say: "Using my robot vision I can see P2 is the only reachable exit. Aim for P2."; and the ToM robot would say: "I suspect you think P2 is correct. I agree, we should follow your instinct and go left to reach it."

To study the effect of ToM on the development of trust between the player and the robot, multiple variables were recorded: (1) Decision Time, i.e. the time participants took to decide which exit path to choose following Pepper's advice (the time participants took to make their decision from the moment the suggestion video ended to the moment participants selected their path of choice); (2) Self-reported Decision Confidence for each mini-maze decision, reported before learning whether the robot decision was correct; (3) Robot Suggestion Adherence, whether participants decided to follow the advice offered by the robot; (4) Robot Capacity Trust; (5) Robot Moral Trust. Robot capacity and moral trust were measured at the end of the game using the MDMT questionnaire (Ullman & Malle, 2019). Moreover, a trust-breaking moment was added in mini-maze, where Pepper would offer a wrong

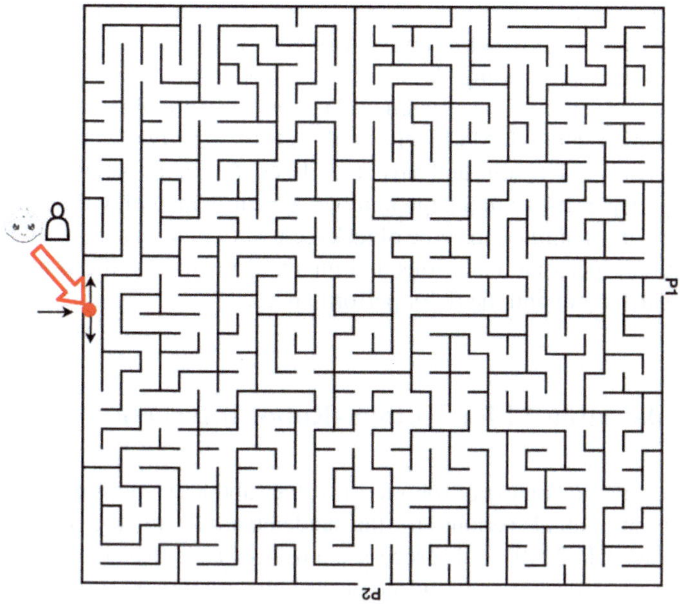

Fig. 9.8 A mini-maze example, indicating where the puzzle starts and where the two different exits (P1 and P2) that participants could choose from are located in the maze (from Romeo et al., 2022)

advice (independently on the condition participants were in). This additional event was added to verify which of the three robot personas would be more effective in regaining the lost trust. After the mistake, all three conditions saw the same video of Pepper apologising, which did not differ across conditions to not introduce an additional variable. To test whether trust was re-gained, the last mini-maze of the experiment represented an equivalent problem as the one where trust was broken.

Findings from this study depict a slightly contradictory picture with respect to what Mou et al. (2020) report. The MDMT revealed no statistical difference between the three conditions (Baseline—Sensor—ToM) with regards to the Robot Capacity or Moral trust, implying that none of the robot personas was perceived as more trustworthy. Participants who experienced the ToM-mimicking robot took more time to decide which exit path to follow in the mini-mazes, and expressed lower confidence in their decision, particularly when the robot made its mistake. In addition, no differences were found when examining the Robot Suggestion Adherence across the three conditions: participants followed a very similar path when adhering with the robot's suggestions and all of the robot personas experienced a significant drop in adherence at the last mini-maze, which was designed to study whether participants would follow the robot's advice in a situation recalling the scenario in which trust was broken. These results showed that participants in the ToM group had a greater sensitivity to the robot's performance relative to the other groups, and that participants were more confident and quicker to decide which exit path to follow when the robot interacted with them as if it was a machine and did not possess cognitive abilities (Baseline and Sensor personas).

The discourse surrounding the effects of ToM in the development of human-robot trust is yet to be fully explored and understood, possibly by developing new computational model of ToM (Tavella et al., 2024b). The two works presented here have shown equivocal results and have underlined the complexities of the ToM-trust relationship, depended from a large number of factors including the type of experiment (in-person vs online), the type of tasks (collaborative vs competitive), the level of vulnerability, personal conscious and unconscious biases, the context in which the task is carried out and the robot performances.

9.6 Explainable AI for Human-Robot Interaction

Explanations, in the context of robotics, involves abductive reasoning that connects the robot's individual actions to the understanding of the human observer (Anjomshoae et al., 2019). This process can be seen as both a cognitive activity and a computational procedure within robotic systems. As robots become more autonomous and intelligent, the ability to explain their actions, decisions, and behaviours to humans becomes increasingly crucial. This capability is especially important in environments where robots work alongside humans, such as collaborative manufacturing, healthcare, and domestic settings. The development of methods for robots to explain their actions is vital for several reasons. Explanations enhance the predictability, user-friendliness, debugging effectiveness, and overall transparency and trustworthiness of robotic systems. In scenarios where human-robot interaction is frequent, clear explanations can significantly improve collaboration and safety, fostering a more reliable and understandable interaction between humans and robots (Fig. 9.9).

Explainable robotics (Setchi et al., 2020) is a field dedicated to making the actions and behaviours of robotic systems comprehensible and trustworthy to humans. It seeks to bridge the gap between the complex internal workings of robots and human cognitive processes. Inspired by eXplainable Artificial Intelligence (XAI) (Das & Rad, 2020), explainable robotics shares the goal of creating systems that can provide meaningful, accurate, and user-tailored explanations of their actions. This field focuses on developing computational models, methods, and algorithms that enable robots to operate autonomously while effectively communicating their decisions to humans.

XAI refers to AI systems that can elucidate their behaviour in ways humans can understand. This ability is essential for collaboration, as it helps humans grasp why an AI system might fail to achieve a goal or unexpectedly complete a task. Explanations provided by XAI enable human users to comprehend the dynamics leading to the AI's actions, facilitating better decision-making regarding the AI's behaviour. In safety-critical applications, such as healthcare or autonomous driving, XAI ensures transparency, accountability, and trust. XAI can be categorized into

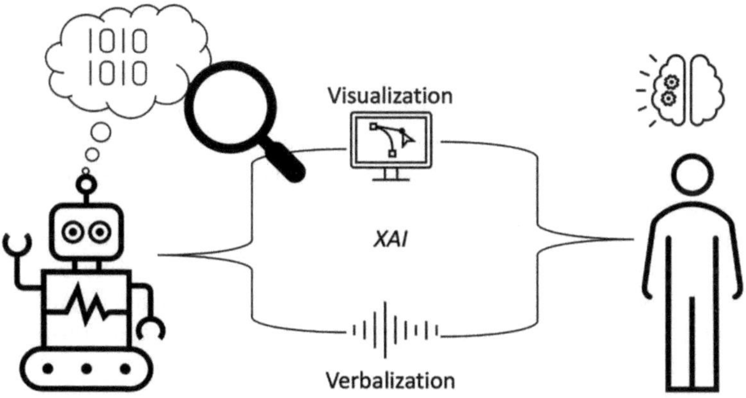

Fig. 9.9 Visualisation of the process and benefits of XAI, so that humans can understand the decisions and behaviours of robots during interaction

data-driven and goal-driven approaches. Data-driven XAI (Li et al., 2020a, 2020b) focuses on explaining decisions made by black-box machine learning systems based on input data. In contrast, goal-driven XAI (Sado et al., 2023) aims to create robots or agents that can justify their behaviours to lay users, assisting them in developing a Theory of Mind (ToM) (Scassellati, 2002) about the agent's behaviour. A well-formed ToM enables users to understand the agent's limitations and capabilities, thereby enhancing confidence, safety, and collaboration.

Explainability is critical in robotics due to the complexity and high dimensionality of data involved, such as images, videos, sounds, and sensor readings. Advanced algorithms like deep neural networks, reinforcement learning, and computer vision further complicate this landscape. Without clear explanations, trust, accountability, and reliability in robotic systems are compromised, potentially leading to ethical, legal, or social issues if robots make erroneous or harmful decisions based on opaque models.

Achieving explainability in robotics is particularly challenging due to the complex, high-dimensional data and sophisticated algorithms involved. Methods to address this include:

- Model-based explanations, like Grad-CAM (Selvaraju et al., 2017) or LRP (Bach et al., 2015), which provide explanations based on the internal models or representations;
- Rule-based explanations, as Decision Trees (Guidotti et al., 2018) or Anchors (Ribeiro et al., 2018), provide explanations by using predefined rules or logical statements;
- Data-based explanations, like counterfactual explanations (Wachter et al., 2017) or influence functions (Koh & Liang, 2017), focus on capturing and visualizing the data and information that influenced the robot's actions; and
- Natural language explanations (Han et al., 2021, Zhu et al. 2022) that Robots can generate explanations in natural language to communicate with humans.

Explainable robotics has numerous applications, notably in human-robot interaction (Ambsdorf et al., 2022), where it enhances collaboration and trust by clarifying robot actions and decision-making processes. In autonomous vehicles (Atakishiyev et al., 2021), XAI ensures compliance with safety standards and aids in incident analysis. In healthcare, it allows robotic systems to explain diagnostic processes and treatment recommendations, thereby supporting healthcare professionals in making informed decisions (Loh et al., 2022).

The primary research challenge in explainable robotics is identifying the appropriate level and type of explanation required for different users and contexts. Developing new algorithms that leverage past experiences, analogies, and real-time data to tailor explanations to specific audiences is essential. Additionally, creating computational models of situational and learned trust (Chamola et al., 2023), alongside algorithms for real-time trust sensing, is critical for advancing this field.

The field of explainable robotics is integral to the development of autonomous systems that are not only capable but also transparent and trustworthy. By focusing on creating robots that can explain their actions in a comprehensible manner, researchers aim to enhance the safety, reliability, and effectiveness of human-robot interactions across various domains.

9.7 Conclusion

This chapter provides an overview of the potential applications of robotics and AI models in a diverse set of domains. These applications range from social assistive robots for health and social care, to manufacturing scenarios with human-robot collaboration, and in the field of education. Overall, the different studies demonstrate the potential use of AI and machine learning methods to help design social and cognitive skills in interactive and collaborative robots.

The chapter considers the important issues for the design of human-centred, ethical and trustworthy robots. In particular, its focus on the concepts of trust and explainable AI (XAI) in human-robot interaction supports a human-centric view of this field. Effective and trustworthy human-robot collaboration is essential for the successful integration of robots and autonomous systems in our homes and workplaces.

The analysis of the state of the art on social robotics applications, as reviewed above, lacks a critical focus on cultural aspects of the design and use of these technologies. But an important contribution of this chapter, in the context of technology as cultural mediator, is the modelling of the cognitive skills of the Theory of Mind (ToM). As we have seen, ToM contemplates two aspects of trust in HRI. In the first case, we have to consider people's ToM of the social robots, that is their perception and believes on the robot's capabilities, goal and positive intent. The other side of the coin focuses on artificial ToM—i.e., robot's ToM representation of the human's intent and joint goals, which can also include their cultural characteristics and knowledge. ToM can thus be used to consider the cultural differences between different people and groups of users, so that robots can adapt to the individual cognitive and cultural preferences of each user. People's and robots' ToMs and access to XAI will help reduce uncertainty in joint collaboration and decision-making, and allow users and machine to share common cultural context, therefore making the interaction more efficient, personalised and effective.

Finally, an important consideration if the potential for current robotics research to convert into everyday applications. Although this chapter shows that prototypes of robots are being developed and tested in various application domains, the current state of the art on AI and robotics is still at an early stage. Transferring the capabilities of the AI-endowed social, cognitive and cultural capabilities from a constrained laboratory-based evaluation study to an open, dynamic real-world setting will require further theoretical and technological efforts towards the design of human-centre trustworthy social robots.

References

Abdi, J., Al-Hindawi, A., Ng, T., & Vizcaychipi, M. P. (2018). Scoping review on the use of socially assistive robot technology in elderly care. *BMJ Open, 8*(2), e018815. https://doi.org/10.1136/bmjopen-2017-018815

Adikari, M., Cangelosi, A., & Gomez, R. (2023). Social robot mediator for multiparty interaction. *HRI Workshop, arXiv preprint arXiv:2310.13508.*

Ajoudani, A., Zanchettin, A. M., Ivaldi, S., Albu-Schäffer, A., Kosuge, K., & Khatib, O. (2018). Progress and prospects of the human–robot collaboration. *Autonomous Robots, 42*, 957–975.

Alves-Oliveira, P., Arriaga, P., Paiva, A., & Hoffman, G. (2021). Children as robot designers. In *Proceedings of the 2021 ACM/IEEE International Conference on Human-Robot Interaction* (pp. 399–408). ACM. https://doi.org/10.1145/3434073.3444650

Ambsdorf, J., Munir, A., Wei, Y., Degkwitz, K., Harms, H. M., Stannek, S., et al. (2022). Explain yourself! Effects of explanations in human-robot interaction. In *2022 31st IEEE International Conference on Robot And Human Interactive Communication (RO-MAN)* (pp. 393–400).

Anjomshoae, S., Najjar, A., Calvaresi, D., & Framling, K. (2019). Explainable agents and robots: Results from a systematic literature review. In *18th International Conference on Autonomous Agents and Multiagent Systems (AAMAS 2019), Montreal, Canada, May 13–17, 2019* (pp. 1078–1088).

Atakishiyev, S., Salameh, M., Yao, H., & Goebel, R. (2021). Explainable artificial intelligence for autonomous driving: A comprehensive overview and field guide for future research directions. *arXiv preprint arXiv:2112.11561.*

Bach, S., Binder, A., Montavon, G., Klauschen, F., Muller, K.-R., & Samek, W. (2015). On pixel-wise explanations for non-linear classifier decisions by layer-wise relevance propagation. *PLoS One, 10*(7), e0130140.

Baños, R. M., Etchemendy, E., Castilla, D., García-Palacios, A., Quero, S., & Botella, C. (2012). Positive mood induction procedures for virtual environments designed for elderly people. *Interacting with Computers, 24*(3), 131–138.

Baron-Cohen, S., Leslie, A. M., & Frith, U. (1985). Does the autistic child have a "theory of mind"? *Cognition, 21*(1), 37–46.

Baxter, P., Ashurst, E., Read, R., Kennedy, J., & Belpaeme, T. (2017). Robot education peers in a situated primary school study: Personalisation promotes child learning. *PLoS One, 12*(5), e0178126.

Belpaeme, T., Kennedy, J., Ramachandran, A., Scassellati, B., & Tanaka, F. (2018). Social robots for education: A review. *Science Robotics, 3*(21), eaat5954. https://doi.org/10.1126/scirobotics.aat5954

Bjorling, E. A., Thomas, K., Rose, E. J., & Cakmak, M. (2020). Exploring teens as robot operators, users and witnesses in the wild. *Frontiers in Robotics and AI, 7*, 5. https://doi.org/10.3389/frobt.2020.00005

Botella, C., Mira, A., Moragrega, I., García-Palacios, A., Bretón-López, J., Castilla, D., et al. (2016). An Internet-based program for depression using activity and physiological sensors: Efficacy, expectations, satisfaction, and ease of use. *Neuropsychiatric Disease and Treatment*, 393–406.

Breazeal, C., Dautenhahn, K., & Kanda, T. (2016). Social robotics. In *Springer handbook of robotics* (pp. 1935–1972).

Briggs, P., Scheutz, M., & Tickle-Degnen, L. (2015, March). Are robots ready for administering health status surveys' first results from an hri study with subjects with Parkinson's disease. In *Proceedings of the Tenth Annual ACM/IEEE International Conference on Human-Robot Interaction* (pp. 327–334).

Budd, D., Burns, L. C., Guo, Z., L'italien, G., & Lapuerta, P. (2011). Impact of early intervention and disease modification in patients with predementia Alzheimer's disease: A Markov model simulation. *ClinicoEconomics & Outcomes Research, 3*, 189–195. https://doi.org/10.2147/CEOR.S22265. Epub 2011 Oct 7. PMID: 22046104; PMCID: PMC3202482.

Buzzega, P., Boschini, M., Porrello, A., Abati, D., & Calderara, S. (2020). Dark experience for general continual learning: A strong, simple baseline. *Advances in Neural Information Processing Systems, 33*, 15920–15930.

Cabi, S., Colmenarejo, S. G., Novikov, A., Konyushkova, K., Reed, S., Jeong, R., et al. (2019). A framework for data-driven robotics. *arXiv preprint arXiv:1909.12200.*

Calvo, M. G., & Nummenmaa, L. (2016). Perceptual and affective mechanisms in facial expression recognition: An integrative review. *Cognition and Emotion, 30*(6), 1081–1106.

Calvo, R. A., & Peters, D. (2014). *Positive computing: Technology for wellbeing and human potential*. MIT Press.

Caselli, N. K., Sehyr, Z. S., Cohen-Goldberg, A. M., et al. (2017). ASL-LEX: A lexical database of American Sign Language. *Behavior Research, 49*, 784–801. https://doi.org/10.3758/s13428-016-0742-0

Cavallo, F., Esposito, R., Limosani, R., Manzi, A., Bevilacqua, R., Felici, E., Di Nuovo, A., Cangelosi, A., Lattanzio, F., & Dario, P. (2018). Robotic services acceptance in smart environments with older adults: User satisfaction and acceptability study. *Journal Medical Internet Research, 20*(9), e264. https://doi.org/10.2196/jmir.9460

Chamola, V., Hassija, V., Sulthana, A. R., Ghosh, D., Dhingra, D., & Sikdar, B. (2023). *A review of trustworthy and explainable artificial intelligence (XAI)*. IEEE Access.

Chang, C. Y. C., Díaz, M., & Angulo, C. (2012). The impact of introducing therapeutic robots in hospital's organization. In *Ambient Assisted Living and Home Care: 4th International Workshop, IWAAL 2012, Vitoria-Gasteiz, Spain, December 3–5, 2012. Proceedings 4* (pp. 312–315). Springer.

Charalambous, G., Fletcher, S., & Webb, P. (2016). The development of a scale to evaluate trust in industrial human-robot collaboration. *International Journal of Social Robotics, 8*, 193–209.

Chi, W., Liu, J., Rafii-Tari, H., Riga, C., Bicknell, C., & Yang, G. Z. (2018). Learning-based endovascular navigation through the use of non-rigid registration for collaborative robotic catheterization. *International Journal of Computer Assisted Radiology and Surgery, 13*, 855–864.

Churamani, N., & Gunes, H. (2020). Clifer: Continual learning with imagination for facial expression recognition. In *2020 15th IEEE International Conference on Automatic Face and Gesture Recognition (FG 2020)* (pp. 322–328). IEEE.

Churamani, N., Kalkan, S., & Gunes, H. (2020). Continual learning for affective robotics: Why, what and how? In *2020 29th IEEE international conference on robot and human interactive communication (RO-MAN)* (pp. 425–431). IEEE.

Churamani, N., Axelsson, M., Caldır, A., & Gunes, H. (2022, October). Continual learning for affective robotics: A proof of concept for wellbeing. In *2022 10th International Conference on Affective Computing and Intelligent Interaction Workshops and Demos (ACIIW)* (pp. 1–8). IEEE.
Colim, A., Morgado, R., Carneiro, P., Costa, N., Faria, C., Sousa, N., et al. (2021). Lean manufacturing and ergonomics integration: Defining productivity and wellbeing indicators in a human–robot workstation. *Sustainability, 13*(4), 1931.
Coradeschi, S., Cesta, A., Cortellessa, G., et al. (2014). GiraffPlus: A system for monitoring activities and physiological parameters and promoting social interaction for elderly. In *Human computer systems interaction: Backgrounds and applications* (Vol. 3, pp. 261–271). Springer.
Das, A., & Rad, P. (2020). Opportunities and challenges in explainable artificial intelligence (XAI): A survey. *arXiv preprint arXiv:2006.11371.*
Davey, J. (2006). *"Ageing in place"—The views of older homeowners about housing maintenance, renovation and adaption.* Technical Report.
Deng, Z., Mi, J., Han, D., Huang, R., Xiong, X., & Zhang, J. (2017, December). Hierarchical robot learning for physical collaboration between humans and robots. In *2017 IEEE International Conference on Robotics and Biomimetics (ROBIO)* (pp. 750–755). IEEE.
Deng, E., Mutlu, B., & Mataric, M. J. (2019). *Embodiment in socially interactive robots.*
Diyas, Y., Brakk, D., Aimambetov, Y., & Sandygulova, A. (2016). Evaluating peer versus teacher robot within educational scenario of programming learning. In *2016 11th ACM/IEEE International Conference on Human-Robot Interaction (HRI)* (pp. 425–426). IEEE.
Ekman, P., & Oster, H. (1979). Facial expressions of emotion. *Annual Review of Psychology, 30*(1), 527–554.
El Ayadi, M., Kamel, M. S., & Karray, F. (2011). Survey on speech emotion recognition: Features, classification schemes, and databases. *Pattern Recognition, 44*(3), 572–587.
European Commission. (2021). The 2021 ageing report. Economic & budgetary projections for the EU member states (2019–2070). *European Economy Institutional Papers.*
Fisher, C. D. (2014). *Measuring wellbeing at work.*
Fong, T., Nourbakhsh, I., & Dautenhahn, K. (2003). A survey of socially interactive robots. *Robotics and Autonomous Systems, 42*(3–4), 143–166. https://doi.org/10.1016/S0921-8890(02)00372
Freedy, A., DeVisser, E., Weltman, G., & Coeyman, N. (2007). Measurement of trust in human-robot collaboration. In *2007 International Symposium on Collaborative Technologies and Systems* (pp. 106–114). Ieee.
Gaggioli, A., Cipresso, P., Serino, S., Campanaro, D. M., Pallavicini, F., Wiederhold, B. K., & Riva, G. (2014). Positive technology: A free mobile platform for the self-management of psychological stress. *Annual Review of Cybertherapy and Telemedicine, 199, 25–29.*
Gambetta, D. (1988). Can we trust trust? In *Trust: Making and breaking cooperative relations* (pp. 213–237). Basil Blackwell.
Gauthier, L., Dehaut, F., & Joanette, Y. (1989). The Bells test: A quantitative and qualitative test for visual neglect. *International Journal of Clinical Neuropsychology, 11*, 49.
Gendron, M., Roberson, D., van der Vyver, J. M., & Barrett, L. F. (2014). Perceptions of emotion from facial expressions are not culturally universal: Evidence from a remote culture. *Emotion, 14*(2), 251.
Gillet, S., van den Bos, W., & Leite, I. (2020). A social robot mediator to foster collaboration and inclusion among children. In *Robotics: Science and Systems XVI. Robotics: Science and Systems Foundation.* https://doi.org/10.15607/RSS.2020.XVI.103
Gillet, S., Winkle, K., Belgiovine, G., & Leite, I. (2022). Ice-breakers, turn-takers and fun-makers: Exploring robots for groups with teenagers. In *2022 31st IEEE International Conference on Robot and Human Interactive Communication (RO-MAN)* (pp. 1474–1481). IEEE. https://doi.org/10.1109/ROMAN53752.2022.9900644
Gillet, S., Vázquez, M., Andrist, S., Leite, I., & Sebo, S. (2024). Interaction-shaping robotics: Robots that influence interactions between other agents. *ACM Transactions on Human-Robot Interaction.*

Guertler, M., Tomidei, L., Sick, N., Carmichael, M., Paul, G., Wambsganss, A., et al. (2023). When is a robot a cobot? Moving beyond manufacturing and arm-based cobot manipulators. *Proceedings of the Design Society, 3*, 3889–3898.

Guidotti, R., Monreale, A., Ruggieri, S., Pedreschi, D., Turini, F., & Giannotti, F. (2018). Local rule-based explanations of black box decision systems. *arXiv preprint arXiv:1805.10820.*

Han, Z., Phillips, E., & Yanco, H. A. (2021). The need for verbal robot explanations and how people would like a robot to explain itself. *ACM Transactions on Human-Robot Interaction (THRI), 10*(4), 1–42.

Hancock, P. A., Kessler, T. T., Kaplan, A. D., Brill, J. C., & Szalma, J. L. (2021). Evolving trust in robots: Specification through sequential and comparative meta-analyses. *Human Factors, 63*(7), 1196–1229.

Hochreiter, S., & Schmidhuber, J. (1997, November 15). Long short-term memory. *Neural Computation, 9*(8), 1735–1780. https://doi.org/10.1162/neco.1997.9.8.1735

Hoffman, G. (2019). Evaluating fluency in human–robot collaboration. *IEEE Transactions on Human-Machine Systems, 49*(3), 209–218.

Johansson, M. M., Marcusson, J., & Wressle, E. (2015). Cognitive impairment and its consequences in everyday life: Experiences of people with mild cognitive impairment or mild dementia and their relatives. *International Psychogeriatrics, 27*(6), 949–958.

Jones, G. R., & George, J. M. (1998). The experience and evolution of trust: Implications for cooperation and teamwork. *Academy of Management Review, 23*(3), 531–546.

Kanazawa, A., Black, M. J., Jacobs, D. W., & Malik, J. (2018). End-to-end recovery of human shape and pose. *Computer Vision and Pattern Recognition (CVPR).*

Kanazawa, A., Zhang, J. Y., Felsen, P., & Malik, J. (2019). Learning 3D human dynamics from video. *Computer Vision and Pattern Recognition (CVPR).*

Kennedy, J., Baxter, P., & Belpaeme, T. (2015). The robot who tried too hard: Social behaviour of a robot tutor can negatively affect child learning. In *Proceedings of the Tenth Annual ACM/IEEE International Conference on Human-Robot Interaction* (pp. 67–74).

Khavas, Z. R., Ahmadzadeh, S. R., & Robinette, P. (2020). Modeling trust in human-robot interaction: A survey. In *International Conference on Social Robotics* (pp. 529–541). Springer.

Kingma, D. P. (2013). Auto-encoding variational bayes. *arXiv preprint arXiv:1312.6114.*

Koh, P. W., & Liang, P. (2017). Understanding black-box predictions via influence functions. In *International Conference on Machine Learning* (pp. 1885–1894).

Kollias, D., & Zafeiriou, S. (2019). Expression, affect, action unit recognition: Aff-wild2, multi-task learning and arcface. *arXiv preprint arXiv:1910.04855.*

Konijn, E. A., & Hoorn, J. F. (2020). Robot tutor and pupils' educational ability: Teaching the times tables. *Computers & Education, 157*, 103970.

Law, T., Chita-Tegmark, M., & Scheutz, M. (2021). The interplay between emotional intelligence, trust, and gender in human–robot interaction: A vignette-based study. *International Journal of Social Robotics, 13*(2), 297–309. https://doi.org/10.1007/s12369-020-00624-1

Lee, J. D., & See, K. A. (2004). Trust in automation: Designing for appropriate reliance. *Human Factors, 46*(1), 50–80. https://doi.org/10.1518/hfes.46.1.50/_30392

Lee, H. R., Sabanovic, S., Chang, W.-L., Nagata, S., Piatt, J., Bennett, C., & Hakken, D. (2017). Steps toward participatory design of social robots: Mutual learning with older adults with depression. In *Proceedings of the 2017 ACM/IEEE International Conference on Human-Robot Interaction* (pp. 244–253). ACM. https://doi.org/10.1145/2909824.3020237

Leslie, A. M. (1987). Pretense and representation: The origins of "theory of mind". *Psychological Review, 94*(4), 412.

Li, S., & Deng, W. (2020). Deep facial expression recognition: A survey. *IEEE Transactions on Affective Computing, 13*(3), 1195–1215.

Li, D., Rodriguez, C., Yu, X., & Li, H. (2020a). Word-level deep sign language recognition from video: A new large-scale dataset and methods comparison. In *The IEEE Winter Conference on Applications of Computer Vision* (pp. 1459–1469).

Li, X.-H., Cao, C. C., Shi, Y., Bai, W., Gao, H., Qiu, L., et al. (2020b). A survey of data-driven and knowledge-aware explainable AI. *IEEE Transactions on Knowledge and Data Engineering, 34*(1), 29–49.

Loh, H. W., Ooi, C. P., Seoni, S., Barua, P. D., Molinari, F., & Acharya, U. R. (2022). Application of explainable artificial intelligence for healthcare: A systematic review of the last decade (2011–2022). *Computer Methods and Programs in Biomedicine, 226*, 107161.

Luperto, A., Romeo, A., Lunardini, F., Monroy, J., Hernández García, D., Abbate, C., Cangelosi, A., Ferrante, S., Gonzalez-Jimenez, J., Basilico, N., & Borghese, N. A. (2024). Exploring the viability of socially assistive robots for at-home cognitive monitoring: Potential and limitations. *International Journal of Social Robotics*. https://doi.org/10.1007/s12369-024-01158-6

Maharjan, R. S. (2022). Continual learning for adaptive affective human-robot interaction. In *2022 10th International Conference on Affective Computing and Intelligent Interaction Workshops and Demos (ACIIW)* (pp. 1–5). IEEE.

Maharjan, R. S., Romeo, M., & Cangelosi, A. (2023). Faces are domains: Domain incremental learning for expression recognition. In *Proceedings of IJCNN24 International Joint Conference on Neural Networks, Queensland June 2023* (pp. 1–8). IEEE.

Maharjan, R. S., Romeo, M., & Cangelosi, A. (2024a). Continual facial features transfers for facial expression recognition (Submitted).

Maharjan, R. S., Romeo, M., & Cangelosi, A. (2024b). Sigh!!! There is more than just faces and speeches to recognize emotion in human-robot interaction. In *31st IEEE International Conference on Robot and Human Interactive Communication (RO-MAN)*.

Matheson, E., Minto, R., Zampieri, E. G., Faccio, M., & Rosati, G. (2019). Human–robot collaboration in manufacturing applications: A review. *Robotics, 8*(4), 100.

Mayer, R. C., Davis, J. H., & Schoorman, F. D. (1995). An integrative model of organizational trust. *Academy of Management Review, 20*(3), 709–734.

Mollahosseini, A., Hasani, B., & Mahoor, M. H. (2017). Affectnet: A database for facial expression, valence, and arousal computing in the wild. *IEEE Transactions on Affective Computing, 10*(1), 18–31.

Mou, W., Ruocco, M., Zanatto, D., & Cangelosi, A. (2020). When would you trust a robot? A study on trust and theory of mind in human-robot interactions. In *Proceedings of the 29th IEEE International Conference on Robot and Human Interactive Communication (RO-MAN), Naples, Italy* (pp. 956–962). https://doi.org/10.1109/RO-MAN47096.2020.9223551

Neuhaus, R., Ringfort-Felner, R., Dorrenbacher, J., & Hassenzahl, M. (2022). How to design robots with superpowers. In *Meaningful futures with robots—Designing a new coexistence* (1st ed., pp. 43–54). Chapman and Hall/CRC. https://doi.org/10.1201/9781003287445-3

Peng, X. B., Abbeel, P., Levine, S., & van de Panne, M. (2018a). DeepMimic: Example-guided deep reinforcement learning of physics-based character skills. *ACM Transactions on Graphics, 37*(4), 143:1–143:14. https://doi.org/10.1145/3197517.3201311

Peng, X. B., Kanazawa, A., Malik, J., Abbeel, P., & Levine, S. (2018b). SFV: Reinforcement learning of physical skills from videos. *ACM Transactions on Graphics, 37*(6). https://doi.org/10.1145/3272127.3275014

Piazza, E. A., Cohen, A., Trach, J., & Lew-Williams, C. (2021). Neural synchrony predicts children's learning of novel words. *Cognition, 214*, 104752.

Rau, P. P., Li, Y., & Li, D. (2009). Effects of communication style and culture on ability to accept recommendations from robots. *Computers in Human Behavior, 25*(2), 587–595.

Reitan, R. M. (1958). Validity of the trail making test as an indicator of organic brain damage. *Percept Mot Skills, 8*(3), 271–276.

Ribeiro, M. T., Singh, S., & Guestrin, C. (2018). Anchors: High-precision model-agnostic explanations. In *Proceedings of the AAAI Conference on Artificial Intelligence* (Vol. 32).

Romeo, M., McKenna, P. E., Robb, D. A., Rajendran, G., Nesset, B., Cangelosi, A., & Hastie, H. (2022). Exploring theory of mind for human-robot collaboration. In 2022 31st IEEE International Conference on Robot and Human Interactive Communication (RO-MAN), Napoli, Italy, pp. 461–468. https://doi.org/10.1109/RO-MAN53752.2022.9900550

Rong, Y., Shiratori, T., & Joo, H. (2021). FrankMocap: A monocular 3D whole-body pose estimation system via regression and integration. In *2021 IEEE/CVF International Conference on Computer Vision Workshops (ICCVW)* (pp. 1749–1759).

Sado, F., Loo, C. K., Liew, W. S., Kerzel, M., & Wermter, S. (2023). Explainable goal-driven agents and robots-a comprehensive review. *ACM Computing Surveys, 55*(10), 1–41.

Salem, M., Lakatos, G., Amirabdollahian, F., & Dautenhahn, K. (2015). Would you trust a (faulty) robot? Effects of error, task type and personality on human-robot cooperation and trust. In *ACM/IEEE International Conference on Human-Robot Interaction (HRI)* (Vol. 2015, pp. 1–8).

Sander, T. (2010). Positive computing. In *Positive psychology as social change* (pp. 309–326). Springer.

Sanders, T., Kaplan, A., Koch, R., Schwartz, M., & Hancock, P. A. (2019). The relationship between trust and use choice in human-robot interaction. *Human Factors, 61*(4), 614–626.

Sandler, W. (2017). The challenge of sign language phonology. *Annual Review of Linguistics, 3*(1), 43–63.

Santhoshkumar, R., & Geetha, M. K. (2019). Deep learning approach for emotion recognition from human body movements with feedforward deep convolution neural networks. *Procedia Computer Science, 152*, 158–165.

Sauer, V., Mertens, A., Heitland, J., & Nitsch, V. (2019). Exploring the concept of passenger well-being in the context of automated driving. *International Journal of Human Factors and Ergonomics, 6*(3), 227–248.

Scassellati, B. (2002). Theory of mind for a humanoid robot. *Autonomous Robots, 12*, 13–24.

Schneiders, E., Cheon, E., Kjeldskov, J., Rehm, M., & Skov, M. B. (2022). Non-dyadic interaction: A literature review of 15 years of human-robot interaction conference publications. *ACM Transactions on Human-Robot Interaction (THRI), 11*(2), 1–32.

Selvaraju, R. R., Cogswell, M., Das, A., Vedantam, R., Parikh, D., & Batra, D. (2017). Grad-cam: Visual explanations from deep networks via gradient-based localization. In *Proceedings of the IEEE International Conference on Computer Vision* (pp. 618–626).

Semeraro, F., Griffiths, A., & Cangelosi, A. (2022). Human-robot collaboration and machine learning: A systematic review of recent research. *Robotics and Computer-Integrated Manufacturing, 79*(C), 1016/j.rcim.2022.102432.

Semeraro, F., Carberry, J., & Cangelosi, A. (2023a). Towards multi-user activity recognition through facilitated training data and deep learning for human-robot collaboration applications. In *2023 International Joint Conference on Neural Networks (IJCNN)* (pp. 1–9). IEEE.

Semeraro, F., Carberry, J., & Cangelosi, A. (2023b). Simpler rather than challenging: Design of non-dyadic human-robot collaboration to mediate human-human concurrent tasks. In *AAMAS2023 Extended Abstract Proceedings, London.*

Semeraro, F., Carberry, J., Leadbetter, J., & Cangelosi, A. (2024). Good things come in threes: The impact of robot responsiveness on workload and trust in multi-user human-robot collaboration. In *2024 IEEE/RSJ International Conference on Intelligent Robots and Systems (IROS).*

Semeraro F., Leadbetter J., & Cangelosi A. (2025). TriHRCBot: A Robotic Architecture for Triadic Human-Robot Collaboration through Mediated Object Alignment. In 2025 IEEE International Conference on Robotics and Automation (ICRA).

Setchi, R., Dehkordi, M. B., & Khan, J. S. (2020). Explainable robotics in human-robot interactions. *Procedia Computer Science, 176*, 3057–3066.

Simões, A. C., Pinto, A., Santos, J., Pinheiro, S., & Romero, D. (2022). Designing human-robot collaboration (HRC) workspaces in industrial settings: A systematic literature review. *Journal of Manufacturing Systems, 62*, 28–43.

Simon-Thomas, E. R., Keltner, D. J., Sauter, D., Sinicropi-Yao, L., & Abramson, A. (2009). The voice conveys specific emotions: Evidence from vocal burst displays. *Emotion, 9*(6), 838.

Steptoe, A., Deaton, A., & Stone, A. A. (2015). Subjective wellbeing, health, and ageing. *The Lancet, 385*(9968), 640–648.

Stoican, R., Cangelosi, A., Goerick, C., & Weisswange, T. H. (2022). Learning human-robot interactions to improve human-human collaboration. In *IEEE/RSJ International Conference on Intelligent Robots and Systems (IROS 2022)-Workshop on Human Theory of Machines and Machine Theory of Mind for Human-Agent Teams (TOM4HAT)*.

Stoican, R., Cangelosi, A., & Weisswange, T. (2023). MEWA: A benchmark for meta-learning in collaborative working agents. In *Proceedings of the 2023 IEEE Symposium Series on Computational Intelligence (SSCI 2023)* (pp. 1435–1442). IEEE.

Story, M., Webb, P., Fletcher, S. R., Tang, G., Jaksic, C., & Carberry, J. (2022). Do speed and proximity affect human-robot collaboration with an industrial robot arm? *International Journal of Social Robotics, 14*(4), 1087–1102.

Tassi, F., Iodice, F., De Momi, E., & Ajoudani, A. (2022). Sociable and ergonomic human-robot collaboration through action recognition and augmented hierarchical quadratic programming. In *2022 IEEE/RSJ International Conference on Intelligent Robots and Systems (IROS)* (pp. 10712–10719). IEEE.

Tavella, F., Galata, A., & Cangelosi, A. (2022a). Phonology recognition in American Sign Language. In *ICASSP 2022–2022 IEEE International Conference on Acoustics, Speech and Signal Processing (ICASSP)* (pp. 8452–8456). https://doi.org/10.1109/ICASSP43922.2022.9747212

Tavella, F., Schlegel, V., Romeo, M., Galata, A., & Cangelosi, A. (2022b). WLASL-LEX: A dataset for recognising phonological properties in American Sign Language. In S. Muresan, P. Nakov, & A. Villavicencio (Eds.), *Proceedings of the 60th Annual Meeting of the Association for Computational Linguistics (Vol. 2: Short Papers)* (pp. 453–463). Association for Computational Linguistics. https://doi.org/10.18653/v1/2022.acl-short.49

Tavella, F., Galata, A., & Cangelosi, A. (2023). Signs of language: Embodied sign language fingerspelling acquisition from demonstrations for human-robot interaction. In *2023 32nd IEEE International Conference on Robot and Human Interactive Communication (RO-MAN)* (pp. 1137–1143). IEEE.

Tavella, F., Galata, A., & Cangelosi, A. (2024a). Bridging the communication gap: Artificial agents learning sign language through imitation. In *Social robotics. ICSR 2024. Lecture notes in computer science*. Springer.

Tavella, F., Manzi, F., Vinanzi, S., Di Dio, C., Massaro, D., Cangelosi, A., & Marchetti, A. (2024b). Towards a computational model for higher orders of Theory of Mind in social agents. *Frontiers in Robotics and AI, 11*, 1468756. https://doi.org/10.3389/frobt.2024.1468756

Tripathi, M. A., Sawant, P. D., Kaur, H., Almahairah, M. S., Chandel, P. S., & Balakumar, A. (2024). Human-robot collaboration in the workplace: Assessing the impact on employee well-being and productivity. In *2024 Third International Conference on Intelligent Techniques in Control, Optimization and Signal Processing (INCOS)* (pp. 1–7). IEEE.

Ullman, D., & Malle, B. F. (2019). Measuring gains and losses in human-robot trust: Evidence for differentiable components of trust. In *Proceedings of the 14th ACM/IEEE International Conference on Human-Robot Interaction (HRI). Association for Computing Machinery* (pp. 618–619).

United Nations. (2022). *International day of sign languages*. United Nations. https://www.un.org/en/observances/sign-languages-day

Vanderbilt, K. E., Liu, D., & Heyman, G. D. (2011). The development of distrust. *Child Development, 82*(5), 1372–1380.

Vinanzi, S., Cangelosi, A., & Goerick, C. (2021). The collaborative mind: Intention reading and trust in human-robot interaction. *Iscience, 24*(2).

Wachter, S., Mittelstadt, B., & Russell, C. (2017). Counterfactual explanations without opening the black box: Automated decisions and the gdpr. *Harvard Journal of Law & Technology, 31*, 841.

Wang, J., Sun, K., Cheng, T., Jiang, B., Deng, C., Zhao, Y., Liu, D., Mu, Y., Tan, M., Wang, X., Liu, W., & Xiao, B. (2021). Deep high-resolution representation learning for visual recognition. *IEEE Transactions on Pattern Analysis & Machine Intelligence, 43*(10), 3349–3364. https://doi.org/10.1109/TPAMI.2020.2983686

Weisswange, T. H., Javed, H., Dietrich, M., Pham, T. V., Parreira, M. T., Sack, M., & Jamali, N. (2023). *What could a social mediator robot do? Lessons from real-world mediation scenarios*.

Winkle, K., Senft, E., & Lemaignan, S. (2021). LEADOR: A method for end-to-end participatory design of autonomous social robots. *Frontiers in Robotics and AI, 8*, 704119. https://doi.org/10.3389/frobt.2021.704119

World Health Organization. (2024). *Deafness and hearing loss*. WHO. https://www.who.int/news-room/fact-sheets/detail/deafness-and-hearing-loss

Xu, A., & Dudek, G. (2016). Towards modeling real-time trust in asymmetric human–robot collaborations. In *Robotics Research: The 16th International Symposium ISRR* (pp. 113–129). Springer.

Zaga, C., Lohse, M., Truong, K. P., & Evers, V. (2015). The effect of a robot's social character on children's task engagement: Peer versus tutor. In *Social Robotics: 7th International Conference, ICSR 2015, Paris, France, October 26–30, 2015, Proceedings 7* (pp. 704–713). Springer.

Zhu, H., Yu, C., & Cangelosi, A. (2022). Explainable emotion recognition for trustworthy human-robot interaction. In *HRI2020 Workshop on "Context-awareness in HRI—Approaches and Challenges", Sapporo/Online, 7–10 March*.

Afterword

Michael Cole and Maria Falikman

Encountering Technologies in Cultural and Historical Context

The central fact about our psychology is the fact of mediation (L.S. Vygotsky)

The collection of articles in this volume creates a highly diverse and multifaceted interdisciplinary perspective on the postindustrial digital era with a focus on its cultural, social, and psychological aspects. It provides a broad overview of the general state of research and includes a variety of illustrations of different spheres and domains of human lives being reorganized.

The rapidity and ubiquity of the changes we witness on a daily basis are captured by Moore's law, the observation regarding the development of digital technologies that the number of transistors per square inch on integrated circuits doubles every year since their invention, with the consequence that the power of computers increases exponentially (Moore, 1975). This unprecedented speed of technological development, combined with the merging of digital and wireless technologies with human daily routines worldwide, has transformed the human ecological and experiential niche and created a hybrid reality, both biophysical and digital, which has altered our experience of space and time. Understanding the full scope of these changes is a daunting task. It took humankind millennia to invent and introduce literacy and numeracy and millennia to make them widespread, but the internet took over human life within several decades.

M. Cole (✉)
University of California, San Diego, USA
e-mail: mcole@ucsd.edu

M. Falikman
The University of the South, Tennessee, USA
e-mail: mafalikm@sewanee.edu

M. B. Ligorio (ed.), *Technology as Cultural Mediator*, Culture in Policy Making: The Symbolic Universes of Social Action,
https://doi.org/10.1007/978-3-031-97673-5

Twenty years ago, when Cole and Derry wrote an afterword devoted to the then-new technologies in a similar volume, they could assume that "the term *technology* evokes thoughts of computers, telecommunications networks, and spaceships, the technologies that occupy 99.9% of the story in [the movie] *2001*" (Cole & Derry, 2005, p. 2). Today the term "technology" evokes the smartphone, social media, large language models, and lives intimately linked to the Internet of Things. Sometimes 'state-of-the-art' technologies come and go before their effects can be systematically understood.

The way of thinking we are going to provide in this essay will be based on one of the central theoretical principles of cultural historical psychology, an approach first introduced a century ago by Lev Vygotsky and Alexander Luria, which is to trace the *history* of the phenomenon if we wish to understand its current, ever-changing state. The inclusion of history in our inquiry forces us to think about the change in temporality and space-time relations that is characteristic of modern life. The phenomenon of interest in this case is the rapid reconfiguring of social life associated with the spread of digital media in recent decades. As clearly demonstrated by the unique case of St. Helena island presented by Whitworth in this volume, a case of creating an interface for keeping the nineteenth-century colonial existence in the world of modern technologies, the influence of newly introduced technologies is not deterministic; there are multiple factors at play. Still, the origins of this phenomenon are in the insertion of tools and language into the way that *Homo sapiens* interacted with its conspecifics in their collective ecological niche.

As a starting point, we are going to examine some of the concepts that will structure our discussion, beginning with the word "*technology*". Some argue that the everyday meaning of this term has morphed so quickly in recent decades that it has become virtually synonymous with the digital technologies transforming patterns of human life globally. Like the authors of this volume, we believe that focusing on new forms of technology while ignoring earlier forms will blind us to the lessons of earlier historical times when technology-related revolutions reordered social life.

Pea and Cole (2019) started their recent discussion of technology and human development with the Ancient Greeks, for whom a technology combined two features: *techne*—an art or craft, and *technologia*—the systematic treatment of such arts and crafts. A technology, then, includes both the doing of something and the theorizing about that doing, both a practice and a theory of that practice. We will use this distinction to order our thoughts about the role of technology in human life, starting with the theory side.

When the term "technology" began to spread in the English language in the late eighteenth century, it referred to "a branch of *knowledge* dealing with the mechanical arts and applied sciences" (Oxford English Dictionary, n.d., italics added)—the *technologia* part of the process. Mechanical arts referred to practical, hands-on disciplines that involved craftsmanship, engineering, and applied sciences. For example, one encounters statements such as, "His technology consists of weaving, cutting canoes, making rude weapons, and in some places practicing a rude metallurgy" (taken from an ethnographic description in the mid-nineteenth century, Oxford English Dictionary, n.d.). Seamanship was considered a mechanical art because sailors used mathematical instruments and navigational theories in their maritime practices.

These examples unequivocally caution us not to think that a technology can be reduced to a particular tool or machine. Although tools are constituents of a technology, it is the way in which the technology is deployed that is crucial to understanding their consequences for the people who use them.

In order to lay the groundwork with respect to the issue of technology's role in human affairs, we approach the study of technology and human life starting from the concept of an *artifact* and what Vygotsky and his colleagues referred to as *mediation*.

Whether speaking of a rudimentary stone axe or a smartphone, the fundamental characteristic of any artifact/tool/technology is that it *mediates* human action, a process conventionally represented by a triangle such as that below (Fig. A.1).

The diagram depicts a person, S, a subject, seeking to obtain a goal that is unachievable or demands disproportionate efforts to achieve by directly acting upon it.

Unable to complete the action, S acts indirectly to achieve its goal by incorporating a mediating artifact into the action. This is an elementary, instrumental act, or what Wertsch (1998) refers to as 'agent-acting-with-mediational-means,' in order to highlight the focus on the agent—technology relationship. Examples might include lifting a heavy load by using a lever or calculating the total cost of purchases by using a smartphone app.

An artifact, from this perspective, is "an aspect of the material world that has been modified over the course of its incorporation into goal-directed human activity. By virtue of the changes wrought in the processes of their creation and use, artifacts are simultaneously ideal (conceptual) and material. They are material in that they have been created by modifying physical material in the process of goal-directed human actions. They are ideal in that their current material form has been shaped by their participation in the interactions of which they were previously a part and which constitute their environment in the present" (Cole, 1996, p. 117).

Alexander Luria (1928) opens his discussion of the transformation that occurs when artifacts are incorporated into action in the following terms: "The tools used by man not only radically change his conditions of existence, they *even react on him* in that they effect a change in him and in his psychic condition" (p. 496, italics added). The tool, or the artifact, is a medium for this reciprocal relationship.

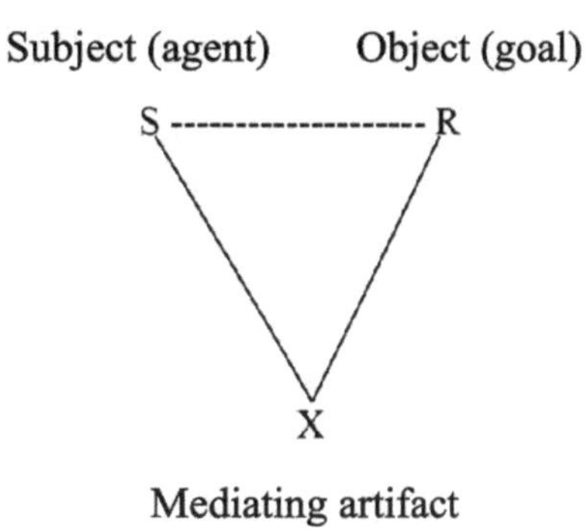

Fig. A.1 Vygotsky's mediated action triangle (Vygotsky, 1978)

Artifacts, while being immanent to human practice, shape our daily activities at the same time, just like an ant's walk on the beach is shaped by the structure of the environment (Simon, 1969).

In his in-depth analysis of human niche construction, Chris Sinha (2015) adds that artifacts are always made, rather than simply found. He emphasizes that artifacts embody human intentionality, conceptualization, and imagination, and that they have canonical functions that are physically realized in their design or culturally produced affordances—something *for what* the artifact was designed, or "*its socially standard function*".

There is broad agreement that to understand a technology is to know the reason and purpose behind it (e.g., Bakhurst, 1990). Put differently, every technology has been created *to achieve some goal, for a purpose,* as part of a particular activity (Kaptelinin & Nardi, 2009). Michael Schiffer (1992) seconds this idea from the archaeological perspective, arguing that the study of technology "must focus on behavior and artifacts in the context of activities" (p. X), emphasizing the art/craft of combining theoretical and practical knowledge, a key feature of a technology. Consequently, when we speak of a technology, we have in mind what might be referred to as a sociotechnical system—an entanglement of humans with each other, the tools, arts, crafts, practices, and the systematized, institutionalized ways of life of their time and space. As Cole (1996) points out, "artifacts and artifact systems exist as such only in relation to 'something else' variously referred to as a situation, context, activity, and so on" (p. 144).

Neuroarchaeologist Lambros Malafouris goes even further by suggesting to treat the human brain not as a biological organ but as a "bio-artifact" (Malafouris, 2013), shaped by culture and 'enacted' cultural practices of many centuries, both in the course of evolution and during individual development, through educational practices, vocational training, hobbies, etc. An excellent example of this process can be found in the work of Dehaene and his colleagues, who have documented the way that the acquisition of the ability to read is accompanied by the reorganization of the brain and the development of new functional regions and inter-regional systems (Dehaene, 2010).

Homo sapiens is thus a "cyborg species," imbued with technologies in a broad sense. Moreover, as Joseph Feigenberg (2011) notices, humans are not viable without all technologies they create in the course of cultural evolution, or "add-ons" they use to extend their capabilities. Feigenberg's definition of our species as *"Homo sapiens se ipsum perimplens"* (or *Homo sapiens* constantly extending themselves) emphasizes this idea of the never-ending cultural evolution of the human being.

Like some of the authors of this volume, we have found it fruitful to employ Wartofsky's (1979) idea of a hierarchy of artifacts. As described in detail by Ligorio in her chapter, primary artifacts are tools used in production (such as axes or needles); secondary artifacts consist of representations of primary artifacts and of modes of action mediated by primary artifacts, from visual symbols to rituals 'explaining' their use. Tertiary artifacts are basically the worlds of 'imaginative practices' involving primary and secondary artifacts, or representations of primary artifacts—for example, through a constructive play, or a scientific paradigm, or a work of art or fiction (for the discussion, see Cole, 2019). Digital technologies bring new opportunities for creating tertiary artifacts, or imaginary worlds operating with secondary artifacts. Digital game worlds, such as Minecraft, provide excellent examples, as discussed in the chapters by Ritella and Lund.

This discussion of technology and artifacts as its 'stem cells' embedded in a cultural context necessarily raises a problem of the definition of culture, which varies with and across different research fields, from philosophy to primatology. As early as the 1950s there were dozens, if not hundreds, of definitions, descriptive and normative, historical and psychological, structural and genetic (Kroeber & Kluckhohn, 1952), focusing on norms, learned behavioral patterns, symbols, or artifacts.

In Vygotsky's cultural historical psychology, which takes it as axiomatic that "a mind cannot be independent of culture" (Vygotsky, 1978, p. 90), culture necessarily became one of the foundational concepts. According to Vygotsky, "culture creates specific forms of behavior, it modifies the activity of mental functions, it constructs new superstructures in the developing system of human behavior" (Vygotsky, 1997, p. 18). Through the prism of this function, culture might be understood as an ensemble of artifacts available to people to interact with the world, or "history in the present" (Cole & Engeström, 1993, p. 10). Packer and Cole (2020) later add another dimension to the definition of culture by demonstrating that it includes not only affordances and constraints but also 'deontic powers' associated with those affordances (obligations, duties, rights, etc.). This makes culture "a key characteristic of the human niche, rather than a characteristic of the human mind" (p. 12).

Even with this revised interpretation of culture, Vygotksy's triangle (Fig. A.1) makes it clear that it is via (by means of) the mediating *artifact* or *tool* that culture shapes interactions of the subject with the world through a process of meaning making. In his early analysis of mediation, Vygotsky contrasts *material tools* (used by humans to control the nature, or the changing environment), or Wartofsky's 'primary artifacts', with *psychological tools* (aimed at controlling oneself or one's own mental processes), later referred to as "cognitive artifacts" by Norman (1991). At the early stages of evolution, both kinds of tools are external. Early humans would use stone cleavers and axes to increase their physical capacities and clay tokens for counting or knots for remembering to increase their mental capabilities. However, eventually the fate of psychological tools would be to become internalized, with clay tokens or knots being replaced by mental calculation or mnemonics. This would happen both through the course of human cultural evolution and in individual development. Both material and psychological tools would first be introduced by adults, or 'knowledgeable others', and both would need to be mastered by children, but while material tools become a part of the physical interactions of a child with the world, modifying their 'natural' movements but increasing their scope and power, psychological tools modify one's mental functions by becoming their intrinsic to them. Those mediated, or higher, psychological functions include mental tools that make them controllable. A popular example is recall supported by mnemonics, which does not rely on natural retention anymore: the information can be retrieved anytime, like with a popular DISHES mnemonic for Spanish irregular verbs or "My Very Educated Mother Just Served Us Nachos" for the order of planets.

Digital mediation seems to be special (Falikman, 2021). While external by nature, digital technologies equip our cognitive functions (retrieval of information, recall of intentions, paying and shifting attention while searching for keywords, comparing options to make a choice, and so on) rather than physical interactions with the world. Sometimes they 'merge' with human cognitive processes (Clark & Chalmers, 1998; for the discussion of 'extended memory,' see Ward, 2013), just as during a medical investigation with an endoscopic probe, a surgeon's sensitivity shifts towards the tip of the probe (Leontiev, 1983), or in Gregory Bateson's famous example of a blind man with a stick, discussed by Ligorio in her introduction to this volume, a physical stick or cane becomes an extension of the blind man's sensorimotor system rather than an external 'material tool'. Moreover, digital technologies create a new *ecological niche* for contemporary humanity, which is sometimes referred to as the "ecology of artifacts" (Bødker & Klokmose, 2011). Those artifact ecologies could be described as "environments where multiple heterogeneous technologies co-exist and are interlinked as a unified system" (Vasiliou et al., 2015, p. 55), and multiple agents are connected via those multiple technologies and media.

In his contribution to this volume, Erstad considers it useful to combine the concepts of *mediation* and *mediatization* to address this transformation of human life in the digital era. Mediatization refers to the fact that Vygotsky's "social situation of development," which determines acquisition of cultural tools and practices, or mastering mediated actions, becomes shaped by multiple media. Hyperconnectivity as a characteristic of the modern world, when everyone is connected to everyone and to everything via multiple devices and digital networks, together with hypersociality and spatiotemporal uniformity (for a recent discussion, see Kirjakovski, 2023), creates highly specific conditions for education, intergenerational relationships, and so on. Those multiple media *"intertwine"* in such a way that four of five different media might interact over time, shaping shared goals of their users through collaboration.

Turning from theory to practice, there are numerous domains of contemporary social life where new digital technologies are used in a helpful manner, including medicine, education, and politics (peace research, conflict resolution, etc.). Several of the articles in this volume are focused on new technologies in education, which is understandable. Education occupies the central role in passing on the experience of prior generations and preparing for the future.

One of the most remarkable transformations of education through the use of digital media, which surged during the pandemic, is the change of its *chronotope* or the consistent interrelation of spatial and temporal coordinates of a particular event or type of events. This term was introduced in 1925 by the Russian physiologist Alexey Ukhtomsky (for a detailed historical discussion, see Chebanov, 2015), and applied to literary studies by Mikhail Bakhtin in late 1930s. The concept of chronotope, illustrated in this volume by Ritella to investigate digital technology-mediated learning, captures the idea of the unity of space and time—a feature of activity that requires reconsideration if we think about new digital instruments of education and the chronotope of a class. "Being in the classroom", "having a museum tour," or even "mediating a conflict" no longer means physical presence anymore. In addition to bringing together students from different physical locations and belonging to different communities to the same virtual space to collaborate and study together (as thoroughly demonstrated in the chapters by Ritella and Lorusso, Austin and Hunter, and Lund), modern technologies allow for asynchronous forms of education (a student 'joining' their class later in the day or in the week if they could not make it to the virtual classroom on time), or working together in the same virtual workspace (such as a collaborative virtual whiteboard) at different times. Moreover, a person can act at several spatial locations simultaneously via different devices. Importantly, these transformations resulting from hyperconnectivity increase *access/accessibility* for different populations not only in school education but also in discovering cultural heritage. As Marti and Recupero show in their chapter, new multisensory technologies and digital connectivity are bringing museum exhibits and artworks to those who cannot come to the museum. Similarly, augmented reality, as demonstrated by Kumpulainen and her colleagues, enhances access of urban children to the natural world and improves their ecological awareness.

In some respects, the most interesting technology, robots, was discussed in some detail in the chapter by Cangelosi and his colleagues. Robots have been used in industry for decades, but *social robotics* is a recent area of research and practice. Social robots are designed to interact and communicate with humans in a variety of domains, such as healthcare, companionship, industrial collaboration, and education. They are often equipped with AI learning algorithms to adapt to novel tasks, environments, and users. In education, social robots are starting to be used as tutors, peers, and novices to be tutored by students.

What makes robots special? Whereas most technologies are tools or extensions of the human body or mind, with a human subject being an agent and technologies being the means for humans to achieve their goals (e.g., to *mediate* this process—see Fig. A.1), robots may be perceived as separate 'agents' interacting not only with the environment on behalf of humans but also collaboratively *with* humans.[1] Large Language Models (LLMs) are similar to robots in this respect. Interestingly, this seemed to be true even for very early and primitive chatbots like Eliza developed by Joseph Weizenbaum in the 1960s, a simple computer program that was strongly anthropomorphized by most users and even led to emotional attachment (Weizenbaum, 1976). LLMs are currently used as *tools* in education, industry (IT, first of all), and general information search. However, they are also broadly used as communicative *partners* or even *"the knowledgeable other"* to increase the number of perspectives on a certain problem under consideration, to receive informed advice, and even to share experiences.

What makes generative AI notable in this discussion is that it seems to represent 'pure culture,' being trained not by engaging with reality (or with primary artifacts), as humans do, but solely on the stories/narratives or images representing reality

[1] The collaborative industrial robots described by Cangelosi et al., which are capable of mediating human interaction and collaboration on a given task, are also technologies that go beyond pure 'extension'. They operate or build on shared intentions, rather than assisting in the achievement of individual goals.

(secondary artifacts), without actually making any difference between the former and the latter. While engaging with LLMs, humans enter a dialogue with this generalized cultural experience. Looked at in Vygotskian terms, LLMs are meta-artifacts, but they are grounded in memory of past uses of language irrespective of context, which, as we have seen, is an absolutely essential aspect of any psychological tool.

By way of a conclusion

Ligorio begins her introduction to this volume by asking us to consider the role of new digital media in the current global political and economic crisis that is shaking the foundations of the world order and reconfiguring the daily lives and experiences of billions of people. "What," she asks, "has technology got to do with all this?" Her answer is, "Yes, technologies do contribute to these problems, and they have a great responsibility for some of these trends, but technologies are not solely responsible."

Addressing the problem of parsing responsibility for any mediated action, Drain and Strong argue that "agency must be de-fused from any local," contained "subject and be understood as a situational property in which subjects and objects can both participate. Any technological artifact should thus be understood as a complex of agential capacities that function relative to any number of social and material factors" (Drain & Strong, 2015, p. 188). Given this state of affairs, assigning responsibility for the changes wrought by incorporating new technologies into our social order and personal lives often becomes fraught with uncertainties and contradictions. The growing polarization of opinions noted by Erstad in his contribution is more than understandable, but what is considered good and bad depends on the context, as the saying goes.

Having read the contributions to this volume, it should be clear that any precise answer to this question is complicated by the fact that many, perhaps all, human actions are mediated by artifacts from the past that embody human purpose and serve as the "starter toolkit" of cultural experience for each new generation. Having changed nature, the artifact-mediated world changes the conditions of life and hence the nature of those who inhabit it. As Cole and Derry put it, "We have encountered technology, and it is us."

References

Bakhurst, D. (1990). *Consciousness and revolution in Soviet philosophy: From the Bolsheviks to Evald Ilyenkov*. Cambridge University Press.

Bødker, S., & Klokmose, C. N. (2011). The human-artifact model—An activity theoretical approach to artifact ecologies. *Human-Computer Interaction, 26*(4), 315–371.

Chebanov, S. V. (2015). Ukhtomsky's idea of chronotope as frame of anticipation. In M. Nadin (Ed.), *Anticipation: Learning from the past. Cognitive systems monographs* (Vol. 25, pp. 137–150). Springer.

Clark, A., & Chalmers, D. (1998). The extended mind. *Analysis, 58*(1), 7–19.

Cole, M. (1996). *Cultural psychology: A once and future discipline*. Harvard University Press.

Cole, M. (2019). Re-covering the idea of a tertiary artifact. In *Cultural-historical approaches to studying learning and development societal, institutional and personal perspectives* (pp. 303–321). Springer.

Cole, M., & Derry, J. (2005). We have met technology and it is us. In R. J. Sternberg & D. D. Preiss (Eds.), *Intelligence and technology: The impact of tools on the nature and development of human abilities* (pp. 209–227). Lawrence Erlbaum Associates.
Cole, M., & Engeström, Y. (1993). A cultural-historical approach to distributed cognition. In G. Salomon (Ed.), *Distributed cognitions: Psychological and educational considerations* (pp. 1–46). Cambridge University Press.
Dehaene, S. (2010). *Reading in the brain*. Penguin Group.
Drain, C., & Strong, R. C. (2015). Situated mediation and technological reflexivity: Smartphones, extended memory, and limits of cognitive enhancement. In F. Scalambrino (Ed.), *Social epistemology and technology: Toward public self-awareness regarding technological mediation* (pp. 187–195). Rowman & Littlefield International.
Falikman, M. (2021). There and back again: A (Reversed) Vygotskian perspective on digital socialization. *Frontiers in Psychology, 12*, 501233.
Feigenberg, J. M. (2011). *Homo sapiens se ipsum perimplens and ethics*. Medical Information Agency. [In Russian].
Kaptelinin, V., & Nardi, B. A. (2009). *Acting with technology*. MIT Press.
Kirjakovski, A. (2023). Rethinking perception and cognition in the digital environment. *Frontiers in Cognition, 2*, 1266404.
Kroeber, A. L., & Kluckhohn, C. (1952). Culture: A critical review of concepts and definitions. *Papers of the Peabody Museum of American Archaeology and Ethnology, 47*(1).
Leontiev, A. N. (1983). Image of the world. In A. N. Leontiev (Ed.), *Selected psychological works* (Vol. 2, pp. 251–261). Pedagogika. [In Russian].
Luria, A. R. (1928). The problem of the cultural behavior of the child. *The Pedagogical Seminary and Journal of Genetic Psychology, 35*, 493–506.
Malafouris, L. (2013). *How things shape the mind: A theory of material engagement*. MIT Press.
Moore, G. E. (1975). Progress in digital integrated electronics. In *Proceedings of the IEEE Electron Devices Meeting* (Vol. 21, pp. 21–25). San Francisco.
Norman, D. A. (1991). Cognitive artifacts. In J. M. Carroll (Ed.), *Designing interaction* (pp. 17–38). Cambridge University Press.
Oxford English Dictionary. (n.d.). https://www.oed.com/
Packer, M., & Cole, M. (2020). The institutional foundations of human evolution, ontogenesis, and learning. In N. S. Nasir, C. D. Lee, R. Pea, & M. McKinney de Royston (Eds.), *Handbook of the cultural foundations of learning* (pp. 3–23). Routledge/Taylor & Francis Group.
Pea, R., & Cole, M. (2019). The living hand of the past: The role of technology in development. *Human Development, 62*, 14–39.
Schiffer, M. B. (1992). *Technological perspectives on behavioral change*. University of Arizona Press.
Simon, H. (1969). *The sciences of the artificial*. MIT Press.
Sinha, C. (2015). Language and other artifacts: Socio-cultural dynamics of niche construction. *Frontiers in Psychology, 6*, 1601. https://doi.org/10.3389/fpsyg.2015.01601
Vasiliou, C., Ioannou, A., & Zaphiris, P. (2015). An artifact ecology in a nutshell: A distributed cognition perspective for collaboration and coordination. In J. Abascal, S. Barbosa, M. Fetter, T. Gross, P. Palanque, & M. Winckler (Eds.), *Human-computer interaction—INTERACT 2015. Lecture notes in computer science* (Vol. 9297, pp. 55–72).
Vygotsky, L. S. (1978). *Mind in society*. Harvard University Press.
Vygotsky, L. S. (1997). The history of the development of higher mental functions. In R. W. Rieber (Ed.), *The collected works of L. S. Vygotsky* (Vol. 4). Plenum Press.
Ward, A. F. (2013). Supernormal: How the internet is changing our memories and our minds. *Psychological Inquiry, 24*(4), 341–348.
Wartofsky, M. (1979). *Models: Representation and the scientific understanding*. D. Reidel.
Weizenbaum, J. (1976). *Computer power and human reason: From judgment to calculation*. W.H. Freeman.
Wertsch, J. V. (1998). *Mind as action*. Oxford University Press.

MIX
Papier aus verantwortungsvollen Quellen
Paper from responsible sources
FSC® C105338

If you have any concerns about our products,
you can contact us on
ProductSafety@springernature.com

In case Publisher is established outside the EU,
the EU authorized representative is:
Springer Nature Customer Service Center GmbH
Europaplatz 3, 69115 Heidelberg, Germany

Printed by Libri Plureos GmbH
in Hamburg, Germany